Mauriac
The Poetry of a Novelist

FAUX TITRE

240

Etudes de langue et littérature françaises
publiées sous la direction de

Keith Busby, M.J. Freeman,
Sjef Houppermans, Paul Pelckmans
et Co Vet

Mauriac
The Poetry of a Novelist

Paul Cooke

AMSTERDAM - NEW YORK, NY 2003

For my parents

The paper on which this book is printed meets the requirements of
'ISO 9706: 1994, Information and documentation - Paper for documents
- Requirements for permanence'.

Le papier sur lequel le présent ouvrage est imprimé remplit les prescriptions de "ISO 9706:1994, Information et documentation - Papier
pour documents - Prescriptions pour la permanence".

ISBN: 90-420-0848-2
©Editions Rodopi B.V., Amsterdam - New York, NY 2003
Printed in The Netherlands

Acknowledgements

I am extremely grateful to the Arts and Humanities Research Board and to the University of Exeter for funding the study leave that enabled me to write the majority of this book. I was able to test certain ideas in papers delivered to the Société Internationale des Etudes Mauriaciennes, the Association Européenne François Mauriac, the University of Exeter French Department, and the University of Oxford Graduate Research Seminar. My thanks to the participants at these various events (too numerous to mention individually) for their comments and encouragement. I am grateful both to Jean Mauriac for giving me permission to consult archival material and to the unfailingly obliging staff of various libraries: the Bibliothèque Nationale de France and the Bibliothèque Littéraire Jacques Doucet in Paris, the Bibliothèque Municipale in Bordeaux, the Taylor Institution in Oxford, and the University Library in Exeter. Finally, I must thank individual friends and colleagues who were kind enough to help me in various ways: John Flower, Toby Garfitt, James Kearns, and Mary Orr provided invaluable support for funding bids; Zoe Boughton, Malcolm Cook, Aidan Coveney, David Cowling, Mike Holland, Melissa Percival, Clarisse Stouvenot, Andrea Williams, and Elizabeth Woodrough helped me find material and provided answers to specific queries; and the following were kind enough to respond to a general e-mail request: Adrian Armstrong, Frédéric Brayard, Peter Cogman, Steve Goddard, Naomi Segal, Bernard Swift, and Rebecca Zorach. Any errors in what follows are entirely my own responsibility.

Contents

Abbreviations and references

References to most primary sources are given in parentheses in the main body of the text. For most of Mauriac's verse, references are to volume VI of his *Œuvres complètes* published by Fayard in 1951. Where necessary, page references (or occasionally line references) are preceded by the following abbreviations:

AA	*L'Adieu à l'adolescence*
Dis	'Le Disparu'
EE	'Ebauche d'Endymion'
MJ	*Les Mains jointes*
Or	*Orages*
SA	*Le Sang d'Atys*
VAL	'La Veillée avec André Lafon'

An abbreviation is also used for the following poem not included in the Fayard *Œuvres complètes*:

MP	'Les Morts du printemps'

The following abbreviations all concern prose texts by Mauriac, full details of which are given in the bibliography (wherever possible, all references to these items will be given in the main body of the text):

BN	*Bloc-notes*, 5 vols
DAM	D'Autres et moi
LV	*Lettres d'une vie (1904–1969)*
MAM	*Mauriac avant Mauriac*
NLV	*Nouvelles Lettres d'une vie (1906–1970)*
OA	*Œuvres autobiographiques*
OC	*Œuvres complètes*, 12 vols
ORTC	*Œuvres romanesques et théâtrales complètes*, 4 vols
PC	*La Paix des cimes: chroniques 1948–1955*
PR	*Les Paroles restent*
SR	*Souvenirs retrouvés: entretiens avec Jean Amrouche*

The following abbreviations are used for secondary sources in the footnotes:

> CFM   *Cahiers François Mauriac*
> CM   *Cahiers de Malagar*
> NCFM *Nouveaux Cahiers François Mauriac*
> TCER *Travaux du Centre d'études et de recherches sur François Mauriac*

Unless otherwise stated, books in French are published in Paris and books in English are published in London.

Introduction

François Mauriac, one of twentieth-century France's most prominent writers, was awarded the Nobel Prize for Literature in 1952 specifically for his achievements as a novelist.[1] In the post-war period, he became increasingly influential as a journalist, building a reputation as perhaps 'le plus grand polémiste du XXᵉ siècle'.[2] But despite all his success as a novelist, a journalist, an essayist, and even (briefly) as a dramatist, he received very little recognition as a poet. Looking back over his career in 1965, Mauriac marvelled that, despite his unpromising background as a provincial bourgeois with limited intellectual horizons and a sedentary nature, he had managed to achieve so much as a writer. The secret of his success, he suggests, could be summed up in a single word: 'poésie'. He continues:

> Le nom de poète, je me moque bien qu'on me l'ait dénié! J'en suis un et je n'aurai même été que cela; et dans la mesure où je n'ai pu m'imposer comme poète, j'ai manqué ma vie,—ou plutôt je l'aurais manqué, si la nappe secrète n'avait alimenté tout ce que j'ai écrit: romans, essais, mais même le moindre article de journal. (*OA* 772)

Despite his protestations of indifference, Mauriac *was* disappointed by the lack of interest in his verse. He clearly derived some comfort from the thought that his poetry found expression in his prose, but he always felt that the verse of his maturity had been unjustly neglected.

How great was this neglect? One way of answering this question is to see how frequently Mauriac's poems feature in standard anthologies and general histories of French verse. None of Mauriac's work features in the general collections edited by Gide, Fouchet, Pompidou, Décaudin, and Bercot, nor in the specifically religious anthologies edited by Aury and Maxence.[3] On the other hand, Mauriac's verse is

---

[1] See Jean Lacouture, *François Mauriac*, 2 vols (Editions du Seuil, 1990), II: *Un citoyen du siècle: 1933–1970*, p. 242.

[2] Jean Daniel, 'François Mauriac et le journalisme', in *Mauriac* (Hachette, 1977), pp. 141–59 (p. 142).

[3] See, respectively, *Anthologie de la poésie française*, ed. by André Gide (Gallimard, 1949); *Anthologie thématique de la poésie française*, ed. by Max-Pol Fouchet, 12ᵗʰ

included in a large, anonymous anthology from the 1920s that focuses generally on more avant-garde authors; in Aury and Paulhan's postwar collection; in a recent general anthology edited by Delvaille, and in a specifically Catholic anthology edited by Mauriac's friend, Vallery-Radot.[4] So, although his poems are not entirely absent from anthologies, they are certainly not included in most of the more important ones. When we turn to major general surveys of modern poetry, the situation is even less favourable for Mauriac. His name is not even mentioned in passing in the studies by Raymond, Lemaitre, Lalou, Rousselot, and Boisdeffre.[5] Indeed, the only significant surveys in which I have found reference to Mauriac are those by Dérieux and Sabatier.[6] This rapid overview would seem to suggest, therefore, that

edn (Seghers, 1958); *Anthologie de la poésie française*, ed. by Georges Pompidou (Hachette, 1961); *Anthologie de la poésie française du XXe siècle: de Paul Claudel à René Char*, ed. by Michel Décaudin (Gallimard, 1983); *Anthologie de la poésie française: XVIIIe siècle, XIXe siècle, XXe siècle*, ed. by Martine Bercot, Michel Collot, and Catriona Seth (Gallimard, 2000); *Anthologie de la poésie religieuse française*, ed. by Dominique Aury (Gallimard, 1997); *Anthologie de la poésie mystique contemporaine*, ed. by Jean-Louis Maxence (Presses de la Renaissance, 1999). It is worth pointing out that Aury's anthology was originally published in 1943 and only included the work of dead poets. However, in the 1997 edition referred to above, the decision was taken to include the work of at least one poet (Claudel) who had died since 1943.

[4] See, respectively, *Anthologie de la nouvelle poésie française*, new edn (Kra, 1928), pp. 384–89; *Poètes d'aujourd'hui*, ed. by Dominique Aury and Jean Paulhan (Editions de Clairefontaine, 1947), pp. 136–38; *Mille et cent ans de poésie française: de la 'Séquence de Sainte Eulalie' à Jean Genet*, ed. by Bernard Delvaille (Laffont, 1991), pp. 1477–79; *Anthologie de la poésie catholique (des origines à 1932)*, ed. by Robert Vallery-Radot (Les Œuvres Représentatives, 1933), pp. 372–75.

[5] See, respectively, Marcel Raymond, *De Baudelaire au surréalisme*, rev. edn (Corti, 1952); Henri Lemaitre, *La Poésie depuis Baudelaire* (Colin, 1965); René Lalou, *Histoire de la poésie française*, 8th edn (Presses Universitaires de France, 1967); Jean Rousselot, *Histoire de la poésie française, des origines à 1940* (Presses Universitaires de France, 1976); Pierre de Boisdeffre, *Les Poètes français d'aujourd'hui (1940– 1986)*, 3rd edn (Presses Universitaires de France, 1987). Despite the dates in Boisdeffre's title, his survey begins with a chapter entitled 'Un renouveau chrétien' which deals with poets such as Claudel, Noël, and Jouve who, like Mauriac, published much of their verse before 1940.

[6] See Henry Dérieux, *La Poésie française contemporaine: 1885–1935* (Mercure de France, 1935), p. 178 and Robert Sabatier, *La Poésie du XXe siècle*, 3 vols (Albin Michel, 1982–88), I: *Tradition et évolution* (1982), pp. 85–90.

Mauriac's verse has indeed been largely neglected by literary history in general.

But what of studies focusing specifically on Mauriac's *œuvre*: is his verse well represented here? The answer would have to be a qualified negative. Although numerous studies of Mauriac the novelist, the dramatist, the journalist, and the religious apologist appeared during his lifetime, his poems attracted virtually no critical interest apart from the various reviews that accompanied the publication of each collection. However, during the last decade of his life, Mauriac had the pleasure of seeing this neglect remedied in part by Alyn's monograph and Le Hir's conference paper.[7] Contributing to the 'Hommage à Mauriac' published a few days after the author's death, Alyn suggested that 'la poésie de François Mauriac—toujours relativement méconnue chez nous—est devenue objet d'étude à l'étranger, et les témoignages d'admiration pour *Orages* et *Le Sang d'Atys* se multiplient de tous côtés'.[8] Although this claim is somewhat exaggerated, it is true that a young Belgian scholar, Marc Quaghebeur, was working on Mauriac's poetry at this time and his articles of the early- to mid-1970s constitute the most substantial body of work on Mauriac's verse so far published by an individual researcher.[9] One or two other general appreciations of Mauriac the poet appeared in minor journals shortly after his death in 1970,[10] but the next significant assessment of

---

[7] See Marc Alyn, *François Mauriac* (Seghers, 1960) and Yves Le Hir, 'La Versification de François Mauriac', in *Le Vers français au 20ᵉ siècle* (Klincksieck, 1967), pp. 65–84. As is standard in the 'Poètes d'aujourd'hui' series, Alyn's book combines a general introductory essay with an anthology of Mauriac's poems. Le Hir's study is a far more academic piece of work. For Mauriac's reaction to these appraisals, see *OA* 1139 and *BN*, IV, 180 respectively.

[8] Marc Alyn, 'Avant tout, un poète', *Le Figaro littéraire*, 7–13 September 1970, pp. 11–12 (p. 11).

[9] See Marc Quaghebeur, 'Mauriac poète', *La Quinzaine littéraire*, 1–15 October 1970, pp. 14–15; 'Mauriac ou la poésie', *Revue générale*, 10 (1970), 13–22; 'Mauriac poète: interstices', *Les Lettres romanes*, 25.2 (1971), 178–99; 'Méandres créateurs de Mauriac poète', *La Revue nouvelle*, 55 (1972), 354–64; 'Yves Frontenac désert', *Cahiers Internationaux de Symbolisme*, 21 (1972), 39–50; 'Une lecture du *Sang d'Atys*', in *François Mauriac 1: la poésie de François Mauriac*, ed. by Jacques Monférier (Lettres Modernes/ Minard, 1975), pp. 51–68.

[10] See, for example, François Pradelle, 'Les Feuillets gallicans du *Cerf-Volant*', *Le Cerf-Volant*, no. 72 (1970), 38–45 and Philippe Chabaneix, 'François Mauriac poète', *Bulletin de la Librairie Ancienne et Moderne*, no. 140 (December 1971), 254–55. A

Mauriac's verse did not appear until 1975. This was when *La Revue des lettres modernes* launched its 'François Mauriac' series. The choice of Mauriac's poetry as the focus for the first number in this series is revealing. As the editor puts it: 'Notre premier volume, [...], a délibérément choisi d'aborder l'œuvre par ses aspects les moins connus et les plus discutés, mais aussi peut-être les plus révélateurs'.[11] Over a quarter of a century later, this volume still constitutes the high watermark of critical interest in Mauriac's verse. There have, of course, been various articles in specialist Mauriac journals and, in-deed, sporadic attempts to introduce Mauriac the poet to a wider audi-ence: one thinks in particular of the section in Sabatier's survey of twentieth-century poetry referred to earlier, of an article by Séailles, and of an anthology of Mauriac's poems edited by Curtis.[12] Overall, though, Mauriac continues to languish in poets' purgatory and there has been very little detailed work carried out on his verse since the articles published during the period 1967–75. The three most original contributions since then have all appeared in studies with a broader focus: Guyonnet's unpublished doctoral thesis on Mauriac's fascina-tion with the myth of Attis; a chapter in Risse's book on the homo-erotic dimension in Mauriac's *œuvre*; and Swift's survey of the influ-ence of Symbolism on his work.[13] This explains the significance of the present study: it is the first monograph on Mauriac's poetry since

---

series of seven articles under the general heading 'François Mauriac, le poète' were published in *La Voix des poètes*, no. 40 (Winter 1970). The contributions are of varied quality, but Guibert, Simon, and Suffran make some perceptive comments (see the bibliography at the end of this study for full details).

[11] Jacques Monférier, 'Avant-propos', in *François Mauriac 1: la poésie de François Mauriac*, ed. by Jacques Monférier (Lettres Modernes/ Minard, 1975), pp. 4–6 (p. 5). Full details of all the articles—by Décaudin, Touzot, Quaghebeur, Suffran, Séailles, and Leroux—can be found in the bibliography.

[12] See André Séailles, 'Défense et illustration d'un poète', *Revue des deux mondes*, February 1986, 280–303 and François Mauriac, *Le Feu secret*, ed. by Jean-Louis Curtis (Orphée/ La Différence, 1993).

[13] See Anne-Marie Guyonnet, 'Mauriac et le mythe d'Atys', 2 vols (unpublished doctoral thesis, University of Paris IV, 1978); Dorothee Risse, *Homoerotik bei François Mauriac: Zur literarischen Gestaltung eines Tabus* (Heidelberg: Universitäts-verlag C. Winter, 2000), pp. 189–212; and Bernard C. Swift, *Mauriac et le Symbolisme* (Bordeaux: L'Esprit du Temps, 2000).

Alyn's introductory presentation of over forty years ago. This detailed re-assessment of his practice as a poet is long overdue.

After an initial exploration of Mauriac's views on poetry and the poetic, my study will examine Mauriac's verse in chronological order of publication, beginning with his first book, *Les Mains jointes* (1909). Of course, the poems in this collection were not the first Mauriac ever wrote. Both the Bibliothèque Littéraire Jacques Doucet in Paris and the Bibliothèque Municipale de Bordeaux have exercise books containing numerous poems Mauriac wrote as a schoolboy and as a student during the period 1901–05.[14] There are also a few poems that were published in minor journals (organs of Marc Sangnier's *Sillon* movement) between 1905 and 1907. However, since I shall be examining this obscure juvenilia elsewhere,[15] I prefer to begin the present study with an analysis of the collection that, thanks to a famous article by Barrès, marked Mauriac's arrival on the literary scene. After a chapter in which I consider Mauriac's second collection of verse, *L'Adieu à l'adolescence* (1911), two chapters are devoted to poems published in various journals between 1913 and 1918. These poems, perhaps the least well-known in Mauriac's verse corpus (with the exception of the juvenilia mentioned above), could be considered as transitional texts providing a bridge between the pre-First World War collections (which Mauriac repeatedly dismissed) and his last two collections—*Orages* (1925) and *Le Sang d'Atys* (1940)—that he prized so highly. After chapters analysing both of these collections, I conclude my examination of Mauriac's poems with a coda devoted to the 'Ebauche d'Endymion' (1942), an unfinished piece that consti-

---

[14] There is only one such manuscript at Bordeaux: 'Cahiers de "Vers" (1905)'. For details of the Doucet's holdings, see *Catalogue de fonds spéciaux de la Bibliothèque littéraire Jacques Doucet, Paris: Fonds Jouhandeau et Fonds Mauriac*, ed. by François Chapon (Boston, MA: Hall, 1972), pp. 91–92.

[15] In a critical edition entitled *'Les Mains jointes' et autres poèmes (1905–23)* to be published in the 'Textes littéraires' series of the University of Exeter Press.

tutes his farewell to verse. I then go on, in a final chapter, to examine the relationship between Mauriac's verse and his novels. It is at this point that the full sense of my subtitle—*The Poetry of a Novelist*—will become apparent.

1. Mauriac and Poetry

Preliminary remarks

In his 'Richard Wagner et *Tannhäuser* à Paris' (1861), Baudelaire wrote:

> tous les grands poètes deviennent naturellement, fatalement, critiques. Je plains les poètes que guide le seul instinct; je les crois incomplets. Dans la vie spirituelle des premiers, une crise se fait infailliblement, où ils veulent raisonner leur art, découvrir les lois obscures en vertu desquelles ils ont produit, [...].[1]

Most of the major French poets from the second half of the nineteenth century onwards have shared Baudelaire's view.[2] While Mauriac wrote a number of essays and articles in which he reflected both on the novel as a genre and on his own practice as a novelist,[3] there is no equivalent piece of sustained reflection on verse. His reviews as poetry editor for the *Revue du temps présent* during the period 1909–11 show that he was perfectly capable of thinking in critical terms about verse, but he chose never to produce anything along the lines of an *art poétique*. It is significant that the only *art poétique* he can countenance is rather nebulous:

> si jamais nous avons rêvé nous-même de faire œuvre de poète, ce fut pour nous rallier à l'art poétique dont M. Thierry Maulnier nous livre la formule: 'La mission propre de la poésie est d'offrir au plus solide du langage et au plus mystérieux du monde, le lieu d'une miraculeuse coïncidence.' (*OC*, XI, 272)

However, scattered throughout his essays, articles, correspondence, and autobiographical writings, one can find many passages in which Mauriac reveals some of his thoughts about poetry as a 'genre' and

---

[1] Charles Baudelaire, *Œuvres complètes*, ed. by Claude Pichois, 2 vols (Gallimard, 1975–76), II (1976), 793.

[2] See Daniel Leuwers, *Introduction à la poésie moderne et contemporaine* (Bordas, 1990), p. 1.

[3] For example, *Le Roman* (1928), *Le Romancier et ses personnages* (1933), and 'Vue sur mes romans' (1952).

about his own work as a poet.[4] In this chapter, I shall attempt to bring these scattered comments together in order to grasp more clearly Mauriac's thinking about poetry.

Firstly, it is worth pointing out that, like many writers, Mauriac often uses the term *poésie* rather loosely. When he exclaims: 'Quelle puissance de poésie chez ces enfants bourgeois que nous étions' (*OA* 642–43), he is referring to a general quality of experience fostered by a combination of factors related to age, socio-economic status, geographical location, and religious practice. Elsewhere, he can refer to 'une espèce de poésie des bars' (*ORTC*, I, 369); to 'la poésie des vieilles familles campagnardes' (*SR* 75); to 'la poésie d'Argelouse' (*SR* 240);[5] to stage sets 'd'une poésie adorable' (*PC* 214); to 'la poésie de la montagne' (*PC* 240); and even to 'une poésie des bagages' (*MAM* 182). Such 'poetry' in no way depends on a literary text. But, in its narrower sense (that of 'la poésie proprement dite' as Valéry puts it), the word *poésie* 'nous fait songer à un art, à une étrange industrie dont l'objet est de reconstituer cette émotion que désigne le premier sens du mot'.[6] Valéry's clear intellect deplores the confusion that arises from the muddling of these two senses of *poésie*; Mauriac, altogether more intuitive and impressionistic in his responses, never feels the need to distinguish sharply between these two meanings.

Influences

Verse was an important part of Mauriac's life from an early age. When he was no more than about ten, he presented a small collection of poems to the other members of his family.[7] His brother Pierre recalls how, when they were still very young, the four Mauriac boys would declaim whole pages of l'abbé Ragon's *Morceaux choisis* that

---

[4] As Daniel Combe points out, 'poetry' in general is actually a linguistic code rather than a genre as such. See his *Poésie et récit: une rhétorique des genres* (Corti, 1989), pp. 33–34.

[5] Argelouse is a village located in the Landes. It provided the atmospheric setting for Mauriac's novel *Thérèse Desqueyroux* (1927).

[6] Paul Valéry, *Œuvres*, ed. by Jean Hytier, 2 vols (Gallimard, 1957), I, 1459.

[7] Three of the eleven poems are reproduced under the title 'Un poète de dix ans', in *François Mauriac*, ed. by Jean Touzot (Editions de l'Herne, 1985), pp. 59–60.

they had learned by heart.[8] This anthology was used by twelve year
olds in Mauriac's Catholic school, the Collège Sainte-Marie de Grand-
Lebrun. The impact it made on Mauriac is plain from the number of
references to it in his reminiscences.[9] Ragon's anthology ensured that
Mauriac would be deeply influenced by the French Romantics:
Lamartine and Hugo occupying top spot in his schoolboy hierarchy,
followed by Musset and Vigny (*PC* 324). Later in his adolescence, it
was the 'minor' Romantic, Maurice de Guérin, whose influence would
become decisive (*DAM* 163). Vigny was a particular favourite of
Mauriac's elder brother, Raymond, who also introduced him to the
work of Sully Prudhomme (*LV* 27). Mauriac links the latter with Al-
bert Samain, another contemporary poet whose work he esteemed as
an adolescent (*OA* 83). Anna de Noailles was also important to him at
this stage (*OC*, XI, 35). He went on to discover Baudelaire at the age
of fifteen thanks to his father's edition of *Les Fleurs du mal* (*BN*, IV,
503). At about the same time he also discovered the Symbolists and
Verlaine, with Rimbaud coming a little later (*PC* 34). Racine proved a
huge influence on Mauriac from the age of about sixteen (*SR* 57). A
couple of years later came his introduction to Claudel (*MAM* 154).
Other contemporary writers—'Jammes surtout' (*OA* 811)—came with
his reading of an anthology of modern verse.[10] The last significant
influence on Mauriac's verse came in 1917 with the publication of
Valéry's *Jeune Parque*. 'Depuis Valéry,' Mauriac writes, 'aucune
voix ne s'est mêlée au chœur familier de mes poètes' (*OA* 667). The
post-1910 avant-garde left him cold. He had no time for 'les onoma-
topées, la pauvre langue télégraphique des poètes cubistes', arguing
that their typographical experiments were no more than 'des jeux

---

[8] Pierre Mauriac, *François Mauriac: mon frère*, ed. by Jacques Monférier (Bordeaux:
L'Esprit du Temps, 1997), p. 26. Ragon's anthology was first published in 1886, the
year after François Mauriac's birth.

[9] See, for example, *OC*, XI, 273 where Mauriac also states his fidelity to the poets
discovered in a manual used by even younger children, the *Corbeille de l'enfance à
l'usage des maisons d'éducation chrétiennes*. I assume this is the same as *La Corbeille de l'enfance: choix gradué de cent jolis morceaux de poésie*, edited and first
published by Mme M. J. Adolphe Guerard in 1853 with numerous subsequent editions.

[10] *Poètes d'aujourd'hui: morceaux choisis*, ed. by Ad. Van Bever and Paul Léautaud
(Mercure de France, 1900). The anthology was regularly updated throughout the first
part of the twentieth century, but Mauriac himself was never included.

supérieurs et des divertissements esthétiques' (*MAM* 111, 112). And he viewed the Surrealists as no more than pale imitators of Rimbaud (*OA* 268).

I shall not be considering the nature of Mauriac's relationship with his various precursors and contemporaries in any detail: Swift's monograph on Mauriac and Symbolism provides a useful overview of such issues and my bibliography provides details of some of the more relevant articles. For present purposes, I simply wish to emphasize the extent to which Mauriac's youth was marked by these poets: 'J'ai été, dès ma première adolescence et durant toute ma jeunesse, un grand lecteur de vers', Mauriac tells us, adding: 'Ma vie, toute nourrie par la lecture [...] était comme orchestrée par les poètes' (*OA* 399). The themes, language, and rhythms of these poets made a deep impression on Mauriac's mind and haunt his own verse production.[11] As a result of this poetic immersion of his youth, one could say that Mauriac was almost 'naturally' drawn towards verse as a medium of expression. However, this is not to deny the significance of more general cultural factors in Mauriac's attraction to verse: the years when he was developing intellectually, first as a reader, then as a writer, were a period when the novel was perceived as problematic and when poetry was still seen as the noblest literary genre.[12]

Nature and childhood
Given the influence of Romanticism on the young Mauriac, it is not surprising to find him emphasizing Nature and childhood in his discussions of poetic origins. For him, 'la source de toute poésie' was not the urban atmosphere of the capital, but 'cette Cybèle aux deux visages qui [l]'avait enfanté et allaité' (*OA* 456).[13] Malagar, the Mauriac family property surrounded by vineyards and overlooking the Garonne, is the rural location that is generally most readily associated with Mauriac's poetry. As he tells Jean Amrouche: 'Malagar a été, dès mon enfance, une source d'extraordinaire poésie pour moi' (*SR* 39). But, in point of fact, Mauriac rarely visited Malagar before his eight-

---

[11] See Guyonnet, 'Mauriac et le mythe d'Atys', I, 421–64 for numerous examples.

[12] See Michel Raimond, *La Crise du roman: des lendemains du Naturalisme aux années vingt*, 3rd edn (Corti, 1968).

[13] The 'deux visages' in question are the vines around Malagar and the pines of the Landes.

eenth year (*OA* 676). The family properties at Gradignan (Château-Lange) and, especially, Saint-Symphorien were his usual destinations during the school holidays[14]—destinations which remind us of the indirect significance of money and class in Mauriac's poetic formation. While Mauriac says it was the major poets of Romanticism who opened his eyes to the natural world's 'beauté extérieure', it was Maurice de Guérin who introduced him to the 'muettes passions de la terre' (*OC*, XI, 89). This suggests that Mauriac discovered Nature through the grid of poetry. But, when Amrouche asks him whether this was in fact the case, Mauriac insists: 'Ce n'est pas par la poésie que je suis allé à la nature. [...] C'est la nature qui m'a atteint d'abord' (*SR* 48). The truth doubtless lies somewhere in the middle: the sensory impressions experienced by the young Mauriac during the school holidays would have taken on a deeper resonance once he discovered the verbalization of similar impressions in Romantic verse.

Mauriac regards childhood as a privileged period for sensory awareness and imaginative recreation. For him, 'tous les enfants sont des poètes' (*OA* 641). He borrows the title of one of Rimbaud's poems, 'Les Poètes de sept ans', to evoke a child's 'pouvoir de transfiguration' (*OA* 373). This privileged period can last well into adolescence (*MAM* 162). Hence his conviction that 'il n'est guère de poète qui ne demeure un enfant, quelle qu'ait été sa vie'—with the notable exception, he admits, of Mallarmé and Valéry (*BN*, II, 292). As Bethlenfalvay has shown, an emphasis on the superiority of childhood was an important part of literary Romanticism. She also shows that literary Romanticism was influenced in its elevation of the child by the evolution of French Catholic approaches to the Incarnation between the seventeenth and nineteenth centuries.[15] Given the centrality of the Incarnation for Mauriac's own faith (*OA* 685), and his interest as a young man in the possibility of writing a history of Catholic Romanticism (*BN*, III, 34), this religious component of his Romantic heritage is particularly noteworthy.

---

[14] Cf. Jean Mauriac, *Malagar: entretien avec Eric des Garets* (Pin Balma: Sables, 1998), p. 72: 'La poésie de toute son œuvre, mon père le doit à Saint-Symphorien.'

[15] Marina Bethlenfalvay, *Les Visages de l'enfant dans la littérature française du XIXe siècle: esquisse d'une typologie* (Geneva: Droz, 1979), p. 41.

Poetry and religion
Mauriac's Romantic heritage and religious convictions also combine in one of his more extended comments on the concept of poetry:

> Si la poésie se ramène à l'effusion de notre être secret, si elle est le cri d'un cœur plein de désir qui se répand et qui se livre, si elle prend sa source en nous à l'intersection de l'esprit et de la chair, elle ne peut pas ne pas exprimer le drame de l'homme divisé contre lui-même jusqu'à ce qu'il ait compris pour quel amour il a été créé. (*PC* 120)

The notion that poetry involves the expression of our deepest feelings belongs to the tradition of Romantic lyricism. But Mauriac's phrasing is ambiguous: is he suggesting that it is the writer or the reader (or both) who will be led to an appreciation of divine love via such poetry? The context, a discussion of eroticism in literature, suggests that Mauriac is primarily seeking to justify the erotic elements in his own work. But he probably also harboured the hope that his poetry would indeed serve as the vehicle for leading some of his readers to faith.[16]

Romantic religious sentiments also underlie Mauriac's conviction that poets are somehow different from other men and women, fulfilling a quasi-religious function:

> Tout se passe comme si les poètes avaient une mission particulière, un exemple à donner et que seuls ils peuvent donner; comme si leur vie, telle qu'elle est, était voulue. Tous, qu'ils aient cru à la vie éternelle ou, qu'à l'exemple d'Anna de Noailles, ils l'aient niée, ils attestent la grandeur de l'âme humaine, sa vocation divine. (*OC*, XI, 41)

One can compare these words with his comments on Paul Eluard: 'Eluard était un mystique puisqu'il était un poète. L'inspiration a abattu devant son rêve les murs du bagne matérialiste.[17] Quel poème

---

[16] Cf. a comment on one of his novels: 'Un roman trouble comme *Destins* a été à l'origine d'une vocation très sainte et qui a donné de grands fruits' (*OA* 773). The allusion is to the Benedictine Dom Charles Massabki. See his 'François Mauriac et l'abbaye Sainte-Marie', in *François Mauriac*, ed. by Jean Touzot, pp. 425–27.
[17] This image is borrowed from Claudel who, in his 1913 text 'Ma Conversion', writes with reference to Rimbaud's *Illuminations* and *Une saison en enfer*: 'ces livres ouvraient une fissure dans mon bagne matérialiste et me donnaient l'impression vivante et presque physique du surnaturel.' See Paul Claudel, *Œuvres en prose*, ed. by Jacques Petit and Charles Galpérine (Gallimard, 1965), p. 1009.

n'ouvre sur l'invisible une porte cachée, connue du seul poète?' (*PC* 384). Strictly speaking, there are, of course, significant differences between poets and mystics,[18] but, however debatable the association, Mauriac's words clearly reveal his high view of the poet's calling. On one occasion, he even describes the poet's function in christic terms: 'la plupart des hommes sont des sourds, des aveugles-nés; un poète survient, recueille un peu de boue pure au fond de la source, nous touche les paupières, les oreilles, et nous voyons tout à coup, et nous entendons' (*OC*, XI, 176).[19] No wonder Mauriac so frequently refers to Baudelaire's poem 'Les Phares': his indebtedness to nineteenth-century conceptions of the poet's role—as 'a visionary, a magician, a priest, a prophet or even a god'[20]—is obvious.[21]

Briolet has argued that poetic language always derives, whether consciously or not, from a desire to vanquish oblivion and time.[22] This desire could be regarded as essentially religious, though not necessarily in any supernatural sense of the term. It is a view of poetic language with which Mauriac would have agreed, as he believed that poetry involves a desire to 'éterniser les mouvantes apparences' (*MAM* 126). He associated this desire particularly with the work of Proust, describing the last sentence of *Du côté de chez Swann* as a 'phrase qui s'ouvre comme un portail sur le monde unique de la vraie poésie' (*OA* 673).[23] These words suggest that, for Mauriac, the es-

---

[18] See Marc Eigeldinger, 'Formule spirituelle de la poésie de Pierre Jean Jouve', in Jean Starobinski, Paul Alexandre, and Marc Eigeldinger, *Pierre Jean Jouve: poète et romancier* (Neuchâtel: La Baconnière, 1946), pp. 81–153 (pp. 87–95).

[19] Mauriac draws here on the story of Jesus's healing of an 'aveugle-né' in Jean 9. 6–7. There is a secondary allusion to the account of his healing of a deaf-mute (Marc 7. 32–35). Henceforth, unless indicated otherwise, all biblical references will be to the text of *La Bible de Jérusalem*, new edn (Desclée de Brouwer, 1975).

[20] Robert Gibson, *Modern French Poets on Poetry* (Cambridge: Cambridge University Press, 1961), p. 27.

[21] The history of theories of inspiration shows that the association of poetry with religion has existed since Antiquity. In France, the idea of the poet as priest is found in the sixteenth century, but declined under the influence of the Counter-Reformation. See Paul Bénichou, *Le Sacre de l'écrivain, 1750–1830: essai sur l'avènement d'un pouvoir spirituel laïque dans la France moderne* (Corti, 1973), pp. 16–17.

[22] Daniel Briolet, *Le Langage poétique: de la linguistique à la logique du poème* (Nathan, 1984), p. 11.

[23] The sentence in question ends: 'le souvenir d'une certaine image n'est que le regret d'un certain instant; et les maisons, les routes, les avenues, sont fugitives, hélas,

sence of poetry has to do with salvaging certain 'privileged moments', the transformation of the ephemeral into the eternal.

Although Mauriac refers to the liturgy as 'ce poème sublime' (*BN*, IV, 20) and to prayer as 'la seule manifestation de poésie authentique' (*BN*, V, 208), his own verse, unlike that of Claudel or Péguy for example, is rarely directly inspired by the rhythms and language of Catholic devotion.[24] Catholicism's influence on his poetry is evident more in moral than aesthetic terms. But it is important to note that religious anxiety tends to be expressed far more by the lyric *je* than by Mauriac as author reflecting on his craft. While he often agonized over Christianity's compatibility with the novel, he does not appear to have been quite so troubled over the relationship between Christianity and poetry. Despite the 'sinful' lives of the *poètes maudits*, he praises them for having preserved 'le sens du surnaturel' in their work (*OC*, VIII, 26). The reason why he so admires the poetry of Rimbaud, while rejecting that of the early-twentieth-century avant-garde is that, for Mauriac, the latter remains 'éloignée du monde intérieur et du surnaturel, ce qui élargit à l'infini l'œuvre de Rimbaud' (*MAM* 113). His exchange with the Jesuit Paul Doncœur (*NLV* 363, 140) suggests that, for Mauriac, it was novelists, rather than poets, who were more likely to be 'les écrivains du péché' (*LV* 218). Perhaps this was because he believed there was an intensity about poetic creativity that was almost self-purifying.[25] Such an implication seems to underlie his statement that the life of those who enter a monastic community 'comporte le plus de poésie, au sens profond du terme (si, comme je le crois, poésie pure est synonyme d'absolu)' (*OA* 86).[26]

---

comme les années.' See Marcel Proust, *A la recherche du temps perdu*, ed. by Jean-Yves Tadié and others, 4 vols (Gallimard, 1987–89), I (1987), 420. Mauriac would entitle a 1939 essay *Les Maisons fugitives*.

[24] On the other hand, listening to his mother's prayers does seem to have been a particularly important influence on his tone as a writer (*BN*, III, 117).

[25] Cf. l'abbé Bremond's conviction that, in moral terms, there can be no such thing as 'impure' poetry: 'Le feu de la purification poétique—catharsis—consume inexorablement toutes les crasses de la chair.' See Henri Bremond, *Racine et Valéry: notes sur l'initiation poétique* (Grasset, 1930), p. 14.

[26] The reference to 'poésie pure' alludes to the contemporary debate about pure poetry, especially the way in which the term was (mis)used by l'abbé Bremond. For a critique of Bremond's 'confusion', see D. J. Mossop, *Pure Poetry: Studies in French Poetic Theory and Practice, 1746 to 1945* (Oxford: Clarendon Press, 1971), p. 167.

The cult of art

This association of poetry and the absolute is important for Mauriac. He sees writers as different as Baudelaire, Verlaine, Rimbaud, Mallarmé, Claudel, Gide, Jammes, Proust, and Valéry as having one crucial thing in common: their sense of being 'engagés dans une partie dont formidable est l'enjeu' (*OA* 54). And this, implicitly, is where he sees a weakness in his own poetic credentials. Artaud referred to 'l'esprit d'anarchie profonde qui est à la base de toute poésie'.[27] It might seem surprising, but Mauriac would almost certainly have agreed with him. Despite his 'répulsion à l'égard de tout ce qui est onirique en littérature', Mauriac insists: 'Au départ de tout destin poétique, il y a le songe'—a dream-like state that, as in the case of Nerval, can eventually lead to madness. And, Mauriac continues, 'on a beau dire: aucun destin poétique qui ne comporte cette folie' (*OA* 391). It is the influence of bourgeois heredity, he suggests, that saved him from 'l'extrême bord de l'absurde ou de l'irréparable': 'Ils m'ont sauvé,' he continues, 'à moins qu'ils ne m'aient perdu, dans la mesure où pour un poète c'est perdre sa vie que de la sauver' (*OA* 392). Prompted by this biblical allusion,[28] he goes on to develop the thesis that Christianity offers an alternative 'folie',[29] arguing that 'la vie religieuse ne bride pas, elle satisfait au contraire l'exigence poétique' (*OA* 393), but one senses that Mauriac is not altogether convinced by his own argument or, at least, by his own experience. Gide had told Mauriac: 'vous n'êtes pas assez chrétien pour n'être plus littérateur' (*ORTC*, II, 833), and it was perhaps this tendency to *jouer sur les deux tableaux* which led Mauriac to believe he had never quite devoted himself *absolutely* to either.

While Mauriac admires devotion to art, he remains wary of the cult of art, especially in its self-reflexive manifestations. As he writes in his *Mémoires intérieurs*:

> Depuis Mallarmé, nous voyons ceux de sa postérité piquer du nez:

---

[27] Antonin Artaud, *Le Théâtre et son double* (Gallimard, 1985), p. 63.

[28] Cf. Jesus's words in Marc 8. 35: 'Qui veut en effet sauver sa vie la perdra, mais qui perdra sa vie à cause de moi et de l'Evangile la sauvera.'

[29] Cf. Paul's argument in I Corinthiens 1. 17–31.

> Sur le vide papier que la blancheur défend[30]

> et il se défend si bien qu'il leur clôt le bec à jamais. Voilà ce que c'est que
> d'être idolâtre et à quoi mène le culte du verbe qui n'est pas le Verbe […].
> (*OA* 446)

Similar sentiments are expressed in Mauriac's comments on Blanchot's *L'Espace littéraire* (1955): 'Ce livre est l'évangile du Verbe
désincarné, la divination de l'absence' (*PC* 559).[31] While one may
disagree with Mauriac's value judgements in such quotations, he is
surely right to see a metaphysical significance in the 'crisis of meaning' explored by poets such as Mallarmé and critics such as Blanchot.
Steiner, for example, refers to the 'break of the covenant between
word and world' in the late-nineteenth century as 'one of the very few
genuine revolutions of spirit in Western history and which defines
modernity itself'.[32] Mauriac's unease with respect to this revolution
stems from his view of language as a communicative tool, a view that
relates to his fundamental humanism: 'A travers les sons, les couleurs,
les mots, l'œuvre, c'est toujours quelqu'un qui parle à quelqu'un—
c'est toujours quelqu'un qui parle de lui-même à un autre' (*OA* 528).
For Mauriac, one of the few benefits of the Occupation was that it
encouraged poets to rediscover a genuinely popular, intelligible
voice.[33] He defines himself as belonging to 'l'espèce commune: celle
qui croit que le langage n'est pas à lui-même sa propre fin et qu'il
peut, qu'il doit servir' (*PC* 559). In similar vein, a decade later, he
writes: 'Nous ne nous serons pas interrogés sur le langage, nous nous
sommes servis du langage, à la manière du peuple et comme les
"crocheteurs du Port-au-foin"[34] pour nous passer l'un à l'autre ce "cri
répété par mille sentinelles"' (*BN*, IV, 294). This passage offers a good

---

30 A line from Mallarmé's poem 'Brise Marine'. See Stéphane Mallarmé, *Œuvres
complètes*, ed. by Carl Paul Barbier and Charles Gordon (Flammarion, 1983), p. 176.

[31] Cf. Maurice Blanchot, *L'Espace littéraire* (Gallimard, 1989), p. 37: 'Qui creuse le
vers, échappe à l'être comme certitude, rencontre l'absence des dieux'.

[32] George Steiner, *Real Presences: Is There Anything 'in' What We Say?* (Faber,
1989), p. 93.

[33] François Mauriac, *Paroles perdues et retrouvées*, ed. by Keith Goesch (Grasset,
1986), p. 125.

[34] Touzot's footnote is helpful here: 'Au témoignage de Racan, ces portefaix étaient
considérés par le poète Malherbe comme "ses maîtres pour le langage".'

example of the way in which Mauriac combines bluff 'common sense' with cultured allusion. By aligning himself with 'le peuple', he attempts to turn the political tables on the left-wing intellectuals associated with *le nouveau roman* and *la nouvelle critique* who are his implicit targets in this passage. And, by appealing to both Malherbe and Baudelaire, he also attempts to suggest his own continuity with the great tradition of French literature, whether Classical or (post-) Romantic.

Theories of poetry

But does perhaps the relatively utilitarian view of language that emerges from the quotations above automatically invalidate Mauriac's claim to be a poet? Although in certain respects Mauriac is indeed 'an heir to what has proved most durable in French Symbolism',[35] the extent to which he prizes clarity demonstrates his allegiance to a Classical aesthetic.[36] Cohen has gone so far as to suggest that this aesthetic is 'antipoétique'.[37] The formulation may be extreme, but the theory of poetic language underlying it—that poetry can be defined as deviance from 'everyday' language (unhelpfully equated with prose)[38]—is widely accepted, thanks in large part to the work of Roman Jakobson. I want in this section to outline some of the Jakobsonian ideas that have proved most influential in twentieth-century attempts to define what is meant by poetry. This will mean leaving Mauriac's corpus for a while, but will enable me to establish some of the theoretical background that helps explain Mauriac's neglect as a poet.

Writing in 1921, Jakobson defines poetry as 'le langage dans sa fonction esthétique', a concept which he associates with that of deviation, both phonetic and semantic, from 'everyday' language. In poetry, he argues, the communicative function (central in both emotional and

---

[35] Bernard C. Swift, 'François Mauriac and French Literary Symbolism', in *François Mauriac: Visions and Reappraisals*, ed. by John E. Flower and Bernard C. Swift (Oxford: Berg, 1989), pp. 97–115 (p. 97).

[36] This can be seen, for example, in his praise for Aragon's *Elsa* (1959): 'la pensée du poète ne cesse à aucun moment d'être intelligible' (*BN*, II, 223).

[37] Jean Cohen, *Structure du langage poétique* (Flammarion, 1966), p. 20.

[38] *Ibid.*, p. 13. For a critique of the methodological confusion underlying this approach, see Combe, *Poésie et récit*, pp. 32–33.

everyday language) is reduced to a minimum.[39] A decade later, he makes an important distinction between the content of the concept of *poetry* which is 'unstable and temporally conditioned' and the poetic function, *poeticity*, which is 'an element sui generis'.[40] In 1935, Jakobson uses Russian Formalism's concept of the *dominant* (defined as 'the focusing component of a work of art' that 'rules, determines, and transforms the remaining components') to help define his thought more closely. He points out that just as poetry exhibits many other functions in addition to the poetic function (the poet's intentions may be related to philosophy or social didacticism, for example), so the poetic function can be found in many language constructs that one would not normally class as poems: everyday conversations, advertisements, newspaper articles, etc. Thus, a poetic work should be defined as 'a verbal message whose aesthetic function is its dominant'.[41] Jakobson's ideas in 'The Dominant' anticipate his most influential text on the poetic function, originally read as one of the concluding papers at a conference on style held in 1958. The most oft-quoted sentence from this oft-cited essay comes in response to the question: 'What is the empirical linguistic criterion of the poetic function?' Answer: '*The poetic function projects the principle of equivalence from the axis of selection into the axis of combination.*'[42]

Attridge explains why this sentence became so significant in subsequent discussions of poetic language:

> it is impressively technical in its vocabulary, assured in its rhetoric, and free of any interference from the messy world of judgements, values, and power-relations; and it offers an objective and purely linguistic method of identifying what counts as poetry and what doesn't. It provides just what was wanted—a key to the sealed chamber that had baffled literary thought for centuries.[43]

---

[39] Roman Jakobson, *Questions de poétique* (Editions du Seuil, 1973), p. 21, p. 14.

[40] Roman Jakobson, *Language in Literature*, ed. by Krystyna Pomorska and Stephen Rudy (Cambridge, MA: Harvard University Press, 1987), p. 378.

[41] *Ibid.*, p. 43.

[42] Roman Jakobson, 'Closing Statement: Linguistic and Poetics', in *The Stylistics Reader: From Roman Jakobson to the Present*, ed. by Jean Jacques Weber (Arnold, 1996), pp. 10–35 (p. 17); Jakobson's italics.

[43] Derek Attridge, 'Closing Statement: Linguistics and Poetics in Retrospect', in *The Stylistics Reader*, pp. 36–53 (p. 38).

Attridge's analysis provides an important counterbalance to Jakobson's seminal paper. He shows how, despite Jakobson's apparent erasure of the reader's activity (in favour of the text's 'inherent' structures), the reader is in fact constantly presupposed by the language of Jakobson's own formulations. But an acknowledgement of the reader's role in the determination of the poetic inevitably introduces an abundance of potentially unpredictable variables (such as ideology, gender, institutional practices, and the unconscious)[44]— variables that pose serious, possibly insurmountable problems for any methodology aiming for 'scientific objectivity'. And since poetry is 'a historically mobile cultural practice', we also need to be aware, Attridge argues, that there are 'ceaseless historical changes at work, shifting the boundaries between the poetic and the non-poetic, which Jakobson, in his grand synchronicity, ignores'.[45] This may not be entirely fair to Jakobson. Although he regards poeticity as a transcultural, supra-historical phenomenon, he does acknowledge the historical variability of the concept of poetry.[46] Perhaps, though, the two are not as distinct as Jakobson would have us believe. Nevertheless, Attridge's comment at least shows how important cultural and historical factors are in relation to this subject.

This point is well understood by literary historians. In terms of the French tradition, Kibédi Varga's account is particularly lucid. He sees three main conceptions of poetry at work in post-Renaissance France: the discursive, the sentimental, and the associative/ analogical. He associates the first of these with Classicism:

> claire et facile, destinée à plaire et à être utile et cherchant à représenter des modèles d'une grande abstraction, la poésie classique est essentiellement un embellissement et une réglementation du discours; elle reste essentiellement linéaire.[47]

---

[44] As Attridge himself reminds us (p. 47), the Jakobson of the 1920s was, in fact, more alert to such considerations than the Jakobson of the late 1950s.

[45] *Ibid.*, p. 46, p. 39.

[46] He acknowledges, for example, that 'the marks disclosing the implementation of the aesthetic function are not unchangeable or always uniform' (*Language in Literature*, p. 43).

[47] Aron Kibédi Varga, *Les Constantes du poème: analyse du langage poétique*, 2nd edn (Picard, 1977), p. 252. The next two quotations are from pp. 256–57 and p. 262, respectively.

The sentimental conception (that one might associate with Romantic lyricism) is rather different:

> l'ordre des sentiments n'est pas linéaire. Aussi la clarté et la facilité ne sont-elles plus considérées comme des mérites, mais plutôt comme les marques d'un esprit superficiel: la poésie demande l'obscurité mystérieuse et confuse des sentiments. [...] La poésie sentimentale cherche notamment à exprimer certains registres spécifiques du sentiment, la mélancolie, la tristesse. En outre, elle a une tendance, [...], passéiste.

The associative/ analogical conception of poetry is seen as an essentially post-Romantic phenomenon, developing from Hugo, via Baudelaire and Rimbaud, to the Surrealists:

> ce qu'elle perd en étendue, la poésie associative le gagne en densité ou, si l'on veut, en profondeur. [...] La poésie associative est non-narrative, et si elle ne cherche pas précisément à éliminer le temps, le temps, et par conséquent le mouvement temporel que toute linéarité implique, lui est indifférent: elle s'installe dans le moment.

This conception of poetry (or something like it) proved dominant in twentieth-century aesthetics. Yet, as Todorov reminds us, despite the popularity of this associative theory (or *symbolist* theory as he calls it), it is important to remember that it is only *a* theory, and not 'la vérité enfin révélée'.[48]

In his own sketch of the evolving concept of poetic language, Mauriac demonstrates a clear sense of the post-Romantic revolution of poetic language. In fact, though, it is the Romantic poet Vigny whom he sees as providing a bridge between old and new views. He suggests that while many of Vigny's poems have a strongly discursive dimension—communicating 'une pensée qui aurait pu être exprimée par la prose'—the final stanza of 'La Maison du berger' offers 'un portique ouvert sur la poésie moderne', that is, the new sort of poetry exemplified by Baudelaire in which 'le mot se détachait de ce qu'il avait reçu mission de nous transmettre', in which the poetic image 'ne correspondait plus à l'idée claire du poète', but 'vivait pour elle seule, de sa propre vie' (*BN*, III, 495). Although the practitioners of this new form of verse ('Symbolist' poets in the broadest sense of the term from

---

[48] Tzvetan Todorov, *Les Genres du discours* (Seuil, 1978), p. 101.

Baudelaire to Valéry) were the poets Mauriac most admired, his own verse also demonstrates the continuing influence of Classical and Romantic models. Perhaps this is one of the reasons why he never achieved any significant recognition as a poet—he was out of step with the dominant aesthetic of his contemporaries, an aesthetic which finds its clearest expression in the writings of Jakobson. However, as the preceding paragraphs have shown, efforts to define precisely what counts as 'poetic' are extremely problematic. Any attempt to dismiss Mauriac's verse purely on the grounds that it fails to correspond to a particular aesthetic would be short-sighted and doctrinaire. There are certainly legitimate grounds on which his poetry could be criticized, but non-conformity to a predetermined model should not be one of them.

Poetry and prose
Mauriac's statement that much of Vigny's thought could have been expressed in prose brings us to the question of the relationship between poetry and prose. The vast majority of twentieth-century theorists tended to accentuate the difference between the two codes. Valéry, for example, develops Malherbe's idea that poetry is to prose as dancing is to walking:

> La marche comme la prose a toujours un objet précis. Elle est un acte dirigé *vers* quelque objet que notre but est de joindre. […] La danse, c'est toute autre chose. Elle est, sans doute, un système d'actes, mais qui ont leur fin en eux-mêmes. Elle ne va nulle part.[49]

In prose, Valéry argues, language is used in an instrumental fashion such that, once communication has taken place, the language that served as a vehicle for that communication is instantly discarded (or, if necessary, can be reformulated using different, but equivalent, terms). He continues: 'La poésie ainsi entendue est radicalement distincte de toute prose: en particulier, elle s'oppose nettement à la description et à la narration d'événements qui tendent à donner l'illusion de la réalité'.[50] This distinction between poetry and prose is not, how-

---

[49] Valéry, *Œuvres*, I, 1371.
[50] *Ibid.*, p. 1374. The quotations in the next two sentences are from p. 1370 and p. 1457 respectively (the italics in the second sentence are Valéry's).

ever, absolute. Valéry is well aware that the twin poles of prose and verse 'se rejoignent et s'enchaînent par une foule de degrés inter-médiaires', but, for the sake of clarity, he tends to view them 'dans leurs états extrêmes' when engaging in theoretical discussions. In reality, all texts contain 'poetic' elements insofar as their language 'montre *un certain écart* avec l'expression la plus directe'; and, con-versely, although poets should strive to achieve the ideal of pure po-etry (that is, poetry devoid of non-poetic elements), such a state re-mains an unattainable ideal: 'ce qu'on appelle un *poème* se compose pratiquement de fragments de *poésie pure* enchâssés dans la matière d'un discours.' This point is also conceded by subsequent theorists such as Sartre and Bonnet, despite their strong conviction that poetry and prose are fundamentally different 'genres'.[51]

Once again, we find Mauriac swimming against the tide in rela-tion to this discussion. Rather than emphasizing the distinction be-tween the codes, he generally underlines their similarity, saying of the poet and the novelist: 'je les ai toujours confondus' (*OA* 523). After reading Guy Dumur's first novel, Mauriac writes to him: 'vous êtes un poète et c'est par là que vous pouvez être un grand romancier' (*NLV* 254). Proust's creativity is defined as 'un des plus grands miracles poétiques de notre littérature' (*OC*, XI, 152). Of Giraudoux, he writes: 'ce prosateur est un unique poète' (*MAM* 155); the Queneau of *Zazie dans le métro* is said to be a poet (*BN*, II, 225); and Sollers is a 'poète de la prose' (*BN*, III, 81). More generally, he writes: 'je crois qu'il n'y a *que* la poésie et que c'est par les éléments poétiques qu'elle ren-ferme qu'une œuvre d'art, à quelque genre qu'elle se rattache, peut durer et mérite de durer' (*PR* 121). Mauriac therefore adopts what might be called a 'universalist' position—one that is fairly common among other authors and critics.[52] Such a perspective may lack nu-ance, but it could perhaps claim the support of etymology (the word *poet* deriving from the Greek *poiein*, to make).

---

[51] See Jean-Paul Sartre, *Qu'est-ce que la littérature?* (Gallimard, 1986), p. 48 and Henri Bonnet, *Roman et Poésie: essai sur l'esthétique des genres. La littérature d'avant-garde et Marcel Proust*, 2nd edn (Nizet, 1980), p. 97.

[52] See, for example, Aragon and Queneau quoted by Combe, *Poésie et récit*, pp. 110–11; Georges-Emmanuel Clancier, *La Poésie et ses environs* (Gallimard, 1973), p. 66; and Henri Suhamy, *La Poétique* (Presses Universitaires de France, 1986), p. 87.

Although, towards the very end of his life, Mauriac refused to distinguish between his own status as novelist and as poet (*BN*, V, 15), he was not always quite so insistent. In a letter of 26 March 1927, Roger Martin du Gard distinguished ('arbitrairement, j'en conviens') between Mauriac the novelist and Mauriac the poet (*LV* 406). Although he prefers the former—'[le] Mauriac observateur' responsible for secondary characters—he also admires the latter (responsible, he suggests, for the central character in Mauriac's novels). In his reply, Mauriac comments: 'je crois profondément juste votre distinction entre le romancier et le poète… quoique beaucoup de mes personnages procèdent des deux' (*LV* 144). The idea that his observational side is to the fore in his novels also emerges in Mauriac's conversations with Jean Amrouche:

> j'ai d'abord été poète et [...] mes premières tentatives de prose exprimaient certainement une recherche du poète en moi. Mais, en même temps, j'étais un poète attentif, [...], à ce que disaient, à ce que faisaient, à ce que pensaient les grandes personnes; [...]. Le romancier est né peu à peu du désir de fixer et d'exprimer toutes ces découvertes presque inconscientes que j'avais faites, petit garçon observateur et attentif. (*SR* 80)

In terms of content, therefore, Mauriac is aware that he pays much closer attention to social interaction as a novelist than he does as a poet. But, in terms of structure, he sees far less of a distinction:

> je crois que je compose mes romans un peu comme des poèmes, et que ce besoin que j'ai de m'isoler, de me concentrer, de les écrire d'une coulée en quelque sorte, vient de ce que c'est le poète chez moi qui compose et qui crée. (*SR* 137)

He would later relate this preference for 'de brefs récits orchestrés comme des poèmes' to Valéry's contempt for the traditional novel (*PC* 499–500). Yet, in his later verse at least, Mauriac did not proceed in this 'inspirational' manner at all. His painstaking approach was much closer to that of Valéry, whom Amrouche cites as a counterexample of the mechanics of poetic creation. Mauriac concedes the point, adding: 'mais je pensais au poète romantique, au sens le plus vague; je parlais d'une certaine famille de poètes dans la lignée de laquelle je me trouve' (*SR* 137–38). However, this rather stereotyped literary model actually reflects the practice of Mauriac's fictional poets such as Yves Frontenac and Augustin (*Préséances*) rather than his own.

Mauriac's tendency to blur the distinctions between poetry and prose at a time when major theorists were keen to emphasize these distinctions provides another reason why his verse received so little attention during his lifetime. While his career as a novelist was probably enhanced by the lyrical quality of his prose, the narrative dimension of his verse contradicted 'le refus du récit' that lies at the heart of many modern theories of poetry.[53] This was a rejection not just of narrative *per se*, but of the various elements that so often accompanied it, so that the theorists of 'pure poetry' wished to 'faire abstraction de l'expérience quotidienne, des contenus didactiques ou utilitaires, des vérités pratiques, des sentiments de tout un chacun, des ivresses du cœur'—in other words, the very features that are so prominent in much of Mauriac's verse. Combe suggests that the supremacy of 'pure poetry' can be seen as something of a parenthesis in the history of French poetics: a parenthesis that opened in the 1870s and seemed to be closing again in the 1970s.[54] It was Mauriac's misfortune as a poet that his career happened to fall within this hundred-year period.

Music and silence
Like many other lyric poets,[55] Mauriac made an explicit association between verse and music. Musicality was something he associated particularly with the work of Racine (*OA* 491). Mauriac nowhere attempts to define in linguistic terms precisely what he means by Racine's 'music' (he doubtless believed it defied analysis), but he does return to the idea a few years later in terms which emphasize the importance of Racine's clarity:

> En fait, la source première de mes poèmes est dans Racine. Le miracle dont je suis presque seul demeuré hanté parmi les poètes, c'est, à travers une musique, à quoi tout est soumis, une pensée qui se développe, une pensée qui dure, qui atteint à son développement logique. Un poème qui n'est que musique et qui pourtant a une signification et enchaîne des idées claires et dis-

---

[53] See Combe, *Poésie et récit*, p. 12. The next quotation is from Hugo Friedrich, quoted by Combe, p. 25.
[54] *Ibid.*, p. 186.
[55] See David Lindley, *Lyric* (Methuen, 1985), pp. 25–30.

tinctes, cela paraît aussi absurde et démodé aujourd'hui que la peinture
d'histoire, mais c'est peut-être ce qui me laisse une chance d'être redé-
couvert... (*BN*, IV, 180)

Leaving aside the self-dramatization of this passage (in his later years,
Mauriac was keen on presenting himself as an isolated figure), it is
important to note Mauriac's unwillingness to sacrifice reason and
intelligibility to the dictates of 'pure' musicality.[56] This had already
been his position over forty years earlier when he had celebrated the
musicality of Valéry's verse, but had added: 'il y a plus ici qu'une
émotion, mieux qu'une tristesse ou qu'une joie: il y a une pensée.'[57]
For Mauriac, the logical coherence of Valéry's verse means that he is
'moins fils de Mallarmé que petit-fils de Corneille, de Racine et de La
Fontaine'. Such statements help explain why, when he came to consider the connection between music and poetry four decades later, he
preferred to do so via a Classical author such as Racine, rather than
the poets of Symbolism who might have provided a more obvious
point of reference.[58]

There is an apparent paradox between this stress on the link between poetry and music and Mauriac's belief that: 'Toute grande
œuvre naît du silence et y retourne' (*OA* 446). Blanchot had written
much the same thing a few years earlier, describing 'la parole confiée
à la recherche du poète' as 'ce langage dont toute la force est de n'être
pas' adding: 'il vient du silence et il retourne au silence.'[59] We have
seen that Mauriac knew *L'Espace littéraire* (1955). Could he have
been (unconsciously?) quoting Blanchot in his *Mémoires intérieurs*
(1959)? Whatever the answer to this question, it is certain that, despite
the similarity of his formulation, Mauriac's understanding of 'silence'
in this context differed radically from Blanchot's sense of a fundamental metaphysical void. Although Mauriac nowhere provides an
explicit definition of what he means by 'silence', a hint is provided in

---

[56] Mallarmé's line 'Aboli bibelot d'inanité sonore' (from the poem 'Ses purs ongles
très haut...') comes to mind. See Mallarmé, *Œuvres complètes*, p. 356.

[57] François Mauriac, 'L'Acte de foi', *Le Divan*, no. 79 (May 1922), 276–78 (pp. 276–
77). The next quotation is from p. 277.

[58] One thinks, for example, of the opening line of Verlaine's 'Art poétique' (*Jadis et
naguère*): 'De la musique avant toute chose'. See Paul Verlaine, *Œuvres poétiques*,
ed. by Jacques Robichez (Garnier Frères, 1969), p. 261.

[59] Blanchot, *L'Espace littéraire*, p. 38.

a quotation that he makes from Maurice de Guérin's *Journal*—a quotation made in the context of a general discussion of silence in literature. In this passage, Guérin refers approvingly to the man who 'garde [...] le secret de son âme et des habitudes intimes de ses pensées' (*OA* 446–47). Mauriac then goes on to discuss the poetry of André Lafon—whom he elsewhere describes as Guérin's 'frère' (*OA* 11)—stating that Lafon's poetry sprang from 'un recueillement et [...] une contemplation intérieure [...] soutenue et [...] jalousement défendue' (*OA* 447). It would appear, then, that what Mauriac really envisages when he refers to creative 'silence' is something like a spirit of quiet contemplation, a period of self-communion for 'the soul' (*l'âme* is generally far more than a metaphor for Mauriac).

But silence is also related for Mauriac to the exigencies of poetic craft:

> La solidité, la dureté, la transparence de la poésie racinienne et valéryenne préservent le silence au cœur de l'œuvre. C'est ce qui sépare le vers de Racine, le vers de Valéry, du vers romantique: celui-ci fait du bruit, le leur est chargé de silence. Et de même la prose de Maurice de Guérin. (*OA* 447)

This passage needs to be compared with one penned over thirty years earlier:

> Il existe un rapport certain entre la discipline intérieure et la perfection poétique; et ce que beaucoup haïssent sous le nom de romantisme, c'est le péché: le péché se trahit dans l'enflure, dans l'égarement, dans le désordre des images, dans le mépris du verbe, dans l'abus des épithètes. Le romantisme est le péché qui s'ignore: Charles Baudelaire domine son siècle parce que, chez lui, le péché se connaît. (*OA* 19)

Despite the strange conflation of moral, cognitive, and aesthetic categories, Mauriac's primary focus here is on poetic practice: Baudelaire is judged superior to the Romantics not because he was a more devout Catholic, but because he combined honest self-appraisal with careful attention to his craft. *Le péché* in the passage above and *le bruit* in the previous quotation are more or less synonymous terms for Mauriac; as he matures as a writer, he increasingly prizes the Classical values of precision and sobriety.

Versification

This leads me, finally, to the question of Mauriac's attitude towards the formal aspects of poetry. It is not my intention to offer a general survey of Mauriac's approach to versification. Excellent work in this area has already been conducted by Le Hir and Guyonnet;[60] and I shall supplement their observations where appropriate in subsequent chapters when I examine Mauriac's verse in more detail. For the time being, I shall content myself with a brief consideration of some of the reasons for Mauriac's fidelity to traditional verse forms.

'Is there, in French poetry,' asks Dunstan Martin, 'a connexion between the certainties of belief and the use of formal metre?'[61] If there is, it is not something that loomed large in Mauriac's consciousness. It is true that, when discussing Claudel's *Vers d'exil* (1912), he does seem to posit some kind of connection between 'le joug de la métrique ancienne' and 'celui de la loi catholique' (*BN*, IV, 166), but this is an isolated reference. If Mauriac remains wedded to formal metre, it is not overtly because of any religious concerns.

A more likely reason emerges from the conversation in which Mauriac told Le Hir that he needed the constraints imposed by Classical versification: 'A partir du moment où je les supprime, je deviens romancier.'[62] Although, as we have seen, Mauriac often refused to separate the poet from the novelist, there was a part of him that continued to view verse as the most prestigious of the literary arts. Hence the disappointment when he confesses to Le Hir that his poems 'se perdent dans la prose'. Re-reading *Les Mains jointes* in 1927, Mauriac was extremely critical of the 'facilité' of his technique (*MJ* 323). But if verse offered the temptation of facile self-indulgence to the young Mauriac (one remembers his censure of Romanticism's aesthetic 'sinfulness'), it also provided a challenge to the mature poet of developing a more rigorous style, one that would prove more aesthetically satisfying.

---

[60] In, respectively, 'La Versification de François Mauriac' and 'Mauriac et le mythe d'Atys', I, 421–64.

[61] Graham Dunstan Martin, 'High Formal Poetry', in *Poetry in France: Metamorphoses of a Muse*, ed. by Keith Aspley and Peter France (Edinburgh: Edinburgh University Press, 1992), pp. 204–18 (p. 217).

[62] Le Hir, 'La Versification de François Mauriac', p. 74. The next quotation is from p. 75.

Ultimately, though, perhaps the most important factor in Mauriac's fidelity to conventional verse forms is simply the influence of the prolonged poetic immersion of his childhood and adolescence. He absorbed the language and rhythms of his precursors so profoundly that it made it difficult for him to envisage deviating too far from their formative example. He could certainly appreciate other formal approaches (hence his admiration for Guérin, Rimbaud, and Claudel), but, as far as his own practice as a poet was concerned, there was an umbilical attachment to rhyme and isosyllabism. Hence his comment to Duhamel when thanking him for a copy of *Elégies* (1920): '[je suis] gêné seulement par l'absence de la rime—qui est, je vous l'accorde, indéfendable en théorie—mais nos oreilles y sont accoutumées depuis des siècles...' (*NLV* 84). His preference for rhyming verse is intimately bound up with the simple but powerful issue of memorability. As he wrote in December 1969:

> Commentant les grands honneurs funèbres rendus à Paul Valéry, Claudel dit drôlement dans son *Journal* que ce furent les funérailles solennelles du vers alexandrin. Mais il se trompe, parce que le vers alexandrin est ami de la mémoire. Je pourrais citer à l'infini des vers de Racine et de tous les romantiques français, de Hugo à Musset et à Vigny, de Baudelaire à Verlaine. Aucun d'Eluard et des autres. Le vers libre est libre en ceci surtout qu'il s'évade librement de la mémoire, qu'il n'y reste pas. (*BN*, V, 289)

If the purpose of poetry is indeed to 'éterniser les mouvantes apparences' (*MAM* 126), then one can understand why Mauriac should have desired the forms employed to achieve this end to be as memorable as possible.[63]

Conclusion

It is clear from the foregoing that Mauriac had an extremely high regard for poetry. Given this lofty conception of the poet's art, one can understand why he was so keen to be thought of as a poet himself. His views on verse are strongly influenced by the theories and practice of his nineteenth-century forebears and by the Classical tradition to which he was also heir. His reactions, however, are never inspired

---

[63] Mauriac writes at greater length about the memorability of conventional verse in an article from 1947 entitled 'La Jeune Parque réveillée'—see his *Journal V* (Flammarion, 1953), pp. 232–33.

purely by aesthetic concerns; as with all his writing, there is an important moral/ spiritual dimension to his various pronouncements on poetry. This can make some of his judgements (especially those delivered as part of a polemic) seem rather reactionary. But it is also worth noting that, on other occasions, he was capable of praising the work of modern poets such as Pierre Emmanuel, Jean-Claude Renard, and Luc Estang (*BN*, IV, 422). It was no doubt the Christian dimension of these poets' work that appealed to him, but, elsewhere, one also finds him expressing admiration for the work of Henri Michaux and quoting at length from René Char—'pour ma délectation'.[64] This will come as quite a surprise for those familiar with Mauriac's tastes. As I turn now to an analysis of Mauriac's own verse, I hope there might be some further surprises in store for readers who have never thought of him as a poet.

---

[64] See, respectively, *François Mauriac et Jean Paulhan: Correspondance, 1925–1967*, ed. by John E. Flower (Editions Claire Paulhan, 2001), p. 115 and François Mauriac, 'Le Bloc-notes', *L'Express*, 12 January 1961, p. 40. However, it should be pointed out that Mauriac's religious preoccupations are in evidence here as well. Although he faithfully transcribes ten stanzas from Char's poem 'Les Dentelles de Montmirail', he adds a capital letter to the word 'ciel' in stanza 4, commenting: 'Il semble que ce soit le Ciel qui ait le dernier mot. Mais il le prononce à voix si basse que nul ne l'entend jamais.' The word 'ciel' is printed in lower case both in the issue of the *NRF* that was Mauriac's source (the number of 1 January 1961) and in the Pléiade critical edition—see René Char, *Œuvres complètes*, ed. by Lucie Jamme and others (Gallimard, 1983), p. 413.

2. The Birth of a Poet: Les Mains jointes

Publication and reception

In September 1907 Mauriac left Bordeaux for Paris with the ostensible aim of gaining a place at the Ecole des Chartes. Although he achieved this goal just over a year later (having failed at his first attempt), his extra-curricular literary interests occupied him to such an extent that he abandoned his studies in March 1909. In May of the same year he became the poetry reviewer for the *Revue du Temps Présent*, a journal which also published some of his own verse. The journal's young editor, Francis-Charles Caillard, offered Mauriac the opportunity of publishing his poems in book form for the sum of five hundred francs. Mauriac had been writing verse since his schooldays and the note-books he brought with him to the capital provided him with some of the material he needed for his first collection.[1] In his diary, the would-be *homme de lettres* adopts a tone of self-mockery to describe his literary debut: 'J'ai pris place dans cette armée d'impuissants aux prétentions exaspérées qui payent 500 frs à un imprimeur pour que leurs amis et connaissances aient communication de leur vague à l'âme, de leurs désirs de coït etc. etc.'[2] Nevertheless, the money paid to Caillard turned out to be a wise investment.

Mauriac sent a copy of *Les Mains jointes* to the novelist Paul Bourget who, in turn, lent it to his fellow Academician, Maurice Barrès. On 8 February 1910, Barrès wrote to the young poet: 'Monsieur, Vous êtes un grand poète que j'admire, un poète vrai, mesuré, tendre et profond qui n'essaie pas de forcer sa voix faite pour nous attendrir sur notre enfance. Je voudrais le dire au public' (*OA* 170–71). And this is precisely what he went on to do in a review published in *L'Echo de Paris* of 21 March 1910—'mon premier titre de noblesse', as Mauriac would later call it (*BN*, II, 81). However, although the review is broadly positive, it is not as unequivocally supportive as the

---

[1] The precise nature of the relationship between the poems of *Les Mains jointes* and the verse contained in Mauriac's unpublished notebooks from the period 1901–05 has never been examined. My forthcoming critical edition of *Les Mains jointes* will shed light on this question.

[2] François Mauriac, 'Ecrits de jeunesse', ed. by Jean Touzot, *CFM*, 10 (1983), 7–55 (p. 31).

earlier letter. Alongside the plaudits ('Beaucoup de mesure, nul mensonge, la plus douce et la plus vraie musique de chambre'), there is
also a challenge to the young poet: 'Saura-t-il mûrir? C'est là le grand
problème. [...] Il faut quitter d'un pas assuré notre jeunesse et trouver
mieux. Ce n'est pas bien malin d'être une merveille à vingt ans!' (*OA*
195, 197).

Barrès was not the only contemporary to praise Mauriac's early
verse. The young poet received words of warm encouragement in
letters from fellow-poets such as Francis Jammes (*LV* 385), Jean de la
Ville de Mirmont (*DAM* 53), Robert Vallery-Radot, and Anna de
Noailles.[3] Perhaps epistolary etiquette and the influence of friendship
dictated some of the sentiments expressed in these letters. Nevertheless, there were also more objective, public expressions of approval,
notably from Pierre Quillard and Marc Lafargue, whose favourable
reviews (positively glowing in Lafargue's case) do not appear to have
sprung from any religious or affective proximity to the poet.[4] Mention
should also be made of the eminent critic Emile Faguet who saw in
Mauriac 'un poète de rare essence', even though, like Barrès, he detected the need for 'un peu de maturité et de quelque effort, [...] pour
que cette belle promesse soit tenue'.[5] It is clear, therefore, that there
were a number of genuine contemporary admirers of Mauriac's early
verse.

There were also more hostile responses among the early critics.
Mauriac himself quotes from what he calls Alain-Fournier's 'note
assez fielleuse' that appeared in *Paris-Journal* in the spring of 1912
and which criticized the young poet for excessive conventionality (*OA*
192). He also quotes the reaction of Alain-Fournier's brother-in-law,
Jacques Rivière (a fellow Bordelais): 'Je trouve très bien ta note sur
Mauriac, lequel nous embête avec son ordre et sa discipline' (*OA*
193). However, the harshest comments on his early verse were to
emanate from the poet himself in a preface dating from 1927: 'Si jamais je n'ai consenti jusqu'à ce jour à rééditer *Les Mains jointes*,

---

[3] For the last two, see 'Ecrits de jeunesse', p. 47 and p. 49.
[4] See Pierre Quillard, 'Les Poèmes', *Mercure de France*, no. 304 (February 1910),
685–90 (pp. 686–87) and Marc Lafargue, 'La Poésie', *Les Marges*, no. 25 (January
1911), 15–28 (pp. 25–28).
[5] Emile Faguet, 'Les Poésies de M. François Mauriac', *Revue des Deux Mondes*, 1
November 1912, 196–204 (p. 204).

c'était sans doute que j'avais en horreur ces vers sans vertèbres, ces poèmes flasques' (*MJ* 323). Mauriac would continue in similar vein little more than a year later: 'Les faciles délices d'une sensibilité religieuse me dictèrent *Les Mains jointes*. [...] Mais déjà, dans le secret, je n'éprouvais que dégoût pour cette dévotion jouisseuse, pour cette délectation sensible à l'usage des garçons qui n'aiment pas le risque' (*ORTC*, II, 787–88). Subsequent negative assessments of *Les Mains jointes* have often been heavily dependent on Mauriac's own criticisms—too dependent, perhaps.[6]

Over recent decades, however, critics have begun to rediscover certain qualities in Mauriac's early verse. In his survey of French twentieth-century poetry, Sabatier comments that the Mauriac of *Les Mains jointes* 'méritait plus d'approfondissement' than Alain-Fournier allowed; he also underlines the fact that much that characterizes Mauriac's later work is found 'en puissance' in these early poems.[7] Pény was the first to attempt a detailed re-evaluation of these early 'vers mal aimés', dismissing Mauriac's own criticisms as the result of an excessive concern for the opinion of others and for literary fashion.[8] A similar point is made by Curtis who suggests that, with the passing of time, the imperatives of 1920s modernity no longer seem so urgent, which means that we can read Mauriac's early verse and appreciate 'ce qu'il y avait d'original et de charmant dans ce chant ingénu'.[9] Most recently, O'Connell has offered an equally positive re-assessment: 'These poems are a minor treasure today, for they offer an exquisite and faithful reflection of the Catholic worldview of an era whose remaining vestiges were completely swept away by Vatican II.'[10]

Whether critics defend or attack *Les Mains jointes*, it is rare for them to transcend rather vague generalizations and actually seek to analyse how the collection as a whole, or individual poems in par-

---

[6] See, for example, Alyn, *François Mauriac*, pp. 73–74 and the same critic's '"Si je suis né poète"', in *Mauriac*, Génies et Réalités (Hachette, 1977), pp. 115–39 (pp. 120–21).

[7] Sabatier, *La Poésie du XXe siècle*, I, 85, 86.

[8] Jean-Marie Pény, 'Plaidoyer pour des vers mal aimés', *CFM*, 10 (1983), 174–89 (p. 175).

[9] In his preface to Mauriac, *Le Feu secret*, p. 9.

[10] David O'Connell, *François Mauriac Revisited* (New York: Twayne, 1995), p. 161.

ticular, function as pieces of literature.[11] I hope my comments in the rest of this chapter will go some way towards remedying this situation. Before turning to a more detailed analysis of the poems, however, I shall consider two broader issues that will prove to be significant for all of Mauriac's verse.

The autobiographical dimension

Although relatively rare, versified autobiography does exist: Wordsworth's *Prelude* (1805) and Betjeman's *Summoned by Bells* (1960), for example. Mauriac's early verse is not of this kind, but it does contain an autobiographical dimension. Although there is no autobiographical pact,[12] the lyric *je* is prominent in most of the poems and this encourages the reader, almost 'naturally' as it were, to identify the author with the voice of this poetic persona.[13]

Such an identification was made particularly readily during the Romantic period. One thinks, for example, of Madame de Staël's classic definition in *De l'Allemagne*: 'la poésie lyrique s'exprime au nom de l'auteur même; ce n'est plus dans un personnage qu'il se transporte, c'est en lui-même qu'il trouve les divers mouvements dont il est animé.'[14] A diary entry for 28 August 1908 suggests that the young Mauriac shared this perspective: 'Je suis resté longtemps sans écrire ici à cause que je me suis ces temps-ci beaucoup exprimé dans des vers.'[15]

Nevertheless, as Vadé has shown, the status of the Romantic lyric subject is ultimately more complex than the poets themselves sometimes appeared to believe:

> Le sujet lyrique apparaît finalement comme la résultante des différentes postures d'énonciation assumées par le 'je' du texte. Il n'est identifiable ni à l'écrivain, ni à un personnage fictif. Il est bien, comme le dit Käte Ham-

---

[11] An exception is provided by Jean Touzot in his article 'Analogie et poème, ou les deux saisons de l'imagerie mauriacienne', in *François Mauriac 1: la poésie de François Mauriac*, pp. 25–49.

[12] On this notion, see Philippe Lejeune, *Le Pacte autobiographique* (Editions du Seuil, 1976).

[13] Cf. Alain Vaillant, *La Poésie: initiation aux méthodes d'analyse des textes poétiques* (Nathan, 1992), p. 100.

[14] Quoted by Combe, *Poésie et récit*, p. 161.

[15] Mauriac, 'Ecrits de jeunesse', p. 28.

burger, un sujet d'énonciation réel, mais décalé par rapport au 'je' autobio-graphique.[16]

This statement could be applied to Mauriac's lyric *je* as well.

When he says that he describes *himself* ('tel que je me décris') as a provincial adolescent in *Les Mains jointes* (*SR* 114), it is clear that he regards the collection as having some kind of autobiographical significance. However, one of the dangers of seeking to use Mauriac's verse as a direct source of autobiographical information emerges ear-lier in his conversations with Jean Amrouche. The interviewer asks him why, in *L'Adieu à l'adolescence*, he described his childhood as being 'trop douce' (*AA* 367). Mauriac replies: 'c'est uniquement, du moins je l'imagine, parce que j'avais besoin du mot "douce" au mo-ment où je faisais ce très mauvais vers!' (*SR* 18). In other words, the dictates of prosody, not to mention aesthetic concerns, problematize attempts to read verse as a straightforward medium of self-expression. This is why I shall refer to the lyric subject either as 'the lyric *je*' or as 'the poet', but not as 'Mauriac'.

However, it seems to me that any attempt to dismiss the autobio-graphical dimension of *Les Mains jointes* in order to safeguard the 'autonomy' of the text would be too extreme. As Combe reminds us, the *énonciation* of lyric poetry is fundamentally ambivalent: 'La référence du JE lyrique est un mixte indécidable d'autobiographie et de fiction.'[17] The notion that biographical information might help inform a reading of an author's work has been viewed with suspicion in certain theoretical circles for many decades now. However, I would agree with Burke that the connection between *bios* and *graphé* cannot simply be erased because of the 'bad biographicist practices of the past'.[18] The reduction of literary texts to more or less rhetorically ornamented versions of life-events can certainly obscure their interest and value as linguistic artefacts. But to ignore the biographical dimen-

---

[16] Yves Vadé, 'L'Emergence du sujet lyrique à l'époque romantique', in *Figures du sujet lyrique*, ed. by Dominique Rabaté (Presses Universitaires de France, 1996), pp. 11–37 (p. 36).

[17] Combe, *Poésie et récit*, p. 162.

[18] Seán Burke, *The Death and Return of the Author: Criticism and Subjectivity in Barthes, Foucault and Derrida* (Edinburgh: Edinburgh University Press, 1992), p. 170.

sion entirely is surely to ignore an important component of certain texts, particularly when, as in the case of Mauriac's early verse, the inclusion of autobiographical elements may be part of an overarching textual strategy.

The lyric *je* of the early verse seems very close in many ways to what we know of the young Mauriac. When the poet, addressing his mother, refers to 'ton dernier enfant que tout désarme' (*MJ* 334), one thinks immediately of François, the benjamin of the Mauriac family, described by his brother Raymond as 'un enfant tranquille, tendre, aimant, et qui pleurait facilement'.[19] The second section of *Les Mains jointes* echoes the sense of melancholy and isolation that the young Mauriac experienced when he arrived in Paris.[20] When the poet writes of:

> Ma peine inconnue et qu'on n'aime pas,
> Ma médiocrité dans la solitude,
> Et la pauvre laideur de mon front las... (331)

one is reminded of Mauriac's confession: 'Par-dessus tout, à dix-huit ans, je me croyais laid et incapable d'être aimé' (*OA* 170). The description of José Ximenès in *Les Beaux-esprits de ce temps*, which Mauriac later identified as a portrait of himself aged twenty-five (*ORTC*, I, 1379), has obvious relevance for Mauriac's practice as a poet around 1910: 'il ne se lasse pas de rappeler son enfance dont les plus menus souvenirs pour lui demeurent sans prix. C'est vrai que merveilleusement il en extrait la poésie secrète' (*ORTC*, I, 951). When we are further told that he is attracted to 'le vieux romantisme de René', we are reminded of the comparison which the poet draws between his schoolboy self and Chateaubriand's hero in 'L'Ecolier' (*MJ* 326). The poet who looks back longingly to his 'Ame blanche d'enfant' and who deeply regrets 'l'horreur de [s]a descente' (327), is reminiscent not only of José Ximenès (*ORTC*, I, 950), but also of Mauriac himself in his epistolary confessions to Robert Vallery-Radot (*LV* 33). Other autobiographical elements relate to people and places

---

[19] Quoted by Lacouture, *François Mauriac*, I, 39.
[20] See François Mauriac, 'Lettres à sa mère (1907–juin 1911)', in *François Mauriac*, ed. by Jean Touzot, pp. 61–77 (p. 61). Cf. the diary entries in 'Ecrits de jeunesse', pp. 22–23.

that Mauriac loved. A letter to Madeleine Le Chevrel (*NLV* 37) makes it plain that the 'vieux domaine' and 'vieux parc' (*MJ* 329, 351) are the family property at Malagar. And the R. L. commemorated in the final two poems of *Les Mains jointes* is Raymond Laurens, Mauriac's sixteen-year-old cousin and holiday companion who died of tuberculosis in June 1909.

The foregoing provides ample evidence of a connection between (auto)biographical detail and the poet's self-dramatization in his first collection of verse. My intention in highlighting the connections is not to encourage a 'decoding' of the poetry into biographical data; rather it is to suggest that Mauriac's poems should be considered as part of that 'espace autobiographique' to which Lejeune has referred in relation to the work of both Gide and Mauriac.[21] In fact, Lejeune limits his concept of an autobiographical space to their 'production narrative', but, in the case of Mauriac at least, it needs to be recognized that the structure of his verse collections means that they too should be included in the narrative corpus.

This relationship between verse and narrative is the second and final broader question I shall consider before turning to Mauriac's practice as a poet in *Les Mains jointes*.

The narrative dimension

Décaudin comments that the similarity of themes and tone throughout *Les Mains jointes* makes the collection seem 'un seul poème'.[22] But the sense of following an unfolding narrative is an equally important factor in the creation of this impression. The forty-two poems are divided into four sections as follows:[23]

I.	'L'Ecolier': 8 poems
II.	'L'Etudiant': 6 poems
III.	'L'Ami': 14 poems
IV.	'Une retraite': 14 poems

---

[21] Lejeune, *Le Pacte autobiographique*, p. 41. The next quotation is from p. 43.

[22] Michel Décaudin, 'Les Premiers Poèmes de Mauriac', in *François Mauriac 1: la poésie de François Mauriac*, pp. 9–23 (p. 9).

[23] There were slightly more poems in the 1909 and 1910 editions of the collection. My figures are based on the 1927 edition, the one followed by the Fayard *Œuvres complètes*. I shall not engage here with discussions of textual variants etc. (these will be dealt with in the critical edition mentioned in note 1 above).

For Quaghebeur, these 'quatre moments prémonitoires' sketch out 'le parcours du poète': after 'une enfance religieuse et blottie' (I) comes the student's departure (II), sealing 'un déchirement jamais accepté'; then, after the failure of the attempt to establish a relationship with a woman (III), the poet turns instead to the eternity of God (IV): 'cette éternité connue jadis avec la mère'.[24] This ordering creates a sense of narrative progression.[25] Although Mauriac has not yet started his ca-reer as a novelist, it is interesting to note this narrative dimension to his poetry. It will be helpful to trace the plot line of this macro-narrative in a little more detail as this will allow me to draw attention to a number of themes that will recur in my analysis of Mauriac's verse.

The collection opens with evocations of childhood. In this re-spect, the verse is a direct expression of Mauriac's own obsession with the past. He had barely turned twenty when he wrote to André Lacaze of 'ceux qui, comme nous, ont cette tendresse du passé, ce goût de revivre par la pensée toutes les naïvetés si charmantes de l'adole-scence' (*LV* 16). However, in *Les Mains jointes*, such memories are characterized by a sense of alienation; hence the repetition of the phrase 'l'enfant que je fus' (325, 327) emphasizing the distance be-tween past and present via the grammatical distinction between third and first person singular. The reason for this sense of alienation is a conviction of a moral fall from grace, evoked in the phrase 'l'horreur de ma descente' (327). The penitent poet wishes to rediscover his 'Ame blanche d'enfant' (327) and escape his 'grave adolescence et toutes ses ferveurs' (328). One way to achieve this is to take up resi-dence in 'le vieux domaine' (329), but this is to condemn himself to a life of 'solitude' and 'tristesse' (330). As these themes of solitude and existential emptiness are explored further, the evocations of childhood become less significant. Despite the greater serenity seen in the poem 'Vacances de Pâques', it is clear that the poet is ready to leave home and to seek another 'destinée' to which to join his own (332).

---

[24] Quaghebeur, 'Yves Frontenac désert', pp. 47–48.

[25] A manuscript (MRC 8) at the Bibliothèque Littéraire Jacques Doucet bearing the trace of an earlier arrangement of the poems indicates that Mauriac thought carefully about how best to order his material. See *François Mauriac: Manuscrits – Inédits – Editions originales – Iconographie*, ed. by François Chapon (Bibliothèque Littéraire Jacques Doucet, 1968), p. 55.

As the second section opens, however, the student-poet remains as lonely as ever in the city to which he has moved, afflicted by a 'morne lassitude' (334). When an addressee appears, it is unclear whether the *tu* in question is a real or an as yet virtual friend, but he (it seems unlikely that a woman is being evoked) is remarkably similar to the poet himself: 'mon isolement cherche ta solitude' (335). What the poet seeks in the other is a self-reflection.[26]

The heading of the third section, 'L'Ami', is ambiguous: does it refer to the poet as friend, to the friend that the poet was seeking in the previous section, or to both? The ambiguity is continued by the use of *tu* in the section's first two poems: is this a genuine address to another person, or is it simply an alternative form of self-reference for the poet?[27] Given that he has so far used *je* quite freely, the latter option is perhaps less likely. But the similarity noted above between the poet and his friend makes the situation less clear-cut. Whatever the identity of the poet's addressee, it is evident that the friend he desires is male:

> Tu ne désires plus celle pour qui chantonne
> > Dans les cœurs de seize ans le premier vers d'amour.
> > [...]
> Tu rêves d'un ami, celui qui n'est pas rude,
> Et qui te viendra voir à la chute du jour,
> > Un enfant simple et bon, aux regards étonnés... (339)

This could be read as raising a question over sexual orientation, especially as in the next poem, 'L'Ami II', the addressee's dreams (and it is presumably still the same *tu* as in 'L'Ami I') are said to have 'cherché les tombes | De l'éphèbe pensif et de la lesbienne' (340). It is true that the classical references give way to an image of a mass celebrated in the catacombs and that Christ emerges as 'le seul ami qui soit toujours fidèle' (340), nevertheless the ambivalence remains over the addressee's sexuality.

---

[26] The influence of Musset, prominent throughout the collection, is very strong in this section. See, in particular, the evocation of a black-clad figure in 'La Nuit de décembre' who, the poet says, 'me ressemblait comme un frère'. The figure is ultimately revealed as the embodiment of 'la Solitude'. See Alfred de Musset, *Poésies complètes*, ed. by Maurice Allem (Gallimard, 1957), p. 310, p. 315.

[27] Mauriac uses the latter technique in a contemporaneous diary entry—see 'Ecrits de jeunesse', pp. 28–29.

There is no evidence that Mauriac himself ever engaged in a homosexual relationship. However, it may be that there was a certain
homoerotic dimension to some of his friendships during this period.
He certainly had a number of gay male friends, including Lucien
Daudet, Jean Cocteau, and François Le Grix, and Lacouture suggests
that such friendships may have been one of the reasons why Marianne
Chausson broke off their short-lived engagement on 17 June 1911.[28]

It is not until the sixth poem in this section, 'Souvenir', that the
lyric *je* returns to centre stage, introducing for the first time a figure
that will be important in later poems: the friend who has died young.
Perhaps it is at least partly because of this loss that the poet's heart
displays such a 'solitude morne' and that he fears that his addressee in
'Le Désert' (a female (?) *vous*) will judge him incapable of love (345).
However, he also fears that the would-be lover her(?)self (this time
addressed as *tu* in 'Trahison') may harbour the memory of a dead
loved one: 'D'autres baisers que les miens | Au fond de toi
s'éternisent' (346).[29] The ambiguity over the gender of the addressee
continues in the 'Veillées' cycle. The *vous* of the first poem who
lightly strokes the poet's forehead on her(?) knees would appear to be
a woman (346). But, in the next poem, the 'tendresse obscure' that is
'violente mais pure' and which remains unspoken seems to relate to a
man: 'C'est l'heure, | Il va venir... c'est lui qui sonne...' (347). The *tu*
of the cycle's third poem is definitely male—'Mon petit' (347)—but
that of the next poem, 'Chanson', is clearly female: 'Ah! comme je
t'aimerais morte!' (348). The violence of the sentiment comes as
something of a shock in this collection and is in itself perhaps symp-
tomatic of a certain perplexity in the realm of sexuality. Problematic
relationships with women are also hinted at in 'Contrition' with its
oxymoronic reference to 'l'amertume des joies' and its refrain of 'la
femme chantante et toujours poursuivie' (349). The section's final
poem returns to the theme of ambiguity, addressed to a 'petite âme
douce' (349) who is also a 'petite âme vaine' (350). This emotional tie
(the addressee's gender is again unclear, but one assumes a woman is

---

[28] Lacouture, *François Mauriac*, I, 144.

[29] This will be Louis's concern in Mauriac's 1932 novel *Le Nœud de vipères*.

intended)[30] is contrasted with 'le grand devoir', her (?) 'yeux chan-
geants' (an adjective which could suggest fickleness) with 'la cause
austère' (350). It is time for the poet to move on once again.

However, as the title of the fourth section suggests, this move is,
in fact, something of a step backwards. This retreat to 'le vieux parc'
is quite deliberate: 'Las de tant d'amitiés et d'amours, j'ai voulu |
Faire un peu de silence en mon âme inquiète' (351). The juxtaposition
of the etymologically-linked *amitiés* and *amours* reminds us of the
ambiguities of the previous section ('L'Ami'). The poet apparently
needs to distance himself from these human affections to concentrate
on his relationship with God. He practises 'l'examen particulier',[31]
plumbing the depths of a soul which he likens to 'une trouble et profonde lagune' (353). His main weakness is highlighted in the following couplet, isolated typographically from the quatrains and quintains
that make up the other stanzas: 'Je songe à tout le bien que mon âme
eût pu faire | A l'âme rencontrée et qu'elle n'a pas fait' (354).[32] Here
is an echo of that Christian conscience which encouraged the young
Mauriac to flirt with Marc Sangnier's *Sillon* movement a few years
earlier. His active participation did not last long, however. The main
obstacle seems to have been Mauriac's aestheticism, hinted at in the
verse following the couplet just quoted: 'Avec les vers en moi chan-
tant, et la musique, | J'étouffais les appels et les sanglots humains'
(354).

'L'Examen particulier' ends on a spiritual high with the poet
comparing his experience to that of the disciples on the road to Em-
maus (354). Thereafter, any sort of narrative progression in this final
section becomes increasingly hard to identify. 'Les Sables' finds the
poet back in the spiritual doldrums, incapable of locating 'La route en
moi qui va vers la mer infinie' (355).[33] Some poems ('La Pécheresse'

---

[30] Though one should note that Mauriac uses the construction *petite âme* + adjective
on several occasions in his correspondence to refer to men. See, for example, 'Lettres
de François Mauriac à Robert Vallery-Radot', ed. by Yves Leroux, *CFM*, 12 (1985),
29–81 (p. 34, p. 70).

[31] The 'particular examen' is a key element in Ignatian spirituality. See *The Text of
the Spiritual Exercises of Saint Ignatius*, 4th edn (Burns and Oates, 1913), p. 13.

[32] Cf. 'Lettres de François Mauriac à Robert Vallery-Radot', pp. 37–38.

[33] This line, isolated typographically and thus emphasized, introduces an image that
will become a leitmotif in Mauriac's 1939 novel *Les Chemins de la mer*.

and 'L'Inconnu') abandon the quasi-autobiographical *je*, focusing rather on a third person; others ('Faiblesse', 'L'Immuable', 'L'Illusion', and 'La Peine') hesitate between a subjective and an objective approach by using 'l'âme' as the dominant grammatical subject. It is only in the final poem, 'A la mémoire de R. L.', that Mauriac returns to the lyric *je*. The collection therefore ends as it began: with an evocation of the past. The final stanza suggests, however, that as a result of his faith, the poet need not regard the past as irremediably lost:

> Mon Dieu, Vous avez pris cet enfant plein de foi
> Qui mêlait votre nom à ses cris d'agonie,
> Et son âme Vous fut si tendrement unie
> Que souvent, le cœur lourd d'un ineffable émoi,
> Je le retrouve en Vous qui Vous donnez à moi… (363)

This return to the divine at the very end of a collection is a feature we will encounter repeatedly in Mauriac's verse.

Poetic practice

My remarks in the previous section were designed to provide an overview of Mauriac's first collection of verse. I want now to consider his poetic practice in more detail. In order to do this, I shall focus particularly on the poem 'L'Ecolier'. Without wishing to suggest that this poem is any way normative for the collection as a whole, it remains true that, as the volume's opening piece, it helps set the tone for much of what follows. I shall therefore use it as a springboard for discussing issues of general significance for *Les Mains jointes*. For ease of reference, the whole poem is reproduced below (subsequent references will be to line numbers):

> Soirs de mois de Marie, étouffants de parfums,
> Samedis d'autrefois… Pour aller à confesse
> Les petits écoliers viennent l'un après l'un
> Dans la chapelle douce et dans le jour qui baisse.
>
> 5   Dehors ce sont les cris stridents et les vols fous
> Des martinets se poursuivant dans l'azur pâle
> Et l'enfant que je fus vient le dernier de tous
> A la chapelle en fleurs dont l'arôme s'exhale.
>
> Il vient, lui que la vie inquiète et repousse

10   Et qui veut du silence autour de sa tristesse,
        Profiter pour pleurer de ce que le jour baisse,
        Rêver sur ses péchés dans la chapelle douce…

        Pourquoi pleurer?—Il ne sait pas. Il veut pleurer
        Comme René, dont il connaît les grandes plaintes.
15   Il se trouble dans le parfum évaporé
        Des fleurs qui vont mourir et des cires éteintes.

        Dans cette âme exhalée et des fleurs et des cires,
        Il sent intensément l'adorable présence
        Du seul ami qui voit, sans jamais en sourire,
20   Couler les tendres pleurs de son adolescence.

        C'est l'Ami qu'il suivait aux Fêtes-Dieu brûlantes,
        Quand les foins hauts rendaient les sentiers plus étroits.
        Et le soleil mettait des flammes sur les croix
        Dans l'odeur de l'encens, de jonchée et de plantes.

25   La veille, on s'effarait autour du reposoir.
        L'enfant portait avec grand soin les fleurs dorées,
        Et l'on disait: 'Seigneur, empêchez de pleuvoir…'
        L'orage au loin grondait dans la lourde soirée.

        Mon Dieu, c'est bien celui que des soirs anciens
30   Menaient vers vous à la Chapelle du Collège
        Et dont l'âme captive et frêle en vos liens
        Etait blanche comme un paysage de neige…

        A l'étude du soir quand le soleil décline
        Et qu'on entend piailler les moineaux dans la cour,
35   Mon Dieu, c'est bien celui qui défaillait d'amour
        En s'enchantant avec 'le Lac' de Lamartine…

        Je sais encore les vers qu'il aimait dans ses fièvres,
        Il y traîne toujours comme un parfum de lys…
        Peut-être ont-ils gardé cette douceur des lèvres
40   De l'enfant que je fus qui les chantait jadis.

The poem's first stanza contains a number of lexical items belonging to semantic networks that are particularly significant in Mauriac's early verse. The very first word, 'Soirs' (l. 1),[34] points to the poet's predilection for the evening hours. This is clearly a poetically

---

[34] 'Soirs' is also the first word of the collection's final poem (362).

charged moment for the lyric *je*: the reference to 'le jour qui baisse' (l. 4) means that the first stanza as a whole is enveloped by the night as it closes in. There are also further references to this time of day in lines 11, 28, 29, and 33. Table 1 provides an overview of the frequency of different times of day in Mauriac's various collections of poetry:

Table 1:

	MJ	AA	CAF	WP	Or	SA
aube	2	2	1	5	5	5
matin	5	0	1	3	2	0
midi	0	0	0	1	0	2
après-midi	4	6	0	1	3	0
crépuscule	15	18	3	3	2	0
soir	46	59	9	15	1	1
nuit	27	21	6	14	8	6

Notes
- The figures in this and all subsequent tables need to be read in relation to the general statistics given in Table 10 (Chapter 4).
- In this and all subsequent tables, titles have been included in the search corpus, except in the case of *L'Adieu à l'adolescence* whose titles are provided by the opening words of each poem. Epigraphs, however, have been excluded from the search corpus.
- In this and all subsequent tables, unless stated to the contrary, no distinction has been made between literal and metaphorical usage of the terms counted.
- In this and all subsequent tables, *CAF* indicates the two poems published in *Les Cahiers de l'Amitié de France*, namely 'Nocturne' and 'Elégie'.
- In this and all subsequent tables, WP stands for 'War Poetry', that is, 'La Veillée avec André Lafon', 'Les Morts du printemps', and 'Le Disparu'.
- 'Ebauche d'Endymion' has been omitted from this and all subsequent tables due to its relative brevity.
- The totals for *aube* include occurrences of the terms *aurore, soleil levant, jour naissant, le jour va poindre*, and *petit jour*.
- The totals for *matin* include occurrences of the words *matinal* and *matinée*.
- The totals for *après-midi* include occurrences of the term *quatre heures*.
- The totals for *crépuscule* include occurrences of the word *crépusculaire* and various combinations of *jour/ journées* with the following terms (and their derivatives): *baisser, chute, éteint, mourir, s'achever, tomber, finir*, and *déclin*.
- The totals for *soir* include occurrences of the word *soirée*.
- The totals for *nuit* include occurrences of the word *nocturne*.

While the figures make it difficult to draw any firm conclusions with respect to the first four terms in the columns above, it is clear that Mauriac's early verse is firmly located in the twilight and evening hours in a way that his later verse is definitely not. This penumbral period is a time when forms lose their sharpness of contour and when colours merge into shades of grey. Here again, a comparative table might prove helpful:

Table 2:

	MJ	*AA*	*CAF*	WP	*Or*	*SA*
ombre	13	9	6	7	3	4
gris	5	2	0	0	0	0
brume	4	7	0	3	0	1
terne	0	3	1	0	0	0
noir	4	2	2	1	3	5
obscur	2	3	0	2	0	5
sombre	1	3	3	5	5	5
ténèbres	0	1	1	4	1	3

Notes
- The totals for *ombre* include occurrences of the word *ombrages*.
- The totals for *brume* include occurrences of the word *brouillard*.
- The totals for *terne* include occurrences of the word *terni*.
- The totals for *noir* include occurrences of the word *noirci*.
- The totals for *obscur* include occurrences of the words *s'obscurcir* and *obscurci*.
- The totals for *sombre* include occurrences of the word *assombri*.
- The totals for *ténèbres* include occurrences of the words *ténébreux* and *enténébrant*.

Table 2 shows that while the terms associated with darkness (*noir* and *sombre*) become more numerous in the later collections, those associated with muted tones and blurred outlines are much more frequent in the early verse. This offers further justification for Barrès declaring Verlaine to be Mauriac's poetic father.[35] Dusk is a time that accords well with the poet's gently melancholic nostalgia. It also provides a contrast with the scorching sun evoked in 'Grandes Vacances II' when

---

[35] Barrès actually refers to 'un Verlaine qui n'a pas de remords' (*OA* 195). In the light of this quotation, it is interesting to note that Jean-Pierre Richard sees the post-conversion Verlaine as having lost his 'misty', ambiguous quality—see his *Poésie et profondeur* (Editions du Seuil, 1976), p. 184.

'Tout ce qui souffre et vit rêve de crépuscule' (330). In Mauriac's later work, this stultifying heat of the summer sun over the Landes will be related to the burning drive of sexual desire.

The evenings referred to in line 1 of 'L'Ecolier' are specifically May evenings. Does Mauriac's verse reveal preferences for particular seasons? Table 3 suggests that it does:

Table 3:

	MJ	AA	CAF	WP	Or	SA
printemps	5	4	0	8	3	1
été	9	11	2	8	0	1
automne	11	10	1	1	1	1
hiver	3	6	2	3	4	0

Notes
- The totals for *printemps* include occurrences of the words *mars*, *mai*, *mois de Marie*, and *Pâques*.
- The totals for *été* include occurrences of the words *juin*, *juillet*, *août*, *la Saint-Jean*, and *Fêtes-Dieu*.
- The totals for *automne* include occurrences of the words *septembre*, *octobre*, and *novembre*.
- The totals for *hiver* include occurrences of the terms *décembre*, *Noël*, and *nouvel an*.

The most striking contrast concerns the abundance of references to autumn in the early verse, compared to the later collections where it is hardly mentioned at all. The pre-War Mauriac could have followed his near contemporary, Apollinaire, in claiming autumn as his 'saison mentale'.[36] In Mauriac's imagination, autumn is the seasonal equivalent of dusk, a time of mist and fog when the bright 'day' of summer fades into the 'night' of winter, a melancholic season associated with the dreaded *rentrée*.[37] The other important feature to note is the general lack of specific calendar references in the later verse. There are frequently references in these poems to heat, damp, cold etc., but par-

---

[36] The quotation is from 'Signe' (*Alcools*). See Guillaume Apollinaire, *Œuvres complètes*, ed. by Michel Décaudin, 8 vols (Balland et Lecat, 1966), III, 127.

[37] Cf. the 1934 article 'Adieu paniers…' in which Mauriac comments that, at the age of twenty, 'la tristesse est une passion' which is only savoured fully 'à certaines heures du déclin de l'été' (*OC*, XI, 115).

ticular months and seasons are not often mentioned. This seems to be part of a tendency in Mauriac's poetic development (especially in *Le Sang d'Atys* where the absence of calendar markers is most marked) towards greater generalization.

The next term from 'L'Ecolier' that forms part of a major semantic network is the word 'parfums' (l. 1). There are further references to aromas in lines 8, 15–17, 24, and 38. Mauriac's sensitivity to smells has long been recognized by critics. Bendz, writing over half a century ago, referred to him as being 'sujet à une hyperesthésie du sens olfactif'.[38] Palante also draws attention to Mauriac's 'prodigieuse sensualité olfactive' (adding 'et tactile'), but contrasts this with a 'sensualité visuelle […] à peu près nulle' and a 'sensualité auditive [qui] n'est guère plus développée'.[39] The final part of this statement seems particularly unfair. Although Mauriac may not have woven many references to sound into his writing, and while it is true that he once described himself as 'un illettré de la musique' (*PR* 221), he was certainly sensitive to the power of music and to the musicality of verse. [40] It is clear from the phonemic clusters at the start of 'L'Ecolier' that he is also attentive to the potential effects created by the sounds of his own poetry. The sounds of /swaʀ də/ are clearly mirrored by those of /mwa də/, with /maʀi/ repeating three of the four sounds already used. In line 2, /fwa/ echoes /swaʀ/ and /mwa/ and the sounds of the first hemistich of line 1 are further echoed in the opening /sam/ and the double /d/ and /ə/ sounds. The second hemistich of line 1 adds to this phonemic density with the repetition of the sequence /f/ + nasal vowel, together with the third occurrence of both /də/ and the /aʀ/ sequence. The repetition of the combination /f/ + nasal vowel helps create the desired effect of heavy, scent-laden evening air, especially as both instances of this combination constitute stressed syllables coming after two unstressed syllables.

---

[38] Ernst Bendz, *François Mauriac: ébauche d'une figure* (Gothenburg: Elanders Boktryckeri Aktiebolag, 1945), p. 95.

[39] Alain Palante, *Mauriac: le roman et la vie* (Editions Le Portulan, 1946), p. 68, p. 69.

[40] He was a soloist in his school choir. See François Mauriac, *Mozart et autres écrits sur la musique*, ed. by François Solesme (La Versanne: Encre Marine, 1996), p. 11.

This careful attention to sound is frequently in evidence in Mauriac's verse. Without undertaking an exhaustive analysis of the collection, one might also mention, still from the opening poem, the sequence of four fricatives (/ʃ/, /s/, /ʒ/, and /s/ again) which has the effect of emphasizing the soft haziness of line 4. This then contrasts immediately with lines 5–6 where the /kʀi/-/stʀi/ sounds, straddling the caesura and echoed in the /ʀti/ sequence in 'martinets', create an altogether different aural effect. In the next stanza, the four-fold repetition of /i/ in line 9 serves to reinforce the sense of anxiety, while two lines further on the alliteration in /p/ is perhaps a rather facile means of capturing the boy's blubbing (/p/ occurs a further nine times in lines 11–15).

Not surprisingly, phonemic patterning is particularly marked when the poet is describing sounds. Thus, in 'Grandes Vacances II', we read that: 'L'herbe bruit d'une vie infinie et fleurit | Eclatante et chantante au soleil qui la brûle' (330). The /ʀbə bʀ/ sequence in 'herbe bruit' draws the reader's attention to the theme of sound; the five-fold repetition of /i/ serves to emphasize the sheer profusion of life in the grass; and the four /t/ sounds in the second line just quoted underline the sharpness and clarity of the sounds. Another sound is heard in this section's last poem:

> Dans l'après-midi clair d'un paisible dimanche,
> Le chant persiste encor d'une cloche qui tinte.
> On plante le croquet autour des villas blanches. (333)

Once again, the interplay of sounds (/ã/, /i/, /k/, /ʃ/, /l/, and /t/ in particular)—not just in the first two lines describing the bell's chimes, but also in the third line where the repetition of phonemes creates a kind of resonance—provides clear evidence of Mauriac's attention to the sonorities of his verse.

Returning to 'L'Ecolier', the next key semantic term to consider from the opening stanza is 'autrefois' (l. 2), a word that signals the importance of the past and memory for the poet. Again, the prevalence of these concepts in Mauriac's early verse is most easily seen via a table showing numerical occurrences of related lexical items:

Table 4:

	MJ	AA	CAF	WP	Or	SA
souvenir	18	18	1	4	6	0
ancien	8	11	1	1	0	0
passé	7	10	3	5	0	0
jadis	7	3	0	0	0	0
autrefois	5	11	2	4	0	1
naguère	0	1	0	2	0	0

Notes
- The totals for *souvenir* include occurrences of the verbs *se souvenir* and *se rappeler* in their various forms.
- The totals for *passé* include occurrences of both the noun and the adjective.

Once again, there is a clear distinction here between Mauriac's first two collections of verse and his last two, with the poems from *Les Cahiers de l'Amitié de France* and the War Poetry marking a kind of transitional period. This will prove to be a recurring feature of these comparative tables.

The three dots that follow 'autrefois' in 'L'Ecolier' further underline the significance of the past as the focus of the poet's attention. They serve here as the typographical equivalent of a pause, lending emphasis to his evocation of the past. Elsewhere in the poem, the dots serve to suggest unexpressed thoughts (l. 12), an abbreviated prayer (l. 27), a wistful nostalgia for the purity of childhood (l. 32), the delights inspired by Romantic poetry (l. 36), and the synaesthetic experience of poetry evoking a scent (l. 38). Such dots are ubiquitous in Mauriac's early verse:

Table 5:

	MJ	AA	CAF	WP	Or	SA
End	52	160	11	12	6	6
Middle	5	12	0	3	0	2
Start	0	3	0	0	0	0

Notes
- 'End', 'Middle', and 'Start' refer to the position of the three dots within the line of verse.

It could well be that this excessive recourse to suspension points is part of what Mauriac had in mind when he criticized the 'poèmes flasques' of his first collection (*MJ* 323). They certainly contribute to the sense of enervated languor that permeates his early verse.

Revisiting the scenes of childhood, whether in imagination or reality, held a quasi-religious significance for Mauriac. In a letter to Robert Vallery-Radot in 1909, having extolled the benefits of the forthcoming summer holidays ('que j'ai chantées dans mes poésies') he adds: 'C'est la vieille province qui nous sauvera, et dans les domaines étouffants et tristes de notre enfance, nous entendrons des sources chanter encore en nous...'[41] It comes as no surprise, therefore, that religious vocabulary should feature prominently in the first stanza of 'L'Ecolier' where the terms 'Marie' (l. 1), 'confesse' (l. 2), and 'chapelle' (l. 4) point to a highly significant semantic field in Mauriac's poetry. Table 6 provides figures for a representative sample of terms belonging to this field:

Table 6:

	MJ	AA	CAF	WP	Or	SA
Dieu	16	32	0	5	7	4
chapelle	10	2	0	1	0	0
prière	8	28	3	2	1	0
Christ	6	2	0	1	3	3
péché	2	2	2	2	12	1
pardon	2	0	3	0	1	0
croix	1	6	1	2	3	2
grâce	1	1	0	0	3	1
Marie	2	1	0	0	0	0
Esprit	0	0	0	1	0	0

Notes

- The totals for *Dieu* include occurrences of the words *Père*, *Pater*, and *Seigneur* (except when used in the combination 'Seigneur Jésus'), but exclude occurrences of the word *dieu(x)*.
- The totals for *chapelle* include occurrences of the word *église*.
- The totals for *prière* include occurrences of the words *oraison* and *litanies*, the verb *prier* in its various forms, and various forms of the expression *joindre les mains*.

---

[41] 'Lettres de François Mauriac à Robert Vallery-Radot', p. 30.

- The totals for *Christ* include occurrences of the words *Jésus, Christus, chrétien, Fils*, and *Agneau*.
- The totals for *péché* include occurrences of the words *pécheresse* and *faute*.
- The totals for *pardon* include occurrences of the word *pardonné*.
- The totals for *croix* include occurrences of the nouns *gibet* and *Arbre* (capitalized), and the verb *crucifier* in its various forms.
- Occurrences of the word *grâce* have only been counted when used in the specifically Christian sense.
- The totals for *Marie* include occurrences of the word *vierge* when the reference is to Mary.

God is clearly named far more frequently in Mauriac's early verse than in his later poetry. This often takes the form of a direct appeal to the Deity: the phrase 'mon Dieu' is particularly prominent in the early verse with ten occurrences in *Les Mains jointes* and twenty-three in *L'Adieu à l'adolescence*. There are only two occurrences in the War Poetry and the phrase does not figure at all in the two later collections. Sin, on the other hand, is particularly prominent in *Orages*.

What the poet misses most from his childhood is the 'Ame blanche d'enfant' apostrophized in 'L'Ame ancienne' (327), a soul whose whiteness has already been compared, rather predictably, to 'un paysage de neige' in 'L'Ecolier' (l. 32). The word *âme* is used repeatedly by Mauriac in his early verse, as can be seen from Table 7. Although not directly synonymous, I have also included the number of references to the term *cœur(s)* since its semantic territory is often similar to that of *âme(s)* in Mauriac's verse.[42]

Table 7:

	MJ	AA	CAF	WP	Or	SA
âme(s)	16	32	7	2	3	2
cœur(s)	10	2	14	21	18	15

The frequency with which the term *âme* in particular is used in the early poetry provides a clear indication of its religiosity (*cœur* relating

---

[42] As one dictionary of synonyms puts it, *âme* refers to the 'ensemble des facultés morales de l'homme', whereas *cœur* 'désigne davantage les facultés sensibles'—see Emile Genouvrier, Claude Désirat, and Tristan Hordé, *Nouveau Dictionnaire des synonymes* (Larousse, 1977), p. 38. Mauriac's usage is by no means so clear cut.

more to sentimentality). Although the word *âme* sometimes signifies
little more than an individual consciousness in the early verse (as in
the poem 'Faiblesse', for example), there are times when it has a much
fuller religious significance, as in 'L'Ame ancienne':

> Vous que je porte au fond de moi comme un remords,
> Qui pleurez doucement l'horreur de ma descente,
> Témoin de mon passé—vierge toute puissante
> Qui pouvez me ressusciter d'entre les morts! (327)

The poet's childhood soul assumes here both the role of Mary ('vierge
toute puissante') and of Christ (as the one who, from a biblical perspective, has power to raise the dead). The soul's miraculous power is
emphasized through the way in which the verb 'ressusciter' spans the
caesura. The other point to note from this quotation is the poet's
strong sense of having fallen from grace ('l'horreur de ma descente').

A religious awareness of alienation from the purity and innocence
of childhood is an important element in Mauriac's work, as it is for
many Christian writers (one immediately thinks of Bernanos, for example). Yet the poet's picture of childhood is far from being uni-
formly luminous, as can be seen from lines 9–13 of 'L'Ecolier': life is
experienced as essentially hostile (an impression that will gather mo-
mentum as the collection develops); the child is sad (another common
theme); he is already a sinner; and he is keen to cry. A little later (ll.
19–20), the boy's solitude is highlighted via the reference to Christ as
the 'seul ami' who sees his tears without mocking him. Once again,
we are in the presence of semantic networks that are particularly
prominent in the early verse:

Table 8:

	MJ	AA	CAF	WP	Or	SA
enfant	24	75	9	19	6	14
adolescence	14	24	8	8	8	8
pleurer	46	53	6	12	2	9
triste	39	37	3	1	5	2
solitude	30	22	4	1	2	2

Notes:
• The totals for *enfant* include occurrences of the word *enfance*.

- The totals for *adolescence* include occurrences of the words *adolescent*, *jeune*, and *jeunesse*.
- The totals for *pleurer* include occurrences of the words *pleuré*, *pleurs*, *larmes*, *sanglots*, and *sangloter*.
- The totals for *triste* include occurrences of the words *tristesse*, *attrister*, *peine*, *mélancolie*, *mélancolique*, and *détresse*.
- The totals for *solitude* include occurrences of the words *isolé*, *s'isoler*, *isolement*, *seul* (in the sense of *alone*, rather than *sole*, *single*, or *only*), and *solitaire*.

As the reference to Chateaubriand's René in line 14 of 'L'Ecolier' suggests, this rather doleful self-image projected by the poet is derived, at least in part, from literary models. In lines 35–36, the poet also mentions the importance his younger self attached to the poetry of Lamartine. Later in the collection, there is a reference to the 'brûlantes lettres' that l'abbé Perreyve (a representative of Romantic Catholicism) sent to young acolytes (329), and a reference to 'les vers du pauvre Verlaine assagi— | Ces vers lourds des sanglots d'un amour ineffable' (351). Claudel once suggested that there was a lack of joy in nineteenth-century French poetry.[43] Whether this is a fair judgement or not, it is certainly true that Mauriac tends to pick up on the more dolorous traits of his predecessors (the exception being the lighter, fresher notes inherited from Jammes). He is well known as the heir of Racine's *amour-souffrance*, but this does not find much expression in his verse until the time of *Le Sang d'Atys*. In earlier collections, Romantic melancholy and tearfulness, Baudelairean spleen and rebellion, Verlainean religiosity, and *fin de siècle* world-weariness[44] are more obvious sources of inspiration.

The reference to René in 'L'Ecolier' is placed within lines whose rhythm also harks back to the greater prosodic freedom instigated by the Romantics. Lines 13–14 are both ternary alexandrines (4 + 4 + 4 syllables), while in line 15 the sixth syllable of a twelve-syllable line is formed by the definite article. From the point of view of traditional versification, proclitics such as articles, prepositions, auxiliary verbs,

---

[43] Claudel, *Œuvres en prose*, p. 61.

[44] Note, in this connection, the distribution of the words *las*, *lassitude*, *lasser*, *fatigue*, and *fatigué* in Mauriac's verse: eleven and twelve occurrences respectively in the first two collections; one in each of the last two; and none at all in 'Nocturne', 'Elégie', or the War Poetry.

and non-disjunctive personal pronouns should not occur immediately
before the caesura. Yet this is a convention that Mauriac breaks repeatedly in *Les Mains jointes*;[45] he also makes extensive use of the
rejet interne and not infrequently has a single word running over the
caesura. The most extreme example is the poem 'Evocation' in which
the poet reflects on some of the figures from Port-Royal. All the lines
in the first six stanzas fall into one of the three non-standard categories
just mentioned. It is only in the final stanza (with the exception of the
final line), that the conventional alexandrine returns. Significantly,
this is the stanza in which the poet evokes Pascal for the first time:

> Dans sa chambre là-bas, que déjà l'ombre noie,
> Pascal, en une extase où son corps ne vit plus,
> Jette aux brises du soir avec des pleurs de joie
> Les cris d'amour de son 'Mystère de Jésus'. (338)

Pascal is therefore distinguished prosodically from the Jansenists
mentioned earlier in the poem. Is this Mauriac's way of 'saving' his
greatest literary influence (*OA* 610) from the taint of heresy, or, given
the allusion to the mystical experience that gave birth to 'Le Mystère
de Jésus', is this a suggestion that the 'order' of conventional versification need not be seen as inimical to the 'adventure' of spiritual experience?[46]

   Although Mauriac adheres to rhyming lines with a fixed number
of syllables in all his published verse,[47] he is clearly at pains, in *Les
Mains jointes*, to adopt a flexible approach towards tradition. Although the dodecasyllabic used in 'L'Ecolier' is Mauriac's preferred
line in the collection (twenty-seven poems in total), we find him ex-
perimenting with other line lengths as well, both even: the octosyllabic (six poems), decasyllabic (four poems), hexasyllabic (three poems); and odd: the heptasyllabic and hendecasyllabic in one poem

---

[45] In the final poem, Mauriac goes so far as to place the preposition 'sur' at the end of
a line (362).

[46] Cf. Jean-Pierre Landry, 'Mauriac, lecteur de Pascal', *CFM*, 14 (1987), 111–31 (p.
120). The terms 'order' and 'adventure' are, of course, borrowed from 'La Jolie
Rousse', the final poem in Apollinaire's *Calligrammes* (1918).

[47] However, among Mauriac's manuscripts at the Bibliothèque Littéraire Jacques
Doucet (MRC 51bis and MRC 56), there are two versions of a free verse poem entitled 'Heurtebrise (Stèle pour Cocteau)'.

each.[48] The latter is unique in Mauriac's verse production,[49] but the heptasyllabic line will feature again in *Le Sang d'Atys*. The desire for variety also dictates his choice of rhyme schemes. 'L'Ecolier' is not untypical in the way in which it shifts from one rhyme pattern to another: it starts with two stanzas of *rimes croisées* alternating masculine and feminine rhymes, the only 'unusual' feature being the rhyme of 'fous' (l. 5) with 'tous' (l. 7) in stanza 2—a type of rhyme described by Lewis as 'irregular but valid'.[50] This pattern is repeated in stanzas 4, 7, and 8. In stanzas 3 and 5, however, we find exclusively feminine rhymes that are *embrassées* and *croisées* respectively. Stanzas 6 and 9 maintain the *alternance des rimes*, but begin with the feminine rhyme and follow the *abba* pattern. Finally, stanza 10 returns to the *rimes croisées* of the first two verses, but leads with a feminine rhyme.

The final aspect of *Les Mains jointes* that I wish to mention emerges from the inside/ outside contrast found in the first two stanzas of 'L'Ecolier'. The comforting interior of the 'chapelle douce' (l. 4) is juxtaposed with the 'vols fous' of the swifts in the evening sky (l. 5). The birds symbolize the freedom of the natural world, as opposed to the circumscribed experience of the pious schoolboy. The term 'fous', emphasized because of the *enjambement* between lines 5 and 6, seems to connote more than just the dizzying acrobatics of flight. This is borne out by the fact that Mauriac recycles this description of the swifts to describe the behaviour of the bacchantes after Atys's self-emasculation: 'Les ménades couraient sur sa trace vermeille | Avec des rires fous et des appels stridents' (*SA* 461). The swifts seem to suggest the 'folly' of the world *extra ecclesia*, a folly that was at once disturbing and attractive to Mauriac. Elsewhere in the collection, nature's disturbing otherness is tamed through integration into a religious perspective. Thus, in 'Grandes Vacances I', 'Les coteaux sont des

---

[48] The first line of stanza 3 in 'Grandes Vacances I' (the hendecasyllabic poem) is dodecasyllabic (329).
[49] The penultimate line of 'A la mémoire de R. L. I'—'Jusqu'au dimanche de juin où tu mourus' (362)—appears to be hendecasyllabic, unless 'juin' has two syllables here (which would be most unusual). Given the significance of this personal loss for Mauriac, the loss of a syllable in the line that narrates the death would be entirely appropriate.
[50] Roy Lewis, *On Reading French Verse: A Study of Poetic Form* (Oxford: Clarendon Press, 1982), pp. 142–43.

vagues d'ombre immobiles | Où toute rumeur se divinise et prie' (331) and in 'Vacances de Pâques':

> Tout le printemps avec ses fleurs est en prière
> Au reposoir qui n'est qu'une immense lumière:
> C'est le recueillement de la Semaine Sainte. (332)

Mauriac would not always see the relationship between natural cycles and the liturgical calendar quite so harmoniously.[51]

Conclusion

Although I would not want to make any great claims for *Les Mains jointes*, I do feel that critics have often been too quick to follow Mauriac's own dismissive judgements of the late 1920s. Yes, there is too much self-indulgent tearfulness here, too much 'Sulpician' religiosity, too many languorous laments, but the collection is by no means devoid of interest. Any reader familiar with Mauriac's world will find here some of the earliest traces of many of his major themes: his fascination with a childhood that is at once a haven and a prison; the role of family properties as triggers for his imagination; the competing influences of faith and desire; and the ambivalence over sexual orientation. The narrative that Mauriac constructs for the first time here provides an early sketch for what I have elsewhere termed his myth of the poet,[52] that is, a semi-autobiographical, semi-fictive dramatization of the evolution of the poet-figure. In addition to all this, I have tried to show that the collection reveals a poet who is more than competent in the practice of his craft. His willingness to work with different line lengths and rhyme schemes, his ability to exploit the semantic possibilities offered by the constraints of versification, and his attention to the relationship between sound and sense all suggest that Mauriac was perfectly at home in this form of self-expression.

---

[51] See Chapter 4 of Mauriac's 1931 essay *Le Jeudi Saint* (*OC*, VII, 171–76).

[52] See Paul Cooke, *Mauriac et le mythe du poète: une lecture du 'Mystère Frontenac'* (Lettres Modernes/ Minard, 1999).

3. Goodbye to All That? *L'Adieu à l'adolescence*

Introduction

Mauriac's second volume of poems was published by Stock in June 1911. *L'Adieu à l'adolescence* was not the original choice of title. On 2 April 1910, Mauriac wrote to Barrès about '*le pain quotidien*, mon prochain poème' (*NLV* 21). This title, connoting both religious preoccupations (via the allusion to the Lord's Prayer) and quotidian simplicity, was later rejected in favour of one focusing on the idea of the past. In a letter of 3 January 1911, Mauriac told Vallery-Radot that he was looking for a title that would express the idea '"Adieu à l'adolescence" ou "Adieu aux beaux jours"' (*LV* 42). On 1 February 1911, he thought he had found such a title, writing to his mother: 'mon livre de vers est fini (il s'appellera "*les traces bien-aimées*")'.[1] In fact, these words (a quotation from Maurice de Guérin) would ultimately feature in the volume's epigraph: 'Vous savez, mon ami, le charme des pas qu'on mène sur des traces bien-aimées...' (*AA* 365). Since this epigraph appears on the same page as the dedication, 'A MAURICE BARRES', one almost has the impression that the words are directed to the great man himself.[2] Although the volume's definitive title signals an intention to rise to the challenge laid down in the Academician's review of *Les Mains jointes*,[3] the Guérinian epigraph suggests that the process of bidding a definitive farewell to the past will be far from easy.[4] A further dedication, 'A MA MERE', at the head of the collection's opening section and a further epigraph—'O mon enfance, c'est vous toujours que je retrouve' (367)—add to the sense that this is 'plus un *retour sur* qu'un *adieu à*'.[5] This second epigraph establishes yet another link with Barrès since it comes from

---

[1] Mauriac, 'Lettres à sa mère', p. 74.

[2] Mauriac had originally intended dedicating his first novel to Barrès (*NLV* 26), but since *L'Adieu à l'adolescence* was ready for publication when Mauriac was still working on what would become *L'Enfant chargé de chaînes*, he decided to dedicate the verse to his 'cher maître' (*NLV* 32).

[3] 'Il faut quitter d'un pas assuré notre jeunesse et trouver mieux' (*OA* 197).

[4] As late as 1962, Mauriac would see this as 'un adieu qui, pour moi, n'a jamais fini' (*BN*, III, 259).

[5] Jean de Fabrègues, *Mauriac* (Plon, 1971), p. 77.

the pen of his nephew, Charles Demange. Indeed, Barrès had himself quoted these very words in his review of *Les Mains jointes* (*OA* 195).[6] There can be no doubt therefore that Mauriac's second collection is to be read as a response to Barrès's review of his first, but it remains to be seen to what extent the title is justified. Did Barrès himself feel that the young poet had risen successfully to his challenge? While a letter dated 12 April 1912 is certainly supportive—'Vos deux livres de vers sont délicieux'[7]—Barrès's public silence with regard to *L'Adieu à l'adolescence* suggests that the charm he had felt on reading its predecessor was beginning to wear off. Without the public enthusiasm of a figure such as Barrès, *L'Adieu à l'adolescence* made relatively little impact. A couple of months after its publication, Mauriac refers to his second volume of verse as 'ce petit livre qui est passé bien inaperçu' (*NLV* 37).

No doubt one of the main reasons for the book's failure to provoke interest is the fact that, in many ways, it was too similar to *Les Mains jointes*. As the various tables included in the previous chapter demonstrated, there is much lexical and thematic overlap between these two collections. Mauriac commented in 1951 that '*L'Adieu à l'adolescence* ne marque aucun progrès et exprime assez bien ce piétinement qui devait durer près de dix années' (*OC*, VI, iii). This judgement was subsequently endorsed by most critics.[8] One of the few positive judgements comes from Speaight who sees the poems as having 'much accomplishment', but even he admits that 'their languorous romanticism enervates after a little'.[9]

---

[6] Demange had committed suicide in August 1909, aged twenty. With great lucidity, Mauriac would later write that 'à travers l'auteur des *Mains jointes*, Barrès, tandis qu'il écrivait son article, ne cessait de voir son enfant que l'amour avait tué' (*OA* 199).

[7] Mauriac, 'Ecrits de jeunesse', p. 50.

[8] E.g., Pierre-Henri Simon, *Mauriac par lui-même* (Editions du Seuil, 1953), p. 14; André Séailles, *François Mauriac* (Bordas, 1972), p. 11; and Lacouture, *François Mauriac*, I, 164.

[9] Robert Speaight, *François Mauriac: A Study of the Writer and the Man* (Chatto and Windus, 1976), p. 49. He also suggests that Mauriac did not 'disown' the poems of his second collection since they were republished in the year of his death (p. 49). In his article 'Mauriac poète: interstices', however, Quaghebeur states that Stock's decision was taken 'malgré les volontés du poète' (p. 178).

However, when these poems were actually being written, the young author was clearly pleased with the way in which his poetry was developing. He considers the poems published by the *Mercure de France* in 1910 to be 'plus "faits" que ceux des *Mains jointes*' (*NLV* 26).[10] Formally, the poems of *L'Adieu à l'adolescence* differ from those of the previous collection to the extent that alexandrines are used virtually throughout—the single exception being a decasyllabic line (a quotation from one of Lully's operas) in the opening poem (468). However, Mauriac's approach to versification remains as flexible as it was in his opening collection: virtually every poem in *L'Adieu à l'adolescence* displays some form of (generally minor) irregularity with respect to issues such as the rhyme scheme, the alternation of masculine and feminine rhymes, the treatment of the caesura, and the choice between diaeresis and syneresis in syllable-counting. Apart from the more extensive use of the alexandrine, verse is handled very much in the second collection as it was in the first, that is, with a view to retaining a high degree of prosodic variation within traditional forms.

Oddly, perhaps, the poems of *L'Adieu à l'adolescence* strike Mauriac as more original than those of *Les Mains jointes*: 'C'est je crois *nouveau*'.[11] Perhaps, though, it is the overtly religious dimension of the verse which he has in mind here, the adjective 'nouveau' needing to be understood in terms of the 'reactionary revolution' of the time.[12] This possibility receives some support from a letter written during the summer of 1910 in which Mauriac, writing to Vallery-Radot about their project for a Catholic literary journal (the *Cahiers de l'Amitié de France*), asks: 'n'est-ce pas à nous, Robert, de préparer le monde à une poésie nouvelle?'[13] Barrès had detected 'une note folle de volupté' in *Les Mains jointes* (*OA* 195). Twenty years later, Mauriac would be delighted with this discovery, the only thing which,

---

[10] The poems in question are: 'Le crépuscule lent...'; 'Ma mère me sourit...'; 'Le salon de famille...'; 'Les grands vents d'équinoxe...'; and 'Nous nous sommes encore...'. See François Mauriac, 'Poèmes', *Mercure de France*, 85 (May–June 1910), 420–24.

[11] 'Lettres de François Mauriac à Robert Vallery-Radot', p. 33.

[12] See Richard Griffiths, *The Reactionary Revolution: The Catholic Revival in French Literature 1870–1914* (Constable, 1966).

[13] 'Lettres de François Mauriac à Robert Vallery-Radot', p. 38.

in his eyes, saved 'ce fade cantique' (*ORTC*, II, 787). But, at the time of preparing *L'Adieu à l'adolescence*, he seems deliberately to have shied away from this aspect of the first collection. As he writes to Vallery-Radot (12 January 1911): 'ces poèmes écrits une année de griserie, auront plus d'accent chrétien que *Les Mains jointes* et seront dépouillés de ce trouble un peu sensuel dont s'ornait bien dangereusement mon jeune mysticisme' (*LV* 43).

This overtly Christian orientation of the poems will become apparent in my subsequent remarks. Because of the many similarities between this collection and its predecessor, this chapter will be shorter than the one devoted to *Les Mains jointes*—it would be superfluous to labour points already established. For reasons explained in the next section, my approach to reading the poems will be structured by their narrative dimension.

Autobiography and narrative development
As shown in the previous chapter, Mauriac's first collection of verse contained a clear autobiographical dimension. The same is true of his second collection. Malagar again appears as 'ce domaine triste' (379) and the spectre of Raymond Laurens continues to haunt a number of poems in the first two sections of *L'Adieu à l'adolescence*. If anything, the number of autobiographical markers seems higher in the 1911 collection. The unnamed port evoked in 'Nous nous sommes encore...' (372–73) is obviously the Bordeaux of Mauriac's adolescence.[14] The fragments of evening prayer spoken by the children (*AA* 368) are the same as those voiced by Mauriac's mother (*OA* 70). Other family members evoked in the verse include Germaine Mauriac, the sister who plays the piano in 'C'est l'époque...' and 'Le salon de famille...' (371, 384). This latter poem also refers to 'mon frère l'abbé' (384)—an allusion to l'abbé Jean Mauriac. The picture of the mother—devoted to her son and deeply religious—corresponds to what we know of Claire Mauriac. The Cardinal Donnet mentioned in a description of the family photograph album (*AA* 404) was one of the many clergymen who visited the family home during Mauriac's childhood (*BN*, IV, 97). Providing precise identifications for any other

---

[14] Cf. *OA* 93. The poems devoted to the port of Bordeaux represent one of the few genuinely original features of this collection compared to *Les Mains jointes*.

figures in the poems would be a hazardous business; indeed, Mauriac has deliberately written in such a way as to make such identifications problematic. However, it is possible that some of the poems in *L'Adieu à l'adolescence* contain oblique references to Marianne Chausson (daughter of the composer Ernest Chausson), the eighteen-year-old to whom Mauriac was engaged for less than a week in June 1911.[15] Certainly the female presence evoked in 'Le long de la tapisserie...'—'sérieuse et calme' (404)—is paralleled by Mauriac's description of Marianne in a letter to his mother of 10 June 1911: 'Cette petite fille [...] extraordinairement sérieuse et grave' (*NLV* 33). As with *Les Mains jointes*, therefore, I would suggest that this second collection also contributes to the delineation of an 'espace autobiographique'.

Like its predecessor, *L'Adieu à l'adolescence* consists of four parts, each of which is prefaced by an epigraph highlighting certain themes shared by the poems in that particular part. If *Les Mains jointes* can legitimately be viewed as a single poem, the same is true of *L'Adieu à l'adolescence*.[16] Once again, the structure encourages a narrative approach to the collection—a semi-autobiographical narrative with the lyric *je* as protagonist. I shall use this plot line as a means of structuring my reading of the poems in the remainder of this chapter.

Part I

Like the first section of *Les Mains jointes*, the first section of this second volume, governed by the epigraph from Charles Demange quoted earlier, focuses on the poet's childhood. The main difference between this collection and the earlier one is that evocation of the past has become more problematic. The section opens with an anxious question: 'Mon Dieu, dois-je oublier mes amours anciennes?...' (367). And, despite the vigorously negative answer given to this question, the poet is still concerned about his heart being 'le prisonnier d'une enfance trop douce' (367). The word 'prisonnier' is em-

---

[15] See 'La Correspondance entre François Mauriac et Claire Mauriac, sa mère [Extraits, 1907–1914]', ed. by John Flower, *NCFM*, 5 (1997), 25–48 (p. 35).

[16] One notes the use of the singular in Mauriac's description of the collection as 'mon prochain poème' (*LV* 42).

phasized in this line through its position immediately before the cae-sura. The notion of imprisonment is echoed a few lines later when the poet exclaims: 'Tous les départs sont vains' (368), a theme that will receive fuller treatment in the last seven lines of 'Je vous donne l'humble trésor...' and throughout 'Pourquoi faut-il...' (370, 387). The poet's initial question is then transformed into a petition at the start of the second stanza: 'Mon Dieu, mon Dieu, délivrez-moi de mon enfance' (368). The repetition of 'Mon Dieu', itself picked up from the opening question, highlights the tension and anxiety that will characterize much of the collection. This is highly emotive language: precisely the kind of language, in fact, that has traditionally been associated with lyric poetry.[17] Some of the most obvious markers of emotive language are the presence of exclamation marks, apostrophes, and interjections. As Table 9 shows, these markers are particularly prevalent in L'Adieu à l'adolescence:

Table 9:

	MJ	AA	CAF	WP	Or	SA
Exclamation marks	20	48	2	31	17	19
ô	11	53	5	17	11	7
Ah	2	15	0	3	1	0
hélas	2	3	0	0	0	0

Mauriac's preference for the muted tones of dusk, already noted with respect to Les Mains jointes, is again in evidence in this collec-tion:

> Le fumeux horizon et ses roses fanées,
> Et les tons adoucis du ciel crépusculaire
> Ont évoqué les soirs de ma douzième année... (369)

Here, as so often in this first section, a moment in the present serves as a springboard for a memory of the past. The emphasis is generally on the continuity between past and present. Sometimes, though, terms such as même and pareil are used so frequently that the insistence

---

[17] See Combe, Poésie et récit, p. 166.

serves to reactivate the carceral image noted above.[18] However, there are also hints of a way out of this impasse. The reference to 'ce pressentiment d'un amour inconnu' in the opening poem (367) is twice echoed in this opening section: 'Mon simple cœur d'enfant vous pressentait déjà | O musique inconnue, amour, douceur de vivre!' (370); 'pressentant l'amour inconnu' (371). The terms *pressentir* or *pressentiment* do not occur at all in *Les Mains jointes*; their presence here suggests that this second collection will be oriented towards a revelation of this 'amour inconnu'. In this opening section, however, it is not yet apparent how such a revelation might be possible. Perhaps the relationship with the addressee of the poem that begins 'Je vous donne l'humble trésor de mon passé' (370) might enable this revelation of love to take place, but it is not clear whether this *vous* is a potential human lover or the God to whom so many of the collection's poems are addressed.

As the first section draws to a close, the mention of the names of Racine and Baudelaire (375) suggests an irrevocable distancing from the world of childhood, 'où la vie était simple et réglée' (369), to a world of passion and sexual desire. 'Soir complice…' evokes a childhood self who is 'maître encor d'un cœur fatigué d'être sage' (376), implying that the poet no longer retains this wearisome control in the present. This is made explicit in the next poem, where the contrast between memories of the school chapel ('Je songe à la chapelle où le collège chante') and life outside its walls ('Loin d'elle, […]') is reminiscent of the internal/ external opposition noted in connection with 'L'Ecolier' in the previous chapter. In the sixth stanza, the poet's reverie about his religious childhood is suddenly interrupted:

> C'est la vie, aujourd'hui, les livres trop connus,
> La facile et médiocre vie où le cœur s'use
> — Et malgré les amours dont ma langueur s'amuse,
> C'est une solitude, hélas! où Dieu n'est plus. (377)

---

[18] E.g., in the last five lines of 'Mon Dieu, c'est avec vous…' (371) where the fourfold repetition of the adjective *même*, coupled with terms such as *comme* and *trop pareil à* (the adverbial modifier is significant here), emphasizes the restrictive nature of the link between childhood and the present. A similar pattern marks the last five lines of the first stanza of 'Un peu de lune pâle…' (379), the last poem in Part I.

The absence of God marks a significant break with the world of the past. The poem concludes with the poet addressing himself in terms reminiscent of the earlier 'pressentiment d'un amour inconnu', but with a decidedly lustful twist (emphasized by the multiple /d/ and /t/ sounds): 'Tu trembles de désir dans cette nuit complice, | Et devines un monde inconnu de délices' (377). It is true that the next poem sees him returning to God, but the poet hardly seems confident about his position: 'Mais un souffle, un regard peut l'éloigner de vous...' (378).[19] The uneasy tension is summed up in the concluding image of the Prodigal: 'Cet enfant retrouvé mais si souvent perdu...' (378).

Part II

This is prefaced by a Latin quotation from the liturgy for the memory of the dead. The main focus here will be on lost loved ones. It has been prepared by the final line of the previous section: 'L'ami pensif et doux qui ne devait pas vivre' (379), probably another allusion to Raymond Laurens. This death has become something of an obsession for the poet, as can be seen from the double alliteration in the opening lines of 'Si je ne peux marcher...', where the poet says he can only walk 'la tête tournée | Vers un pauvre passé' (382). This poem is dated 'Grandes vacances 1909' (383). This coincides with the date given in *Les Mains jointes* for the composition of 'A la mémoire de R. L.'—'Juillet-Août 1909' (*MJ* 363)—and it is evident that the poems have the same subject matter. A little later, this lost friend is referred to as 'Celui qui fut ma peine et ma joie ici-bas' (*AA* 384). Leaving aside the question of a homoerotic dimension to this friendship, there is clearly a considerable degree of emotional investment on the poet's part, an investment that helps explain his solitude and melancholy in the narrative present and his desire to take refuge in memories of the past. It is the persistence of such memories (underlined by the positioning of the adjective before the noun in the following quotation) that will make it so difficult for the poet to respond to the title of his second collection: '— Inconsolable deuil dont mon âme est blessée, | O mon adolescence à qui je dis adieu!' (382).

---

[19] Cf. Mauriac's letter of 6 October 1910 to Vallery-Radot: 'Comment ne pas la perdre [sa foi]? Je la sens si vacillante en moi, pauvre petite flamme qui ne me réchauffe plus...' (*LV* 39).

Part III

As in *Les Mains jointes*, the third section of *L'Adieu à l'adolescence* centres on the theme of friendship. Mauriac takes for his epigraph three lines from 'Elégie', a poem from Vallery-Radot's collection *Les Dents du Sylvain*:

> Et vous fûtes la fleur intime et préférée
> Où savamment, les yeux fermés, fut respirée
> La divine amitié plus douce que l'amour. (*AA* 387)

The sexual ambivalence found in this third section and already encountered in the earlier collection encourages us to see this epigraph as contrasting male friendship with male–female love. But, in fact, Vallery-Radot's poem bears the dedication 'Pour Ariane'—a *female* friend, whose 'tendresse maternelle' and sisterly qualities are mentioned in the next poem ('Les Adieux').[20] In other words, the male–female contrast and the resulting sexual ambivalence are very much Mauriac's creation.

In terms familiar from *Les Mains jointes*, the poet portrays himself as lonely and lachrymose. Tears, indeed, even function as surrogate friends (387–88). He goes on to reveal his passion for 'le mystère des âmes' (389). As we have seen, *âme* is an extremely common term in Mauriac's early verse. As well as reflecting a general religiosity, it also points to Mauriac's interest in the Barrésian *amateur d'âmes*.[21] It is only with 'Le crépuscule lent...', however, that another specific human presence appears in this third section.[22] The *vous* referred to in the first line is almost certainly a male figure (389). The epigraph from l'abbé Henri Perreyve, which appears to refer to a spiritual fra-

---

[20] Robert Vallery-Radot, *Les Grains du myrrhe: 'Les Chants de Chryseis', 'Les Dents du Sylvain', 'Au seuil de la Demeure' (1904–1906)* (Bibliothèque Internationale d'Edition/ Sansot, 1907), p. 77, p. 80.

[21] 'Un amateur d'âmes' is the title of the opening text in Barrès's *Du Sang, de la volupté et de la mort* (1894). For its influence on Mauriac, see *OA* 172.

[22] It is true that a 'servante' speaks in 'O lassitude...' (*AA* 388), but, from the poet's perspective, her presence is evidently insignificant. A reading of Mauriac's poetry impelled by socio-economic concerns would, of course, see considerable significance in this very marginalization.

ternity, supports this impression.[23] By the start of the second stanza, the *vous* has become a *tu* as his soul is united to the poet's in the intimate experience of shared prayer (389). By the end of the poem, the addressee has become 'mon enfant' for the poet who celebrates 'Une pure amitié qui se sent éternelle' (390)—a clear contrast to the unlocatable bones of the dead lovers evoked at the end of the first stanza (389). 'Mon enfant' is a useful form of address for Mauriac: it can be applied metaphorically to either men or women (he never uses it in his verse to refer to actual children) and it expresses a deep affection apparently devoid of sexual connotations. He has already used the term in *L'Adieu à l'adolescence* (it does not figure in *Les Mains jointes*) in what I take to be a reference to Raymond Laurens (383). It will be used twice more in this third section, in the poem 'La chambre te retient...', where the addressee also appears to be male (391–92).

Moving ahead to Part IV for a moment, the term 'mon enfant' occurs no fewer than four times in 'Les heures, comme un flot...' (395). This poem is dedicated to André Lafon, another Catholic poet-novelist from Bordeaux, and it could well be that the *tu* here is Lafon himself. Despite their common geographical origin, Mauriac and Lafon did not meet until March 1910 and their friendship would be cut short by Lafon's death only five years later. However, looking back on his life in the 1960s, Mauriac would write that, of all his friends, Lafon was 'le plus près de mon cœur, et en même temps celui que j'admirais le plus' (*OA* 813). On the basis of Lafon's broken engagement with the novelist Jeanne Alleman (who wrote under the pseudonym of Jean Balde), Lacouture suggests that Lafon may have felt no sexual attraction for women in general.[24] The suggestion receives some support from the fact that Mauriac uses Lafon as the model for Nicolas Plassac in his 1952 novel, *Galigaï*—not, as Flower notes, 'sans une suggestion d'homosexualité.'[25] The words that Mau-

[23] Cf. Mauriac's 1913 comments on Perreyve: 'cœur à la fois virginal et viril—de toute pureté, mais consumé d'amour. Des lettres qu'il écrivait à des jeunes hommes du second Empire aident encore un jeune homme d'aujourd'hui à vivre selon l'Esprit' (*ORTC*, I, 931). Perreyve's 'brûlantes lettres' have already been mentioned in *Les Mains jointes* (329).

[24] Lacouture, *François Mauriac*, I, 154.

[25] *François Mauriac et Jacques Rivière: Correspondance 1911–1925*, ed. by John E. Flower (Exeter: University of Exeter, 1988), p. 11. In 1956, Mauriac states explicitly

riac has Agathe (partly modelled on Jeanne Alleman) say to Nicolas are particularly relevant in the light of Lacouture's suggestion: 'Je vous dégoûte? Mais quelle femme ne vous dégoûte pas?' (*ORTC*, IV, 434). Perhaps none of this had any bearing on the nature of Lafon's friendship with Mauriac, but, if one wished to pursue the possibility mentioned earlier of a certain homoerotic dimension to some of Mauriac's friendships (reflected, perhaps, in his early verse), then these factors would need to be taken into consideration.

Returning to the text of *L'Adieu à l'adolescence*, we find that in the latter part of the final section the term 'mon enfant' is used exclusively (and for the first time) in connection with the poet's beloved (402, 408). There is only one other occurrence of the term in Mauriac's verse corpus: in the sexually charged poem 'Assassin' from *Orages* where the reference is definitely to a female lover (431). The ambiguity surrounding this term provides further evidence of sexual ambivalence in Mauriac's early verse.

The addressee is apparently male throughout Part III. His friendship provides an important step towards the achievement of the farewell announced in the title. The friend allows the poet to form an emotional attachment with somebody other than his mother:

> Ma mère me sourit dans la photographie,
> D'un sourire qui dit tout ce que fut ma vie
> Jusques au soir où tu entras dans cette chambre,
> Un crépuscule pâle et doré de septembre. (390)

The /m/ and /i/ sounds that dominate the first two lines (centred on the mother) in this quotation are transferred to the friend in the next stanza: 'Mon ami, mon ami, tu seras là bientôt' (390).[26] The next two lines—'La chambre, qui le sait, s'apaise et se recueille… | De son feu, de sa lampe douce elle t'accueille' (390)—use a typically Mauriacian personification,[27] to create the kind of enclosed, intimate space that

---

that Nicolas is modelled on Lafon and admits that the fictional friendship between Nicolas and Gilles 'rappelle par plus d'un trait celle qui nous unissait durant les cinq années qui ont tant compté dans ma vie: 1910–1915' (*DAM* 48).

[26] This line, the thirteenth out of a total of nineteen, uses a masculine rhyme for the first time in the poem.

[27] The poet's room is also personified in the apostrophe at the end of 'En ces jours de vacances tristes…' (374).

Mauriac so often associates with the mother's bedroom.[28] In the next poem, it is 'sous le regard d'une âme bien-aimée' that the poet no longer feels so attached to his childhood past (391).[29] The poet sees in his friend a kindred spirit: 'Nous avons tant besoin l'un de l'autre! La vie | Est si dure aux enfants comme nous, que tout blesse' (392).[30] As these lines suggest, the poet is certainly not concerned about identifying himself with traditional images of masculinity. Perhaps this is one of the reasons why only feminine rhymes occur in this poem.

However, despite the poet's dependence on his male addressee, it is also clear that their friendship is a rather fragile affair, since the poet refers to 'ton amitié morte' (391) and 'l'amitié que nous avons pleurée' (392). It comes as little surprise, therefore, that the section should end as it began—with an evocation of the poet's isolation in a poem in which the word 'solitude' provides the penultimate rhyme and in whose three quatrains the term 'désert' is used twice (393).[31]

Part IV

The collection's final and longest section has an epigraph from a poem by André Lafon: 'Dis, c'est assez rêver au bord des vitres pâles, | C'est assez se meurtrir le cœur à ce qui fut!' (394).[32] Whereas the title of the fourth section of *Les Mains jointes*, 'Une retraite', suggested a return to the past, this epigraph suggests the need to transcend it. Perhaps religious experience will offer a way of achieving this transcendence. The poet begins this section with an appeal which partly echoes the epigraph's second line: 'Mon Dieu, reprenez-moi

---

[28] Cf. J.-M. Bataille, 'La Chambre de la mère', in *Présence de François Mauriac* (Bordeaux: Presses Universitaires de Bordeaux, 1986), pp. 131–40.

[29] It is worth noting the verbless style adopted in the second stanza to evoke the past in a quasi-impressionistic manner. The same style is used for the same purpose elsewhere (*AA* 369, 396, 406).

[30] Cf. the lines from the collection's opening poem: 'Mon Dieu, ce faible cœur que tout blesse et repousse, | Est le prisonnier d'une enfance trop douce' (367).

[31] This poem is something of a rarity in Mauriac's verse corpus in that it employs *rimes plates* (all feminine) throughout. Mauriac would recycle the poem's final line ('— Et ce carré de ciel par la fenêtre ouverte…') in an article entitled 'Méditation sur Henri Perreyve' (1912). See François Mauriac, *Lacordaire*, ed. by Keith Goesch (Beauchesne, 1976), p. 138.

[32] The poem, taken from Lafon's *Poèmes provinciaux* (1908), is reproduced by Mauriac in *OA* 17.

dans ma misère, | Reprenez-moi meurtri, blessé, mais tout en larmes'
(394). However, the prodigal poet ('Comme un enfant prodigue abîmé
dans son Père') does not receive the welcome reserved for the son in
the parable. Nor does his self-offering receive the type of divine response accorded to Samuel or Isaiah:

> Me voici... me voici... Vous ne répondez pas.[33]
> Aucun souffle. L'air est pesant sous le ciel bas.
> Un ami qui devait venir, ne viendra pas. (394)

The *rejet interne* in the second line just quoted underlines the oppres-
sive nature of divine silence. The third line signals the definitive
breakdown of the friendship celebrated in Part III. In the absence of
his friend, and of any divine response, the poet falls back again on
sounds from the past: 'les airs oubliés des vieilles chansons tendres',
'les voix du passé qui fredonnent en toi', and 'les sanglots perdus de
ton premier émoi...' (394). Perhaps this section is to be another *retraite* after all...

Yet such memories do not long suffice. Only a couple of pages
later, and in terms which allude directly to those just quoted, the exas-
perated poet asks: 'Ah! Pourquoi m'endormir au chant des autrefois |
Dont les brumes ne valent pas qu'on les regrette?' (396). At the end of
the poem, as in the fourth section of *Les Mains jointes*, the poet finds
his self-contained indolence challenged by the possibility of social
action:

> O faible cœur, dont beaucoup d'autres ont besoin,
> Quitte la chambre tiède où ton rêve s'isole,
> Songe à l'enfant malade et laid que tu consoles:
> L'heure est déjà tardive et le faubourg est loin... (396)

Although this Sillonist solution will not be pursued, it does seem to
signal a definitive change of mood. In the next couple of poems, not
only is the poet once more reconciled to his God, but he resigns himself to the fact that the personified bedroom of his childhood no
longer recognizes him and that he is no longer 'le cœur terrifié d'avoir
déjà vingt ans | Qui veillait et pleurait sur son enfance morte' (397).

---

[33] Cf. I Samuel 3. 8 and Isaïe 6. 8.

The poet sees this trajectory in terms of divine providence: 'O mon
Dieu, vous avez tout fait pour que je change, | Vous avez clos les yeux
des amis que j'aimais' (396–97) and

> O mon Dieu, Vous avez voulu que je connaisse
> Cet ineffable espoir et cette certitude
> Que l'amour a tendu les bras vers ma jeunesse. (397)

This is the first allusion to the female presence who will dominate most of the remaining poems and who appears directly for the
first time in 'Vous venez jusqu'à moi...'. Future tenses abound as the
poet imagines the unfolding of their relationship. Firstly, there will be
the presentation of a house and grounds closely associated with the
poet's memories of growing up. The references to 'la charmille' and
'la terrasse' strongly suggest that Malagar serves as a model here
(399). The poet also offers less tangible tokens of his past to his beloved: 'J'ai des morts dans mon cœur, je vous les donne aussi' (399).
One is reminded of the opening line from a poem in Part I: 'Je vous
donne l'humble trésor de mon passé' (370). There, it was uncertain
whether the addressee was human or divine; here, there is no longer
any doubt. Dismissing 'le morne attrait de toutes les déroutes' (401),
the poet paints a domestic idyll, suffused with the glow emanating
from a shared faith.[34] In Part I of the collection, the adjective *même*
was frequently used to evoke a sense of continuity with the past. In
Part IV, it is also used to suggest idealized spiritual harmony: 'Nous
recevrons d'un même amour, d'un même cœur, | La joie et la douleur
par vos soins préparées' (400). The prayer that he once shared with
his male friend (389) will now be shared with the beloved (400). In-
deed, 'C'est *elle* qui dira l'oraison à voix haute | En demandant pour
tous le pain de chaque jour...' (401; Mauriac's italics)—words which
remind us of the collection's initial title, *le pain quotidien*. In the
poet's imagination, 'Cette enfant trop longtemps cherchée et atten-
due!...' (401) has by now become the mother of his children. She will
shortly have become a grandmother too (404)! But physical contact

---

[34] Cf. what Mauriac writes to Vallery-Radot on 12 May 1910: 'La famille chrétienne
est la plus émouvante harmonie du monde. C'est elle que je veux vénérer et aimer en
vous et en Ismène' (*LV* 34). Ismène was Vallery-Radot's wife; the husband celebrates
their conjugal love in the third part of his 1909 collection of poems, *L'Eau du puits*.

barely gets beyond hand-holding in these poems (399, 402). Here it is
'âmes' that are 'confondues' (401); in later poems, it will be 'soifs'
(*Or* 429) and 'mondes' (*SA* 455), both of which serve as images for
the lovers' bodies. Significantly, the three references to a kiss (*baiser*)
in Part IV of *L'Adieu à l'adolescence* are all rhymed with the verb
apaiser (395, 399, 403). Desire has been more or less evacuated. With
reference to his soul, the poet writes:

> Elle tue, ô mon Dieu, ses désirs infinis,
> Et vous demande, chaque jour, dans sa prière
> Une compagne simple, grave et ménagère. (400)

Now that his 'anciennes amours' are 'à jamais mortes' (401),[35]
the poet finally appears to have freed himself from the past. But it is
at this very moment that he evokes his mother in a most striking
fashion:

> Si nous voyons, longeant les parterres voilés,
> Ma mère qui récitera son chapelet,
> Que la simple grandeur de cette âme chrétienne
> Fasse dans notre cœur l'amour silencieux…
> Que de voir seulement passer l'ombre bénie,
> Nous sentions dans nos cœurs la présence de Dieu…
> Que nos brûlantes mains un instant désunies,
> En un acte d'amour, d'espérance et de foi,
> Tracent sur nos deux corps le signe de la croix!… (402–03)

The mother to whom the collection as a whole is dedicated continues
to cast a shadow (both literal and metaphorical) over the poet—suffi-
cient, indeed, to evoke the very presence of God. In particular, we see
how her proximity disturbs physical intimacy: hands that had previously been clasped (and 'nos brûlantes mains' is a synecdoche that
merely localizes bodily desire in a way unlikely to offend even the
most prudish of Mauriac's readers) are now separated to make the
sign of the cross. The tension between 'corps' and 'croix', highlighted
by their positions at the end of their respective hemistichs and by their

---

[35] A somewhat different emphasis is given two poems earlier: 'D'anciennes amours
dont je porte le deuil, | Plus douces, revivront dans cet amour unique' (399).

phonemic similarity (two of the three phonemes in 'corps' recur in 'croix'), results in a victory for 'croix' as the poem's last word.[36]

The female presence introduced in Part IV enables the poet to envisage his past with greater equanimity. In terms which offer a conscious echo of his first collection's title, he states: 'Vous avez joint les mains pour la peine inconnue, | Héritage secret de mon adolescence...' (403).[37] In her company, the desire to quit childhood memories is no longer so urgent: the poet can savour 'L'ineffable douceur de n'avoir pas vieilli...' (405). Ultimately, however, imagining standing with his beloved on the threshold of 'la maison de campagne' (407),[38] the poet can, without any sense of bitterness or regret, envisage a time when:

> Je n'aurai plus besoin de vous—ô souvenirs!
> Mon enfance s'éloignera—humble servante,
> Celle qui fut fidèle et ne peut plus servir.
> Je prendrai dans mes bras ta jeunesse vivante,
> Mon enfance dira: je meurs... il est aimé... (408)

This future scenario is as close as he will get to declaring the *Adieu* of the title, before he brings his imagined relationship with his beloved to an end as they are separated by death (409).

Although the poem describing this separation, 'La lente mort...', is the penultimate one in the collection, it might be appropriate to regard it as providing a conclusion to the plot line I have been tracing. In some ways, the poem with which Mauriac concludes his collection, 'Port-Royal...', seems unrelated to the plot I have traced above. Should one regard it simply as a kind of addendum? Perhaps, although the only formal device which might signal its difference from the other poems is the fact that its title does not repeat verbatim the

---

[36] Significantly, this line contains the only occurrence of the word 'corps' in *L'Adieu à l'adolescence*.

[37] Various forms of the expression *joindre les mains* are found on four occasions in *L'Adieu à l'adolescence*: twice in Part I where the subject is the poet himself (368, 374) and twice in Part IV where the subject is the beloved (399, 403). Elsewhere in Mauriac's verse, the expression only occurs in the final stanza of the final poem of 'Les Morts du printemps'.

[38] Those familiar with the Mauriac family's property will recognize this as the holiday home at Saint-Symphorien in the Landes.

first few words of the opening line: 'Port-Royal...' rather than 'O Port-Royal...'. This, however, hardly seems conclusive, especially as, in other ways, the poem seems to make a number of deliberate connections with what has gone before. The epigraph from Maurice de Guérin that prefaces the volume as a whole (365) is echoed in the poet's lament: 'J'ai vainement cherché les traces bien-aimées | Des Solitaires amoureux de controverses' (409). Lest it be thought that the path of memory has finally led the poet down a dead end, it should be remembered that the tension between these two statements is considerably eased by the fact that the poet immediately goes on to say: 'Mais qu'importe? L'allée où ma peine se calme | Garde en son gravier blanc leurs cendres impalpables' (410) and then, via the power of poetic creativity, he goes on to give bodily form to these ashes.[39] The reference to 'ma peine' in the lines just quoted reminds us of many poems in earlier sections; the way in which the lyric *je* describes himself in this last poem is entirely consonant with what we already know. When we read: 'je t'apporte | Un cœur blessé de vivre et chercheur de silence' (409), we are reminded of a line from the very first poem: 'ce faible cœur que tout blesse et repousse' (367). It is almost as though the plot I have been tracing in this section is ultimately revealed as a fiction: the future of domestic bliss which the poet has spent much of Part IV sketching out can never, in fact, become a reality for this heart which is 'pressé de mille peines, | Blessé des mille traits d'un amour décevant' (411). This undermining of an apparent idyll will recur in Mauriac's later work: 'Conte de Noël' challenges the beatific vision at the end of *Le Mystère Frontenac*,[40] and, as we shall see, the 'Ebauche d'Endymion' undermines the orthodoxy imposed at the end of *Le Sang d'Atys*.

Conclusion

It is true that, in terms of tone, lexis, and structure, *L'Adieu à l'adolescence* is very similar to *Les Mains jointes*. The collection's

---

[39] The evocation of various figures falling outside the poet's immediately personal circle anticipates the tendency in the later poetry to work on a broader canvass. A similar effect is already apparent in 'Dès le collège...', in which the poet evokes various figures from Racine's tragedies in a style vaguely reminiscent of Racine's own (375–76).

[40] See Cooke, *Mauriac et le mythe du poète*, pp. 107–13.

title proclaims a desire to move on from the past, but this desire proves difficult to realize. Stylistically, the omnipresence of the twelve syllable line arguably provides *L'Adieu à l'adolescence* with a greater degree of firmness. Thematically, the images of domestic satisfaction (reminiscent of Vallery-Radot's *L'Eau du puits* and Verlaine's *La Bonne Chanson*) do provide at least one new element with respect to *Les Mains jointes*. Nevertheless, it would be impossible to argue that the 1911 collection is either original or adventurous. The degree of continuity with *Les Mains jointes* does, however, provide a clear indication that Mauriac is almost spontaneously drawn to a type of verse production that dramatizes the lyric subject's evolution in quasi-narrative fashion and that the main topoi of narrative interest will be childhood/ adolescence, the mother, religion, friendship, love, and death. Even before he has published his first work of fiction, one senses that Mauriac the novelist and Mauriac the poet will never be very far apart.

4. Transitional Verse (1): 'Nocturne' and 'Elégie'

The two poems to be discussed in this chapter were both originally published in *Les Cahiers de l'Amitié de France*.[1] This was an overtly Catholic cultural journal launched in 1912 by Robert Vallery-Radot, aided by his friends and fellow-Bordelais poets André Lafon, Eusèbe de Brémond d'Ars, and, of course, François Mauriac. In addition to his functions as the journal's *administrateur-gérant*, Mauriac was a regular contributor from March 1912 to July 1914.[2] Although he was rather dismissive about the venture in later years, it is clear from contemporary correspondence that Mauriac invested considerable time, energy, and hope in the *Cahiers*.[3] As he wrote to his mother in June 1911: 'si nous savons nous organiser, d'ici deux ans nous constituerons le seul mouvement littéraire important de France' (*NLV* 34). Such optimism proved ill-founded, not least because of the outbreak of war in August 1914. The impact of this catastrophic event on Mauriac's development as a writer will be considered in the next chapter. My concern here is to assess whether new orientations can already be discerned in his immediately pre-War verse.

'Nocturne'
Mauriac's correspondence reveals that the poem was written for Jeanne Lafon (*MAM* 213), the woman he would marry on 3 June 1913 (with Jammes acting as his *témoin*). The fact that Mauriac chooses to use exclusively feminine rhymes in this poem is possibly intended to highlight the importance of his relationship with his fiancée. Décaudin has described 'Nocturne' as perhaps 'le véritable *adieu à l'adole-*

---

[1] François Mauriac, 'Nocturne', *Les Cahiers de l'Amitié de France*, 2.4 (March 1913), 78–80 and 'Elégie', *Les Cahiers de l'Amitié de France*, 3.4 (April 1914), 201–05. The former is reproduced in *MAM* 41–42. Subsequent references to 'Nocturne' will give line numbers only.

[2] These dates are accurate. The items listed by Keith Goesch, *François Mauriac: essai de bibliographie chronologique, 1908–1960* (Nizet, 1965), pp. 72–73 and Laurence Granger, 'Supplément bibliographique', *NCFM*, 4 (1996), 297–310 (pp. 297–98) are incomplete.

[3] See Jean Touzot, 'Les Trois Avatars de la revue rivale', *NCFM*, 8 (2000), 199–210 (pp. 200–03).

scence'.[4] While justified in some respects, I would suggest that, in others, this judgement is somewhat premature. As in the 1911 collection, the emphasis here lies on the competing calls of past and future, male friends and female beloved. However, it would appear that the scales have tipped significantly in favour of the woman and the future, as is suggested by the balance of adverbs in the opening lines: 'C'est encor la jeunesse et pourtant je m'étonne | De moins souffrir des soirs où ne viendra personne' (ll. 1–2).

It is perhaps line 3—'Je me regarde, au fond de la glace, sourire'—that alerts us to the most important feature of the poem: its reflexivity. The word 'fond' in particular attracts attention, since, although it stands at the end of the first hemistich, it is not immediately apparent whether scansion encourages us to retain the ghost of a caesura at this point (giving a binary alexandrine), or whether we should respect the pressure of punctuation and see the line as having a 4 + 5 + 3 structure (a ternary alexandrine). Perhaps Mauriac has deliberately engineered this indecision in order to focus attention on 'fond' and on the line as a whole in which it appears.[5] The word 'fond' would certainly appear to be significant in this poem, since it occurs on three further occasions. In each case, it is connected with memories of the past (ll. 25–26, 43–44, 49–50). In 'Nocturne', it seems as though the self-regarding poet wishes, as it were, to get to the bottom of things', that is, to establish some kind of a *bilan* with respect to his past and future from his present perspective of relative stability ('d'un cœur qui se sent désormais immobile' (l. 11)). This will involve him, at least in part, in returning to some of those self-dramatizations observed in his first two collections of verse.

Lines 1–2 show that the poet no longer regards his solitude as a major source of suffering (as it generally was in *Les Mains jointes* and *L'Adieu à l'adolescence*). He no longer even desires the presence of his male friend (l. 4). This is reminiscent of the fourth section of *L'Adieu à l'adolescence* where the only occurrences of the words *ami* and *amitié* emphasize absence (394, 395, 397, 404), in contrast to the presence of the *amie* who functions as the addressee (399, 404, 405).

---

[4] Décaudin, 'Les Premiers Poèmes de Mauriac', p. 19.

[5] For a discussion of the ways in which poets can exploit the uncertainty around the caesura, see Clive Scott, *French Verse-Art: A Study* (Cambridge: Cambridge University Press, 1980), pp. 71–74.

In 'Nocturne', the reason for this indifference towards the male friend is an awareness of the love (personified for greater intensity) of the female addressee: 'Car ton amour pour moi veille au loin, et j'y pense' (l. 7).

Yet the poet does not simply jettison the past; he insists he is the same as he ever was (l. 12). But this self-identity is defined specifically in terms of a fidelity to favoured locations (ll. 13–14). Much of the poeticity of Mauriac's writing can be attributed to his ability to exploit what might be called the poetry of place.[6] Childhood relationships too continue to exert a hold on the poet's imagination. A child he sees (or imagines?) is identified with images of the past: 'C'est une âme parmi celles que j'ai connues, | Un ami mort peut-être, ou mon frère, ou moi-même' (ll. 22–23). He then adds, tellingly: 'Comment me distinguer de tous ceux-là que j'aime?' (l. 24). Rather than an *adieu* to adolescence, this is more like a loving recognition of memories that will never leave him. The very use of the word 'âme' here (employed a total of five times in the poem) shows that Mauriac is still quite faithful to the tone of his early verse. Hence the pre-emptive apology to his beloved with which the second stanza ends:

> Il faut me pardonner si souvent je m'arrête,
> Et détournant de vous un visage extatique,
> J'écoute ces rumeurs que le passé me jette… (ll. 28–30)

Does the poet's ecstasy derive from the sight of his beloved, or from the rumours of the past? Although the former is presumably intended, the latter remains a possibility, underlining the poet's ambivalence (an ambivalence which is also suggested by the suspension points at the end of the quotation which seem to leave the question of the poet's emotional orientation *en suspens*).

To a certain extent, this uncertainty is resolved in the final stanza (reproduced below) which focuses more directly on the beloved. Her priority is asserted via an allusion to the story of Jesus walking on the water (ll. 34–37),[7] with the poet playing Peter to the beloved's Christ (an identification which represents an ideal fusion of the themes of

---

[6] Cf. Bernard C. Swift, 'Mauriac et Proust: la poésie de l'endroit', *NCFM*, 7 (1999), 89–100.

[7] See Matthieu 14. 22–33.

love and religion so common in the early verse). The lapse of faith
referred to in line 37 leads on to the simile of lines 39–40 which,
though it remains within the maritime semantic field, is altogether
darker. As the next few lines confirm, this is effectively a death wish
(a recurring theme in Mauriac's work and central to *La Chair et le
Sang*, the novel begun in 1914). And it is at this point that the voices
of the past are reintroduced in lines 43–45. Given the presence of
nautical imagery in the preceding lines, it would not be inappropriate
to regard these memories as siren voices, seeking to lure the poet towards oblivion. It is the beloved who checks this mortal drift. The
three-word sentence placed in emphatic position at the start of line 48,
and which reverts to the *tu* form of the first stanza, functions as a simple but powerful break. When the poet says he will forget 'les lilas
d'autrefois et les roses' (l. 49)[8] whose smell (always the most capti-
vating of stimulants in Mauriac's writing) evokes 'des noms qu'il ne
faut plus entendre' (l. 51), it is as close as he gets to bidding a definitive farewell to the past. But even now the parting is not absolute since
the poet follows the words just quoted with a reference to a child (presumably the poet's younger self) waiting for the beloved on the ter-
race. Certainly the emphasis lies on continuity of location (ll. 52–53),
but the fact remains that the poet is still intent on signalling some kind
of continuity with his past.

At the start of the poem, the beloved is addressed as: 'Cœur
d'ombre, âme nocturne et pleine de silence'—imagery that recurs in
lines 55–56.[9] For Mauriac, as for the Judaeo-Christian tradition generally, darkness and night are often associated with sin: 'cette nuit charnelle, intreprète et complice du désir' (*OC*, XI, 117). But, as this poem
demonstrates, Mauriac also uses nocturnal imagery in more nuanced
fashion.[10] In his early verse, he can describe both a 'jardin nocturne'
and evening hills which are 'des vagues d'ombre immobiles' as being
at prayer (*MJ* 385, 330). In 'Le Disparu', however, the terms *nocturne*

---

[8] Cf. 'Le Disparu' where lilacs and roses are also associated with the past (421).

[9] Cf. the description of the beloved in 'Dans le salon...', where the terms *calme*,
silences/silencieuse, and *nocturne* also appear (*AA* 403).

[10] Cf. Marie-Françoise Canérot, 'Nocturne mauriacien', in *Présence de François
Mauriac*, pp. 149–59 and Philippe Le Touzé, 'Les Trois Nocturnes', in *Pascal–Mauriac: l'œuvre en dialogue*, ed. by Jean-François Durand (L'Harmattan, 2000), 195–
210.

and *ombre* will be utilized in more sensual/ sexual contexts: the woman thinks of her lover's eyes 'Dans l'ombre retombant des nocturnes cheveux' and confesses: 'Comme je perdais cœur sur de neigeuses cimes, | Vallée, Ombre, Péché, vers vous je descendis' (417, 419). Even in the early verse, however, dusk can be associated with sexual desire: 'Je suis l'enfant que trouble une pensée mauvaise | Dans la complicité du louche crépuscule' and 'Le crépuscule lent touche vos yeux tranquilles. | Ils songent aux baisers qu'ils n'ont jamais connus…' (*AA* 376, 389). Again, the connection becomes even more explicit in 'Le Disparu': 'Ils ne sombreront plus au fond des crépuscules, | Nos deux corps enchaînés, meurtris et caressés'; and a few lines later: 'Mais—terreur!—les plus longs crépuscules sont courts. | Mes mains n'erreront plus au contour de ses membres' (419). The description of the woman's love as 'un crépuscule calme' in 'Nocturne' therefore takes on greater significance when read in conjunction with other poems. It is, in fact, another aspect of the beloved's christic associations (all sins are effaced in this 'cœur d'ombre'). As the quotations from 'Le Disparu' have already intimated, this highly idealized presentation of the beloved (inherited from the final section of *L'Adieu à l'adolescence*, but finding its purest expression here) will disappear from Mauriac's later verse.

The final few lines of 'Nocturne' would be used again by Mauriac in 'La Tempête apaisée', one of the poems in *Orages* (442–43). In fact, nearly all the elements in this poem are drawn from the final stanza of 'Nocturne'. I shall therefore conclude my analysis of the latter poem by examining the ways in which it came to be reworked. For ease of comparison, here is the final stanza of 'Nocturne' followed by the whole of 'La Tempête apaisée':

31 Pour venir jusqu'à vous, j'ai fait la traversée
    Des jours de ma jeunesse en tempêtes féconde,
    Je vous tendais une âme amoureuse et blessée.
    Parmi les goëlands, j'ai marché sur les ondes,
35 J'ai marché sur les eaux comme un disciple indigne,
    Vers vous qui m'appeliez et me faisiez des signes.
    Parfois j'ai perdu cœur au cœur de la tempête.
    Les larmes, les embruns aveuglaient ma figure.
    Comme un vaisseau perdu, sans voile ni mâture,
40 J'ai désiré sombrer dans les cris des mouettes.
    Amie, il fut des soirs où, détaché du monde,

J'ai désiré mourir, moi qui souris encore,
Comme les bien-aimés dont le souvenir gronde
Au fond de notre cœur attentif et l'implore
45   — Comme les bien-aimés qui n'ont pas voulu vivre.
Je me penchais sur eux, pris de vertige, et ivre
Du sommeil de la mort et de la nuit sans aube.
Mais te voilà. Devant la maison encor close
J'oublierai les lilas d'autrefois et les roses
50   Dont l'odeur douce au fond de mes jours se dérobe,
Et m'évoque des noms qu'il ne faut plus entendre.
La vieille cour est pleine d'ombre—et la terrasse
Est la même où l'enfant s'asseyait pour t'attendre,
Avec le soleil d'août ruisselant sur sa face.
55   Accueille-moi, cœur d'ombre où tout péché s'efface!
Ton amour me devient un crépuscule calme.
Le clair de lune pèse aux immobiles palmes.
Tu t'étonnes du ciel liquide et de ses signes.
Les dos sombres des bœufs vont émerger des vignes.
60   Et le bouvier adolescent qui les ramène
Et dresse vers la nuit sa pure forme humaine,
Celui dont le soleil a pris la chair pour cible,
Sentira sur ses yeux ton sourire invisible!

1   Caresse maintenant les océans calmés,
Mouette au sage cœur qui ne t'es pas enfuie
D'une chair triste en proie aux péchés bien-aimés.
De leurs perfides nœuds, mes mains faibles délie,
5   Et conjure à jamais le dangereux ennui
De traverser tout seul le sommeil et la nuit.
Quand mon rire emplissait de chaudes matinées,
Je savais moins aimer quand j'étais moins amer.
Aujourd'hui, je resonge aux fautes pardonnées,
10   Et mes yeux, dites-vous, ont le goût de la mer.
Accueille-moi, cœur d'ombre, où tout péché s'efface.
J'oublierai les prénoms que tu ne peux entendre.
La vieille cour étouffe de lys; la terrasse
Est brûlante où j'aimais à quinze ans de m'étendre
15   Pour braver le soleil comme la mort en face.
Tu t'étonnes du ciel liquide et de ses signes;
Les dos sombres des bœufs vont émerger des vignes
Et le bouvier adolescent qui les ramène,
Humble et majestueux, les pieds nus et paisibles,
20   Découvre, face au ciel, sa fauve argile humaine,
Et propose au soleil sa poitrine pour cible.

One obvious difference between the two poems is that, in 'La Tempête apaisée', Mauriac has abandoned the nocturnal setting of the earlier poem; lines 56–57 and the first half of line 61 of 'Nocturne' therefore became naturally redundant when rewriting. The other obvious difference concerns the poems' respective lengths: in the process of rewriting, the text has contracted by about a third. Mauriac has achieved this by deliberate condensation: the final stanza of 'Nocturne' opens with a series of images related to a stormy sea (ll. 31–40) that are confined to the title and opening line of 'La Tempête apaisée'; the first poem's lengthy evocation of a death wish (ll. 39–47) is limited to two rather more elliptical lines in the later poem (ll. 5–6); and whereas the past that needs to be forgotten takes up three lines in 'Nocturne' (ll. 49–51), it occupies only one in 'La Tempête apaisée' (l. 12). This shift towards a more condensed poetic form is typical of *Orages* as a whole, as can be seen from Table 10:

Table 10:

	MJ	*AA*	*CAF*	WP	*Or*	*SA*
No. of poems	42	48	9	8	28	19
No. of lines	812	999	175	382	434	390
No. of words	6582	8696	1534	3107	3403	3271
Av. no. of lines per poem	19.3	20.8	19.4	47.8	15.5	20.5
Av. no. of words per poem	156.7	181.2	170.4	388.4	121.5	172.2

Notes
- *Les Mains jointes* contains several groups of numbered poems with a collective title. I have included each of these separately numbered poems in the total number of poems.
- The total number of words and lines is based solely on the text of the poems (that is, titles, epigraphs, dates of composition, etc. have not been included).
- Lexical items that ordinarily contain an apostrophe (e.g., *aujourd'hui*) count as a single word, but where apostrophes are used to indicate an elision, I have counted two separate words. Thus the line 'C'est encor la jeunesse et pourtant je m'étonne' has ten words. Lexical items that are ordinarily hyphenated (e.g., *peut-être*) count as a single word, but those that are hyphenated to conform to grammatical rules (e.g., inversion) count as two words. Thus, the line 'Peut-être ont-ils gardé cette douceur des lèvres' has eight words. The letters *l* (e.g., *l'on*) and *t* (between verb and subject) used for purposes of euphony have been ignored in

the word count. Thus, the line 'M'aime-t-on? Est-ce que j'aime?' has eight words.

As a result of this process of condensation, there is a greater sense of urgency about 'La Tempête apaisée', reinforced grammatically by the poem's four imperatives.[11] The first of these—'Caresse', emphasized as the poem's opening word—is addressed to a 'Mouette au sage cœur' (l. 2). In 'Nocturne', the references to 'goëlands' (l. 34) and 'mouettes' (l. 40) appear simply as part of the seascape; in the later poem, however, the bird has become a symbol for the beloved. Even though the object of the imperative 'Caresse' is non-human (the becalmed oceans), the verb itself has sensual connotations that inevitably inform the reader's response to the poem.[12] Sexuality is certainly still in the background, but not to the extent that it was in 'Nocturne', as can be seen by comparing the latter's vague reference to 'ma jeunesse en tempêtes féconde' (l. 32) to the more obviously sexual 'chair triste en proie aux péchés bien-aimés' (l. 3) in 'La Tempête apaisée'.[13] There is no apparent contact between the lovers in 'Nocturne', but the later poem alludes elliptically to a kiss (l. 10). However, it is in the final half of 'La Tempête apaisée' (where the language of 'Nocturne' is most clearly recycled) that we can see how Mauriac's verse is developing a more sensual dimension. Here are the major points of comparison in tabular form, followed by comments on each of the eight comparisons in turn:

Table 11:

	'Nocturne'	'La Tempête apaisée'
1	La vieille cour est pleine d'ombre (l. 52)	La vieille cour étouffe de lys (l. 13)
2	la terrasse	Est la même (ll. 52–53)	la terrasse	Est brûlante (ll. 13–14)

[11] See lines 1, 4, 5, 11; there is only one imperative in the final stanza of 'Nocturne' (l. 55).

[12] Elsewhere in Mauriac's verse, the verb *caresser* and the noun *caresse* always have sensual connotations (see *Or* 431, 435; *SA* 449; EE 465). The terms are not found in the first two collections.

[13] Cf. later in *Orages*: 'ma chair, triste abîme de joie' (444). Mauriac is perhaps echoing the opening words of Mallarmé's 'Brise marine': 'La chair est triste, hélas!' (*Œuvres complètes*, p. 176).

3	où l'enfant s'asseyait pour t'attendre (l. 53)	où j'aimais à quinze ans de m'étendre (l. 14)
4	Avec le soleil d'août ruisselant sur sa face (l. 54)	Pour braver le soleil comme la mort en face (l. 15)
5	Et dresse vers la nuit (l. 61)	Découvre, face au ciel (l. 20)
6	sa pure forme humaine (l. 61)	sa fauve argile humaine (l. 20)
7	Celui dont le soleil a pris (l. 62)	Et propose au soleil (l. 21)
8	la chair pour cible (l. 62)	sa poitrine pour cible (l. 21)

1. The abandonment of the nocturnal setting partly accounts for the difference between the two lines. But the verb 'étouffe' is altogether more evocative than the construction 'pleine de'. Although lilies are generally associated with purity in Mauriac's verse (*AA* 398; Dis 421), the emphasis here seems rather to be on their overpowering scent—a distinctly *sensual* experience.[14]

2. The first poem's stress on continuity with the past is replaced by an emphasis on heat. Metaphors associated with heat are frequently used in Mauriac's later verse in connection with human passion.

3. This comparison indicates three shifts in perspective. Firstly, the poet refers to himself in the first person rather than the third. Secondly, we move from childhood to adolescence (the age of the discovery of sexuality as far as Mauriac was concerned).[15] And, finally, the seated position of passive waiting becomes a more dramatic stretching out on the ground.[16]

4. The sun moves from grammatical subject to object as the poet presents himself in defiant, quasi-heroic mode.[17]

5. The difference can again be partly explained by the move away from the nocturnal setting. However, it may be that *le ciel* here is meant to evoke a religious heaven as much as a spatial sky. As we shall see in Chapter 6, the poet borders on religious revolt on a number of occasions in *Orages*.

6. There is an important contrast here at the level of both adjectives ('pure'/ 'fauve') and nouns ('forme'/ 'argile'). The abstraction of the earlier poem gives

---

[14] Cf. the double reference to 'la chambre étouffante' in the strongly sensual 'Lumière du corps' (*Or* 439).

[15] Cf. 'l'adolescence marque une rupture, interrompt le courant, crée parfois une chimère à tête d'enfant et à corps d'homme' (*PC* 262).

[16] The use of *s'étendre* in *Le Sang d'Atys*—'Je m'étends, quand midi luit, | Au feu de ta chair perdue' (448)—suggests that there could be a sensual dimension to the use of the verb in 'La Tempête apaisée'.

[17] The wording in 'La Tempête apaisée' alludes to La Rochefoucauld's twenty-sixth maxim: 'Le soleil ni la mort ne se peuvent regarder fixement.' See La Rochefoucauld, *Maximes*, ed. by Jacques Truchet (Garnier Frères, 1967), p. 13.

way to an altogether earthier vision. Man's integration in the natural world is at the heart of Mauriac's fascination with the figures of Attis and Cybele.[18]

7.   Here again the sun moves from grammatical subject to (indirect) object.
8.   This comparison illustrates the shift from the general to the particular as 'la chair' becomes 'sa poitrine'. The naming of specific body parts is more prominent in *Orages* than in Mauriac's earlier verse.

In conclusion, it can be said that 'Nocturne' has much in common with the final section of *L'Adieu à l'adolescence*. Despite Décaudin's claim, the relationship between the two texts is essentially one of continuity. It is only when we look at how Mauriac reworked the final stanza of 'Nocturne' into 'La Tempête apaisée' that we detect a genuine shift in his practice as a poet. It is, of course, in 'Nocturne' that the figure of 'le bouvier adolescent' is introduced (1. 60), but it is only in the later poem that his role becomes truly significant. The final line of 'Nocturne' reorients the poem back towards the beloved (a shift that is entirely appropriate in the context of the poem as a whole). In 'La Tempête apaisée', however, this line is omitted and attention remains focused on the adolescent who dares to brave the sun (functioning here as a symbol of the divine?).[19] The later poem also adds a line not present in 'Nocturne', describing the youth as 'Humble et majestueux, les pieds nus et paisibles' (1. 19)—terms which mark him out as a potentially heroic (and possibly even christic) figure.[20] He serves to introduce those other young male figures that feature in the poems immediately following 'La Tempête apaisée' in *Orages*—Marsyas, Ganymède, David, and Rimbaud—figures who, in different ways, ultimately point towards Atys and Endymion. It is this turn towards the mythic that characterizes the poetry of Mauriac's maturity; and it reveals itself for the first time, perhaps somewhat incongruously, at the end of 'Nocturne'.

---

[18] In general references to mythological figures, I shall use their English names; when figures from Mauriac's verse are specifically in view, I shall use the French names he gives them.
[19] Cf. the association between the sun and the divine in Psaumes 89. 37; Matthieu 17. 2; and Apocalypse 1. 16.
[20] The New Testament refers to Christ's 'majesté' (2 Pierre 1. 16) and to his being 'humble' (Matthieu 11. 29).

'Elégie'

'Elégie' is a cycle of eight separately numbered, single-stanza poems written entirely in alexandrines.[21] The stanzas vary in length from 9 to 22 lines, giving a total of 111 lines for the cycle as a whole. The first six poems are addressed to a female *vous* who twice becomes a *tu* (II, 9; VI, 10); poem VII apostrophizes '[le] Bonheur'; and, in poem VIII, the poet addresses himself in the second person singular. Although the cycle contains a narrative dimension of sorts, this is less clearly marked than in the preceding collections. Given that the cycle's dominant theme is the poet's love for a woman (presumably the same figure as in 'Nocturne'), the choice of 'Elégie' for the collective title might seem rather odd. However, as we have seen from both *L'Adieu à l'adolescence* and 'Nocturne', the beloved's presence is deemed to be incompatible with those things that characterized the poet's past, and it is the loss of these elements that gives rise to the cycle's elegiac dimension.

The first poem opens with an evocation of overwhelming summer heat—the kind of atmosphere that would be so characteristic of Mauriac's novels of the 1920s. The personification of the natural world—the sun has a heart, the ploughed fields are exhausted, the vineyard is mute, and the earth sleeps (I, 3–4, 7)—provides another stylistic trait that would come to be seen as typically Mauriacian. The general sense of weary enervation is reflected in the casual half rhyme (/ɥe/ and /ɥɛ/) of 'exténués' and 'muet' (I, 2–3). The nine-line poem is a single sentence whose main verb and subject (the lyric *je*) are dramatically delayed until the final line. In the midst of nature's immobility and the prone bodies of the reapers, the poet alone stands erect—his uniqueness emphasized through the isolated adjective and adverb used to describe him at the start of line 6: 'Seul, debout, […]'. But the picture is not quite one of the poet as hero. Unlike the lyric *je* of 'La Tempête apaisée', the poet of 'Elégie' has no desire to 'braver le soleil'; rather, as he puts it: 'Je cherchais votre cœur comme je cherchais l'ombre' (I, 9). The beloved here, then, plays much the same

---

[21] The full text will be reproduced in my forthcoming edition of *Les Mains jointes*. References in this chapter will use an initial Roman numeral to indicate the poem number, followed by an Arabic figure indicating the line number (e.g., VII, 8).

role as she did in 'Nocturne' where reference was twice made to her 'cœur d'ombre' (l. 8, l. 55).

The connections with 'Nocturne' carry over into the next poem where the final line refers to 'ta douceur mêlée à celle de la nuit' (II, 9). By now the poet has apparently obtained the woman whose heart he sought at the end of poem I: 'Je vous possède enfin—chère âme au ciel couvert' (II, 2). Attention is focused on the emerald (engagement?) ring that he has given her. There is no trace in its depths of what the poet refers to as the 'regards que j'ai fuis' (II, 6)—a formulation that recalls the 'noms qu'il ne faut plus entendre' from 'Nocturne' (l. 51) and that seems to return us to the *amitié/ amour* opposition familiar from Mauriac's early verse.

These first two poems would later reappear in *Orages* under the titles 'L'Ombre' and 'L'Emeraude' respectively. Although the text is very similar in both cases, there are lexical changes in three places that show Mauriac's interest in 'polishing' his poems. The three variants are given below in Table 12 with comments on each underneath:

Table 12:

	'Elégie'	'L'Ombre' & 'L'Emeraude'
1	Quand les faucheurs, comme une armée anéantie, | Etendaient sur le sol leurs bras crucifiés (I, 4–5)	A l'heure où des faucheurs l'armée anéantie | Ecrasait l'herbe sous des corps crucifiés (*Or* 442)
2	De toutes les douleurs dont j'ignorais le nombre (I, 8)	Assourdi par le cri des cigales sans nombre (*Or* 442)
3	[l'émeraude] Que je vous ai donnée, un soir du triste hiver. | La mystérieuse eau de cette étrange pierre (II, 4–5)	[l'émeraude] Que nous avons crue morte, au long du noir hiver. | La mystérieuse eau qui dort dans cette pierre (*Or* 442)

1. Mauriac begins by exchanging the neutral 'Quand' for a less banal temporal adverb. He then transforms a basic simile into a metaphor combined with 'poetic' inversion. By so doing, he gives a more pleasing rhythm to line 4, with the caesura falling after 'faucheurs' rather than after the proclitic 'une'. The use of the verb *écraser* in preference to *étendre* gives greater dynamism to the fifth line and the use of 'corps' in preference to 'bras' has the advantage of producing the alliteration in /k/ at the end of the line. In addition, the /k/ and /ʀ/ sounds in 'corps' are echoed in both 'Ecrasait' and 'crucifiés'.

2. The focus shifts from an abstract moral concern ('toutes les douleurs') to a more concrete attention to actual sounds. This is more in keeping with the emphasis on

the stifling summer heat. The threefold repetition of /s/ and, especially, /i/ in the line from 'L'Ombre' succeeds well in conveying the cicadas' shrill noise.

3.   The initial relative clause becomes more dramatic in the reworked poem. Although the adjective 'morte' is perfectly ordinary in many ways, the fact that it serves, somewhat unusually, to qualify a precious stone prepares for the unexpected reference to 'la mystérieuse eau' contained in the gem. The decision to substitute 'au long du' for 'un soir du' and 'noir' for 'triste' illustrates the trends suggested in Tables 1 and 8 (Chapter 2) which show how Mauriac moved away from nocturnal, melancholy vocabulary in his later verse. Finally, one notes that the third adjective in the two lines quoted from the 1914 version is replaced by a metaphor in the reworked poem. Perhaps Mauriac felt the sequence of three adjectives placed before nouns in rapid succession was rather excessive, or perhaps he thought the connotations of 'étrange' were too similar to those of 'mystérieuse'.

In the third poem of 'Elégie', the beloved is described for the first time as 'une enfant' (III, 3), a noun that will be used as part of an apostrophe to her on three further occasions (IV, 1, 5; VI, 1). It is a term that effectively desexualizes the woman, emphasizing her purity and innocence. As well as being referred to as an 'enfant', the beloved is also imagined following in the footsteps of 'les aïeules', joining 'les paysans' in their agricultural activities (III, 12, 13). We see the woman as child and as worker, but never as lover.

The third poem also offers a number of examples of Mauriac's attentiveness to the expressive potential of sound and rhythm. The succession of six nasal vowels in the opening line—'Soirs devant le perron où l'on entend son cœur'—evokes the regular beat of a heart. And the harmonious balance of phonemes in line 7 provides an appropriate aural impression of a calm pastoral scene: 'Déjà, c'est la saison où l'herbe que l'on fauche | Reste sur la prairie et parfume le soir' (III, 6–7). The way in which the adjective 'pétrifiés' straddles the caesura in line 10 ('Autour des bœufs pétrifiés, des sombres meules') emphasizes this bovine immobility.

The fourth poem returns to a number of *topoi* familiar from Mauriac's early verse. 'La chair [...] si faible en face du désir' in the evening setting (IV, 3) is reminiscent of the situation in 'Soir complice...' (*AA* 376). When the poet refers to 'le passé si lourd des amitiés pleurées...' and says that his 'cœur n'ose | S'arracher tout entier à ses bonheurs perdus' (IV, 4, 5–6), one is reminded of the tearfulness and the pull of the past in the earlier collections. However, the poem's final four lines would later be incorporated by Mauriac in 'La Tem-

pête apaisée' (ll. 7–10) in an altogether more sensual context. The
only lexical difference between the two sets of lines is that 'claires
matinées' (IV, 9) becomes 'chaudes matinées' (*Or* 442). The only
reason for the change appears to be that Mauriac never uses the adjective *clair* in his later verse: it occurs three times in *Les Mains jointes*,
six times in *L'Adieu à l'adolescence*,[22] and three times in the War
poetry, but is entirely absent from the last two collections.

At the end of poem IV, there is a suggestion that the beloved
kisses the poet on his eyes (IV, 12). This is echoed in the next poem
by the hint of a kiss on the mouth, when the poet comments that his
beloved's lips have prayed so much that they have 'conservé le goût
de miel des litanies' (V, 7). Once again, therefore, one sees how the
beloved is desexualized, not this time by being referred to as a child,
but through her association with religious devotion. Furthermore, the
kiss is taken while the beloved is asleep: 'un sommeil aussi doux que
la mort' (V, 6). In contrast, waking up is viewed in terms of re-
entering 'l'importune vie' (V, 8)—the location of the adjective underlining the poet's sense of alienation from quotidian existence. The
words the beloved speaks on waking—'"Pour venir, le chemin fut
bien rude… | J'avais peur de moi-même et de ma solitude…"' (V, 9–
10)—echo the kind of sentiments expressed by the lyric *je* himself in
his first two collections. There is perhaps a degree of narcissism about
his attraction to his female addressee.

The sixth poem reveals a certain distance with respect to the past.
Rather than agonizing over bidding farewell to his adolescence, the
poet is now sufficiently removed from this situation to be able to nar-
rate it as a past event: 'Mon enfant, je vous dis alors ce que me furent |
Ces jours où ma jeunesse hésitait à mourir' (VI, 1–2). The *rejet interne* in the second of these lines nicely encapsulates the central
problematic of *L'Adieu à l'adolescence*, but the tenses suggest that
now, in the narrative present, the lingering demise of the poet's youth
is finally over.

The penultimate poem is unusual in Mauriac's verse corpus in
that it takes the form of an apostrophe to an abstract concept: 'Bonheur, tu es […]' (VII, 1). The fact that happiness is such a rare com-

---

[22] Not including two references to the *Sonate au clair de lune*.

modity in Mauriac's verse makes the poem doubly unusual.[23] The poet's happiness is partly due to the beloved's influence, hinted at in the first person plural grammatical forms (VII, 8, 9, 20) and alluded to in the phrase 'l'onde d'une présence' (VII, 4). There is also a reference to 'L'immobile berceau [qui] dit l'attente ineffable | De l'âme déjà là qui bientôt sera née' (VII, 6–7), but this highly allusive evocation of marital union is clearly focused on the result rather than the process or the participants.[24] But happiness for the poet is also associated with the past. Hence the use of a comparison that draws on the memory of Raymond Laurens to describe the way in which '[le] Bonheur' smiles at the poet:

> Derrière moi, tu me souris au fond des glaces,
> Comme l'ami défunt, pur visage détruit,
> Dont la vingtième année est fidèle et me suit. (VII, 14–16)

True happiness for the poet is characterized by this fusion of past, present, and future horizons in a moment of silent reverie just before the onset of sleep (VII, 20).

The mode of the beloved's presence in poem VII could be described as all-pervasive though barely tangible. The same is true in the final poem where, although she appears in the poem's central section (lines 9–11), she is evoked simply as 'Une amour' leaning over the poet's book (VIII, 9). Her reassuring, quasi-maternal presence allows the poet to address himself as follows: 'Dors maintenant et songe aux tempêtes finies, | Mouette au sage cœur que les vagues ont fui...' (VIII, 12–13).[25] The metaphor would be recycled at the start of 'La Tempête apaisée': 'Caresse maintenant les océans calmés, | Mouette au sage cœur qui ne t'es pas enfuie' (*Or* 442), but whereas in the later poem the seagull represents the beloved, in 1914 it refers to the poet

---

[23] See my article 'Les Obstacles au bonheur dans la poésie de François Mauriac', in *Le Bonheur dans la littérature européenne contemporaine*, ed. by Michel Reffet (Sarrebourg: Association Européenne François Mauriac, 1998), pp. 36–45.

[24] The use of the term 'âme' to refer to the unborn child is a good example of the kind of ethereal spiritualizing that may have appealed to readers of the *Cahiers*, but that Mauriac himself would increasingly abandon after the War.

[25] The beloved's quasi-maternal status is reinforced a few lines later when her 'genoux étroits' are said to await the poet's 'front sage' (VIII, 16).

himself. The marine metaphor paves the way for the poem's conclusion:

> Et tu seras, dans les muettes fins de jour,
> Comme un marin moins jeune à son dernier retour
> Qui s'asseoit sous la lampe et renonce au voyage. (VIII, 17–19)

This static image demonstrates that the poet's painful *adieu* to adolescence has hardly resulted in a liberating voyage of discovery. Here is a classic example of what Quaghebeur terms 'cette catégorie "thanatique" à laquelle aspire tout le mauriacisme'.[26] The poet's evening lamp-light meditations at the end of 'Elégie' recall the student's situation early in *Les Mains jointes*: 'Je suis tout seul avec ma lampe dans la nuit' (*MJ* 337). The only difference is that the poet is no longer alone. This picture of domestic quietude will be challenged in the opening poem of *Orages* where the image of the poet as sailor will be put to radically different use.

Conclusion

In many ways, the two poems considered in this chapter merely continue debates opened in Mauriac's earlier collections: elements such as the pull of the past, the tension between friendship and love, and the pleasures of domesticity are all familiar from *L'Adieu à l'adolescence* in particular. But there are newer elements too: the introduction of a quasi-mythical figure at the end of 'Nocturne' and the powerfully stifling imagery used in the opening poem of 'Elégie', both of which look forward to characteristics of Mauriac's work during the 1920s. One is, then, justified in viewing these poems as transitional texts, even if Mauriac is still much closer to the pole of *Les Mains jointes* than to that of *Orages*. Perhaps the greatest interest of these poems lies in the way in which Mauriac rewrites parts of them for his 1925 collection. The changes that he makes reveal his drive towards greater density and intensity of poetic expression. However, it would take the events of 1914–18 to encourage this reorientation of his work. It is to this second transitional period that I now turn.

---

[26] Quaghebeur, 'Mauriac poète: interstices', p. 185.

5. Transitional Verse (2): The War Years

As a result of the severe pleurisy he contracted in 1903, Mauriac was declared unfit for military service when war was declared in 1914. However, his desire to serve his country led him to volunteer as a medical auxiliary. He was finally invalided out of the Red Cross in May 1917 following an extremely dangerous voyage (undertaken against medical advice) to Salonica where he immediately contracted malaria. While he may not have had first-hand experience of the horrors of life at the Front, his menial medical duties involved exposure to blood, pus, and excrement as he tended the wounded; endless piles of clothes to be laundered; and frequent opportunities to hone his louse-slaying skills.[1] It is clear from Mauriac's correspondence and his *Journal d'un homme de trente ans* (1948) that the events of 1914–18 made a profound impression on him. It has often been observed that the First World War marks something of a watershed in his literary production. Attention is drawn to the contrast between *L'Enfant chargé de chaînes* and *Le Baiser au lépreux*, for example, or between *Les Mains jointes* and *Orages*.[2] It should also be noted that transitional novels such as *La Chair et le sang* (1920), *Préséances* (1921), and *Le Mal* (1924) were all begun during the War years. The poetry produced by Mauriac during this period has, however, almost entirely escaped critical attention. The following examination of his war poetry is an attempt to fill this gap.

'La Veillée avec André Lafon'

Although written in 1915, this poem was not published until after the War. It functions as a kind of preface to the original edition of Mauriac's *Petits Essais de psychologie religieuse*.[3] The poem would disappear when the essays were republished in 1933, only to reappear as

---

[1] See Lacouture, *François Mauriac*, I, 183–207 and Violaine Massenet, *François Mauriac* (Flammarion, 2000), pp. 120–40.

[2] See François Durand, 'Mauriac devant la grande guerre', in *Présence de François Mauriac*, pp. 81–87 (p. 84).

[3] François Mauriac, *De quelques cœurs inquiets: petits essais de psychologie religieuse* (Société Littéraire de France, 1919), pp. 5–7; republished as *Petits Essais de psychologie religieuse*, 2nd edn (L'Artisan du Livre, 1933).

a kind of coda when Mauriac's final collections of verse came out in a single volume[4]—hence its inclusion as the last verse text in the 1951 *Œuvres complètes*.[5] The strategic location occupied by the poem is a testimony to the deep friendship that existed between the two men.[6] As Mauriac wrote to his wife: 'Je ne peux vous dire quelle *adoration* j'éprouve pour lui.'[7] Lafon's death from scarlet fever in Bordeaux's military hospital on 5 May 1915 struck Mauriac as '*l'irréparable perte* d'une amitié telle que la vie ne nous en renouvelle pas la faveur…'[8] By the end of the War, Mauriac had already published articles commemorating his friend (*OA* 833) and would later produce a more extensive appreciation entitled *La Vie et la mort d'un poète* (1924).

André Lafon is both the subject and the addressee of 'La Veillée avec André Lafon'. The whole poem is an attempt to deny the definitiveness of death and the threat that it poses to a precious friendship. The poem begins: 'Entre comme autrefois' (l. 1), as though Lafon had just knocked on the poet's door. Although addressed to his dead friend, the invitation is also an invitation to the reader to enter a textual world of imagination and memory where death loses some of its power. Hence the paradoxical affirmation that follows this invitation: 'Tu vis encor.' Lafon's continued existence is stressed particularly at the start of the second stanza which pictures him having accepted the poet's invitation to enter: 'Tes lourds souliers au feu fument d'un long chemin, | Mais sur ton front rayonne une paix éternelle' (ll. 5–6). Even though Lafon is dead, line 5 stresses his embodied existence with the heavy, steaming footwear evoking physical effort. This focus on the point where the body makes direct contact with the earth is replaced in line 6 with a reference to the forehead—behind which, of course, lies the centre of consciousness that allows man to transcend bodily limitations. The eternal peace streaming from Lafon's forehead speaks of spiritual, heavenly experiences. This picture of Lafon there-

---

[4] François Mauriac, *Orages* (Grasset, 1949), pp. 98–100.

[5] Subsequent references will give line numbers only. Where necessary, the abbreviation VAL will also be used.

[6] See André Bourcheix, 'François Mauriac et André Lafon', *CFM*, 4 (1976), 27–41.

[7] Quoted by Massenet, *François Mauriac*, p. 109.

[8] Quoted by Pierre Mauriac, *François Mauriac*, p. 49; Mauriac's italics.

fore unites the earthly and the heavenly, the physical and the spiritual in an attempt to rob death of its victory. As is made clear by the two temporal adverbs used in the opening line ('autrefois' and 'encor'), time will not be viewed in an exclusively linear fashion in this poem with an *avant* opposed to an *après*. Although there is certainly a temporal framework to the poem, its frames are not watertight. Thus, in stanzas 1–4, although the verbs are predominantly in the present tense, past verbs also figure in lines 4, 9, and 16. This situation is then reversed in stanzas 5–9 where the verbs are mostly in the past tense, but with present verbs in lines 18, 25, and 34. The final three stanzas revert to a preponderance of present verbs with just two in the past (lines 39 and 41), but there is a difference here in that the present verbs used in the last stanza have a future significance.

An analysis of these verb forms would show that the relationship between past and present in the poem is characterized by both similarity and difference. The opening line may well highlight continuity, but elsewhere the poet recognizes that there is discontinuity too. Despite the confident 'Tu vis encor' (l. 1), he can twice refer to a time 'où tu étais vivant' (l. 17, l. 25) with the obvious implication that this life is no longer being lived. The poet can also make use of negative constructions to emphasize the distance between the peaceful past and the violent present: 'Le sang ne souillait pas les cheveux des enfants, | L'hiver ne glaçait pas d'immobiles poitrines' (ll. 27–28). But more important than this temporal contrast are those which exist between the poet and his friend. Another negative construction is used in the first stanza to allude to Lafon's unmarried state: 'tes mains où ne luit pas d'anneau' (l. 2). Perhaps this is just an incidental detail, but it may be more than that: although Mauriac himself enjoyed a long and apparently happy marriage, there was a part of him that, influenced no doubt by his 'Jansenist' up-bringing, had difficulty in forgetting Pascal's definition of marriage as 'la plus basse des conditions du christianisme, […], vile et préjudiciable selon Dieu' (*OA* 117). Whether biographically accurate or not, Mauriac espoused a vision of a virginal Lafon who had retained a purity he himself had lost.[9]

---

[9] Hence his description of him as being 'pur parmi les purs' (quoted by Massenet, *François Mauriac*, p. 81).

Although Mauriac certainly appreciated his friend's literary gifts, it seems that his response to Lafon's writing was usually filtered through this idealized image of him as a 'pure' poet.[10] Hence a final contrast in the first stanza of 'La Veillée avec André Lafon' where Lafon is addressed as 'toi qui te taisais pour que l'on pût t'entendre...' (l. 4). The paradox is one of the first examples of a theme that would become increasingly important for Mauriac: the idea that poetry is intimately bound up with silence and that the greatest poets (Racine and Rimbaud) ultimately chose to *se taire* (*OA* 444–48). Although at this early stage, Mauriac has not yet begun to develop his concept of poetic silence in aesthetic terms, it is noticeable that whenever he uses the term *silence* in this poem, he does so in a context that draws attention to his language by overt repetition of certain sounds:

(i)   Tes yeux ont le silence et le sommeil de l'eau,
        Toi qui te taisais pour que l'on pût t'entendre... (ll. 3–4)

(ii) [...] quand les brusques piverts
        S'éloignaient dans le bois en blessant le silence. (ll. 15–16)

(iii) Mon André, ton silence emplit ce soir l'espace. (l. 37)

(iv) Et pourtant, tu es là, silencieuse Face. (l. 40)[11]

Perhaps, then, we can see here a foreshadowing of Mauriac's later remarks about poetic silence, where, as we saw in Chapter 1, *silence* functions as a metaphor for certain kinds of spiritual/ aesthetic experience rather than signifying a literal absence of sound. Nevertheless, Lafon's silence is certainly also that of the grave in this poem. The

---

[10] Cf. *BN*, IV, 112: 'c'était bien son âme que je chérissais, non son intelligence ni même son inspiration poétique'.

[11] In (i), the fricative and liquid sounds of line 3 (/s/ occurs three times and its voiced equivalent /z/ once; /l/ occurs four times) contrast effectively with the occlusives of line 4: /t/ occurring five times, its voiced equivalent /d/ once, and /k/ and /p/ both twice. In (ii), /l/ occurs six times; /s/ and /ã/ five times each; there are also three occurrences of /b/ with its unvoiced equivalent /p/ being used once. In (iii), we find six occurrences of /s/ and five nasal vowels (/ã/ three times and /ɔ̃/ twice). In (iv), there are three occurrences of /s/ and its voiced equivalent /z/ is used once.

fact that this silence was not self-imposed (as Mauriac thought it was for both Racine and Rimbaud) does not seem to matter;[12] death has transfigured his friend in a way that will always be denied Mauriac, the 'survivant' (*OA* 5).

If Mauriac is a survivor, it is primarily because he has been spared the 'combats inhumains' referred to in line 7 of 'La Veillée avec André Lafon'. As this adjective makes plain, Mauriac, although a keen patriot, was too much of a humanist to adopt a gung-ho attitude to the brutality of war. Indeed, there are several references in his correspondence to his disgust at the appalling slaughter and suffering he witnessed in his medical duties.[13] However, he is also acutely aware that he has never really had to make any sacrifices on behalf of others during what he calls his 'égoïste vie' (*LV* 69) and therefore suffers from a continual sense of guilt about not participating in direct combat. As he writes to his brother Pierre after his exemption in December 1914: 'Il faudra payer d'une manière ou de l'autre, et quelquefois je suis terrifié à la pensée que j'échappe à l'expiation universelle...'[14] Something of this seems to surface in 'La Veillée avec André Lafon' when the poet seeks refuge in his friend's gaze from the horrors of war (ll. 10–12). The next line presents this flight as a kind of desertion, with the poet temporarily abandoning 'les martyrs'—a term whose religious connotations would obviously have been significant for Mauriac. The word is further emphasized by the fact that the line in which it occurs is the first that does not allow for a natural pause at the caesura: 'Une heure délaissant les martyrs, à travers | Les branches du passé touffu, mon cœur s'avance' (ll. 13–14). Perhaps this shift in rhythm (that continues into line 14) itself conveys something of Mauriac's psychological discomfort.

As the poet travels back into his memories in stanza 5, we find a typically Mauriacian touch in that his first sense impression is olfactory (ll. 17–18).[15] However, the most important memory is that contained in stanza 6 (which brings us up to the poem's mid-point):

---

[12] But cf. Mauriac's comments in his essay on Lafon: 'la sainteté, c'est presque toujours le silence. J'entrevois qu'André Lafon vivant n'aurait plus guère écrit que de fervents et brefs poèmes' (*OA* 61). Similar thoughts are expressed in *DAM* 49.

[13] See *LV* 76, 84, 86, 91–92; *NLV* 59, 62; cf. *OA* 224, 227, 253.

[14] Pierre Mauriac, *François Mauriac: mon frère*, p. 44.

[15] Elsewhere, Mauriac also stresses Lafon's acute sense of smell (*DAM* 45).

> La houle qui berça mes voyages d'antan
> Savait moins consoler ma souffrante insomnie
> Que celle qui gonflait ta poitrine endormie,
> O dormeur étendu dans l'herbe du printemps! (ll. 21–24)

We find here a further contrast between the poet and his addressee. Curiously perhaps (given the relative scarcity of significant journeys in Mauriac's life), the poet casts himself in the role of an insomniac voyager. Lafon, on the other hand, is earth-bound and asleep. The poet suggests he can only find comfort with his head resting on his friend's slumbering chest. Although there may be a vaguely homoerotic dimension to the image, the use of the verbs *bercer* and *consoler* imply that Lafon plays an almost maternal role here. But, above all, he recalls Rimbaud's 'Dormeur du val'. Like Lafon, the latter is described as being 'étendu dans l'herbe' and the poem also employs the verb *bercer*: 'Nature, berce-le chaudement: il a froid.'[16] Rimbaud's description of the dead young soldier, apparently sleeping so peacefully, clearly haunted Mauriac and, as we shall see, it is an image to which his War poetry returns on a number of occasions.[17]

Lying in the spring grass, Lafon's pre-War 'poitrine endormie' contrasts with the 'immobiles poitrines' being chilled by winter (VAL, l. 28). The term employed to describe these dead soldiers is significant: they are 'enfants' (l. 27).[18] The term is obviously designed to heighten the pathos of the slaughter and, once again, we shall see that it recurs under Mauriac's pen. In this poem, it is identified particularly with the figure of the herdsman already encountered in 'Nocturne': 'Un bouvier presque enfant passait, d'ombre vêtu: | Comme ils étaient vivants encor, les jeunes hommes!' (VAL, ll. 31–32). The *rejet interne* in the second line just quoted heightens the sense of tragedy over so many wasted young lives.

---

[16] Arthur Rimbaud, *Œuvres*, ed. by Suzanne Bernard and André Guyaux (Garnier Frères, 1981), p. 76.

[17] Mauriac may also have known the photograph of his friend Jean de La Ville de Mirmont (taken in 1913) in which the latter, who would be killed in the first few months of the War, posed as the *dormeur du val*. See Jean de La Ville de Mirmont, *Œuvres complètes*, ed. by Michel Suffran (Seyssel: Champ Vallon, 1992), p. 6.

[18] Cf. a letter in which Mauriac tells Vallery-Radot about the wounded soldiers in hospital: 'Ils sont bons, reconnaissants, affectueux. Ce sont de *petits enfants* qui malheureusement ont conscience d'avoir un sexe' (*LV* 76; Mauriac's italics).

I suggested earlier that, when Mauriac reused 'Nocturne' in 'La Tempête apaisée', the figure of the herdsman was beginning to assume quasi-mythical proportions. While this is not the case in 'La Veillée avec André Lafon', the poem does manage to transcend the immediately personal. It does this not only by evoking the general context of the War, but also by locating the horror of war within a long tradition of human violence stretching back into a past that could be regarded as 'mythical' in the broadest sense of the term:[19] 'Ainsi nous poursuivons cette étrange veillée, | Loin d'un monde à jamais souillé du sang d'Abel' (ll. 41–42). This, of course, is an allusion to the story in Genesis in which Cain introduces violence into human society by murdering his brother Abel. Significantly, the term 'souillé' then recurs in the poem's final stanza:

> Jusqu'à ce que, tremblant de vertige et d'effroi,
> Surgissant de ma couche au brusque appel du Père,
> J'apparaisse souillé et nu dans ta lumière,
> O mort! et me découvre aussi vivant que Toi. (ll. 45–48)

By applying the adjective 'souillé' to himself in this evocation of the Last Judgement, the poet is implicitly locating himself within the lineage of Cain.[20] If he was earlier '*Loin* d'un monde à jamais souillé du sang d'Abel', it was presumably because he was then in the company of Lafon who, metaphorically, might be said to be in the line of Seth—the son who replaced Abel and who, in the New Testament, figures in the genealogy of Christ.[21] There can certainly be little doubt that Lafon fulfils a quasi-christic role in this poem. When the poet writes: 'Ce calme en moi, c'est bien ton éternelle paix' (l. 38), it is reminiscent of two passages in John's gospel. In the first, Christ tells his disciples about 'l'Esprit de Vérité' that they will know 'parce qu'il demeure près de vous et qu'il est en vous'; then, later in the same

---

[19] Cf. John C. L. Gibson, *Genesis*, 2 vols (Edinburgh: The Saint Andrew Press, 1981), I, 10–14.

[20] The term 'nu' suggests additional biblical allusions: to Adam and Eve's postlapsarian self-awareness (Genèse 3. 7) and to Christ's reproof to the church of the Laodiceans (Apocalypse 3. 17–18).

[21] See Genèse 4. 25 and Luc 3. 38 respectively.

chapter, he tells them: 'Je vous laisse ma paix'.[22] Lafon's christic
status is further suggested by the capitalization of the words 'Face'
and 'Toi' with respect to him (lines 40 and 48). This should be compared with the way in which Mauriac capitalizes 'Agneau', 'Paix, and
'Fils' at the end of *Le Sang d'Atys* with respect to Christ (*SA* 463).

These kinds of allusions clearly serve to heighten the by now familiar contrast between the poet and Lafon. Whereas the latter enjoys
eternal peace, the former is 'tremblant de vertige et d'effroi' (l. 45).
Lafon's light exposes the poet's filth and nakedness. And Lafon,
though dead (and the word 'mort' is finally applied to Lafon for the
first time in the poem's last line), is still far more alive than the poet is
at present—an affirmation that returns us to where the poem started.
Despite his fear and self-abasement, however, the poet sees his ultimate destiny in terms of being reunited with his friend on an equal
footing: 'aussi vivant que Toi' (l. 48). This recourse to a transcendent
religious perspective by way of a conclusion is a technique that we
find on several occasions in Mauriac's work. It can sometimes appear
rather contrived, but, in this particular poem, where the emphasis
throughout has been on the paradox of Lafon's continuing presence
despite his physical death, the conclusion does not seem out of
place.[23]

'Les Morts du printemps'

This is the general title given to six poems published in *Le Mercure
de France* on 1 November 1915. These are among the least well
known of all Mauriac's poems, never having been republished.[24]
Mauriac himself says virtually nothing about them in his letters or
autobiographical writings, and specialists of his work have remained

---

[22] Jean 14. 17, 27.

[23] It appears to reflect Mauriac's own convictions concerning Lafon: 'Il s'est porté
notre garant auprès du Père' (*OA* 5) and 'Sa présence est en moi, autour de moi. Je ne
me consolerai jamais de l'avoir perdu et sans doute, au moment de mourir, je ne
doute pas que ce soient ses bras tendus vers moi qui aident à me détacher de tout ce
que j'ai aimé ici-bas' (*NLV* 69). However, Mauriac's faith was not always this strong,
as is demonstrated by a quotation from an as yet unpublished *cahier*: 'Où est André?
Qu'est-ce que cette vie mystérieuse en Dieu? Nous voit-il? Sait-il que nous l'aimons
dans la mort mieux que dans la vie?' (quoted by Massenet, *François Mauriac*, p.
126). Cf. the last verse of the first poem in 'Les Morts du printemps'.

[24] They will be included in my forthcoming edition of *Les Mains jointes*.

equally silent.[25] The authorial silence (which helps explain that of the critics) is no doubt due to the fact that Mauriac did not rate these verses very highly. In a letter dated 3 November 1915, he wrote: 'Mon poème a paru au *Mercure* de ce mois. Que je le trouve pauvre!' (*MAM* 58). But the cycle does not strike me as being markedly different in quality from poems such as 'La Veillée avec André Lafon' and 'Le Disparu' that were republished during Mauriac's lifetime. Perhaps, then, there is another reason why Mauriac subsequently decided to ignore these poems. It emerges from the 'frame narrative' that we find in the opening text.[26]

As in 'La Veillée avec André Lafon', the poem opens with an invitation to enter, but the addressee here is a woman. We saw at the end of *L'Adieu à l'adolescence* how a female presence allowed the poet to bid farewell to his childhood, but the situation here is different: the beloved may be invited into the 'domaine' (I, 1; another echo of the earlier collections), but she is to enter 'Sans effacer avec la traîne | Les pas d'enfant que j'ai tracés' (I, 3–4). One is reminded of the Guérinian epigraph to *L'Adieu à l'adolescence*: 'Vous savez, mon ami, le charme des pas qu'on mène sur des traces bien-aimées...' (365). The War has had the effect of turning the clock back for the lyric *je*. He no longer wishes to flee his past, but to cherish memories of times with his male friends: 'les bien-aimés' (I, 6, 10). The fivefold repetition of the /a/ sound in line 9—'Tu n'effaceras pas la trace' (intensified even further as a result of the octosyllabic line)—suggests an almost aggressive insistence on the poet's part that the woman can never cause him to relinquish his past. Critics invariably see the War years as a period during which Mauriac matured as both an artist and a man.[27] While this is certainly true, it is difficult to fit the introductory poem of 'Les Morts du printemps' into such a framework, and this may be one of the reasons why Mauriac later preferred to consign the cycle to oblivion.

---

[25] The exception being Quaghebeur who offers a brief reading of the cycle in 'Mauriac poète: interstices', pp. 186–88.

[26] References will take the form of a Roman numeral indicating the poem number, followed by an Arabic numeral indicating the line number(s).

[27] See Massenet, *François Mauriac*, p. 128, for example.

Although the opening words of the second poem—'Mon Dieu, […]'—also hark back to the style of Mauriac's earlier verse, the focus now shifts to the consequences of the War. Mauriac makes effective use of sound to help capture the bright excitement of the recruits: 'ils riaient lorsque l'aurore a lui' (II, 2). There are a number of connections here with 'La Veillée avec André Lafon'. Firstly, negative constructions are used to emphasize the distance between a radiant past and a dark, bloody present: 'Mais au zénith la voie lactée erre et s'encombre | D'astres que ne voient plus leurs yeux emplis de nuit' and 'Le sang ne souillait pas leurs visages imberbes' (II, 3–4, 8). Secondly, there are allusions to Rimbaud's 'Dormeur du val':

> Aux printemps d'autrefois, dans les épaisses herbes,
> Les premières chaleurs faisaient sombrer leurs corps.
> Ils dormaient face au ciel comme de jeunes morts […]. (II, 5–7)

And, thirdly, the dead soldiers are referred to as 'enfants' (II, 9). There is also a religious dimension throughout that becomes particularly strong at the end. However, the poet's attitude is rather more ambivalent than it was in 'La Veillée avec André Lafon'. When he describes the dead (addressing God) as 'vos morts' (II, 1), it is hard to tell whether the tone is supposed to be indignant (i.e., God is responsible for their deaths) or comforting (i.e., the dead have now been welcomed into the divine presence), though comparison with line 15—'Vous preniez en pitié cette chair et ce sang'—lends weight to the second of these possibilities. A similar uncertainty emerges from the repetition of /je/ in the sixth syllable of each of the four lines preceding the poem's concluding alexandrine:

> O mon Dieu qui saviez ce qu'ils ne savaient pas,
> Et, d'avance, comptiez les gerbes moissonnées,
> Vous preniez en pitié cette chair et ce sang,
> Et déjà vous donniez à ces adolescents
> Cet attrait de la mort qu'a la vingtième année. (II, 13–17)

Depending on the position adopted, the reader could see this repetition of /je/ as suggesting either a reassuring divine order or a desperate attempt to impose some kind of coherence on the chaos of war.[28]

God is not mentioned at all in the third poem, where the poet addresses himself to a *tu* born in a 'port sans navire' (III, 2). This port is almost certainly Bordeaux (cf. *AA* 372–73, 380). If one wished to try and put a name to the anonymous addressee, then perhaps the most likely candidate would be Jean de La Ville de Mirmont, a poet from Bordeaux who died in action on 28 November 1914.[29] Mauriac refers to the poet as a 'voyageur immobile, corsaire condamné à ne pas courir les mers' (*OA* 184), a description that would fit in well with the evocation of the port in this poem. Although the dead soldier is addressed as 'Chevalier', he is also, in line with what we have seen in other poems, described as an 'enfant' (III, 13).[30] In his portrait of La Ville (who died aged twenty-seven), Mauriac stresses his friend's childlike qualities. But, in the same portrait, he also writes: 'il vivait, il aimait, il souffrait' (*OA* 184), which, again, would accord well with the reference to 'sa blessure' in the poem (III, 14).

The first half of the poem contains a number of references to sounds: the hubbub of the city, a port siren, the footsteps of a friend, and alarm bells (III, 4–5, 7–8, 12). The second half focuses rather on sight and the eyes: the sequence is introduced and concluded by the verb *voir* (III, 17, 28–29), there are then single references to eyelids

---

[28] Before leaving this second poem, mention should also be made of a relatively rare example of Mauriac's departure from the conventions of verse: the word 'ténèbres' at the end of line 11 has no rhyme. Perhaps Mauriac felt the /ɛbʀ/ ending was sufficiently close to the /ɛʀb/ rhyme used in lines 5 and 8 ('herbes'/ 'imberbes'), or perhaps he thought the anaphora binding lines 11 and 12 together, coupled with the repetition of 'lilas'—'D'invisibles lilas accablaient les ténèbres, | D'invisibles oiseaux chantaient dans les lilas'—provided a sufficient 'anchor' for line 11. Is it just a coincidence that this is the only line in the poem that appeals to the sense of smell?

[29] The first poem in *L'Horizon chimérique* begins and ends with the words: 'Je suis né dans un port' (La Ville de Mirmont, *Œuvres complètes*, p. 115)—words which seem to find an echo in Mauriac's poem (III, 2). The capitalization of 'Ville' (III, 4) is perhaps intended as an allusion to the poet's name.

[30] To be precise, he is described as a laughing child, a combination of terms that will reappear in the picture of Luc (*ORTC*, II, 457), a character in *Le Nœud de vipères* who dies as a teenage soldier in the Great War.

and the eyes (III, 20, 22) before the insistent anaphora of the penultimate quatrain:

> Ces yeux dont le sommeil ne cause aucun désastre,
> Ces yeux brûlés que j'ai rafraîchis de mes mains,
> Ces yeux où je cherchais d'impossibles chemins,
> Ces yeux qui m'étonnaient comme des ciels sans astres… (III, 24–27)

It is unusual for Mauriac to use anaphora in so concentrated a fashion
in his verse (though a similar intensity can be found in IV, 13–15),
and the device clearly makes his addressee's eyes the main focus of
the poem,[31] especially as the last line of the sequence emphasizes the
poet's astonishment and concludes with a particularly rich rhyme:
/zastʀ/.

This insistence on the ocular is coupled with a number of references to the sun, described in line 18 as 'l'indifférent soleil'. Although, semantically, 'indifférent' suggests neutrality, the fact that the
adjective precedes the noun seems to indicate a more malevolent attitude. This certainly seems to be the case in lines 20–23 where the sun
functions as a kind of antagonist, forcing the addressee to close his
eyes in a manner that pre-empts the eternal darkness of death:

> Autrefois, il pesait si fort sur tes paupières,
> Dans l'éblouissement de ces beaux jours éteints,
> Que tu devais fermer les yeux à sa lumière,
> Tels qu'ils sont à jamais, ô mort d'un clair matin!

The lexis of the stanza preceding the one just quoted (*étendre*, *terrasse*, *soleil*, *ruisseler*) recalls what we have already seen at the end of
'Nocturne' and 'La Tempête apaisée':

> Tu ne l'étendras plus sur la chaude terrasse,
> D'où ta jeunesse vit s'obscurcir de beaux jours.
> L'indifférent soleil ruisselle sur ma face,
> Comme si tu vivais encor, cœur plein d'amour! (III, 16–19)

In 'La Tempête apaisée', I suggested that the sun could be seen as a
symbol of the divine. Perhaps the same is true of this poem from 'Les

---

[31] Elsewhere, Mauriac mentions La Ville's 'yeux brûlants et doux' (*DAM* 53).

Morts du printemps'. As already mentioned, there is no overtly religious element in this poem at all. The final quatrain, in particular, is
strikingly different from what we found at the end of the second poem
in this cycle and at the end of 'La Veillée avec André Lafon'. Rather
than references to God or eschatological transformation, we find the
poet imitating the death of his friend by closing his own eyes (III, 29)
so that he will not have to see the latter's shade (in the ghostly sense
of the term). The /ɔ̃/ sound of the word *ombre* is found five times in
lines 29–30 ('Je fermerai les miens pour ne pas voir t*on* *om*bre, | A
l'heure où frémir*ont* au f*ond* des lilas s*om*bres') and is echoed to some
extent by the threefold use of /ɔ/ in line 31 ('Les r*o*ssign*o*ls qui nous
délivraient du s*o*mmeil'). These back vowels provide a powerful contrast with the six-fold repetition of front /y/ in the final stanza of 'La
Veillée avec André Lafon'. If the addressee of this third poem is indeed Jean de La Ville, this non-Christian conclusion would be perfectly appropriate since, unlike Lafon, he remained an agnostic.[32]

Having commented in some detail on the first three poems in the
cycle, I shall now pass rather more rapidly over the final three, mentioning only those aspects that add something new to the points already made.

The fourth poem differs from the others in that it is addressed to
a 'mort d'avant la guerre' (IV, 1). The allusion is clearly to Raymond
Laurens, the cousin whose death influenced a number of the poems in
Mauriac's first two collections. Indeed, the use of terms such as 'vacances', 'chapeau de paille', and 'salon' (IV, 6, 7, 10) plunges us back
into the atmosphere of these early poems. One feature of this poem
rarely found elsewhere in Mauriac's writing is an apparent celebration
of what he refers to as the 'pure gloire' of dying in battle (IV, 4). As
we have seen, Mauriac was generally only too aware of the horror of
war. Despite initial appearances, perhaps a similar dimension can be
sensed in this poem too, since the /gl/ sound at the start of 'gloire' in
line 4 is mirrored by the /gl/ in the middle of 'sanglots' in line 5 (and,
in both cases, this sound provides the start of the sixth syllable). Ab-

---

[32] In his idealized portrait of La Ville, Mauriac claims: 'Jean croyait en Dieu parce
que sa mère priait Dieu' (*OA* 185). But Massenet's description of the poet as 'ce
rêveur agnostique' (*François Mauriac*, p. 123) seems more objective. His family was
Protestant (*BN*, IV, 546).

stract glory is inseparable from human pain. Perhaps then, rather than an uncharacteristically jingoistic reference to the glory of war, Mauriac is writing in a semi-ironic tone. On the other hand, it could be that we see here a re-emergence of that sense of guilt discussed earlier: Laurens's peacetime death from tuberculosis lacks the sacrificial dimension (and hence the 'glory') that Mauriac associates with death in combat. Like his dead cousin, Mauriac is excluded from that 'peuple adolescent' that answers 'l'appel lointain aux armes' (IV, 26, 22).

The theme of guilt is certainly present in the next poem's reference to 'l'humilité d'être des survivants' (V, 3). The emphasis in this fifth poem is on the mother–son bond, another theme that was frequently evoked in *Les Mains jointes* and *L'Adieu à l'adolescence*.[33] Again, it is noticeable how Mauriac makes use of sound-patterning to underline this relationship: the tenfold repetition of /m/ (V, 25–28), echoing the initial sound of 'mères', being balanced by the eleven occurrences of /v/ (V, 29–32), emphasizing the first sound of 'vous' (that is, the dead sons to whom the poem is addressed):

> Vos *m*ères avaient revêtu leurs sombres robes
> Pour entendre la *m*ê*m*e *m*esse, la pre*m*ière,
> Redit les *m*ots connus de la *m*ê*m*e prière,
> Et, co*mm*e hier, leurs *m*ains se joignaient sur leurs yeux.
> *V*ous, ren*v*ersés, face aux étoiles pâlissantes,
> *V*ous appeliez encor de *v*otre *v*oix mourante,
> De la terre et du sang souillaient *v*os doux che*v*eux.
> *V*os lèvres se tendaient *v*ers des lèvres absentes [...]. (V, 25–32)

These two key sounds and concepts are brought together in the noun phrase 'vos mères' which occurs three times in this poem (V, 8, 12, 25). There is perhaps a further allusion to 'Le Dormeur du val' in this poem, since reference is made to the dead soldiers' 'poitrines traversées' (V, 24). Also, the line 'Et l'aube n'était qu'un baiser à votre chair' (V, 21) recalls the opening words of Rimbaud's 'Aube': 'J'ai embrassé l'aube d'été.'[34]

---

[33] It is also stressed in Mauriac's presentation of La Ville (*OA* 185).
[34] Rimbaud, *Œuvres*, p. 284. Cf. a line from 'Fils du Ciel', Mauriac's homage to Rimbaud: 'Et l'aube t'imposait la glace de ses bras' (*Or* 446).

The final poem is similar in form to the first: the latter being composed of four octosyllabic quatrains and the former of five hepta-syllabic quintains (the intervening poems are all written in alexandrines arranged in stanzas of various length). This sixth poem continues the trend begun in the first poem of evoking images from Mauriac's earlier collections of verse. The opening line—'Le vent pleure sous la porte' (VI, 1)—is reminiscent of a line from *Les Mains jointes*: 'C'est un peu de vent sous la porte...' (348). And when the poet pictures himself crying, 'mains jointes sous la pluie' (VI, 21), there is an obvious allusion to the title and general tearfulness of Mauriac's first book.[35] In the first poem, the poet had concluded by asking the night stars: 'Que ne rallumez-vous les yeux | Dans les visages éphémères?' (I, 15–16). This question now receives an answer of sorts in the third stanza of the final poem where the night lights up for the young victims of the War: 'Et pose sur vos poitrines | Les yeux fixes des planètes' (VI, 14–15).

Not surprisingly, perhaps, the female addressee of the first poem, absent from poems 2–5 where the emphasis is on male friendship and mother–son love, remains out of sight in this final text (though the rhymes are exclusively feminine). The poet's attention is entirely focused on his vigil for the dead.[36] Indeed, they quite literally have the last word in this cycle: 'Je veille aussi, je vous veille | Au fond de mon cœur, hosties!' (VI, 24–25). This concluding image suggests that the poet feeds on his dead friends as he does on the eucharistic wafer, that token of another young male body that met a premature and violent end. This bold metaphor, whose directness exceeds the christic allusions found in 'La Veillée avec André Lafon', fully deserves the exclamation mark that follows it.

'Le Disparu'

I shall conclude this chapter by examining 'Le Disparu', published in *Le Mercure de France* on 16 May 1918. Touzot regards the poem as

---

[35] The reference to rain in this quotation provides a further link with the first poem— 'L'immense patience des pluies' (I, 7). The only other occurrence of the term 'pluie' in this cycle also occurs in the final poem (VI, 3).

[36] The verb *veiller*, used on three occasions in this poem (VI, 16 and 24 (twice)), obviously brings to mind 'La Veillée avec André Lafon'.

belonging to the 'cycle André Lafon',[37] which presumably means he would identify the *disparu* in question as Lafon himself. This identification is supported by the fact that, elsewhere, Mauriac explicitly refers to Lafon as 'le disparu' (*OA* 6).[38] The identity only really becomes important if pursuing a psychobiographical approach. Although 'Le Disparu' was never incorporated in any of Mauriac's verse collections, it is reprinted in his *Œuvres complètes*, located between *L'Adieu à l'adolescence* and *Orages*. Nevertheless, as Durand points out, it remains a 'poème peu connu'.[39] Lacouture, who dismisses 'Le Disparu' as another example of 'cette littérature inchoative et maniérée' begun with *Les Mains jointes*,[40] is untroubled by the poem's relative obscurity, but Durand clearly sees it as regrettable, stating that the poem is not only 'peu connu', but '*trop peu* connu'.[41] I share Durand's perspective, not because 'Le Disparu' is an artistic triumph (it is not), but because it functions as a genuinely transitional text in Mauriac's verse corpus.

Formally, the poem is unique in Mauriac's *œuvre* since he chooses to cast his alexandrines entirely in dialogue form. The association of this style with French Classical drama possibly indicates a desire on Mauriac's part to start distancing himself from the more sentimentalized, introspective style of his earlier verse. The essence of drama is conflict, and conflict lies at the very heart of 'Le Disparu' with its juxtaposition of two opposing voices. In this connection, it is worth remembering that, at more or less the same time that he was writing this poem,[42] Mauriac was also working on two plays with his

---

[37] Touzot, 'Analogie et poème', p. 31.

[38] The same term is used with some insistence in *Le Nœud de vipères* to describe Luc, another 'pure' victim of the War: 'déjà disparu [...]. Il a disparu; c'est un disparu' (*ORTC*, II, 458). Luc is trained at Souges, the camp where Lafon contracted the illness from which he died (*ORTC*, II, 456, 1210).

[39] François Durand, 'Les Jeunes Héros de Mauriac devant l'amitié', *CFM*, 11 (1984), 147–56 (p. 153).

[40] Lacouture, *François Mauriac*, I, 203.

[41] Durand, 'Les Jeunes Héros', p. 153; my italics.

[42] Although it is difficult to know exactly when the poem was composed, a fragment of it is reproduced in Mauriac's diary as part of the entry dated 7 August 1917 (*OA* 241). The final text differs slightly from this fragment.

friend, Jacques-Emile Blanche.[43] Although the tone and style of these (unpublished and unperformed) comedies is far removed from those of 'Le Disparu', it could be argued that both creative avenues imply a new interest on Mauriac's part in heightening the degree of drama and conflict in his imaginative world (an interest that is also discernible in his novelistic production during this period). The nature of this conflict is also significant. The exchanges between *l'Ami* and *l'Amie* foreground in exemplary fashion that tension between *amitié* and *amour* that we have seen running through all of Mauriac's previous verse. In the verse published after 'Le Disparu', this tension no longer receives any overt attention: the term *amitié* does not figure at all in either of the last two collections of verse. It is as if the very explicitness of the debate here exhausts the desire to continue pursuing this theme from within this genre. Of course, this does not mean that the tension simply disappears. It could be argued that it continues to haunt the verse at the level of a latent content. More straightforwardly, we could look to novels such as *Les Chemins de la mer*, *La Pharisienne*, *Galigaï*, and *L'Agneau* where we find the typically Mauriacian triangle in which a man and a woman struggle to possess a young man.

In 'Le Disparu', this young man is physically absent, a victim of the War. The latter is only significant as the cause of death of the 'enfant mort' (Dis 422). Apart from some incidental references to the victim's helmet, knapsacks, boots, and gas mask (417, 422), a fleeting allusion to 'cette boue et ce sang' (418), and the use of the term 'survivant' to describe *l'Ami* (421), the War itself is not mentioned at all. Interest resides rather in the ways in which the dead soldier is remembered by his male friend and female lover. Authorial sympathy would appear to lie with the friend, who not only opens and concludes the poem, but also speaks the majority of the lines (98 out of 182).[44]

The poem begins with the friend bringing the lover an old school photograph showing the *disparu* at the age of thirteen. The main

---

[43] Mauriac and Blanche collaborated on these plays during the autumn of 1917. See *François Mauriac–Jacques-Emile Blanche: correspondance (1916–1942)*, ed. by Georges-Paul Collet (Grasset, 1976), pp. 49–60.

[44] I have arrived at this total by counting separately alexandrines that are divided between the two voices. Although contrary to standard practice, this method of counting allows the total number of lines allotted to each voice to be calculated more easily.

function of this ostensibly friendly gesture is to reveal the woman's ignorance of her lover, emphasized by her opening word—'Lui?' (415)—as she fails to recognize him. To be more precise, it is the schoolboy's gaze that she fails to recognize and this allows the friend's negative attitude towards women to emerge for the first time:

> Ce regard
> De treize ans, ce regard effrayant d'innocence,
> Quelle femme aurait su le voir? (416)

The woman's ignorance, standing in stark contrast to the detailed memories of the male friend (416), is further underlined in her three interventions that follow the question just quoted:

> Enfance, enfance
> Du bien-aimé, pourquoi ne t'ai-je pas connue? (416)

> Je ne l'ai pas connu lorsqu'il était enfant. (416)

> Ah! que je t'eusse aimé dans ta seizième année!
> Si je t'avais connu, tu me l'aurais donnée
> Comme un bouquet de roses pourpres son arôme... (417)

This thought of the dead friend giving his adolescence to the lover[45] is the trigger for another misogynous comment on the part of the *Ami*, and, as in the first of these comments, we find emphasis being laid upon the gaze: 'Dès qu'il vous regarda, ce ne fut plus qu'un homme' (417).[46] The *Ami* then extrapolates from this experience to formulate a general maxim regarding the relationship between men and women:

> Ainsi que dans les nuits trop chaudes, les lilas,
> Notre enfance toujours vient mourir dans vos bras
> Et vous nous exilez du candide Royaume. (417)

---

[45] Cf. 'Je vous donne l'humble trésor de mon passé' (*AA* 370).

[46] It is worth remembering at this point the significance placed on the young victim's eyes in the third poem of 'Les Morts du printemps'. Cf. further references to eyes or the gaze in MP, I, 10, 15; II, 4; IV, 8, 21; V, 28, 35, 36; and in VAL, ll. 3, 10, 44. Risse draws attention to the homoerotic connotations of the male gaze in Mauriac's novels (*Homoerotik*, pp. 69–70).

The allusion to the story of the expulsion from Eden is plain; the *Ami* even echoes Adam by blaming the woman for this fall from grace.[47] And, when the woman responds by remembering her last meeting with her lover, her words are clearly intended to make the reader question her worthiness:

> Comme si pour l'entendre, il eût toute la vie,
> Mon cœur demeurait calme au chant de cette voix.
> Ignorant que sa main me dût être ravie
> Et ne me ferait plus de signes, ici-bas,
> — Sa main que je touchais, je ne la serrai pas. (417)

Such confessions of ignorance and lukewarm love are no doubt delib- erately intended to make the exile from Eden appear all the more tragic.

The *Ami*, by contrast, appears as a model of attentiveness in his account of how he bade farewell to *le disparu*: 'J'écoutais un à un, comme des oiseaux ivres, | Jaillir vers moi ses vers pleins de douces ténèbres' (418). Whereas the woman has confessed to a less than adequate final touch between herself and her lover, the *Ami* speaks of a much deeper communion:

> Mais l'orage enchaîné des musiques futures,
> En nos cœurs séparés et déjà confondus,
> Grondait... (418)[48]

It seems to me that there is an undeniably homoerotic dimension to this, although, of course, the poem itself never overtly encourages such an interpretation.[49] *L'Ami* contrasts the woman's sexual desire with his own ostensibly platonic feelings for the young soldier: 'Je n'aimais que son âme et je n'ai cherché qu'elle' (419). He later rein- forces this point via two contrasting water-related images:

---

[47] Cf. Genèse 3. 12.

[48] We see a further example here of how Mauriac will often emphasize certain sounds when using words associated with the semantic field of sound (or its absence): the vowels /e/ (six occurrences), /y/ (four occurrences), and /ɔ̃/ (three occurrences) are particularly noticeable in these lines.

[49] Quaghebeur refers to the purity of *l'Ami*'s affection as being 'fort équivoque' ('Mauriac poète: interstices', p. 190).

> Et vous êtes pareille à ces plages de sable
> Que ronge l'océan d'un amour inlassable.[50]
> L'amitié, ce pur fleuve, a de plus doux méandres. (419)

He then adds: 'Amitié, qu'au premier amour j'ai méconnue' (420).
Although this is the only line in the poem to suggest a heterosexual
dimension to the male friend's experiences, it is foregrounded by the
fact that no rhyme is provided for *méconnue*.[51]

However, other imagery tends to blur the distinction between
l'Ami's 'platonic' feelings and *l'Amie*'s overtly sexual desire. There
is, for example, the rather more ambivalent use of water imagery in
the following passage that *l'Ami* addresses to his dead friend:

> Car mon cœur te jetait ses premières marées,
> Ces vagues d'amitié de si loin déferlées
> Que le cœur bien-aimé comme un phare est battu. (420)

In *Orages*, the image of the tide (437), of the wave (440), and of the
lighthouse (430) will all be used in poems focusing on sexual desire.
Moving away from the maritime semantic field, one thinks also of
l'Ami's apostrophe to friendship: 'Feu chaste qui brûlais mon cœur
adolescent' (420). The adjective 'chaste' is intended to emphasize the
purity of this passion, but the reader has just encountered the terms
'feu' and *brûler* in the mouth of the female lover: 'Présence dans ma
chair de l'absent, tu me brûles. | Je suis marquée au feu de nos baisers
passés' (419), and it is difficult not to feel a trace of these sexual connotations when the terms are reused by the male friend. There is also
an unusual prosodic feature that should be noted in connection with
this subject. Although the male friend is sure that the young victims of
the War are now in the presence of God, he adds: 'Mais leur corps
sans sépulcre est parmi nous, il erre | Obsédé de nos accablants retours
des jeudis soirs' (421). The first of these lines is an alexandrine, but
the second contains fourteen syllables. While it is not unusual for
Mauriac to intersperse his alexandrines with shorter lines (there are

---

[50] This image will recur twice in *Le Sang d'Atys* (447, 449).
[51] The title term *disparu* occupies the rhyme position five lines further on, but, tech-
nically, this forms a masculine rhyme with *plus* (tradition would require *méconnue* to
be part of a feminine rhyme pair).

occasional six- and eight-syllable lines in 'Le Disparu', for example), this is the only occasion in his verse corpus in which he employs a line longer than the alexandrine. The concept of obsession, already foregrounded by the term 'Obsédé' at the start of the line, is given still greater prominence as a result of the length of the line.

It is a (curiously collective) male *body* that is said to experience this obsession. This underlines the fact that there is a physicality about 'Le Disparu' that was lacking from the first two collections, but that will become standard in the two later ones. Table 13, giving the frequency of key terms related to the physical, illustrates this trend very clearly:

Table 13:

	corps	*chair*	*sang*
MJ	2	2	0
AA	1	0	0
CAF	0	2	0
Early War poetry	4	2	5
Dis	7	10	3
Or	25	15	10
SA	27	10	15

Notes
• 'Early War poetry' refers to 'La Veillée avec André Lafon' and 'Les Morts du printemps'.

This increased emphasis on the corporeal from the time of the War poetry is no doubt partly due to Mauriac's exposure to bodies as part of his medical duties.[52] But it also coincides with an increased fascination with all that was bound up with the terms he foregrounded in the title of the novel begun during the War years, *La Chair et le sang*.[53] As he confesses on 15 January 1915: 'je suis soumis à la chair et au sang' (*LV* 76).[54]

---

[52] See 'Lettres de François Mauriac à Robert Vallery-Radot', p. 78.

[53] In an article demonstrating the general significance of the body in Mauriac's novels published during the 1920s and early 1930s, Edward Welch provides statistics based on the (admittedly incomplete) 'Frantext' database showing that the terms *corps* and *chair* are far more common in Mauriac's novels than in the work of his

In 'Le Disparu', it is the woman who expresses this sexual obsession. She is therefore represented as occupying the moral low ground:
'Comme je perdais cœur sur de neigeuses cimes, | Vallée, Ombre,
Péché, vers vous je descendis' (419). As a non-Christian, she can
present 'un corps délivré du remords' (419) to the capitalized trio of
terms just mentioned. Yet the fact that the poet makes 'remords'
rhyme with 'mort' and that the same /mɔʀ/ sound is also present at the
beginning of the line ('Morne assouvissement, parfait comme la
mort...') indicates his own fear of sexuality, underlined by *l'Ami*'s
moralizing response: 'Vous n'aimiez que sa chair et la chair n'est que
cendre' (419).

As the poem approaches its conclusion, the religious dimension
becomes increasingly apparent. In response to the woman's aggres-
sive, agnostic question: 'Qu'est-ce que *votre* Dieu a fait des dis-
parus?' (420; my italics), the male friend sketches an astonishingly
naïve vision of the after-life: 'Devant Lui, comme au clair collège de
naguère, | Ils balancent, fronts hauts, le lys et l'encensoir' (421). The
woman, by contrast, is presented as a thorough-going materialist.[55]
The repetition of the /ʀ/ sound in the two quatrains beginning 'Rien ne
reste des morts, pauvre cœur,—rien ne reste | Des rires ni des voix'
(422) emphasizes her refusal to countenance the possibility of anything beyond the tangible. For a moment, the male friend seems to
share her perspective, echoing the earlier anaphora of 'Rien ne [...]'
as he remembers a dawn scene in Paris in the company of his dead
friend: 'Rien n'est que sur ce banc, devant la Madeleine, | Ton corps
qui reposait' (422).[56] Once again, we notice how attention is focused

---

near contemporaries, Gide and Colette—see 'Le Carnaval perverti de François Mauriac', in *Masque et carnaval dans la littérature européenne*, ed. by Edward Welch
(L'Harmattan, 2002), pp. 39–53 (pp. 52–53). Mauriac's predilection for these terms is
no doubt partly due to their general nature (which would have appealed to his Classicism) and partly to their strong religious connotations.

[54] The two terms are found together on a number of occasions in Mauriac's verse
(MP, II, 15; Dis 420, 422; *Or* 433; *SA* 462).

[55] Apart from her question quoted above, the only time that the woman uses the term
dieu is in a metaphorical context designed to emphasize (via an octosyllabic line) the
intensity of her love (*eros* as opposed to *agape*): 'Je suis en proie au dieu que tu fus'
(418). Cf. the male friend's reference to 'ta face divine' (420).

[56] A very similar scene will be used by Mauriac nearly forty years later in *Galigaï*
(*ORTC*, IV, 408).

on the male body. Durand quotes this passage to show that, for Mauriac, 'l'amitié peut contenir en elle-même cette contemplation, sans
possession ni désir, de la beauté humaine.'[57] This strikes me as an
overly hasty denial of the presence of homoerotic desire in the poem.
Indeed, when the following quatrain begins 'Non, non, [...]', even
though the denials are grammatically associated with what follows
('tu n'étais pas un héros, cœur frivole'), it is almost as if *l'Ami* is
seeking to distance himself from the unacknowledged desire that
briefly surfaced a few lines earlier. Almost immediately, therefore,
l'Ami sublimates his emotions by returning to the reassuring image of
heaven as 'un collège immense, une chapelle' (422), which serves as
a prelude to the final quatrain:

> O mon ami qui disparus d'entre les hommes,
> Plus qu'aucun autre mort, tu survis—pur Esprit!
> C'est une Ascension qui t'ouvre le royaume.
> Ton sépulcre est vacant comme celui du Christ. (423)

This conclusion is reminiscent of what we found at the end of 'La
Veillée avec André Lafon', though the christic allusions are made
even clearer in 'Le Disparu' as a result of the final comparison. After
the verbal jousting of the male and female characters, it is Christ who
has the last word by *being* the last word.

Conclusion
The poems considered in this chapter are among the least well-known
in Mauriac's verse corpus, mainly because they were never made into
a distinct collection. Nevertheless, they are important transitional
poems that help bridge the gap, as it were, between *L'Adieu à
l'adolescence* and *Orages*. There are certainly a number of areas of
continuity with Mauriac's early verse: the continuing nostalgia for
childhood and adolescence, for example, and a degree of sentimentalized religiosity. But, as we move through the War years, we can
also see new elements beginning to emerge: in particular, a sense of
loss and suffering that goes beyond the rather narcissistic melancholy
of the early verse, and, in 'Le Disparu', the emergence of the authen-
tic voice of sexual desire. The final reference to Christ in this poem is

---

[57] Durand, 'Les Jeunes Héros', p. 153.

clearly intended to have a definitive ring to it, silencing *l'Amie*'s passionate memories. But, as is so often the case in Mauriac's work, an overtly religious conclusion seems to function as a trigger to further debate.[58] This debate will be taken up in the next collection, *Orages*.

---

[58] I have argued this in detail with respect to the most famous of Mauriac's 'pious endings', that of *Le Mystère Frontenac*. See my *Mauriac et le mythe du poète*, pp. 100–07.

6. Storms of Passion: *Orages*

Introduction

Although *Orages* was published in 1925,[1] a bibliographical note explains that the volume's poems were written between 1912 and 1923 (*Or* 426). These years were extremely significant in terms of Mauriac's evolution as a writer. In 1912 he was just a minor Catholic poet, seen as part of the marginal 'école spiritualiste' that was dedicated to serving the cause of Catholic literature via *Les Cahiers de l'Amitié de France*. By 1923, *Le Baiser au lépreux* had been published to widespread critical acclaim and Mauriac had had the pleasure of seeing his next novel, *Le Fleuve de feu*, serialized in the *Nouvelle Revue française*—the very journal the *Cahiers* had aimed to rival.[2] When reading *Orages* it should come as no surprise, therefore, to discover that the volume embraces a number of different perspectives.

This is not to say that the collection lacks cohesion. Although there are no 'narrative' divisions such as those found in the first two volumes of verse, Mauriac has not simply reproduced the poems in chronological order of composition. Rather, he has arranged them in such a way as to suggest a broad sense of narrative progression. Although I would not want to place too much significance on questions of ordering, it seems to me that the poems are grouped along the following lines. The first four poems (from 'Sédentaire' to 'Autre péché') provide a kind of overture, introducing the main themes that will be explored in the rest of the volume. The next seven (from 'Faune' to 'Petit chien sombre') centre on the most obsessive of these themes: sexual desire. After four poems (from 'Renoncement' to 'Le Regret du péché') focusing on the poet's unsuccessful attempt to renounce 'sin', the next four (from 'La Marée infidèle' to 'Le Désir') show how desire returns, though in a way that leaves the poet unsatisfied since he cannot abandon his faith. 'Sacré-cœur' and 'Le Corps

---

[1] Mauriac had initially hoped that Gallimard would take the collection (*LV* 125), a view shared by Jacques Rivière—see *François Mauriac et Jacques Rivière*, p. 33. In fact, they were finally published by Champion.

[2] Mauriac notes concerning the *NRF*: 'Il me fallut donc douze ans […] pour rejoindre enfin le groupe littéraire avec lequel je me sentais le mieux accordé' (*OA* 192).

fait arbre' then evoke the possibility of the sublimation of desire. The next three poems (from 'L'Ombre' to 'La Tempête apaisée'), deriving from material published in 1913–14, suggest the possibility of finding peace in a woman's love. The final four poems (from 'Marsyas ou la Grâce' to 'Fils du ciel') focus on characters that could be described as mythic in some sense,[3] and all relate to the question of religious conversion, though certainly not in unproblematic fashion.

The poems of *Orages* were the first with which Mauriac would later declare himself satisfied:

> *Orages, Le Sang d'Atys, Endymion*, ne me déçoivent pas. Que mes lecteurs les récusent ou non, ce sont mes modestes titres de poète; je les revendique devant ceux qui s'intéresseront encore à moi lorsque j'aurai quitté ce monde. C'est ce chant qu'il faut bien entendre pour me connaître. C'est au fond de cette eau endormie que repose l'anneau de Mélisande et bien d'autres bagues perdues et tous les secrets, et tous les remords et toutes les douleurs et tous les songes dont nous nous berçons jusqu'à notre dernier jour. (*OC*, VI, iii–iv)[4]

The question of the collection's autobiographical significance is a difficult one. In an unpublished letter (11 September 1925), Mauriac tells the Catholic critic Henri Guillemin that in *Orages* he will discover the poet's '*cœur mis à nu*'.[5] One can understand, therefore, why Monférier claims that the poems 'contiennent en germe les éléments

---

[3] Marsyas and Ganymède are properly mythological. David the shepherd-king of Israel became the model of an ideal Messianic ruler in the Judaeo-Christian tradition (see Luc 1. 32–33 and II Samuel 7. 12–16) and could therefore be regarded as a mythic figure in much the same way as Alexander the Great or Napoleon, for example. Rimbaud's status as a modern myth has been examined by Etiemble, *Le Mythe de Rimbaud*, 5 vols (Gallimard, 1952–67).

[4] The reference to 'l'anneau de Mélisande' is an allusion to the scene in Maurice Maeterlinck's Symbolist drama *Pelléas et Mélisande* (1892), turned into a famous opera by Debussy in 1902, in which the heroine drops her wedding ring into a fountain as she talks with her lover, Pelléas. The lost wedding ring symbolizes the loss of fidelity (an important theme in Mauriac's later verse). Mauriac adored Debussy's opera, referring to it as 'notre histoire à tous' (*PR* 224).

[5] 'Lettre à Henri Guillemin [extrait]', in Maison Charavay, *Bulletin d'autographes à prix marqués*, no. 828 (2000), p. 41; Mauriac's italics. The phrase is obviously an allusion to Baudelaire's text, 'Mon Cœur mis à nu' (published posthumously in 1917).

de la crise de 1928'.[6] However, when Mauriac read the proofs of an article published in March 1930,[7] he took exception to the ease with which the critic moved from *l'œuvre* to *l'homme*, objecting that: '*Orages* n'exprime que des états de sensibilité—des temps de repos— à aucun degré mon attitude devant la vie' (*NLV* 127). Given that the main cause of Mauriac's *crise* was almost certainly his struggle with latent homosexual desires, Risse has recently argued that the poems in *Orages* should be read in the light of this struggle. She points out that, in many poems, the addressee is described in terms that are non gender-specific. This is true, though her statement that the addressee is identified as female in only three of the poems in *Orages* is less accurate: the correct figure is seven.[8] Nevertheless, Risse's general thesis is convincing. Her observation that the last four poems in *Orages* all deal with figures who have been associated with homosexuality is particularly significant. Marsyas ('Marsyas ou la grâce') is a Phrygian satyr with whom Socrates is compared in Plato's *Symposium* and Risse therefore suggests that the figure should be seen as referring to an older man who, with God's help, manages to master his homo-erotic inclinations.[9] Mauriac's presentation of a 'Ganymède chrétien' is seen by Risse in terms of a 'deliverance' from homosexual love that serves as a model for the lyric *je*.[10] Although King David ('David vaincu') is never presented as homosexual in the Bible, later writers would choose to interpret his relationships with Saul and Jonathan in

---

[6] Jacques Monférier, *François Mauriac du 'Nœud de vipères' à 'La Pharisienne'* (Geneva: Editions Slatkine, 1985), p. 11.

[7] Jean Prévost, 'De Mauriac à son œuvre', *La Nouvelle Revue française*, 34 (January–June 1930), 349–67.

[8] Risse, *Homoerotik*, p. 197. The relevant quotations are as follows: 'Si je te couchais, morte' (*Or* 430); 'mon endormie' (431); 'O mon enfant, morte inconnue' (431); 'Je t'ai dit non, à toi, plaintive' (434); 'quand vous m'étiez sujette' (437); 'toi, ma triste amour' (440); and 'Le parfum de ta robe' (441). One could add 'La Tempête apaisée', derived, as we have seen, from the earlier 'Nocturne' where the addressee is Jeanne Lafon, and 'L'Emeraude' where reference is made to 'mon amour dernière' (442).

[9] Risse, *Homoerotik*, pp. 200–01.

[10] *Ibid.*, p. 201. She uses the term 'Erlösung' (deliverance) merely to present the issue from Mauriac's own moral perspective.

homoerotic terms.[11] The homosexuality of Rimbaud ('Fils du ciel'), on the other hand, is well documented. Risse is surely right that Mauriac's choice of these particular mythic characters is significant in terms of his own sexuality. Nevertheless, in my reading of the poems, the emphasis will be on sexual desire in general, rather than on homo- or heterosexual desire in particular. This is because the most significant tension for Mauriac is between sexual desire (of whatever kind) and the Christian ideal of purity.[12]

Having offered some introductory comments, I shall now turn to my analysis of the collection. This will be divided into three sections dealing respectively with water imagery, the struggle between sexual and religious desire, and myth. I shall begin each section by looking in some detail at one of the poems from the 'overture' identified above. This will serve as a starting point for a more general discussion of the issues raised.

Water imagery
The significance of imagery for *Orages* is already signalled by the metaphorical nature of the collection's title: the poet is interested, not in meteorological phenomena, but in the storms of passion. The term *orage* or its derivatives is used four times in the collection (432, 435, 439, 441), but, in addition, 'Le poète mobilise tout le champ lexical de la perturbation atmosphérique: passages nuageux, tonnerre, fulgurations'.[13] Touzot's article picks up on the wish formulated by Barrès that the author of *Les Mains jointes* would in time yield 'ses quatre saisons de fleurs et de fruits' (*OA* 197). For Touzot, however, the imagery employed by Mauriac in his verse corresponds to only two seasons: autumn and summer, the former reflected in the early verse (including the War poetry), the latter in *Orages* and *Le Sang d'Atys*.[14]

---

[11] *Ibid.*, pp. 170–71. From an Old Testament perspective, David's famed love for Jonathan (see, for example, I Samuel 18. 1 and II Samuel 1. 26) is viewed purely as an ideal of male friendship.

[12] Cf. his letter to Gide of 28 June 1924: 'Ce qui importe ce n'est pas ce que nous désirons—mais le renoncement à ce que nous désirons. L'objet de notre tentation, il ne dépend pas de nous que ce soit celui-ci ou celle-là—mais ce qui dépend de nous, c'est le refus…' (*LV* 132).

[13] Touzot, 'Analogie et poème', p. 38.

[14] *Ibid.*, p. 26.

Touzot ably demonstrates how Mauriac's handling of imagery develops through the various collections, and there is no doubt that imagery associated with fire, heat, and light is particularly prevalent in Mauriac's later verse. However, in this section I want to focus rather on the semantic field of water (antithetically related on occasions to the field of heat), since this is the element that strikes me as being most significant in *Orages*.

It emerges immediately in the collection's opening poem, 'Sédentaire', which is short enough to be quoted in full:

1   Si jamais je ne fus sur l'Océan amer,
          C'est que mon univers a tenu dans les êtres.
          Un corps était un monde où je régnais en maître,
          Des yeux avaient les bords ravagés d'une mer.

5   Haleines, tièdes vents sur ma poitrine heureuse!
          J'ai vu des lacs dormir aux lisières des cils
          Et, plus qu'aucun marin, j'ai connu les périls
          D'un corps que le sommeil soulève, abaisse et creuse. (427)

The natural world here (Ocean, sea, shores, lakes) provides a metaphorical mirror for the human body. Mauriac was never a great traveller and the title 'Sédentaire' accurately reflects this.[15] But, the poem suggests, it would be a mistake to confuse physical immobility with spiritual tranquillity. Just as the poem begins by drawing a contrast between the vast oceans and the even vaster space of human relationships, so it ends by suggesting that one does not have to be at sea to be imperilled (ll. 7–8).

In its brief compass, 'Sédentaire' repeatedly exploits the possibilities of viewing the human body as a microcosmic version of planet Earth (land and sea). These parallels are presented in terms of metaphor (as opposed to simile).[16] And, as the poem progresses, the type

---

[15] Mauriac describes himself as a 'sédentaire' on several occasions (*OC*, XI, 24; *OA* 772; *BN*, IV, 143).

[16] As Touzot points out ('Analogie et poème', p. 31), whereas simile is the dominant figure in the early verse, identification and metaphor become far more important in *Orages*: statistically, similes account for only one in eight of the images (p. 40). Line 7 of 'Sédentaire' does, however, contain an example of a quantitative comparison, a figure which, according to Touzot, is statistically almost as important in the collection

of metaphor changes. In line 2, the concepts 'mon univers' and 'les êtres' are simply laid side by side; there is no metaphorical relationship between them as such. Metaphor is used for the first time in line 3, and it is metaphor of the most direct type: a body *is* a world. The metaphor in line 4 is slightly more complex: eyes are not simply said to be seas, rather they display one aspect ('les bords ravagés') of a sea. Line 5 is different in that it dispenses with the verbs (*être* and *avoir*) that have so far been used to establish a relationship between the *comparé* and the *comparant*. Here the noun phrase 'tièdes vents' is simply in apposition to 'Haleines',[17] thus increasing the directness of the relationship between the two terms. The metaphors encountered so far have all been *in praesentia* (that is, both the *comparant* and the *comparé* have been present). The remaining metaphors are, by contrast, *in absentia*. Thus, in line 6, 'lacs' (the *comparant*) clearly functions as a metaphor for eyes, but the *comparé* is not mentioned. There is, however, a reference to eyelashes that, metonymically, leads us to eyes. Perhaps it would therefore be more accurate to say that this particular metaphor is only half *in absentia*. A similar phenomenon can be observed with respect to the trio of verbs ('soulève, abaisse et creuse') that makes up the second hemistich of line 8.[18] These verbs all describe the motion of the sea, but here they are used metaphorically of a sleeping body. The sea as such (the *comparant*) is not mentioned, but the reference to 'marin' in line 7 again leads us to it metonymically. Here too, then, we have a metaphor half *in absentia*. The main difference on this occasion is that the poet has chosen verbs, rather than nouns, as the vehicle for his metaphor.

---

as 'le *comme* sacro-saint' and which 'convient parfaitement au climat de tension orageuse, de passion qui s'exacerbe' (p. 40).

[17] Mauriac employs the same technique on a number of occasions in *Orages*. Indeed, the very next poem begins: 'Couleuvres, les chemins dormaient dans la lumière' (427). Formally, this example differs from the one in 'Sédentaire' in that the *comparant* precedes the *comparé*.

[18] Mauriac makes effective use of ternary structures on a number of occasions in *Orages*. Cf. 'Une seule cigale éclate, grince et bat' (428); 'Je me penche sur lui. J'ai peur. Je le côtoie' (434); 'Désert intérieur, étouffant crépuscule, | Triste mer qui ne put mouiller que tes genoux' (440); 'La vague gonfle, meurt, puis renaît sur nos corps' (440); 'Le péché que je hais, que je fuis et que j'ose' (444); 'Dieu géant, regardez, honteux, chétif et nu, | Cet enfant' (445); 'Vagabond de seize ans, tout couvert de rosée, | De vermine et de fleurs' (446).

As the opening poem in the collection, 'Sédentaire' suggests that imagery in general will be important in this collection and that water imagery in particular will occupy a privileged position. There are hardly any 'neutral' (that is, purely descriptive) references to water in *Orages*. Perhaps the only example is to be found in 'Ganymède chrétien' where the poet evokes 'La macération des landes inondées, | L'odeur des bois mouillés' (444), in terms reminiscent of the autumnal descriptions in *L'Adieu à l'adolescence* (380–82). Otherwise, the references to water tend to be associated either with sexual desire or with God.[19] This is not always the case: rivers (used to offer a comparison to the blood of a woman metamorphosed into a tree) are referred to as 'La circulation de la terre vivante' (*Or* 441) and, in an evocation of an emerald ring, reference is made to 'La mystérieuse eau qui dort dans cette pierre' (442). However, in the vast majority of instances, the association either with desire or with the divine is clearly present.

Taking the former category first, we find that the title image of 'Les Deux Fleuves' is used to describe two lovers whose passion is never consummated: 'Nous fûmes, tête contre épaule, | Deux fleuves de sang parallèles' (431). This image of flowing water is combined with a marine metaphor: 'Mais nos mains, mouettes perdues, | Ne rasaient pas l'amère écume' (431). In Chapter 4, we saw that the gull in 'La Tempête apaisée' functioned as a symbol of purity (442); here, this purity is compromised (the gulls are lost), but only partly so, for these gulls have *not* made contact with 'l'amère écume'—clearly a synecdoche for the sea of sexual congress.[20] The image of a muddied source would be used on a number of occasions by Mauriac in the late 1920s and early 1930s in connection with sexual desire,[21] the poet uses similar imagery in 'Petit chien sombre' when he refers to 'mes

---

[19] Michel Le Guern, *L'Image dans l'œuvre de Pascal* (Colin, 1969), p. 140 notes that for authors belonging to the 'courant augustinien'—and Mauriac would certainly have to be numbered among them—water imagery often has 'la valeur ambiguë qu'elle a déjà dans la Bible', being used to refer both to good and evil.

[20] Cf. the sexual connotations of the noun phrase 'un flot amer' in 'Renoncement': 'Que ne m'as-tu roulé soudain, d'un flot amer, | Sur le sable où ma marche hésitante est inscrite' (435).

[21] See Paul Cooke, 'Les "Sources" de François Mauriac', *Rencontres avec Jean Sullivan*, 11 (1999), 84–95, 168–70.

secrets décombres, | Cette eau vaseuse et ces remous' (*Or* 432).[22] This
poem contrasts the desire of the lyric *je* with the oblivious innocence
of the beloved whose sleeping head is in his lap. The pulse of this
body becomes for the poet 'L'invisible courant du gave | Qui dans ton
corps frémit' (433), an image whose freshness is clearly meant to
contrast with the poet's own muddy waters.

By contrast, the heart of the woman evoked in 'Renoncement' is
far more like the poet's own, being likened to 'une eau endormie'
(434). He continues:

> Elle m'attire et me repousse. Je me couche
> Au bord de cette eau noire où pourrissent des tiges,
> Et mon cœur baptisé cherche et fuit le vertige
> Au contour de ta bouche. (434)

In addition to the contrast between the life-destroying black water of
the woman's heart and the cleansing, life-giving water of baptism, it
is worth noting the characteristically ambivalent nature of these lines,
underlined through Mauriac's exploitation of the resources of rhythm.
The first line is metrically ambivalent: syntax encourages us to view it
as a ternary alexandrine (4 + 4 + 4), but the rhythm of the Classical
(binary) alexandrine, so important in Mauriac's verse, means that we
might also be tempted to see the syllable pattern as 4 + 2 + 2 + 4. In
the latter case, the caesura falls between 'me' and 'repousse'. From
the perspective of Classical prosody, it is, of course, most unusual for
the caesura to separate an object pronoun from its verb. The effect is
to draw attention to the emotional turmoil of the lyric *je* and, through
the *rejet interne* of 'repousse', to emphasize the contradictory power
of his ambivalent response to the woman.[23] Elsewhere, however, the
poet's ambivalence disappears entirely. In 'Délectation', for example,

---

[22] Cf. 'Le Regret du péché': 'Un reflux de désirs, du plus profond des terres, | Re-
monte en moi, flot trouble et de boue épaissi' (436).

[23] Cf. the third line of stanza 1: 'Il restait pur après la pureté perdue' (433), where the
location of the proclitic 'après' immediately before the caesura emphasizes the paradox enunciated in this line. Sound too plays its part here: there are only two sounds in
the first hemistich (/i/ and /s/) that are not found in the second, and only three in the
second (/ə/, /e/, and /d/) that are not found in the first. This phonemic similarity between the two halves of the alexandrine diminishes the distance between its two
paradoxical clauses.

we read: 'Je plonge en de profondes eaux pour m'assouvir... | Délectation défendue!' (436). The bold caesura in the middle of the word 'profondes' suggests that the poet is in the mood for transgressing the Christian moral code, as well as the rules of Classical versification.

As its title suggests, 'La Marée infidèle' returns to the maritime imagery introduced in 'Sédentaire'. It also picks up on the notion of a sexual power relationship hinted at in this introductory poem ('Un corps était un monde où je régnais en maître'). Here, the relationship between the poet and his lover is viewed in terms of a power struggle: 'J'eusse voulu de vous, quand vous m'étiez sujette, | Ce zèle de la mer que la lune repousse' (437). Rather than the language of love and exchange, the poet draws on the master–servant relationship. As would-be master, he wishes to enjoy the absolute power of inspiring and rejecting desire. But this control fantasy founders on the rocks of the woman's freedom:

> Réticentes amours sans cesse retirées,
> N'épandrez-vous jamais sur mon aride sable
> Cette fidélité grondante des marées,
> Ces retours d'amertume à l'heure inéluctable?
>
> Poursuivi de ton flux, si je me voulais chaste,
> Je fuyais vainement l'écume défendue,
> Mais quand je t'appelais pour que tu me dévastes,
> Tu feignais de dormir, mer étale et perdue. (437)

The repetition of sounds in the first (especially /ʀ/, /t/, /s/, /ə/) and third (/d/, /t/, /e/) lines just quoted nicely captures the ebb and flow of the tide.[24] However, the poet's problem is that the phases of his partner's desire never coincide with his own.

Maritime imagery is also important in 'Le Désir', but here the metaphor of the sea is itself transformed metaphorically into that of the desert. This double metaphor dominates the poem's final three stanzas:

> Désert intérieur, étouffant crépuscule,
> Triste mer qui ne put mouiller que tes genoux,

---

[24] Cf. the last line where the fourfold repetition of /ɛ/ (twice in the first hemistich and twice in the second) emphasizes the woman's feigned calm.

Si je suis son captif, c'est en moi qu'elle brûle:
Le pays de la soif est au dedans de nous.

J'ai cru qu'un Dieu pourrait tarir cette mer morte,
Qu'il suffirait du ciel pour combler cette mer:
Mais on n'échappe pas au désert que l'on porte,
On ne s'évade pas de son propre désert.

La vague gonfle, meurt, puis renaît sur nos corps,
Les souille en les couvrant d'écume, et se retire.
L'antique terre et nous, connaissons ce martyre:
Rien ne peut séparer l'Océan de ses bords. (440)

The first line of the second stanza just quoted would appear to be an allusion to the account in the Book of Exodus in which God dries up the Red Sea so that the Israelites can leave Egypt and make their way to the Promised Land.[25] Indeed, Mauriac even employs a form of parallelism in the following line as if in imitation of the principal poetic feature of biblical Hebrew. It is, of course, true that Mauriac actually refers to 'cette mer morte' which inevitably makes us think of the connotations attaching to the Dead Sea. Although the connection is never made explicitly in the Bible itself, Judaeo-Christian tradition has always associated the Dead Sea with the destruction of Sodom and Gomorrah.[26] Mauriac himself makes use of this tradition (*OA* 60).[27] However, since the final poem in *Orages* contains a reference to 'cette cendre au bord des mers Mortes ou Rouges' (445), it would seem that there is some degree of overlap between the two bodies of water in Mauriac's poetic imagination. The important thing to note is that, in contrast to the biblical exodus, there is no divine deliverance for the poet. He will not be able to escape his inner desert, that Rim-

---

[25] See Exode 14. 21–22. It is still common, in both English and French, to refer to the *Red* Sea in this context, even though more modern translations of the Bible refer rather to the *Reed* Sea (la Mer des Joncs). Mauriac's use of the verb *tarir* recalls Isaïe 44. 24, 27: 'c'est moi ,Yahvé, […] qui dis à l'abîme: "Dessèche-toi, je vais tarir les fleuves"'.

[26] *New Bible Dictionary*, 3rd edn, ed. by I. H. Marshall and others (Leicester: Inter-Varsity Press, 1996), p. 263.

[27] Risse (*Homoerotik*, pp. 169–70, p. 200) explores the homosexual connotations of the imagery.

baldian *désert de l'amour* that would provide Mauriac with the title of his 1925 novel.[28]

This brings us to the association of water imagery with the divine in *Orages*. There are far fewer references to be considered here than when exploring the use of water imagery in relation to sexual desire, a fact that is significant in itself. In fact, there is only one poem in which we see the association clearly, though the reference to 'les océans calmés' at the start of 'La Tempête apaisée' (442) could legitimately be related to the theme. The poem in question is 'Sacré-cœur' which begins as if in direct response to the end of 'Le Désir':

> Il est une autre mer (la mer est à deux pas…)
> Son sel prête à ta lèvre une amertume neuve.
> Cet amour sans rivage attire à soi les fleuves
> Et console les cœurs qui ne se mêlaient pas. (441)

The sea in question is no longer that of sexual desire, but of God's love. This imagery will be developed at considerable length in Mauriac's later writing (one thinks in particular of *Les Chemins de la mer* and the *Nouveaux Mémoires intérieurs*).[29] However, in the sensual context of *Orages*, it is virtually still-born, surviving for only five of the poem's eight lines. The poem continues: 'Son écume nourrit la candeur des mouettes… | Trop tard! Une autre écume a sali mes genoux' (441). The use of the word 'autre' at the start of the poem had signalled the possibility of an alternative way to the obsession of sexual yearning, the second occurrence of the word (again qualifying a noun placed immediately before the caesura) returns us to the fundamental stimulus in *Orages*. The imagery suggests, in particular, a complete reversal of the situation described in 'Les Deux Fleuves': 'Mais nos mains, mouettes perdues, | Ne rasaient pas l'amère écume' (431). The Christian dimension continues to haunt the poet, as can be seen from the despairing alliteration of 'Trop tard!' and the moral connotations of the verb *salir*, but it appears to be an unobtainable

---

[28] 'Les Déserts de l'amour' is the title of some prose texts probably written in 1872 (Rimbaud, *Œuvres*, pp. 185–86). It was a title with which Mauriac readily identified both as a man (*OA* 78) and as a writer (*SR* 90).
[29] See Jean Touzot, 'L'Eau et le rêve chrétien: réflexions sur l'imagerie des *Nouveaux Mémoires intérieurs*', *CFM*, 6 (1979), 77–88.

alternative. Hence the question with which the poem closes: 'Comment se lèveraient pour calmer la tempête | Ces éternelles mains où j'ai fixé des clous?' (441). We have already begun here to think about the tension between the pull of sexual desire on the one hand and a yearning for religious peace on the other. I shall now go on to explore this more fully.

Sexual desire and God

The significance of sexual desire for the collection has already become apparent from my analysis of water imagery. A passage from a letter to Blanche of 9 September 1924 is very revealing in this respect: 'Triste humanité obsédée! car ce que je leur reproche, ce que je *me* reproche, ce qui est notre vice à tous, c'est l'obsession sexuelle: nous sommes obsédés et obsédants.'[30] However, as a letter to the same addressee earlier in the same year makes clear, Mauriac is just as obsessed with God as he is with sex: 'Rien ne me guérira de tout ramener à Dieu, [...]. Je pense que le trait dominant de ma nature (si basse par ailleurs) aura été la bonne foi—oui, le désir, le besoin douloureux de ne pas vivre dans le mensonge...' The tension between these two obsessions marks all of Mauriac's creative writing, but it is perhaps nowhere more clearly displayed than in *Orages*. As he told Amrouche: 'Dans *Orages*, s'exprime la plainte du pécheur non repenti et qui tout de même a la foi' (*SR* 94). Here more than anywhere we see the truth of what he writes to Gide on 11 December 1922:

> Et nous qui ne savons rien concilier en nous, notre œuvre ne saurait être que l'image de cette lutte sans issue, de ce débat dans notre cœur, entre Dieu et la passion à quoi Dieu nous soumet et qui pourtant est voulue de Lui. (*LV* 121)

Among the poems from the introductory 'overture', those which focus most clearly on this struggle are 'Péché mortel' and 'Autre péché'. The former focuses on the contrast between chronological time and the temporal perspective of a lyric *je* consumed by desire. Given the poem's brevity (in keeping with the short-lived moment of consummation), it can be quoted in full:

---

[30] *François Mauriac–Jacques-Emile Blanche*, p. 129; Mauriac's italics. The next quotation is from p. 114.

1   Cette après-midi lourde épouse mon attente,
           Sa rumeur est le bruit d'un amour contenu,
           Mais la marche du temps, désespérément lente,
           Se précipitera lorsque nous serons nus.

5   Un siècle, j'attendrais la seconde où nos corps
           Insulteront le ciel de leurs soifs confondues.
           Si j'épuise une vie à guetter ta venue,
           L'espace d'un baiser me donnera la mort. (429)

The use of the noun 'attente' at the end of a line and of the verb *attendre* at the end of a hemistich conveys the impression of a mind focused almost exclusively on the longed-for sexual encounter. The emphasis on time is apparent from the lexis employed, but Mauriac also makes use of the resources afforded by verse. Syntactically, the placing of the adjective phrase 'désespérément lente' between the subject ('la marche du temps') and its verb ('se précipitera'), thus delaying the action indicated by this verb, adds to the sense of time dragging slowly. The insertion also creates an *enjambement* which allows the verb to explode at the start of a new line. Rhythmically too, there is a striking contrast between the adjective phrase and the verb that adds to the obvious contrast at the semantic level. The final two syllables of 'désespérément lente' both contain the 'long' back nasal vowel /ɑ̃/ (already present in the word 'temps') and could both receive a stress in recitation (in addition to the *accent d'insistance* that might be placed on the first syllable), whereas 'se précipitera', with its succession of front vowels, could easily be read as a single measure. In line 5, the similarity in sound between 'siècle' and 'seconde' (the phonemes /s/, /k/, and /ə/ are common to both words) and their parallel positioning (both occupying the second and third syllables of their respective hemistichs) make their semantic contrast stand out even more starkly. One is reminded of Banville's dictum: 'vous ferez rimer ensemble, autant qu'il se pourra, des mots très-semblables entre eux comme SON et très-différents entre eux comme SENS.'[31] There is a similar contrast in lines 7 and 8 between 'une vie', a whole lifetime evoked in two short words, and 'L'espace d'un baiser'—a moment in

---

[31] Théodore de Banville, *Petit Traité de poésie française* (Charpentier, 1891), p. 75; Banville's capitals.

time that, due to its overwhelming significance, expands to fill a hemistich.

In this poem, Mauriac emphasizes the clash between the physical and the spiritual. The latter is represented metonymically by 'le ciel' (l. 6); the former by the terms 'nus' (l. 4), 'corps' (l. 5), and 'baiser' (l. 8). All of these words are given prominence by being placed either at the end of lines or immediately before the caesura. The terms that occur at the end of lines are especially emphasized through rhyme. 'Nus' seems particularly significant in this respect since its vowel is also used in the rhyme in lines 6 and 8. Indeed, as Table 14 shows, the term *nu* is an important one generally in Mauriac's later verse:

Table 14:

	MJ	AA	CAF	WP	Or	SA
nu	3	3	0	3	6	8
	(0)	(0)	(0)	(0)	(3)	(4)

Notes
- The first figure gives the total number of occurrences of the word *nu*.
- The figure in parentheses indicates the number of occasions on which *nu* is used with sexual connotations.

We have already seen from Table 13 (Chapter 5) that the term *corps* becomes increasingly prevalent in Mauriac's later verse. In 'Péché mortel', it is the rhyme between 'corps' and 'mort' that is particularly significant. Prior to *Orages*, the rhyme only occurs once in Mauriac's verse (MP, II, 6–7), but we find it twice in *Orages* (429, 430) and then three more times in *Le Sang d'Atys* (449, 452, 462). The association of sexual sin with death is already implicit in the title 'Péché mortel'. The death referred to in the poem could be regarded as metaphorical (*la petite mort* of orgasm), but Mauriac certainly took the metaphysical dimension seriously. Only two weeks before the poem was first published (in *La Revue européenne* of March 1923), Mauriac wrote to Jacques Rivière: 'Ne voyez-vous pas autour de vous que le péché tue, et qu'il est mortel, à la lettre?' (*LV* 122). Within the confines of *Orages* itself, the very next poem ('Autre péché', a title that emphasizes the close link between this piece and its immediate predecessor) makes it clear that the death evoked at the end of 'Péché mortel' is not to be seen in purely metaphorical terms. After alluding to the metaphorical sense of *la petite mort* ('La volupté fait mourir: | O seule mort passagère!'), the poet continues:

> Mais tu sais que les morts brèves
> D'où, les yeux blessés, tu sors,
> Nous mènent, de rêve en rêve,
> Jusqu'à l'éternelle mort? (429)

The five-fold repetition of the /ɛ/ sound in these final two lines (a sound that has already occurred four times in the previous two lines) helps the poet create a sense of inevitability about the association between sex and death.

The association features in other poems too, though with a more sinister edge. In 'Faune', we read: 'L'odeur te fait mourir de mon désir tapi' (430)—the twisted syntax caused by the inversion offers a parallel to a vitiated human relationship. In 'Phares' (430), the poet imagines embalming his love and laying out his dead beloved. The grammatical construction used here (two consecutive *si* clauses) makes it plain that neither possibility will ever happen. However, in 'Assassin', the flesh of the woman (described as a 'morte inconnue') to whom the poet has just made love is said to be 'glacée et nue | Comme pour être ensevelie' (431). The lover is cast in the role of murderer. Finally, in 'Délectation', the association receives a new, almost necrophilic, twist:

> Je plonge en de profondes eaux pour m'assouvir…
>   Délectation défendue!
> Fut-il jamais permis aux lèvres de ravir
> Sur des visages morts une douceur perdue?
>
> Visages exhumés, chaque jour moins distincts,
>   Ma délectation vous ronge.
> J'use de mes baisers vos cheveux et j'éteins
> Dans vos yeux trop souvent rouverts le dernier songe. (436)

The exclamation mark at the end of the second line quoted above is certainly deserved, for we find in these verses a three-fold linkage between sex and death. Firstly, there is the quasi-necrophilic relationship between the poet and the dead/ exhumed faces of former lovers.

Secondly, there is implicit here another instance of the idea that 'sinful' sexual activity leads to death (e.g., the coupling of the noun 'délectation' with the verb *ronger*). But thirdly, there is also the specific indication in the final two lines (emphasized in formal terms through the *enjambement* that highlights 'et j'éteins' as a *contre-rejet*) that it is the poet himself who is responsible for this death—a kind of second death, since the victims are already dead.

The reason for this obsessive association between sex and death is, of course, the background of Mauriac's 'puritanical' Catholicism. The poems 'Péché mortel' and 'Autre péché' show the poet in revolt against his faith from the start, but he can never abandon it. Thus we read at the end of 'Autre péché':

> De peur que la Grâce sourde
> En nos cœurs dévotieux,
> J'invoque une étoile sourde
> Au doux nom de mauvais dieu.
>
> En vain! Nous serons vaincus
> Par le Dégoût, ce complice
> Du Dieu qui nous aime plus
> Que nous n'aimons nos délices.[32] (430)

Because, as he puts it in 'La Tempête apaisée', the poet is 'en proie aux péchés bien-aimés' (442), the possibility of experiencing Grace has become a source of anxiety to him. Yet he remains a believer ('nos cœurs dévotieux'). The 'étoile sourde' he invokes is presumably the 'étoile du matin' mentioned by the prophet Isaiah and given the name Lucifer in the Vulgate.[33] This is as far as he goes in revolt against God, imitating the example of Nerval and Baudelaire.[34] But the invocation falls on deaf ears. The contest between God and Satan, emphasized through the extremely rich rhyme /əsuʀd/, is thoroughly one-sided: God's influence is that of an irrepressible spring (the verb

---

[32] Cf. the words of Christ in Pascal's 'Mystère de Jésus': 'Je t'aime plus ardemment que tu n'as aimé tes souillures.' See Blaise Pascal, *Œuvres complètes*, ed. by Jacques Chevalier (Gallimard, 1954), p. 1314.

[33] Isaïe 14. 12.

[34] I am thinking of poems such as Nerval's 'Antéros' (*Les Chimères*) and Baudelaire's 'Les Litanies de Satan' (*Les Fleurs du mal*).

sourdre has the same etymological origin (Latin *surgere*) as the noun *source*), whereas the Morning Star is incapable of response. Ultimately, therefore, the poet's revolt fails as a result of 'le Dégoût', the divine ally whose capital D is echoed in those of 'Du Dieu', contrasting with the lower case letters used at the start of '[mauvais] dieu' and 'délices'. God appears to have the upper hand even at the purely typographical level.

God does not figure overtly in any of the next twelve poems. Christ is mentioned at the end of 'Attendre et se souvenir' as 'l'ami de Lazare' responsible for the resurrection at the Last Day (438). But it is really in the next poem, 'Lumière du corps', that we return to a divine figure reminiscent of the one encountered in 'Autre péché'. Neither God nor Christ is mentioned by name in this poem, the poet preferring to employ various periphrases: 'un Autre', 'Celui' (twice), 'Il', and 'l'Epoux' (439). The capitalization leaves us in doubt as to the divine nature of the referent (and *l'Epoux* is, of course, one of the biblical terms used to refer to the Messiah),[35] but it is as if the poet does not wish to utter an unequivocal term such as *Dieu* or *Christ*. This reticence is very much in keeping with what he says to his lover:

> Aimons-nous sourdement afin que nos étreintes
>   N'attirent pas Celui qui les hait.
> De peur qu'Il ne rallume en nous la lampe éteinte,
> Cachons notre folie à Celui qui la hait. (*Or* 439)

There are two obvious lexical similarities between this quatrain and the fourth stanza of 'Autre péché' quoted above. The adverb 'sourdement' here recalls the use of the adjective 'sourde' in the earlier poem (the lovers' relationship is thereby implicitly linked to the morning star that is Lucifer) and we find a 'De peur que' construction in both poems (in both instances, the connotations of the word 'peur' are actualized far more than is usual with this conjunction). There is also, however, a shift of emphasis with respect to 'Autre péché'. There, God was the subject of the verb *aimer*; here, he is twice the subject of the verb *haïr*. The object of the verb is, of course, different in the two poems: 'nous' in 'Autre péché', but 'nos étreintes'/ 'notre folie' in 'Lumière du corps'. Mauriac's usage corresponds to the or-

---

[35] See, for example, Matthieu 9. 15 and Jean 3. 29.

thodox position according to which God loves the sinner, but hates the sin.

The title 'Lumière du corps' is an allusion to part of Christ's Sermon on the Mount: 'La lampe du corps, c'est l'œil. Si donc ton œil est sain, ton corps tout entier sera lumineux. Mais si ton œil est malade, ton corps tout entier sera ténébreux. Si donc la lumière qui est en toi est ténèbres, quelles ténèbres!'[36] The poet's perspective is, however, rather different. The light of desire is by no means dark in this poem. Indeed, the light of the lover's body, and specifically of the lover's 'jambes *pures*' (my italics), is brighter than the light of the lamp in the bedroom (*Or* 439). The poem's double reference to the lovers' extinguished (spiritual) lamp is clearly intended to evoke the foolish virgins of Christ's parable.[37] From a Christian perspective, the lovers in the poem might be considered 'foolish' precisely because they are no longer virgins. But the poet deliberately shuns this interpretive grid. Once again, therefore, in the final stanza, we find him drawing on the language of Scripture only to undermine it. When he writes: 'Même si notre lampe est éteinte, l'Epoux | Verra la mèche fumer encore' (439), he is no doubt alluding to yet another Matthean description of Christ: '*Le roseau froissé, il ne le brisera pas, et la mèche fumante, il ne l'éteindra pas*'.[38] But the intended comfort of the evangelist's quotation becomes a source of anxiety in Mauriac's poem. The poet would prefer there to be nothing at all to attract the Bridegroom's gaze, for a look from Him will inevitably lead to the termination of the poet's passion: 'La cendre couvrira ton corps laiteux et roux, | La cendre étouffera l'amour qui brûle encore' (439). The use of anaphora and the similarity of the rhythm of these two lines powerfully emphasize the smothering of his 'sinful' relationship.

In the poems examined so far, sexual desire has been a shared commodity. However, this is not always the case in *Orages*. One thinks of the five-line 'Faune', for example:

> Plus sournois qu'un regard, mon silence t'outrage.

---

[36] Matthieu 6. 22–23.

[37] Cf. Matthieu 25. 8: 'nos lampes s'éteignent.' It is noteworthy that this parable also contains the figure of the 'époux' (25. 1).

[38] Matthieu 12. 20; the italics used in the *Bible de Jérusalem* indicate a quotation (from Isaïe 42. 3).

> L'odeur te fait mourir de mon désir tapi.
> Ton corps est violé dans mon cœur, sans répit.
> Prométhée envieux du feu de ton visage,
> Je le vole à toute heure et rien ne me trahit. (430)

Nearly all of the verbs here have violent connotations, and there is a rare brutality about the central line of this quintain. The frequently repeated /i/ sound, prominent at the end of lines and before the caesura,[39] adds to the uneasy impression of an obsessive, almost pathological desire invisible from the outside. A similar impression emerges from the aptly titled 'Tartufe'.[40] But this latter poem also adds the idea of a significant age difference between the poet and the object of his lust: 'Je rôde, orage lourd, autour de ta jeunesse' and 'Ce mensonge charnel que nous enseigne l'âge, | J'en commence d'avoir l'humiliant usage' (432). Something similar, though against a gentler background, emerges from the next poem, 'Petit chien sombre', in which the poet, with reference to himself, evokes: 'Ce vieux cœur hurlant à la mort' (433). Like 'Tartufe', this is a poem about feelings that are not reciprocated: in the former, the poet describes the 'brèves lueurs' of his desires (432); in 'Petit chien sombre', he uses the related image of 'brefs éclairs' (433), but in both poems the result is the same: the light of his desire finds no reflection. The 'prunelles pures' of his innocent beloved therefore provide a (rhyming) contrast with the poet's 'misérable figure' (433).

The age theme also appears in the next poem, 'Renoncement', with the poet describing himself as a 'vieux pauvre au cœur dur' (434). However, the addressee here is very different from the one presupposed in the two preceding poems. This woman has a colourful past including various 'amours' and 'crimes':

> Tu vécus loin de moi des milliers de vies,

---

[39] Scansion demands that the vowel combinations in 'violé' and 'envieux' be treated as diaereses, giving /viɔle/ and /ãviø/.

[40] The element of religious hypocrisy made famous in Molière's play is coupled with an allusion to Rimbaud's poem 'Le Châtiment de Tartufe' (Œuvres, p. 50), where Tartufe is also spelled with a single 'f' (as opposed to Molière's *Tartuffe*). However, one should not make too much of this, since Mauriac's spelling of 'Tartuffe' is erratic: sometimes he uses two 'f's, but generally only one, even when referring directly to Molière's play (see, for example, OC, XI, 81–82).

> Je ne sais quel secret t'habite et te dévore.
> Mais ton sourire faux et tes tempes blanchies
>   L'emportent sur l'aurore. (434)

One is reminded of some of the mature heroines in Mauriac's fiction: Thérèse Desqueyroux in *La Fin de la nuit*, for example, or, from a novel whose composition is closer to that of this poem, Maria Cross in *Le Désert de l'amour*. The woman's experience unsettles the lyric *je*. Her 'cœur chargé de trop de proies', likened to 'une eau endormie', inspires fear (434)—but also, as I showed in the section on water imagery, ambivalence.

This ambivalence suggests that the renunciation evoked in the title of 'Renoncement' and given voice in its concluding lines—'Ne vous refermez plus jamais sur mon tourment, | Ténèbre des caresses' (435)—is unlikely to be definitive. Whereas the next poem, 'Equinoxe', continues in renunciatory mode, this is followed by the reawakening of desire in 'Délectation':

> Je pleure mes péchés et ceux que j'ai commis,
>   Et ceux que j'eusse aimé commettre.
> Pour réveiller la faim dont je ne fus le maître,
> Je trouble ton sommeil, ô mon cœur endormi! (435)

This final line in particular seems a direct response to the poet's appeal in 'Equinoxe': 'Que je retrouve en vous le repos de l'hiver | [...] O nuit de mes deux mains contre le lit désert!' (435). The inadequacy of the poet's renunciation is apparent from the title of the next poem, 'Le Regret du péché'. Once again, ambivalence is to the fore:

> Un reflux de désirs, du plus profond des terres,
> Remonte en moi, flot trouble et de boue épaissi.
> Il recouvre cette âme asservie au mystère,
> Asservie à la chair, et qui n'a pas choisi. (436)

And, once again, Mauriac makes use of the specific resources offered by verse to highlight this ambivalence: the word 'chair' (in stressed sixth-syllable position) rhymes with the word 'mystère'. Sound binds together the two opposing poles of the poet's world.[41]

Although Mauriac drew a considerable part of his inspiration and success from this tension between *la chair* and *le mystère*, it was a tension that troubled him. Hence the question that we have already seen at the end of 'Sacré-cœur': 'Comment se lèveraient pour calmer la tempête | Ces éternelles mains où j'ai fixé des clous?' (441). The use of the conditional in this question makes it seem even more despairing. Yet, in the subsequent poems, there are a couple of potential answers. One is to be found in 'La Tempête apaisée' whose title is itself a response to the question raised in 'Sacré-cœur'. However, since I have examined this poem in Chapter 4, I want now to conclude this section by looking at 'Le Corps fait arbre', the poem in *Orages* that immediately follows 'Sacré-cœur'.

The title suggests an association with the myth of Attis, but the body to be transformed is in fact that of a woman (in a poem where all the rhymes are feminine). She is introduced in very sensual terms: 'Le parfum de ta robe attire les abeilles, | Plus que les fruits mangés que ta sandale broie' (441). Smell has already been associated with sexual desire on at least three occasions in *Orages* (429, 434, 435); the woman's dress inevitably evokes the body it contains; and the reference to fruit that has been eaten, reminding us of the story of the garden of Eden, also has sensual connotations. The verb *attirer* therefore seems to apply as much to the poet as to the bees. The reader too is offered a pleasurable aural experience, largely as a result of the seven /a/ sounds in these two lines.[42] Then comes the transformation, no doubt inspired by Attis's metamorphosis into a tree:

> Rêve que désormais immobile, sans âge,
> Les pieds enracinés et les mains étendues,
> Tu laisses s'agiter aux orageuses nues

---

[41] The poem's final line—'Je regardais contre ma bouche ton épaule' (436)—is also noteworthy from a formal point of view. The *césure lyrique* (which occurs when /ə/ is contained in the sixth syllable) is a rare phenomenon in Mauriac's verse and is used here to emphasize a special moment of physical contact between the lovers (the preceding two lines explain why this moment is special).

[42] The next line contains three more /a/ sounds, including the first and last phonemes: 'Accueillons cet élan de végétale joie' (441).

Une chevelure odorante de feuillage.

Les guêpes voleront sur toi sans que s'émeuve
L'écorce de ta chair où la cigale chante,
Et ton sang éternel sera, comme les fleuves,
La circulation de la terre vivante. (441)

It is significant that the first word used to describe this transformed woman is 'immobile'. No doubt there is an affinity here with those poems in which the lyric *je* prefers a woman's absence to her presence and even, on occasion, dreams of her death. The mobility of female desire is a source of concern to the poet in *Orages*; this dream of immobility is therefore reassuring to him. As a result of the woman's transformation, she has become one with the earth (that is, Cybele). But, since she is pictured with her hands stretched out, an association with Christ is also being established. Implicitly, therefore, we see in this poem a preliminary sketch for the bringing together of Cybele and Christ that marks the end of *Le Sang d'Atys*. The reference to outstretched hands could be taken as an allusion to the crucifixion, but perhaps it is here that we discover an answer to the question posed at the end of 'Sacré-cœur', for not only do we find a reference to outstretched hands in 'Le Corps fait arbre', we also find immediately afterwards a reference to stormy clouds (cf. the reference to 'la tempête' in the earlier poem). Now, it is true that the woman/ tree does not calm the storm around her, but she does not seem at all perturbed by it.[43] As a result of her transformation, she has gone beyond desire, as is made clear by the *enjambement* in which the terms *chair* and *s'émouvoir* are coupled in a negative construction. We might paraphrase the question in 'Sacré-cœur' as follows: 'How can I possibly escape desire?' The answer offered here is: 'Through sublimation.' It is left open whether this sublimation is of a religious nature (the conformity of the body of desire to the tree that is the Cross), or can be achieved through the poet's own art (art, conventionally, being 'sans âge' and 'éternel' as is the transformed woman).

---

[43] Cf. the gospel account, where Christ is pictured as sleeping through the storm until woken by his disciples (Marc 4. 7–39).

Myth

'Le Corps fait arbre' clearly draws on mythical elements, not just in its allusion to the myth of Attis (and to Ovidian metamorphosis in general), but also in its reference to the god Pan. As I have shown elsewhere, this appeal to mythology is a new feature in Mauriac's verse.[44] It is also a feature that reminds us of his indebtedness to Symbolist imagery.[45] Brief references to mythic characters are scattered throughout *Orages*: in 'Faune', whose very title evokes the satyr of Greek mythology, the poet presents himself as Prometheus (430); 'Phares' contains an allusion to the myth of Icarus (430); 'Tartufe' (432), while not related to a character from classical mythology, is an example of one of the 'mythes littéraires nouveau-nés' described by Sellier;[46] and I have already argued that there is a hint of a mythic dimension to the figure of 'le bouvier adolescent' at the end of 'La Tempête apaisée' (443). However, it is in the four concluding poems that follow 'La Tempête apaisée', and in 'Atys' at the start of the volume, that this mythic dimension is particularly prominent, forming a kind of mythic frame around the collection as a whole. I shall bring this chapter to a conclusion through an analysis of these poems.

In 'Sédentaire', the poet's metaphorical imagination sees the body as a world; in 'Atys', it sees the world as a body. The mythological figure of Cybèle, introduced in the poem 'Atys', is Planet Earth personified and embodied: 'Un seul enfant tient l'univers entre ses bras: | Un corps illimité sous l'herbe épaisse plie' (428). The paradox of the first of these two lines is emphasized by the way in which, contrary to Mauriac's standard practice, the caesura falls in the middle of the word 'univers'. And, in the second line, the word 'illimité', already foregrounded phonemically through its three /i/ sounds in quick succession (the same sound that makes up the rhyme at the end of the line), is further emphasized by its position at the end of the first hemistich. By its very nature, a body should not be 'illimité', but Cybèle's is, and the contrast between her vastness and the smallness

---

[44] Paul Cooke, 'Présence des mythes dans la poésie de François Mauriac', *NCFM*, 9 (2001), 67–87 (p. 72).

[45] See Marc Alyn, 'Le Désir, messager de l'irrationnel dans les poèmes d'*Orages*', *CFM*, 15 (1988), 77–87 (p. 83).

[46] Philippe Sellier, 'Qu'est-ce qu'un mythe littéraire?', *Littérature*, 55 (1984), 112–26 (p. 116).

of Atys ('Un seul *enfant*') could hardly be greater. The physical in-compatibility between these two bodies is self-evident. Yet Cybèle is still said to adore Atys (427), and it is the very impossibility of this love that causes her suffering and pain.[47] In this early poem, Atys seems to reciprocate Cybèle's feelings (things are different, as we shall see, in *Le Sang d'Atys*). His deception ('cette bouche déçue') stems from the fact that the 'déesse sans yeux' cannot see or feel him (428). The phrase *tenir entre ses bras* in the quotation at the start of this paragraph has obvious connotations of affection, but there is also an implicitly sexual dimension to Atys's actions:[48]

> Jaloux de ce soleil qui te couve et te boit,
> Atys a caressé tes plus secrètes mousses,
> De sa lèvre renflée et d'un timide doigt,
> Cybèle, ô cœur feuillu, chair verdissante et rousse! (428)

This description of a young man, already referred to in the poem as an *enfant*, jealous of the sun (a standard symbol of the father),[49] explor-ing the body of the adoring earth-mother with both desire ('sa lèvre *renflée*') and timidity ('un timide doigt') is very striking. All the ele-ments of a psychoanalytical drama are here—a little too conveniently, perhaps? As I shall be arguing in more detail in my reading of *Le Sang d'Atys*, it is possible that Mauriac *deliberately* incorporates psy-choanalytic motifs into his treatment of the Cybèle–Atys relationship. This does not mean that it is inappropriate to explore the poems from a psychoanalytic perspective, but it does mean that such an approach needs to be aware of the possibility that Mauriac knowingly engages with the very theories we may be tempted to apply to his work.

Although the presentation of the Earth in terms of the figure of Cybèle is the most striking example of personification in 'Atys', it is by no means the only example. Indeed, personification is the poem's most important rhetorical figure. It occurs as early as the first line:

---

[47] The words 'souffrir', 'douleur', and 'souffrant' are all used in connection with Cybèle (428).

[48] This is where Mauriac's version of the myth diverges from that of Ovid who refers to the shepherd's 'pure love'. See Ovid, *Fasti*, trans. and ed. by A. J. Boyle and R. D. Woodward (Penguin, 2000), p. 89.

[49] See Jean Chevalier and Alain Gheerbrant, *Dictionnaire des symboles*, 2nd edn (Robert Laffont/ Jupiter, 1982), p. 895.

'Couleuvres, les chemins *dormaient* dans la lumière' (427), a figure which takes us back to 'Sédentaire': 'J'ai vu des lacs *dormir*' (427). Elsewhere leaves dream, Earth suffers, clay breathes, grassland cries out, the sun drinks, cicadas sing, and pines bleed (428). The distinctions between the human and the natural world are constantly being dissolved. The 'pathetic fallacy' is omnipresent and will continue to be an important device throughout the collection.

Before leaving this poem, I want to draw attention to the way in which it introduces the figure of Atys. Whereas in *Le Sang d'Atys* the mythological characters are presented to us through their own speech (the lyric *je* is absent), in this poem the lyric *je* is still present and it is he who sees the figure of Atys as offering a parallel to his own situation:

> Comme Atys, le berger que Cybèle adora,
> Crucifiait au sol fendu ses faibles bras,
> Du temps que j'étais fou, j'ai possédé la terre. (427)

The lyric *je* spends much of his time in *Orages* in revolt against the Christian call. However, the lines just quoted provide a hint from the outset that the Christian perspective will ultimately triumph. Firstly, one notes the use of the verb *crucifier*.[50] Although the full implications of this verb will not be revealed until *Le Sang d'Atys*, Atys is already being presented as a christic figure in some sense. The same is also true of the lyric *je* by virtue of the comparison being drawn between himself and Atys. Even though the poet will frequently seek to avoid his faith in this collection, Mauriac's view of the power of the Cross is such that a return is always likely. 'On naît prisonnier de sa croix' is how he puts it, before going on to describe how even those who appear to reject the Cross eventually find themselves brought back to it (*ORTC*, II, 795). His observations are largely autobiographical, but they are also related to his understanding of 'le mystère d'Arthur Rimbaud' (*ORTC*, II, 796): 'Il fut le crucifié malgré lui, qui hait sa croix et que sa croix harcèle;—et il faudra qu'il agonise pour qu'elle vienne à bout de lui' (*ORTC*, II, 797). This helps us understand the appropriateness of the conclusion of 'Fils du Ciel', the last poem

---

[50] The only other two occurrences of the verb in Mauriac's verse are also in *Orages* (442, 444).

in *Orages* and one that centres on the figure of Rimbaud, when the lyric *je* finally returns (albeit somewhat ambivalently) to Christ.

The second (related) point I want to make about the lines quoted above is that the third of them appears to be an allusion to one of the Beatitudes: 'Heureux les doux, car ils posséderont la terre'.[51] There are, however, two significant differences between the gospel saying and Mauriac's alexandrine. Firstly, whereas Christ's words are addressed to 'les doux', the poet refers to a time when he was 'fou'; and secondly, there is a contrast between the future and the *passé composé* of the verb *posséder*. The concept of madness is referred to on three other occasions in *Orages* and each time it is associated with sexual 'sin' (431, 436, 439). I would suggest that the same is true in 'Atys', and that the verb *posséder* in the line quoted above is being used primarily in the sense of *posséder une femme*, except that the woman in question is the earth-mother goddess/ planet, Cybèle (hence the 'madness' of the union).[52] At the end of the poem, in contrast, we read:

> Sous les pins où ton sang ruisselle à chaque tronc,
> Atys d'un corps terreux va cacher la souillure.
> Il ne sait pas encor sa victoire future
> Et qu'en l'unique mort nous te posséderons. (428)

The first two lines of this quatrain allude to the most well-known aspect of Attis's madness: his self-castration. In literary terms, the most enduring evocation of the shepherd's deranged frenzy has come down to us from the Roman poet Catullus. Yet Mauriac's approach to the myth of Attis owes virtually nothing to this illustrious predecessor. His christianization of the myth will not be fully worked out until *Le Sang d'Atys*, but already in this poem we can see an allusion to the Christian doctrine of an Adamic fall in the poet's reference to the 'souillure' of a 'corps terreux'.[53] The 'victoire future', although somewhat enigmatic in this poem, is almost certainly an allusion to

---

[51] Matthieu 5. 4.

[52] Cf. a passage from *Genitrix*: 'Comme un désespéré, qui veut quitter la terre, se couche tout de même contre la terre marâtre, y meurtrit sa face, aspire aux ténèbres de ses entrailles, ainsi cet homme à bout de souffle embrassait sa vieille mère, étroitement' (*ORTC*, I, 621).

[53] Cf. Paul's description of the first Adam as 'terrestre' (I Corinthiens 15. 47).

the Final Resurrection evoked at the end of *Le Sang d'Atys*, an event in which Cybèle shares: 'Innombrables Atys! Vous êtes ma poussière, | Ma poussière, c'est vous qui ressusciterez' (*SA* 462). This vision of an ultimate fusion between Atys and Cybèle allows us to understand the significance of the verb *posséder* when it is used again at the end of 'Atys' (this time, significantly, in the future tense in accordance with the Beatitude). Similarly, the collective Atys of the later poem (*SA* 458–59) helps account for the unexpected 'nous' in the final line of 'Atys' (*Or* 428). Although Mauriac claimed to have started work on *Le Sang d'Atys* only in 1927,[54] it seems clear that the broad lines of his reworking of the myth were already in place as early as 1922 (when part of what would later become 'Atys' was published under the title 'Cybèle possédée').[55]

Mauriac's christianization of mythic figures, a process that is only hinted at in 'Atys', becomes more explicit in the final four poems of *Orages*. I say 'christianization', but, in fact, the traditional image of the Christian God is sometimes difficult to detect in this collection. In 'Marsyas ou la grâce', for example, the central figure— in Greek mythology, a shepherd who was tied to a pine tree and flayed alive for having dared to compete with (and to best) Apollo in a musical challenge—is compared in his suffering with Christ upon the Cross. Marsyas is apostrophized as a 'doux corps qu'un Dieu jaloux torture' (443) and the capitalized 'Dieu' encourages us to equate Apollo with the Christian Father. A little further on, still addressing Marsyas, the poet speaks of 'l'amour de ton Dieu, plus cruel que sa haine' (443) and, again, it seems as though he has difficulty reconciling the doctrine of God's love with what happened to God's Son upon the Cross. This paradox is further highlighted via the *rejet interne* in the following line: 'Il aime tant les corps qui souffrent, ce dur maître' (444).[56] It is true that the doctrine of the Incarnation is also present in this poem, since this same cruel God

---

[54] *Orages* (Grasset, 1949), p. 4.

[55] François Mauriac, 'Poèmes', *Intentions*, 1.6 (June 1922), 1–2 (p. 1).

[56] Cf. the words of the third servant in the Parable of the Talents: 'Maître, je savais que tu es un homme dur', Matthieu 25. 24 in *Traduction œcuménique de la Bible*, new edn (Alliance Biblique Universelle/ Le Cerf, 1991).

'change l'eau en vin et la douleur en joie',[57] but the final image of a Marsyas who 'Sourit au ciel d'airain avec sa blême bouche' (444) still leaves us with an impression of divine indifference that borders on sadistic coldness.[58]

The concept of God's love is less ambiguous in the next poem, 'Ganymède chrétien'. Despite the fact that it concludes with a reference to 'le Dieu de proie'—an allusion to that version of the myth (there are several variants) in which Zeus changes into an eagle in order to abduct Ganymede, the handsome young shepherd with whom he has fallen in love—the Christian God in this poem is associated with an 'autre Amour' quite different from that displayed by the Greek god, since it reflects Christian *agape* rather than pagan *eros* (444). It is the poet himself who, like Zeus, is a slave to *eros*: 'Esclave désolé d'un amour qui me flatte' and 'Serf d'un plaisir si bas qu'il m'arrache des plaintes' (444).[59] These moralizing adjectives explain why the poet declares himself jealous of Ganymède's 'blessures saintes': 'la couronne de sang' about his head and the 'quatre stigmates' that assure his identification with Christ (444). We are clearly at some considerable distance from the classical myth here. Indeed, the only element from the Greek original that seems to interest Mauriac is the concept of 'le Dieu de proie' (444), an image that will resurface in the 'Chasseur divin' of the late-1920s (*OA* 122). In other words, Mauriac is only interested in the figure of Ganymede to the extent that he can use him as a symbol for Christian conversion (which explains why he is relocated from ancient Greece to a bedroom in the rain-drenched Landes).

---

[57] Cf. 'le chrétien sait pourquoi il souffre; en imitation de son Dieu crucifié, en union avec Lui, il a part à son agonie, il coopère à la rédemption du monde. Comme l'eau en vin aux noces de Cana, le Christ transmue la douleur en joie' (*OA* 132). The allusion is to the story recorded in Jean 2. 1–11.

[58] Cf. the reference to 'cieux [...] d'airain' in God's conditional curse against Israel in Deutéronome 28. 23.

[59] The terms 'esclave' and 'serf' provide a significant contrast with the poet's description of himself as a 'maître' in the opening poem (427). In 'Délectation', he is already pointedly *not* a master (435) and, in 'Marsyas ou la grâce', the concept of master is reserved for God (444). In these poems, Mauriac is exploiting the language of Nietzsche's master–slave contrast that proves so significant in *Le Baiser au lépreux*.

His use of David in 'David vaincu' is rather similar. The future
King of Israel mentioned in the title only appears in the poem's fourth
and final stanza. At the outset, the lyric *je* compares himself to a quite
different (though equally mythic) biblical character, Eve: 'Et ma
main, se levant vers l'arbre de science, | A la forme du fruit qu'elle
voudrait saisir' (445). Once again, God is presented in rather ambiguous terms. The Atonement is the result of 'grâce insidieuse, inhumain
maléfice' and Providence is described as being 'implacable, en ruses
si féconde' (445). Although God is addressed as the 'adorable en-
nemi' of the poet's desire, this leads up to what is perhaps the most
surprising of all Mauriac's reworkings of Scripture, since he describes
this desire as 'ce David qui veut être vaincu', an image that means
that God is assigned the role of Goliath: 'Dieu géant, regardez, hon-
teux, chétif et nu, | Cet enfant qui vous brave, et sa fronde sans pierre'
(445). But, in addition to requiring an outcome that is the precise
opposite of that found in the biblical account (in which David fa-
mously slays Goliath),[60] this constitutes a total reversal of the traditional Christian allegorical interpretation of the conflict between
David and Goliath, in which the shepherd-boy's victory over the pagan giant is seen as a type of Christ's defeat of the devil.[61] If the poet
elects to invert tradition in this way, it is presumably to underline his
ambivalence towards the Christian God and because he feels that his
desire, 'ce David qui veut être vaincu', may still gain the upper hand.

Of all the poems in this final section of *Orages*, it is only 'Fils du
ciel' that does not present God in an implicitly negative light. Christ is
mentioned three times in the poem, at the end of three of its four stanzas. On the first two occasions, Christ is the object of the poet's (and
Rimbaud's) waiting: 'Mais comme toi j'attends le Seigneur: il est
tard' (445); 'Pour moi, j'attends aussi le Christ, au noir matin' (446).
There is undoubtedly a certain Beckettian quality (*avant la lettre*) to
this waiting, but, in terms of *Orages* as a whole, what is particularly
significant is that this is now a genuinely religious expectancy as
opposed to the sexual *attente* that marked 'Péché mortel' at the start

---

[60] See I Samuel 17. 48–51.
[61] See, for example, St Augustine, *Expositions on the Book of Psalms*, ed. by C.
Marriott, E. B. Pusey, and H. Walford, 6 vols (Oxford: Parker, 1847–57), I (1847),
344–45.

of the collection. The third occurrence of the verb *attendre* comes in
the final distich: 'A l'heure du CHRISTUS VENIT, au chant du coq, |
Je t'attendrai, Rimbaud qui n'étais pas au monde' (446). The capitalized Latin words (meaning 'Christ is coming') are from the liturgy for
Sunday Lauds.[62] They are incorporated by Rimbaud himself in the
poem 'Délires II': 'Le Bonheur! Sa dent, douce à la mort, m'aver-
tissait au chant du coq,—*ad matutinum*, au *Christus venit*,—dans les
plus sombres villes.'[63] Given the probable allusion to Peter's denial of
Christ ('avant que le coq chante, tu m'auras renié trois fois'),[64] it
seems likely that Rimbaud is here expressing 'un sentiment très complexe de trahison'.[65]

Given the nature of the poet's relationship to his faith in *Orages*,
it could well be that Mauriac's allusion to Rimbaud's text is intended
to evoke a similarly complex sense of betrayal. On the whole, however, the poem seems designed, rather, to outline the possibility of a
return to faith via a meditation on the experience of Rimbaud. It is
important to note that with this third occurrence of the verb *attendre* it
is not Christ for whom the poet waits, but Rimbaud. I have already
suggested that Rimbaud functions as a christic figure for Mauriac, this
is emphasized not only by Rimbaud being substituted for Christ as the
object of the verb *attendre*, but also by the structural parallel that links
the names 'CHRISTUS' and 'Rimbaud' (both occupying syllables
five and six of their respective lines). The description of Rimbaud in
the relative clause following his name is also significant in this respect, recalling what Christ says about his disciples: 'Ils ne sont pas
du monde, comme moi je ne suis pas du monde.'[66]

Why is the poet so keen to associate Rimbaud with Christ in this
way? It is partly to do with what has been called the 'conversion
melodrama' of the time.[67] In the wake of the Catholic literary revival
that had begun in the latter part of the nineteenth century, Catholic

---

[62] See the note in Arthur Rimbaud, *'A Season in Hell' and 'Illuminations'*, trans. by
Mark Treharne (Dent, 1998), p. 55.

[63] Rimbaud, *Œuvres*, p. 234.

[64] Matthieu 26. 34.

[65] Margaret Davies, *'Une Saison en enfer' d'Arthur Rimbaud: analyse du texte*
(Minard, 1975), p. 89.

[66] Jean 17. 16.

[67] Martin Jarrett-Kerr, *François Mauriac* (Cambridge: Bowes & Bowes, 1954), p. 12.

intellectuals were keen both to try and convert their agnostic contemporaries and to emphasize the significance of faith for writers of earlier generations. Claudel, himself a convert, had a particularly prominent role in this dual process, as can be seen from his correspondence
with Gide and from the way in which he promoted the view of a
'Catholic' Rimbaud in a 1912 preface that drew on the account provided by Rimbaud's sister, Isabelle, of the poet's pious death.[68] Mauriac accepts this Catholic version of the Rimbaud myth and contributes to it in this poem by juxtaposing images of the archetypal *poète
maudit* with images that draw on religious connotations.[69] But there is
also a more personal, and ultimately more important, reason why
Mauriac associates Rimbaud and Christ. It is because he sees Rimbaud's destiny as similar to his own. Séailles perhaps goes a little too
far when he suggests that, in this poem, Rimbaud 'joue un rôle
d'intercesseur auprès de Mauriac'.[70] But it is certain that Mauriac
identifies closely with Rimbaud, as can be seen from the first two
'waiting' references considered above ('comme toi', 'moi […] aussi')
and from the poem's opening words: 'Je porte en moi l'enfer où tu
fus' (445). Clearly, Mauriac's biography was altogether different from
Rimbaud's in terms of external events, but, as 'Sédentaire' suggests, it
is the inner world that is of real significance for Mauriac, and it is
here that he senses a deep affinity with Rimbaud. Throughout *Orages*,
the poet has been in a state of anxious revolt against God; that is why
the deathbed scene recounted by Isabelle Rimbaud is of such importance to him. When he asks: 'Quand un dernier rayon brûlera mes
rideaux, | Aurai-je comme toi ce lit encerclé d'anges?' (446), he is
still not in a position to be able to answer with any confidence, but it
is clear that, whatever its historical validity, this image of a penitent

---

[68] See, respectively, Paul Claudel and André Gide, *Correspondance: 1899–1926*, ed.
by Robert Mallet (Gallimard, 1949) and Claudel, *Œuvres en prose*, pp. 514–21.

[69] E.g., 'Vagabond de seize ans, tout couvert de rosée, | De vermine et de fleurs, chère
tête embrasée' followed by 'Ange du grand chemin, que l'on ne voyait pas', and
'Amant des bords maudits sans verdure et sans eau' preceded by 'Fils du ciel qui
cuvais le vin bleu dans les granges' (446).

[70] André Séailles, 'François Mauriac lecteur de Rimbaud: affinités et contrastes',
CFM, 5 (1978), 95–112 (p. 99).

and pardoned *poète maudit* exercises a powerful hold over Mauriac's imagination.[71]

Conclusion

Although largely ignored at the time of its publication, Mauriac always considered *Orages* to be one of his finest achievements as an author. He was right to do so. Speaight comments: 'These are no metrical exercises; the salt of experience is in them, as you taste it in Villon and Baudelaire.'[72] The comparisons are flattering, certainly, but not altogether undeserved. There is an emotional intensity to these short poems not previously encountered in Mauriac's verse. There are also some longer poems with a mythological framework that show a broadening of perspective and that pave the way for *Le Sang d'Atys*. Above all, as I hope my analyses have helped to show, *Orages* offers a rewarding reading experience thanks to Mauriac's evocative use of imagery, lexis, and phonemic patterning, as well as his skilful handling of intertextual allusions and the semantic possibilities afforded by prosody. The poems of *Orages* certainly appeal to the emotions and senses, but they are also offer far more aesthetic satisfaction than the early verse.

---

[71] For further analysis of the significance of deathbed conversions for Mauriac's own myth of the poet, see my *Mauriac et le mythe du poète*, pp. 100–05.

[72] Speaight, *François Mauriac*, p. 93.

7. Christianized Myth: *Le Sang d'Atys*

Background

Mauriac gives the official dates of composition of *Le Sang d'Atys* as 1927–38,[1] but, in a letter to Georges Duhamel dated 17 December 1939, he describes his text as 'un poème pris, repris, déchiré, depuis *quinze ans*, tant il est païen' (*NLV* 193; Mauriac's italics). The same figure of fifteen years is advanced in a letter dated 25 January 1940 in which Mauriac adds: 'mais le meilleur est ce qui date de cette année' (*NLV* 197), presumably a reference to 1939. A period of between eleven and fifteen years is a long time for a writer to whom words generally came easily and who had published no fewer than nine novels between 1919 and 1928. This degree of investment in time and effort is significant. Yet, when *Le Sang d'Atys* was published (in January 1940 in the *NRF* and then in May of the same year by Grasset), it passed virtually unnoticed. This is hardly surprising: looking back over the history of twentieth-century France, May 1940 must rank as one of the worst possible dates for the launch of a new book. Nevertheless, Mauriac saw the poem as his most significant verse achievement and, over recent decades, a number of critics have also come to value it highly. Guyonnet shows in detail that Mauriac's interest in the myth of Attis both pre- and post-dates the actual composition of *Le Sang d'Atys* and argues that it constitutes a personal myth that is ultimately responsible for the unity of the author's universe.[2] Others have described the cycle as 'le chef-d'œuvre de l'entreprise poétique de François Mauriac'; as a 'très beau texte' offering 'un bilan poétique'; as 'le pivot central de l'œuvre de Mauriac, un principe organisateur, une racine essentielle'; and even as a 'joyau méconnu de la poésie française'.[3]

---

[1] *Orages* (1949), p. 4.

[2] Guyonnet, 'Mauriac et le mythe d'Atys', I, 15.

[3] See, respectively, Quaghebeur, 'Une lecture du *Sang d'Atys*', p. 53; Monférier, *François Mauriac*, p. 115; Paule Lapeyre, '*La* [sic] *Sang d'Atys* poème de François Mauriac: mythe fondateur d'une vie, d'une œuvre et d'une pensée', in *Hommage à Claude Faisant (1932–1988)* (Les Belles Lettres, 1991), pp. 267–78 (p. 268); and François Mauriac, *L'Agneau*, ed. by François Durand (Flammarion, 1985), p. 209.

Mauriac's own obsession with the poem can be seen from a preface included in the manuscript, but omitted from the published text:

> j'ai vécu avec ce poème, le défaisant, le recomposant sans cesse. Le fond païen de ma nature s'y découvre jusqu'à l'horreur. Aussi dans des heures d'adoration, de terreur et de scrupule, l'ai-je souvent brûlé... Mais à chaque fois un ange ou un démon me tendait avec un sourire de moquerie, une copie oubliée.[4] Atys renaissait de ses cendres: constance étrange, à laquelle je cède enfin.
>
> Peut-être fallait-il que mes lecteurs connussent clairement l'être que je suis: la grâce dans un poète est surajoutée à la nature; mon œuvre est une de ces sources consacrées aux nymphes, dont l'Eglise transmit à ses saintes et à ses saints l'héritage. (*ORTC*, III, 1418)

What are we to make of this curious document? It holds out the promise of important revelations for the reader, yet this preface was not made available until forty years after the poem's publication. Perhaps Mauriac felt the preface provided *too* honest an insight into his religious struggles? But in that case, why keep it with the manuscript for later researchers to discover? Could this have been a deliberate ploy on his part (he was, after all, very alert to the issue of posthumous reputation)? Or did he perhaps choose not to publish the preface because he felt it was not honest *enough*? If the repeated incineration of the manuscript for moral reasons seems a little too dramatic, the repeated discovery of a 'forgotten' copy defies belief. Did he perhaps feel that he was guilty here of overdramatizing the interplay of conflicting forces? Whatever the reasons behind this preface and Mauriac's decision not to publish it, one thing emerges very clearly from his words: ambiguity and ambivalence are central to his poem. These are concepts to which I shall return.

The myth

As shown in the previous chapter, Mauriac was increasingly turning to mythical figures for his inspiration as a poet. Two important points emerge from Mauriac's handling of mythological material in *Orages*.

---

[4] Margaret Parry's suggestion that Mauriac might here be alluding to D. H. Lawrence seems too specific. Nevertheless, the parallels she adduces between Mauriac's poem and Lawrence's novels certainly open the possibility of the former having been influenced by the latter. See her 'Mauriac and D. H. Lawrence', in *François Mauriac: Visions and Reappraisals*, pp. 181–200 (pp. 191–96).

Firstly, he is primarily interested in those myths which he feels he can most readily relate to his own religious concerns; and, secondly, the only mythological figures in whom he appears to be interested as characters in their own right (as opposed to their symbolic value) are Attis and Cybele. These factors help explain why Mauriac should have chosen this particular myth (rather than that of Marsyas or Ganymede) for the subject of an entire cycle of poems. However, before turning to Mauriac's treatment of the myth, it will be useful to remind ourselves of the classical material he inherited.

Cybele was a Phrygian goddess whose cult went back to the second millennium BC:[5] 'Elle personnifie sous différents noms—Grande Mère, Mère des dieux, Grande Déesse—la puissance végétative et sauvage de la nature.' Apart from the story of her relationship with Attis, she figures little in myth. Her 'major importance lay in the orgiastic cult which grew up around her and which survived to a fairly late period under the Roman Empire'.[6] She is, in other words, a relatively straightforward figure. By contrast, the mythology of Attis is 'complex'.[7] This complexity begins with the story of Attis's father, Agdistis, a hermaphrodite begotten when Zeus spilt some semen on the earth. Agdistis was later castrated by the other gods (or by Dionysus alone) and from his/ her penis (or blood) sprang an almond (or pomegranate) tree. Nana, the daughter of the river-god Sangarius, picked an almond (or a fruit) from the tree and placed it in her lap (or inserted it in her womb), thus becoming pregnant and giving birth to Attis. At Sangarius's behest, she abandoned her son who was cared for by a goat (or taken in by passers-by and reared on honey and goat's milk). Attis grew up to be so beautiful that his father Agdistis, by now entirely female, fell in love with him. Attis was due to marry the daughter of King Midas of Pessinus, but Agdistis appeared (or there was an argument between Agdistis and Cybele) and a frenzied Attis castrated himself (beneath a pine tree in one version) and died. Cybele buried

---

[5] *The Encyclopedia of Religion*, ed. by Mircea Eliade, 16 vols (New York: Macmillan, 1987), IV, 185. The subsequent quotation is from Joël Schmidt, *Dictionnaire de la mythologie grecque et romaine* (Larousse, 1965), p. 86.

[6] Pierre Grimal, *The Penguin Dictionary of Classical Mythology*, ed. by Stephen Kershaw, trans. by A. R. Maxwell-Hyslop (Penguin, 1991), p. 112.

[7] *The Encyclopedia of Religion*, IV, 523. Subsequent details are taken from Grimal, *The Penguin Dictionary of Classical Mythology*, pp. 27–28.

Attis and violets grew from his blood spilt underneath the pine. Zeus granted a distraught Agdistis that her son's body should not decay, his hair should continue to grow, and his little finger should move. This original material was reshaped by the Latin poets Ovid and Catullus to give the most well-known versions of the myth. In Ovid's version, the beautiful 'Phrygian boy' conquers Cybele 'with pure love': 'She wanted to keep him as her shrine's guardian, | And said, "Desire to be a boy always."'[8] Attis, however, cheats Cybele with Sagaritis (a Naiad). In her wrath, Cybele cuts down the tree with which Sagaritis is associated and both tree and Naiad die. Attis goes mad and castrates himself. This act is very much the focus of Catullus's extraordinary poem (in which Sagaritis does not figure at all). Attis emasculates himself 'in the frenzy of his devotion to the Mother Goddess',[9] an act signalled in the Latin text by a change of grammatical gender. The mutilated Attis goes to the sea, but Cybebe (Catullus's name for Cybele) sends a lion to bring the youth back to her.[10]

It is evident that Mauriac knew this source material well. His version of the myth draws on many of the elements mentioned in the previous paragraph, often via quite subtle allusions. There are a number of elements about the Attis–Cybele myth that would immediately have attracted Mauriac: the background of incest and gender confusion; the attraction of a mother-figure for an adolescent male; the association of this mother-figure with the natural world; sexual betrayal and subsequent punishment; and the notion of life after death. The fact that the myth had not proved particularly popular with earlier French poets was an added bonus: Mauriac was in a position to produce a genuinely original work.[11] Most importantly, Mauriac saw how

---

[8] Ovid, *Fasti*, p. 89.

[9] Catullus, *The Poems of Catullus*, trans. by Peter Whigham (Harmondsworth: Penguin, 1966), p. 40.

[10] *Ibid.*, p. 139.

[11] I know of brief references to Atys and Cybèle in the medieval *Ovide moralisé*, in Bouchet's *Jugement poetic de l'honneur femenin* (1538), and in Ronsard's *Franciade* (1572), but it is doubtful whether these texts (with the possible exception of Ronsard's) would have had any impact on Mauriac. It is, however, likely that he knew Lully's *Atys*, a *tragédie lyrique* with libretto by Quinault, first performed in 1676. Among nineteenth-century works mentioning Atys and/ or Cybèle, Mauriac would certainly have been familiar with Maurice de Guérin's *Le Centaure*, Nerval's 'Le Christ aux Oliviers' and 'Horus' (*Les Chimères*), Baudelaire's 'J'aime le souvenir…'

he could relate this pagan myth to his own Christian concerns. In the early-twentieth century, specialists of ancient myth were drawing attention to the parallels between the Attis material and the biblical presentation of Christ's death and resurrection, arguing that the latter story was influenced by the former.[12] While Mauriac's lack of English would have placed Anglo-Saxon scholarship beyond his reach, he may have been familiar with Loisy's argument that 'la métaphore chrétienne et l'idée de régénération du fidèle dans le sang du Christ [...] procèdent de rites comme le taurobole et des idées qui s'attachaient à ces rites'.[13] Whether Mauriac knew Loisy's study or not, we find him in 1940 asserting that: 'Les mythes grecs préfiguraient la vérité chrétienne et le Christ est bien plus annoncé par les Grecs que par les prophètes juifs' (*LV* 242). The assertion is certainly debatable, but it helps account for the ease with which Mauriac could turn mythological material to his own, Christian ends.

Traditionally, however, the Cybele material had never been considered well suited to imparting moral lessons. Pépin explains that in the analysis provided by Varro, a Latin writer of the first century BC who offered an allegorical reading of Roman religion, '[le] dessein est toujours d'excuser l'immoralité, particulièrement rebutante, attachée

---

and 'Bohémiens en voyage' (*Les Fleurs du mal*), Verlaine's 'En bateau' (*Fêtes galantes*), Rimbaud's 'Soleil et chair' (*Poésies*), and with Flaubert's *La Tentation de Saint Antoine*. However, the references in all cases are only very brief and any 'influence' would therefore be quite limited.

[12] See, for example, James George Frazer, *Adonis, Attis, Osiris: Studies in the History of Oriental Religion*, 3rd edn (Macmillan, 1907), pp. 256–60 and John M. Robertson, *Pagan Christs: Studies in Comparative Hierology*, 2nd edn (Watts, 1911). More recently, Jonathan Z. Smith (*The Encyclopedia of Religion*, IV, 523) has pointed out that 'Attis is not, in his mythology, a dying and rising deity; indeed, he is not a deity at all' and suggests that it was probably under the influence of Christianity (the allegory of the *Naassene Sermon* and Firmicus Maternus's *De errore profanarum religionum*) that the notion of rebirth came to be attached to his cult.

[13] Alfred Loisy, *Les Mystères païens et le mystère chrétien* (Nourry, 1914), p. 121. The *taurobolium*, a rite associated with the cult of Cybele from the second century AD, involved the killing and castration of a bull. From the fourth century, the bull's blood was used in a baptismal ceremony for the priest. See *The Encyclopedia of Religion*, IV, 186.

au mythe et à la liturgie de cette déesse'.[14] On Attis and his possible
symbolic value, Varro remains silent; a silence commended by
Augustine who attributed it, not to ignorance, 'mais au dégoût, et à
l'impossibilité de découvrir une interprétation décente de cette peu
ragoûtante légende'. Mauriac was therefore rising to something of a
challenge by adopting this particular myth as the vehicle for an overtly
Christian poem.[15]

Structure
Le Sang d'Atys is made up of nineteen closely connected poems
forming a narrative whole. Sometimes terms or concepts used at the
end of one poem are repeated at the beginning of the next to foster a
sense of narrative continuity.[16] The story is told by four voices: those
of Cybèle, Atys, the narrator, and the author. The author figures only
at a paratextual level, being responsible for the poems' various titles.
These titles convey the broad outlines of the cycle's plot. It is worth
noting that they were a relatively late addition. In the proofs held at
the Bibliothèque Littéraire Jacques Doucet (MRC 2151), the poems
are simply numbered from I to XVIII (the 'missing' poem is ac-
counted for by the fact that 'La Guerre des Atys' is numbered 'XV
bis'). By including the titles, Mauriac underlines the cycle's narrative
dimension. He also emphasizes his Christian treatment of the pagan
myth via the foregrounding of terms such as 'sang', 'péché', 'chrétien', and 'grâce'. Cybèle and the narrator express themselves exclusively in alexandrines; the heptasyllabic line is reserved for Atys.
Table 15 gives an overview of the cycle:

---

[14] Jean Pépin, *Mythe et allégorie: les origines grecques et les contestations judéo-
chrétiennes*, rev. edn (Etudes Augustiniennes, 1976), p. 341. The next quotation is
from p. 342.
[15] Vermaseren highlights the struggle between Christianity and the Cybele cult in the
fourth century and states, *pace* Loisy, that: 'it is obvious that Attis could never be a
true counterpart of Christ.' See Maarten J. Vermaseren, *Cybele and Attis: The Myth
and the Cult*, trans. by A. M. H. Lemmers (Thames and Hudson, 1977), p. 180.
[16] See the transitions between poems 1 and 2 ('argile'/ 'chair'); 7 and 8 ('cheveux'/
'boucles'); 9 and 10 ('je ris'/ 'tu ris'); 10 and 11 ('cieux'/ 'cimes'); 14 and 15
('écorce'/ 'écorce'); and 17 and 18 ('peur'/ 'Je n'ose').

Table 15:

Poem no.	Title	No. of lines	Speaker
1	Plaintes de Cybèle	30	Cybèle
2	Atys à Cybèle	12	Atys
3	Atys vient	4	Narrator
4	Sommeil d'Atys	20	Cybèle (and narrator?)
5	Réveil d'Atys	16	Atys
6	Cybèle découvre qu'Atys n'est plus un enfant	16	Cybèle
7	Cantique de Cybèle	60	Cybèle (and some direct speech from Atys)
8	Les Boucles d'Atys	13	Cybèle
9	Reproches d'Atys à Cybèle	16	Atys
10	Cybèle irritée	8	Cybèle
11	Trahison d'Atys	15	Cybèle
12	Cybèle attend son heure	13	Narrator
13	Atys après le péché	9	Narrator
14	Atys est changé en pin	40	Cybèle and narrator
15	Atys sans nombre	14	Cybèle
16	La Guerre des Atys	16	Cybèle
17	Atys chrétien	12	Narrator
18	Cybèle regrette l'Atys païen	24	Narrator reports Cybèle's direct speech
19	Atys en état de grâce	52	Cybèle

The poems might be grouped together as follows:

(a) 1–3: introduction of the principal characters via the three main narrative voices.
(b) 4–8: Cybèle's desire for Atys.
(c) 9–13: Atys makes love to Sangaris.
(d) 14–16: Atys's metamorphosis.
(e) 17–19: Atys's conversion.

It is clear that the narrative dimension, an important element in all of Mauriac's verse, is particularly strong in *Le Sang d'Atys*, a poem defined by Favre as 'un récit à plusieurs personnages'.[17] Favre goes

---

[17] Yves-Alain Favre, '*Le Sang d'Atys*: poétique et poésie', in *Présence de François Mauriac*, pp. 243–54 (p. 244).

on to identify six characters: three whose voices we hear (Atys, Cybèle, and the narrator) and three who remain silent (Sangaris, the pagan gods, and the Christian God). I would add two more to this list: the curious 'Atys sans nombre' and a small group of miscellaneous minor figures. I shall offer an analysis of the poem by tracing the roles played by these eight (groups of) characters.

Atys
The collection's title implies a central, perhaps even heroic role for Atys. In one sense this is true, and yet: 'Il s'agit [...] d'un héros agi plutôt que d'un héros agissant.'[18] This is immediately evident from the fact that he is the speaker in only three of the cycle's nineteen poems (just over 10% of the total number of lines). However, whenever Cybèle speaks, she either addresses him or speaks about him in the third person. The only poem in which he does not feature directly is 'La Guerre des Atys' in which Cybèle addresses a collective Atys, rather than the individual character.

The poem's very first line is addressed to Atys: 'Ton rire jaillissait, vif entre les eaux vives' (447). The four occurrences of the /i/ sound (three of which fall on stressed syllables), coupled with the positive connotations of the words concerned, offer an immediate impression of joyous vitality on the part of Atys.[19] Of all the life on her surface, the earth-goddess says she can only feel 'les mains écorchées | D'Atys qui caressait l'herbe de mes cheveux' (447).[20] This *enjambement* draws attention to Atys's significance for Cybèle. The reference to him stroking her 'hair' suggests that their relationship is

---

[18] Quaghebeur, 'Une lecture du *Sang d'Atys*', p. 54.

[19] This line also offers an excellent example of Mauriac's careful craft. The four /i/ sounds form a pattern that is elegantly symmetrical without being overly schematic: the first two /i/ sounds occurring in syllables 2 and 5 of the first hemistich; the second two occupying syllables 7 and 12 of the second hemistich. In both cases, even though the /i/ sounds occupy different relative positions within their respective hemistichs, there is mirror symmetry around the hemistich's mid-point.

[20] Cf. the description of Atys's hair as 'l'obscure forêt' (447). Here again we find that blending of the human and the natural spheres that we saw in the poem 'Atys' in *Orages*.

gently sensual;[21] Lapeyre sees it in terms of a quasi-asexual mother–child bond.[22] Atys is certainly referred to in this opening poem as 'enfant' and the reference to his unfurrowed brow ('front désert') also points to his youthfulness, but when Cybèle says that the eyes of the sleeping Atys 'vont brûler sur un autre univers', there is already a hint of dormant sexual passion, especially as the eyes are said to possess 'flammes jumelles' (447).[23] The description of Atys's 'Visage dur, souillé de mûres et de boue' may also be significant in this connection, especially as the corresponding rhyme refers to 'l'argile de ta joue' (448). The terms 'souillé', 'boue', and 'argile' are all terms that Mauriac uses to refer to what he regards as humanity's fallen condition, especially in relation to sexual desire.[24]

In *Orages*, Atys's feelings towards Cybèle were clearly of a passionate nature. In *Le Sang d'Atys*, the situation is less clear. When Atys tells Cybèle that he cannot 'sortir de l'ombre | Que ton corps fait sur ma vie' (448), is this omnipresence something that infuriates or reassures him? The answer is uncertain. There is something rather oppressive about the series of nasal vowels and /ʀ/ sounds in the stanza from which this quotation is taken,[25] but, in the final stanza, the repeated /ʀ/ sounds seem rather to reinforce the notion of intimacy via a mingling of fluids that results in a characteristically Mauriacian emphasis on smell:

> Sous l'herbe, l'argile est dure.
> Ta rosée ou ma sueur
> Donnent au soir son odeur
> De terre et de chair obscure. (448)

---

[21] The verb *caresser* is used in a more overtly sexual context in the antepenultimate verse of 'Atys' (*Or* 428).

[22] Lapeyre, '*La* [sic] *Sang d'Atys*', p. 270.

[23] Such images are hardly original. The terms 'feu' and 'flammes', both used in this poem to describe Atys's eyes (447), were already 'hackneyed' metaphors for passion in seventeenth-century tragedy. See Peter France, *Racine's Rhetoric* (Oxford: Clarendon Press, 1965), p. 63.

[24] Cf. for example: 'Jusqu'à ce que [...] J'apparaisse souillé et nu dans ta lumière' (VAL, ll. 45–47); 'Un reflux de désirs, du plus profond des terres, | Remonte en moi, flot trouble et de boue épaissi' (*Or* 436); 'une pitié d'homme et de Dieu qui sait de quelle argile souillée il a pétri sa créature' (*ORTC*, III, 801).

[25] As if to emphasize Cybèle's influence, the stanza contains only feminine rhymes.

However, this hint that Atys may reciprocate Cybèle's feelings is not pursued. In the fourth poem, a series of negative statements is used to underline the apparent indifference of the sleeping Atys towards Cybèle's suffering (449). The third poem already shows Atys thinking about Sangaris; though she is not named, the 'invisibles bras' are clearly hers (448). We are then explicitly told that it is this nymph 'qu'il accueille en ses songes' (449). This is why, in poem 5, Atys refers to 'Le mensonge et le silence, | Les soldats de mon destin' (449): he wants to hide his desire for Sangaris from Cybèle. This same poem also contains the first reference to Atys's blood: 'Cybèle seule pénètre | Aux bords du fleuve de sang' (450).[26] The image has already been used in *Orages* with reference to sexual desire (*Or* 431); it has the same meaning here.

In poem 6, we see that Atys has definitively passed from childhood to adolescence. It is a transformation that coincides with the birth of spring. A series of sharp plosives signals his arrival on horseback, an arrival that is necessarily painful for the planet–goddess:

> J'eus froid. Je m'éveillai. Mon argile meurtrie
> Tressaillit sous le choc d'un galop furieux.
> De lourds sabots frappaient les chemins pleins de pluie
> […]. (450)

Atys's horse is presented in unmistakably phallic terms:

> Atys parut serrant de ses cuisses dorées
> Un court cheval hirsute, humide et blanchissant
> De l'écume et du sel que laissent les marées.[27] (450)

Although Cybèle can still refer to him as 'l'enfant' (450), the term is either ironic or used for the convenience of rhyme. Atys is naked and his post-pubescent body hair serves metonymically to underline his sexual maturity (as do the metaphors related to fire):

> Mais lui riait, couvert de ce léger pelage
> Dont la flamme montant du ventre jusqu'au cœur

---

[26] Guyonnet ('Mauriac et le mythe d'Atys', I, 362) views the penetration effected by Cybèle in terms of a maternal rape of the child.

[27] Cf. the references to 'écume' in sexual contexts in *Orages* (431, 437, 440, 441).

Embrasait tout son corps d'une fauve lueur. (451)

This laugh is altogether more defiant than the one mentioned in the cycle's opening line (447). Atys laughs again at the end of poem 9; a mocking laugh this time as he tells Cybèle that he thinks only of Sangaris (454). However, as this poem's title suggests ('Reproches d'Atys à Cybèle'), his mockery is born of disappointment. This is one of the rare poems in *Le Sang d'Atys* that gives the impression that Atys would have liked to be able to reciprocate Cybèle's passion, but, as he says to her in his most telling reproach: 'Tu n'es rien, tu n'es personne' (454).

The association between Atys and Christ is hinted at for the first time in poem 7. Humanity's painful co-existence with the earth is evoked in the first two stanzas in terms that recall the divine curse placed on the ground (with inevitable consequences for man) following the biblical story of the Fall. As part of his curse on the serpent, God says: 'Je mettrai une hostilité entre toi et la femme, entre ton lignage et le sien. Il t'atteindra à la tête et tu l'atteindras au talon.'[28] From the second century onwards, Christian commentators have often regarded this passage 'as the Protoevangelium, the first messianic prophecy in the OT'.[29] Cybèle's description of Atys seems to draw on this tradition: 'Mais savaient-ils que tu venais, toi, leur revanche, | M'arracher plus de pleurs qu'ils n'en avaient versés?' (*SA* 451). In the first of these two lines, the *rejet interne* emphasizes the significance of Atys's coming (the verb *venir* is, of course, pregnant with significance from a messianic perspective). It is true that the 'revanche' in question is that of humanity over the earth (not over the serpent), but Cybèle's later hostility towards the Christian God places her, from a biblical perspective, in the serpent's line. It might also be objected that the lines 'Ils ont frayé la route, ils ont coupé les branches, | Atys, pour que tes pieds ne fussent pas blessés' (451) conflict with the Genesis reference to a bruised heel. But here Mauriac is drawing on different messianic material. One thinks, for example, of John the Baptist's task of preparing the way for the Messiah and of the Devil's quotation of a

---

[28] Genèse 3. 15.
[29] Gordon J. Wenham, *Genesis 1–15* (Waco: Word Books, 1987), p. 81.

messianic Psalm as part of his temptation strategy: '*Sur leurs mains, ils te porteront, de peur que tu ne heurtes du pied quelque pierre.*'[30]

Even before his 'conversion', Atys exemplifies the pattern familiar from *Orages* as sated desire immediately gives way to remorse. We are told that, '[...] enfin remonté de l'abîme, il écoute | Les coups sourds de son cœur sous le pelage obscur' (456), and the recurring sounds (/k/, /u/ and /s/ in particular) underline not only the beating of Atys's heart, but also the insistent pulse of moral unease. The very next lines (the first in poem 13) read: 'Atys repu dans les ajoncs s'ouvre une voie. | Il s'y déchire, il fuit une nymphe qui pleure' (456). The $4 + 4 + 4$ rhythm found in the first of the lines is relatively unusual in Mauriac's verse: it draws attention to the significance of this moment when, for the first time, Atys turns his back on sexual desire. Nevertheless, despite his flight from Sangaris, Atys's situation remains ambivalent:

> Le regard de l'enfant où meurt l'immonde joie,
> Cet azur trouble encor où l'âme reprend vie
> Est un ciel tourmenté que le vent purifie.
> Mais sous les cils toujours sommeille une eau confuse,
> Dort un secret d'ardeur, de fatigue et de ruse. (456)

The reference to the purifying wind suggests certain Christian images used to describe the activity of the Holy Spirit;[31] in the case of Atys, the work of imparting prevenient grace (that is, the grace that *comes before* conversion) would be particularly apposite. But ('Mais ...'), at the same time, the image of 'une eau confuse' shows that desire remains part of Atys's experience (the five /d/ sounds give even greater prominence to the ternary structure in the final line quoted above).

This ambivalence is given powerful expression in the next poem when Cybèle transforms Atys into a pine tree:

> Livre en vain tes cheveux à tous les vents du monde!
> Tends tes branches au dieu que tu voudrais saisir!
> Rien, rien n'arrachera ta racine profonde

---

[30] See, respectively, Luc 3. 4–6 (quoting Isaïe 40. 3–5) and Luc 4. 11 (quoting Psaumes 91. 12).
[31] In the Bible, the Hebrew word *ruach* and the Greek word *pneuma* are translated as both *wind* and *spirit*.

A mon immense corps engourdi de plaisir. (457)

Atys is literally caught between heaven and earth. The situation is mirrored to some extent by sound patterning that suggests a balance of forces. Thus, in the first line just quoted, the first hemistich contains three /v/ sounds and one dental stop (/t/), whereas the second contains one /v/ and three dental stops (/t/ once and /d/ twice). And, in line 3, there is an intense cluster of /a/ sounds (five in all) around the caesura. Here this sound is closely connected with Cybèle's desire, but, in the next couple of lines, it is connected rather with divine love: 'Plus tu t'érigeras vers l'azur dont l'abîme | Recèle un pur amour inconnu de nos dieux [...]' (457). Another technique used to show the balance of opposing forces is that of internal rhyme, used at the beginning and end of the following line: 'Sa cime cherche un dieu, mais ses lentes racines [...]' (457), where /sasim/ is echoed by /ʀasin/.

Of course, while there may be syntactical and phonemic balance, the competing forces are far from equal. Cybèle has to cling to Atys's roots, while his branches strain heavenwards: his desire is now vertically oriented. By transforming him into a tree, Cybèle has actually transformed him into the Cross, 'ce gibet vide' (458), hence the capitalization of the word 'Arbre' in poem 14's opening stanza (457). The transformed Atys is not just identified with the Cross, but with Christ himself: the resin that Cybèle imagines flowing from his 'flanc' (457) is clearly reminiscent of the blood and water that flowed from Christ's pierced side.[32]

Although Cybèle enjoys the power of metamorphosis, we learn in poem 15 that she is unable to keep Atys where she wants him: he flees from his prison of bark, emerging as 'un Atys inconnu'. He is said to be 'gracile', to 'resurgir des ténèbres du bois', and to have a raindrop shining on his shoulder (458). Even though Atys has not yet been 'converted', there are lexical links here to Christian terms such as grâce and résurrection, and a connection via the water imagery to the sacrament of baptism.[33] We finally see a Christian Atys in poem 17. It is significant that the narrator should present his conversion primarily in terms of the death of libidinal desire: 'Il ne murmura pas le nom

---

[32] Jean 19. 34.

[33] Cf. in poem 18: 'La Grâce de son Dieu le couvre comme une eau' (460).

d'une mortelle | Ni ses mains ne cherchaient l'ombre d'un corps absent' (460). We learn in the next poem that even his physical appearance has changed: the 'boucles', 'front bas', and 'lèvres épaisses' of the 'Tendre Atys phrygien' whom Cybèle once possessed have all gone (460). There is no specific reference to Atys's self-castration in poem 17, only a periphrastic allusion in a manner reminiscent of Classical respect for *bienséance*: 'Tout désir avait fui de la grappe écrasée | Entre le corps obscur et la terre embrasée' (460).[34]

When Cybèle evokes Atys's self-castration in poem 18, she uses the concept of androgyny to explain the act:

> Cœur double rejeté par la mer des vieux âges,
> Doux être féminin dans un mâle exilé
> Qui, pour atteindre enfin l'impossible partage,
> Te déchiras la chair, d'un silex affilé. (460–61)

This idea is not something encountered previously in the poem, though it reminds us both of the way in which Attis becomes grammatically feminine in Catullus's poem after the act of self-castration and of the fact that Agdistis, Attis's father, was an hermaphrodite. Risse has related the theme to the homoerotic dimension of Mauriac's *œuvre*.[35] However, while it would certainly be legitimate to pursue such an approach, it is important to note that Cybèle is the speaker here and that her reliability as an interpreter is limited by her 'pagan' perspective. This poem begins: 'Je n'ose m'approcher de l'enfant, dit Cybèle. | J'aime les corps mais non les âmes immortelles' and continues: 'Dans la limpidité de cet Atys nouveau | Il ne subsiste rien de toi que je connaisse' (460). Cybèle must keep her distance; her ability to offer lucid comment is impaired. Implicitly, we are being encouraged to question her perspective (though the fact that her perspective exists at all shows that Mauriac does not want it simply to be ignored). The poet seems to be suggesting that the 'impossible partage' has at least as much to do with the body–soul dichotomy alluded to at the start of poem 18 as with issues of gender identity and/ or sexual orientation.

---

[34] Cf. in poem 18: 'La sombre grappe humaine arrachée à la treille' (461). The image reminds us that the blood of Atys is closely associated with the blood of Christ, represented by the juice of the grape in the Eucharist.

[35] Risse, *Homoerotik*, p. 209.

In order to highlight Cybèle's limited perspective, the poet seems on occasion to have given her lines whose significance transcends her intentions. Thus, when she says: 'La terre sèche but, lourdes gouttes d'orage, | Le sang noir que perdait l'éphèbe mutilé' (461), there appears to be an allusion to Luke's account of Christ's agony in Gethsemane: 'sa sueur devint comme de grosses gouttes de sang qui tombaient à terre.'[36] Similarly, in the lines: 'Dans le sable que tu souillais, sous un ciel bas, | Pauvre cœur, tu fuyais malgré ta plaie immonde' (461), the emphasis on the terms 'souillais' (a *rejet interne*) and 'immonde' (the rhyme word) causes us to wonder whether, from a Christian perspective, such terms are at all appropriate. Finally, however, it is as though the poet is unable to maintain Cybèle's pagan perspective, for she concludes with the lines: 'Tu fuyais, ignorant qu'à chacun de tes pas | Le sang trouble d'Atys ensemençait le monde' (461). While this could be an allusion to the way in which Attis's blood caused violets to grow in the original myth (and, indirectly, to the fact that Attis's conception can be traced back to the blood of his father's castration), the words have a much stronger Christian resonance.[37]

The portrait of Atys painted by Cybèle at the start of the final poem is still marked by a degree of uncertainty:

> Ton Dieu t'a délivré du monstre vil et tendre
> Dont tu n'as rien gardé que ce qu'il faut de cendre
> Pour recouvrir un feu qui ne s'éteindra plus.
> Et moi, Cybèle, autour du cœur où ce feu couve,
> J'hésite gémissante et rôde à pas de louve,
> Je pleure de te voir si frêle et si puissant. (461)

The image of fire presumably now refers to religious, rather than sexual desire. Paradoxically, although this fire will never go out, it is still capable of being smothered by the ashes of the 'monstre vil et tendre'. Indeed, these antithetical adjectives themselves (like those at the end of the last line quoted above) point to that essentially Mauriacian quality of ambivalence. Cybèle seeks to exploit this by tempting Atys

---

[36] Luc 22. 44.

[37] Cf. Christ's words in Matthieu 13. 37–38: 'Celui qui sème le bon grain, c'est le Fils de l'homme; le champ, c'est le monde; le bon grain, ce sont les sujets du Royaume' and in Jean 12. 24: 'si le grain de blé tombé en terre ne meurt pas, il demeure seul; mais s'il meurt, il porte beaucoup de fruit.'

with a combination of the smell of Sangaris's body and sultry summer heat: 'Mais en vain! Les genoux salis d'un peu de glaise, | Tu te dresses, plus fort que l'été délirant' (462).[38] The shift in connotation as we move from the first of these lines ('salis', 'glaise') to the second (Atys's triumph) is reminiscent of Paul's comments on the transition from the first to the last Adam.[39] Atys's triumph is explicit by the end of the first stanza as he emerges as finally impervious to the power of the *libido sentiendi*:

> De l'océan livide et des tristes forêts
> Ni ton sang, ni ta chair ne demeurent complices:
> Ton corps n'obéit plus au flux ni au reflux,
> A la sève qui sourd Atys n'obéit plus.
> Cet enfant maigre et dur connaît d'autres délices,
> Un autre brisement, une meilleure mort,
> Que la vague arrachée à l'abîme d'un corps. (462)

This is a rare moment of deliverance in Mauriac's *œuvre*. His verse (particularly in the post-1914 period), has been dominated by terms such as *sang*, *chair*, *complice*, *corps*, and *flux*; they appear now finally to have lost their power. We saw in 'Sacré-cœur' how the adjective *autre* could be used with reference either to God or sexual desire (*Or* 441). In the quotation above, only the former of these possibilities is retained. Indeed, the phrasing of this passage as a whole seems deliberately designed to counter the kind of imagery found in the previous collection.

Cybèle

As befits her status as the earth-goddess, Cybèle speaks most of the poem's lines (nearly 80%). Yet, despite her divine status and textual pre-eminence, we are immediately shown her weakness in the opening poem: 'Atys, tu me brûlais de ta petite bouche, | Je n'avais pas de bras pour enserrer ton corps' (447). Her tragedy lies in her physical incom-

---

[38] The insistent /t/ and /d/ sounds of this second line recall the poem's opening four lines where these same two sounds are used to help emphasize the triumph of the Christian God—'*Ton Dieu*' (461).

[39] I Corinthiens 15. 45–49. The Pauline contrast is made in the context of a general discussion of resurrection (verses 35–57). This whole passage provides a relevant intertext for the conclusion of Mauriac's poem.

patibility with the one she loves: the /p/ plus /b/ combination of 'petite bouche' (emphasizing Atys's human stature) is ironically mirrored in 'pas de bras' (underlining Cybèle's non-human frame).[40] Her frustration will ultimately lead to a violent reaction; this is already prefigured in the very first verb of which Cybèle is the subject: *déchirer* (447). Despite his physical insignificance, a series of hyperboles shows the extent of Cybèle's love for Atys: his face shines more brightly for her than the stars, she feels his hands rather than all the other animal life on the surface of the planet (her body), and a single one of his tears means more to her than all the world's streams and torrents (447–48). The poem's very title ('Plaintes de Cybèle') alludes to her unhappiness, as do lines such as 'Ma douleur sur la mer poussant un cri farouche', 'Enfant qui me dévaste, océan qui me ronge' (447), and 'ô toi qui m'as perdue' (448). This use of the verb *perdre* (with the past participle in the emphatic rhyme position) perhaps provides a hint of the Christian perspective adopted by Mauriac in this poem. This becomes even clearer in the next poem when reference is made to Cybèle's 'chair perdue' (448). But, from Mauriac's Christian perspective, 'le Fils de l'homme est venu chercher et sauver ce qui était perdu'.[41] This theme will become particularly apparent in the cycle's conclusion.

Cybèle's obsession with Atys emerges particularly clearly in her long 'Cantique'. As so often in literature, the imagery of food is used with reference to sexual appetite:

> Nourriture mortelle et pourtant infinie,
> Ce visage de lait, ce visage de sang
> N'est plus qu'un fruit tombé dans mes paumes unies,

---

[40] There is something of a tension between Cybèle's non-humanity and the degree to which she is personified in the poem. There is a sense in which, for Mauriac, nature is indeed human. He disagrees with Newman that nature has nothing to do with the Adamic Fall: 'la nature est devenue humaine', Mauriac insists, 'elle est faite de la cendre du péché humain et ne ressemble en rien à ce qu'elle était lorsqu'elle naquit dans la pensée de Dieu' (*OC*, XI, 21). Such a view helps explain why Mauriac sees Cybèle's redemption as being bound up with the resurrection of the 'innombrables Atys': 'Vous êtes ma poussière, | Ma poussière, c'est vous qui ressusciterez' (*SA* 462). Cf. Daniel 12. 2.

[41] Luc 19. 10. The importance Mauriac attached to these words is evident from the fact that he gave the title *Ce qui était perdu* to one of his novels.

> Qui, dévoré sans cesse, est toujours renaissant. (452)

Cybèle is similar to those 'ogresses' that surface periodically in Mauriac's work: older women ever ready to consume young men.[42] There is, however, a significant difference: Atys's substance is inexhaustible (as emphasized in the paradoxical first line quoted above). Cybèle will therefore never be able to appropriate him: 'Mon soleil ne se couche pas sur ton empire' (453). As the negative verbal construction stretches over this line's caesura, so the influence of Atys over Cybèle knows no bounds. But all he is prepared to offer her is 'le culte affreux' of his piety (453). Cybèle's reaction—'Epargne-moi l'autel, les victimes, les feux...' (453)—is strangely reminiscent of Jahweh's rejection of the formal worship of Israel.[43] However, whereas Jahweh asks rather for 'le droit' and 'la justice', Cybèle wants only the 'feu d'aurore' on Atys's cheek and 'l'animal encens qui naît de [s]es cheveux' (453).

Cybèle may be obsessed with Atys, but she also has her regal pride.[44] In the tenth poem, her tone of lament changes to one of anger in response to Atys's laughter: 'Tremble! Ton souffle naît du souffle de Cybèle' (455). The accent is reminiscent of one of Racine's heroines.[45] The next poem shows us her hatred and fury as she vents her rage against Atys and Sangaris as they make love. Her accent is now that of the puritanical Christian moralist as she refers to 'cette chair souillée' (455), though, of course, it is jealousy, rather than a patristic view of the flesh, that is meant to motivate such terminology.

Her suffering finally drives Cybèle to change Atys into a pine tree. She is careful to present this action not as a product of pique ('J'ai feint d'être jalouse, Atys, et je me flatte | D'avoir d'un faux-semblant joué les dieux du ciel'), but as a means of achieving her own sexual fulfilment: 'Rien, rien n'arrachera ta racine profonde | A mon immense corps engourdi de plaisir' and '[...] Plus tes membres profonds jouiront de leur crime | Dans la nuit de mon corps que j'ai fermé

---

[42] See, for example, *ORTC*, II, 625, 730; IV, 670.

[43] Amos 5. 21–23. The next quotations are from 5. 24.

[44] She is described as a 'reine' in poem 4 (449).

[45] Cf. Esther addressing Aman: 'Tremble. Son jour approche, et ton règne est passé.' See Jean Racine, *Œuvres complètes*, ed. by Georges Forestier, new edn (Gallimard, 1999–), I: *Théâtre. Poésie* (1999), p. 994.

sur eux' (457). The phallic connotations of this language are obvious. Eventually even a tree will rot and die, but Cybèle remains defiant: 'Je tends cet arbre mort aux dieux que je défie. | Je me ramasse toute autour d'un arbre mort' (458). These lines (like so many in this fourteenth poem) are deliberately ironic: Cybèle is unaware that this 'arbre mort' is symbolic of the Cross and that, in Mauriac's theology, the Cross is indeed at the centre of her being.[46] When she says: 'Mes vignes, mes forêts et mes sillons avides | Jaillissent en rayons de ce corps calciné' (458), she unwittingly articulates a vision of a christocentric natural world.[47] This is why Mauriac has her say of Atys's dead roots: 'Reptiles embaumés que rien ne putréfie, | Au cadavre d'Atys ils emmêlent mon sort' (458), though the full significance of these words will not emerge until the final poem.

When Cybèle sees the Christian Atys, she is afraid of the 'Dieu couvert de sang' who indwells 'cet être éphémère' (460). She does not dare approach 'cet Atys nouveau', for 'la Grâce de son Dieu le couvre comme une eau' (460). In the last poem, having failed to reawaken the sensual Atys even when she calls the hated Sangaris to her aid, Cybèle finally admits defeat before this God. This acknowledgement is contained in the poem's first stanza; in the second, Cybèle becomes the unexpected herald of the Christian doctrine of a general resurrection at the end of time:

> Au dernier jour, ces corps confondus en Cybèle,
> Les milliards de morts qui dorment dans la mer,
> Se précipiteront hors de mon flanc ouvert.
> [...]
> C'est pour ne pas mourir que Cybèle éphémère
> Épouse étroitement vos corps ensevelis,
> Innombrables Atys! Vous êtes ma poussière,
> Ma poussière, c'est vous qui ressusciterez. (462)

---

[46] Cf. Mauriac's comments on Rimbaud and the Cross (*ORTC*, II, 795–96).

[47] Cf. 'Cybèle est purifié par Celui que je ne vois pas; elle se referme sur Lui; elle Le cache sous des pierres, dans des feuilles; elle Le contient: l'ostensoir a des rayons de vignes et de forêts' (*OA* 154).

There are unmistakable echoes of biblical language here, especially in the first three lines.[48] The use of the verb *se précipiter* also provides a response to 'Péché mortel': 'Mais la marche du temps, désespérément lente, | Se précipitera lorsque nous serons nus' (*Or* 429). In terms of verisimilitude, Cybèle's sudden transformation from a pagan goddess barely conscious of 'l'Inconnu' (*SA* 462) to an exponent of eschatological orthodoxy is scarcely credible, but, then, verisimilitude can hardly be considered a relevant criterion on which to judge a mythological poem.[49] The purpose of the transformation is clearly to suggest Cybèle's own redemption in terms that do not necessitate her 'conversion'. As Favre puts it: 'Une religion ne vient pas en remplacer une autre. Le Christianisme assume le paganisme et le sanctifie.'[50]

Narrator
The narrative voice is responsible for just under 10% of the poem's lines. The narrator's main function is to provide a moral (and, ultimately, religious) perspective on events. He first intervenes in the third poem, picking up language and ideas already familiar from the two preceding pieces, but adding a specifically moral dimension. For example, when we are told with reference to Atys that 'Cybèle ne sent rien que ce corps *infidèle* | Qui *gémit* et qui *souffre* en d'invisibles bras' (448), the words I have italicized are intended to convey a negative impression of sexual activity. The second intervention (lines 6–7 of the fourth poem) has a similar function: 'Et Cybèle frémit jusque dans ses abîmes | De ce *trouble* abandon sans caresse et sans *crime*'

---

[48] 'Au dernier jour' is a common phrase in John's gospel (Jean 6. 39–40, 44, 54; 11. 24; 12. 48). In the same gospel, Jesus also says: 'elle vient, l'heure où tous ceux qui sont dans les tombeaux entendront sa voix et sortiront: ceux qui auront fait le bien, pour une résurrection de vie, ceux qui auront fait le mal, pour une résurrection de jugement' (5. 28–29). Christ's note of judgement, is absent from Mauriac's vision: as ever, he prefers to privilege the notion of divine mercy. Finally, Cybèle's 'flanc ouvert' recalls the wound Christ received in his side while on the Cross (Jean 19. 34).

[49] When he visited Greece in 1936, Mauriac was struck by how religious the ancient Greeks had been: 'Je ne crois pas à l'impiété de Périclès ni à celle de Phidias', he writes, 'peut-être étaient-ils sensibles à ce vide que l'Incarnation a comblé' (*OC*, XI, 196). In Mauriac's own mind at least, therefore, the christianization of a goddess associated with this pagan culture would not have seemed totally incongruous.

[50] Favre, '*Le Sang d'Atys*', p. 252. This idea owes something to the vision of Mauriac's patron saint, Francis of Assisi (*OC*, XI, 234–35).

(449; my italics). Although the rest of the poem is spoken by Cybèle as she watches Atys sleeping, the italicized terms reveal the narrator's moralizing presence as he momentarily assumes control of the text.

The narrator resumes direct control of the text in poems 12 and 13, whose close relationship is evident from the fact that the title of poem 12, 'Cybèle attend son heure', is actually reproduced in poem 13 (456). Cybèle has just seen Atys and Sangaris making love; the context is ideal for the narrator's moral perspective to be brought to the fore. This is most obviously seen in the title of poem 13: 'Atys après le péché'—sin being a specifically Judaeo-Christian concept. The narrator's moral perspective is also revealed in his choice of highly charged terms such as 'corps impurs', 'déroute', 'abîme', 'proie', 'immonde joie', and 'azur trouble' (456). Surprisingly, perhaps, the narrator's Christian sympathies lie with the pagan goddess. He is anxious to spare her pain: 'Il faut fermer les yeux, Cybèle, ou que tu partes! | Tu souffres trop', and he empathizes with her suffering: 'Tu subis les soupirs jaillis de cette couche | Et ces cris insultant ton ombre et ton azur' (456). Atys, on the other hand, is clearly viewed as guilty (all of the isolated terms listed above relate to him). The narrator also takes this opportunity to prepare for future developments. When he seeks to comfort Cybèle with the words: 'Mais tu sais que ce feu qui brûle les planètes | Meurt parfois au secret des humains et des bêtes' (456), there is a suggestion that Sangaris will not always interest Atys. Similarly, when Atys cuts himself on the reeds when fleeing from Sangaris, the verb (*déchirer*) is the same as will be used to describe his self-castration (456, 461).

The narrator intervenes again for a single stanza in poem 14:

> Mais, brève éternité dont Cybèle s'enchante,
> Toute étreinte a fini quand les dieux l'ont voulu.
> Homme, arbre, sève ou sang ou résine gluante,
> Un jour, fleuve brûlant, tu ne couleras plus. (457)

Cybèle has been exulting in the phallic symbolism of Atys's roots. The narrator immediately undercuts her jubilation with the oxymoronic 'brève éternité'. By introducing the theme of death, he reorients the poem away from Cybèle's libidinal pleasure to the allusions to the Cross that dominate the remaining four stanzas. This type of narratorial intervention is common in Mauriac's novels. Indeed, Sartre had taken him to task for it in the pages of the *NRF* a year before the same journal published *Le Sang d'Atys*.[51]

Given what we have seen so far, it is not surprising that it should be left to the narrator to announce the appearance of 'Atys chrétien'. This poem obviously represents a highly significant turning point, and this is signalled formally by the fact that it is the only poem in the cycle that adheres to a single basic rhyme scheme (alternating feminine–masculine couplets throughout). His moralizing discourse is less in evidence in this poem, though the inversion of 'Tranquille et pur coulait ce flot de jeune sang' (460) emphasizes positive terms that contrast with the more negative judgements seen in earlier poems.[52]

Sangaris

Sangaris is one of the nymphs referred to collectively in the opening poem: 'Les gaves dont les eaux par les cailloux brisées | Agitent les cheveux des nymphes enlisées' (448). She will not remain waterbound for long. As Atys sleeps in the fourth poem, we are told: 'La nymphe Sangaris qu'en un songe il accueille | Agite les bas-fonds sous l'eau qui ne dort pas' (449). Although Atys may be asleep, his unconscious mind (symbolized here by the water) remains active. The image of Sangaris stirs his sexual desires: the term 'bas-fonds' relates both to Christianity's vertical scale of moral values and to the kind of diagrammatic representation used by Freud to explain the workings of the mind.[53] The description of the pair making love shows that Mauriac is not immune to the beauty of human sexuality:

> Deux pâles univers l'un dans l'autre perdus:
> Atys et Sangaris, dont la blancheur humaine,
> L'espace d'un éclair, déconcerta ma haine. (455)

---

[51] Jean Paul [sic] Sartre, 'M. François Mauriac et la liberté', *La Nouvelle Revue Française*, 52 (January–June 1939), 212–32.

[52] One thinks in particular of the line 'Un jour, fleuve brûlant, tu ne couleras plus' (457), a kind of prophecy whose fulfilment we see in the line just quoted from 'Atys chrétien'.

[53] Cf. Sigmund Freud, *The Pelican Freud Library*, trans. and ed. by James Strachey and others, 15 vols (Harmondsworth: Penguin, 1973–86), XI: *On Metapsychology: The Theory of Psychoanalysis*, ed. by Angela Richards (1984), p. 363.

It is perhaps significant that the only occurrence of the word 'bonheur' comes in this same poem with reference to the lovers' post-coital slumber. However, Mauriac's intentions in this poem are such that this happiness cannot be allowed to last.

Sangaris's great advantage over Cybèle is that she has an embraceable body. The poet underlines this in his manipulation of versification:

> Tu souffres trop. La main de Sangaris écarte
> Sur le front du berger les sauvages cheveux,
> Et le vol titubant de sa petite bouche
> Erre sans se poser sur un visage en feu. (456)

In the first of these four lines, the word 'main' is emphasized as a result of its occupying the sixth syllable. Similarly, the nymph's 'petite bouche' is also emphasized because of its position at the end of the line (the rhyme with 'couche' underlines the sexual physicality of this mouth). It should be remembered that attention has already been drawn to Atys's 'petite bouche' in the opening poem as a means of stressing the incompatibility between Atys and Cybèle (447).

After a brief reference to her crying in poem 13 (456), presumably because Atys chooses to flee her, and allusions to 'une mortelle' and 'un corps absent' in poem 17 (460), we do not read of Sangaris again until the final poem when Cybèle causes the wind to bring 'le parfum du corps de Sangaris' to Atys (462). Cybèle refers to the nymph as the 'Rivale que je hais, que j'appelle à mon aide' (462), the paradox finding natural reinforcement through the structure of the alexandrine. Given Mauriac's intense awareness of olfactory impressions, it is hardly surprising that Cybèle should seek to rekindle Atys's desire through a smell. Nevertheless, on this occasion even aromas remain without effect and Sangaris disappears definitively from the poem.

The Collective Atys
Although they are not given the name Atys, the 'mille précurseurs' mentioned in poem 7 (451) are clearly related to the 'Atys sans nombre' who will appear later in the cycle (458–59). The relationship between Cybèle and these ancestors is based on conflict: humanity seeks to tame nature (*posséder, fouler, frayer, couper* are the verbs

used), but progress is painful: 'Les ronces de mon cœur griffaient leurs jambes nues | Et mes branchages fous faisaient saigner leurs mains' (451). As previously suggested, the situation is reminiscent of the cursing of the earth in the Book of Genesis. Yet, if there is conflict, there is also passion: these ancestors are Cybèle's 'amants d'autrefois' (451).

In 'Atys sans nombre', we learn that every age has produced an Atys who was 'infidèle' to Cybèle. Every time Cybèle transforms one of these Atys into a pine, another Atys emerges and, as she says, 'me fixant d'un œil pur et sauvage, | Attend de moi l'aveu de son propre secret' (459). In other words, the story narrated thus far by the poem is part of a recurring cycle. Both Atys and Cybèle are locked into an infinitely repeatable tragedy. There is a parallel here with what Yves Frontenac thinks of as 'la nécessité aveugle, [...] cette chaîne sans fin de monstres tour à tour dévorants et dévorés'. For him, the only way out of this impasse is for the 'adorable bouleversement' of love, 'le mystère du Christ', to interrupt the destructive cycle (*ORTC*, II, 605). This is precisely the element that Mauriac imports into his poem. His Christian perspective does not, of course, belong to the original myth, nor does his concept of an endless series of Atys. The two additions are linked: by turning Atys into a recurring character, Mauriac effectively casts him in the role of Everyman. The Christian redemption of the most recent Atys will therefore apply retrospectively to all his forerunners.

'La Guerre des Atys' is another of Mauriac's additions to the ancient myth. Its function is presumably to show that the tragedy of the human condition resides not only in the sort of problems encountered in the Cybèle–Atys–Sangaris triangle, but also in the horror of war. For Durand, this poem expresses Mauriac's 'angoisse devant la guerre imminente'.[54] While this is probably true, I would suggest that the poem also forms part of his retrospective reflection on the slaughter of the *First* World War. In the first six lines, there are a series of noun phrases in which the adjectives serve to create a sense of foreboding: 'une sanglante gloire', 'ce soupir inhumain', 'la verdure noire', 'leurs aveugles mains', 'adolescents cruels', and 'enfants immolés' (459).

---

[54] François Durand, 'Richesse et ambiguïté mythiques du *Sang d'Atys*', *NCFM*, 9 (2001), 89–99 (p. 98).

The last two examples underline the brutality of combat with particular clarity. The battle itself is not described, but, in the second half of the poem, Cybèle addresses the dead:

> O seins chastes d'Atys, ô poitrine inféconde,
> Purs espaces du corps frémissants et déserts,
> Impénétrable cœur qu'une flèche traverse,
> O cuisses qu'écorchaient les ronces et les houx,
> Devrai-je boire au fleuve pourpre né de vous,
> Moi qui n'eus jamais soif que du froid des averses? (459)

In apostrophizing various body parts, Cybèle implicitly draws attention to the dismembered corpses on the battlefield. Her distress (which is also Mauriac's as he remembers his experiences during the Great War) is seen in the rhetorical question of the last two lines.

Significantly, the cycle concludes by focusing not on the individual Atys who dominates the early poems (*tu*), but on the *vous* of the resurrected 'Innombrables Atys' (462). Since Mauriac regarded Christ's message as having a significance that transcended the confines of Catholicism, it is appropriate that his vision of redemption should be presented in these generalized terms.[55] The final few lines draw on the maritime imagery found in *Orages*, but this imagery is now pressed into unambiguously Christian service:

> Le calme de la mer à vos cœurs enchaînée
> Se mue en cette Paix qu'il vous avait donnée.
> Mes fureurs qui jonchaient les plages de débris
> Et ce halètement de la houle marine
> Dont le souffle arrachait aux pins blessés des cris,
> De tout temps à jamais gonflent votre poitrine
> Lorsque, le front levé, vous contemplez le Fils. (463)

The concatenation of the terms *houle*, *gonfler*, and *poitrine* is also found twice in Mauriac's War poetry (VAL, ll. 21–23 and MP, VI,

---

[55] Although Mauriac never discusses the nature and extent of the Atonement from a theological perspective, in *Ce que je crois* (1962), he reflects on 'toutes les demeures qu'il y a dans la maison du Père' (an allusion to Christ's words in Jean 14. 2) and suggests that there will be room for Protestants, Jews, Muslims, and even for militant atheists who, in their passion for human dignity, unwittingly 'cherchent en dehors de tout intérêt temporel le royaume de Dieu et sa justice' (*OA* 596).

14–15). This supports my suggestion that the collective Atys relates back to Mauriac's sense of horror over the butchery of the Great War. It is important for Mauriac that such pointless destruction should not be presented as the end of the story.

Miscellaneous figures

This category includes a figure such as the Gorgon, mentioned in poem 8: 'Les reptiles tordus au front de la Gorgone | N'ont pas fait tant de mal que tes boucles d'enfant' (453). The reference is essentially decorative: the poet draws on another mythological figure to generate a strongly ironic comparison.

The only other figures occur in poem 18 after Atys has castrated himself:

> Les ménades couraient sur sa trace vermeille
> Avec des rires fous et des appels stridents.
> Et même la plus jeune approcha de ses dents
> La sombre grappe humaine arrachée à la treille.
> [...]
> Les enfants des pêcheurs menaçaient de leur fronde
> Ta chair blessée à mort et qui ne mourait pas [...]. (461)

The reference to the Maenads picks up on an element in Catullus's poem.[56] The Maenads were female devotees of Bacchus (indeed, they are more commonly known as Bacchantes) whose worship was characterized by mystical, wine-induced frenzies. In this poem, they function as the epitome of 'fleshly' desire (their obsession is reflected in the insistent /a/ sound, used fourteen times in the first four lines quoted above), symbolizing the sphere from which Atys seeks to escape via his self-emasculation. 'Les enfants des pêcheurs', on the other hand, do not figure in the original myths, though there is an emphasis on the sea in Catullus's poem.[57] The reference is baffling. Perhaps Mauriac invented them as a means of symbolizing the New Testament view of the hostility between 'le monde' and those associated with Christ.[58] Perhaps he refers to them as 'les enfants des

---

[56] *The Poems of Catullus*, p. 137.

[57] *Ibid.*, p. 139.

[58] See, for example, Jean 15. 18–19 and I Jean 3. 12–13.

pêcheurs' because of the phonemic proximity of *pêcheurs* to *pécheurs*, but this is simply conjecture.

Pagan gods

Although she is herself a pagan goddess, Cybèle's attitude towards her fellow deities is marked by conflict. This emerges in the very first reference to the pagan gods: 'Il dort. Je forcerai les dieux même à se taire. | J'anéantis le monde autour d'Atys qui dort' (449). The *rejet interne* in the first of these two lines underlines the force of Cybèle's will in this matter. She has no personal antagonism towards the gods; the only reason for her aggressive stance is the exclusive nature of her passion for Atys: she wants nothing to distract her from her contemplation of the young shepherd.

The gods are next mentioned in poem 6 when Atys first emerges as an adolescent: 'De lourds sabots frappaient les chemins pleins de pluie | Et jetaient de la boue à la face des dieux' (450). The gods function here as representatives of that symbolic system of order that Atys dares to defy under the impulse of libidinal desire. They have a similar role in poem 11 when Cybèle sees Atys and Sangaris making love: 'Mais l'âpre paradis où ces corps m'avaient fuie, | Le Plaisir, les rendait indifférents aux dieux' (455).[59]

There are a number of references to the gods in poem 14, all of them negative. Cybèle says: 'J'ai feint d'être jalouse, Atys, et je me flatte | D'avoir d'un faux-semblant joué les dieux du ciel' (457). The remark is dismissive: pagan gods are viewed as being motivated by petty emotions; Cybèle implies that she is above such behaviour. The gods are also characterized by their ignorance (and, implicitly, by their impurity): 'un pur amour inconnu de nos dieux' (457). Cybèle is in a state of conflict with them because of her cult for Atys: 'Je tends cet arbre mort aux dieux que je défie' (458). Finally, they appear in a rather unflattering simile: 'Les astres, dans leur nuit cherchant ce gibet vide, | Comme un troupeau de dieux ont vers lui cheminé' (458). The collective noun 'troupeau', usually associated with sheep or goats, leaves little room for divine dignity. There is, however, a hint here

---

[59] It is worth noting how the /p/ sound is used here to illuminate the tension in the oxymoron: from Cybèle's jealous perspective, this 'paradis' is 'âpre' because it consists of the lovers' 'Plaisir'.

that even the pagan gods will benefit from what Paul views as Christ's cosmic reconciliation.[60]

The Christian God

The second stanza of the opening poem begins somewhat obscurely: 'Une ligne de sable, un renflement de dune, | Une frange d'écume et de varech: la mer…' (447). If this were simply a description of a beach, it would seem strangely superfluous. It could be viewed as an oblique evocation of the face of Atys, 'Enfant qui me dévaste, *océan qui me ronge*' (447; my italics), but it could also be the first suggestion of the presence of the Christian God. The words 'la mer' certainly receive considerable emphasis in the lines just quoted: their position at the end of the line means that they are naturally stressed, but they also come after a verbless ternary structure followed by a colon suggestive of expectancy; the three dots after the word 'mer' further encourage us to consider the significance of this reference to the sea. In the Christian tradition, the sea has often been used as a metaphor for God's power and the vastness of his love. It is a symbol that Mauriac employs most memorably in the epigraph and title of *Les Chemins de la mer* (*ORTC*, III, 541). Given the close connections between this novel and Mauriac's poem, it seems probable that the lines in 'Plaintes de Cybèle' do indeed allude to the God of Christianity—a presence that is as yet merely hinted at.

The next reference is almost as veiled. In poem 7, Cybèle cries out to Atys:

> Roule dans ma ténèbre, ô fleuve de lumière,
> De peur qu'un dieu ne jette avec les astres morts
> Cette chair qui sans toi redeviendrait poussière,
> — Cybèle à qui le ciel est caché par ton corps! (452)

Although the identity of this god is far from clear, the use of terms such as 'ténèbre', 'lumière', 'chair', 'poussière', and 'ciel'—all of which have particular resonance in a Christian context—suggests a

---

[60] Cf. Colossiens 1. 19–20: 'car Dieu s'est plu à faire habiter en lui toute la Plénitude et par lui à réconcilier tous les êtres pour lui, aussi bien sur la terre que dans les cieux, en faisant la paix par le sang de sa croix.' My suggestion assumes that the simile in *Le Sang d'Atys* also functions as a kind of identification, i.e., that the stars are not just like pagan gods, but that they somehow represent them as well.

possible link with the God of Christianity. The same is true a couple of stanzas further on when Cybèle detects 'la trace [...] d'un chasseur inconnu' on the body of Atys (452). She interprets what she sees in terms of sexual activity; despite Atys's denials, she may well be correct to do so. Nevertheless, references elsewhere to 'le Dieu de proie' (*Or* 444) and a 'Chasseur divin' (*OA* 122) suggest that the 'chasseur inconnu' in *Le Sang d'Atys* also alludes, at least in part, to the hidden activity of the Christian God.

The allusions to the Christian God become more explicit in poem 14 where the transformed Atys raises his branches towards 'l'essence divine', 'un dieu' (as opposed to the plural *dieux* of mythology), and 'un pur amour inconnu de nos dieux' (457). In the poem's final stanza, Cybèle also alludes to the myth of Zeus and Ganymede:

> Et seule, je ne sais, noire colonne, ô pâtre,
> Doux arbre humain qui fus de feuilles frémissant,
> Sur ton cadavre nu, quel aigle va s'abattre,
> S'agriffer à l'écorce et te couvrir de sang... (458)

The prominent plosives (especially the /t/, /k/, and /g/ sounds) give a certain harshness to the final two lines, especially when set against the alliterative /f/ sounds of line 2. This harshness is perhaps reminiscent of the note of divine sadism suggested in the mythical poems at the end of *Orages*—including, of course, 'Ganymède chrétien'.

Appropriately enough, Mauriac waits until the poem 'Atys chrétien' before alluding directly (via the simple technique of capitalization) to the Christian God: 'Un Dieu souffrait au cœur de cet être éphémère', 'Un Dieu couvert de sang dont Cybèle avait peur' (460). The paradoxes of eternal Deity *suffering* in ephemeral humanity[61] and of a bloody (and therefore apparently defeated) God inspiring fear in a rival goddess point to what is probably the most significant of all Christian doctrines for Mauriac: the Incarnation. In the next poem, the association between Atys and the Christian God is taken a step further: Cybèle refers to 'son Dieu' (460), rather than just 'un Dieu' as in the preceding quotations.

---

[61] The influence of Pascal—'Jésus sera en agonie jusqu'à la fin du monde' (*Œuvres complètes*, p. 1313)—is discernible here.

In the final poem, Cybèle is made to admit the superior power of the Christian God:

> L'Inconnu qui l'habite a, pour se rendre maître
> Du doux serpent lové dans le repli d'un être,
> Des charmes dont Cybèle ignore le secret. (462)

This is the fifth time the term *serpent* has been used in the poem, always with reference to Atys.[62] The allusion to the traditional Christian symbol of sin is transparent (the snake is 'doux' from Cybèle's libidinal perspective); the promise of the Protoevangelium is finally fulfilled. Cybèle's reference to 'L'Inconnu' in the passage just quoted reflects her pagan stance.[63] This is in the first stanza of the final poem. In the second, as already noted, her understanding of Christianity increases dramatically, and it is here that the unknown God is finally revealed via the christological titles of 'l'Agneau' and 'le Fils', both of which appear in the emphatic end-of-line position. Indeed, the poem concludes with this reference to the Son. Christ is the last Word, the Omega of Mauriac's cycle.

The psychoanalytic dimension

It is perhaps significant that one of the first critics to write at length about *Le Sang d'Atys* chose to do so from a psychoanalytic perspective (both Freudian and Lacanian).[64] Freudian concepts are also important in Guyonnet's exhaustive thesis. This is hardly surprising: the poem does, after all, explore the tensions of a quasi-incestuous mother–son relationship;[65] tensions that are only resolved once the son becomes identified with a divine father-figure. Quaghebeur summarizes thus:

> Le recueil présente [...] une évolution psychique et idéologique qu'il développe à travers une histoire structurée par le triangle œdipien. Ce 'roman'

---

[62] For the other references, see 449, 453 twice, and 458.

[63] Cf. Paul's comment on the Athenian altar with the inscription 'Au dieu inconnu' (Actes 17. 23).

[64] Quaghebeur, 'Une lecture du *Sang d'Atys*'.

[65] The term *enfant* is used eleven times to describe Atys and even though he is never explicitly referred to as Cybèle's child, as Magna Mater she is already mother of all that lives. Cf. her words to Atys: 'Ton souffle naît du souffle de Cybèle' (455).

familial, qui est aussi l'histoire d'une initiation, met en vedette un personnage, Atys, allégorie de l'homme et de l'écrivain. Il lui assigne une condition infantile permanente et le fait évoluer au seul gré du conflit opposant
père et mère et leurs différentes valeurs.[66]

The readings of Quaghebeur and Guyonnet are rich and stimulating,
but it seems to me that they ignore an important facet of the debate,
namely the extent to which Mauriac himself was conscious of these
psychoanalytical perspectives when composing his poem.

Mauriac wrote in 1957: 'Depuis un demi-siècle, Freud, quoi que
nous pensions de lui, nous oblige à tout voir, et d'abord nous-même, à
travers des lunettes que nous ne quittons plus' (OA 369). Although it
is important to read these words in the rhetorical context of Mauriac's
problems with the genre of autobiography,[67] it is nevertheless a revealing comment. Mauriac's ambivalent, often critical reaction towards Freudian theory may have fluctuated over the years,[68] but it is
clear that he never underestimated its significance, either for society at
large or for his own situation as a writer. He once described Baudelaire as a 'gibier de choix pour la psychanalyse', adding, by way of a
sideswipe at Sartre's Baudelaire (1947): 'Le complexe d'Œdipe fré-
tille ici à l'œil nu pour les délices des commençants' (OA 402). Mauriac probably also had his own situation in mind when he penned these
words. He would have been well aware that much of his work (and,
indeed, his own biography) could easily have lent itself to a psychoanalytical interpretation. One thinks, for example, of the teasing invi-
tation issued in his 1951 preface to Les Chemins de la mer when Mauriac expresses (feigned?) amazement over the recurring theme of incest in his work: 'Comme il n'est aucune passion qui m'ait été plus
étrangère que celle-là,' he comments, 'il serait curieux de chercher la
clef de ce mystère. Mais c'est l'affaire des psychanalystes et non la
mienne' (ORTC, III, 926). In making such comments, Mauriac seems

---

[66] Quaghebeur, 'Une lecture du Sang d'Atys', p. 59.
[67] See Paul Cooke, 'Problems of Establishing an Autobiographical Identity: The Case
of François Mauriac', in Locating Identity: Essays on Nation, Community and the
Self, ed. by Paul Cooke, David Sadler, and Nicholas Zurbrugg (Leicester: De
Montfort University, 1996), pp. 17–30 (pp. 18–19).
[68] See Paul Croc, 'Lunettes freudiennes', in François Mauriac: Psycholectures/
Psychoreadings, ed. by J. E. Flower (Exeter: University of Exeter Press, 1995), pp.
218–31 (p. 219).

to be pursuing two different objectives. On the one hand, he is seeking to whet the appetite of future critics (thus helping to ensure his continued literary fame), and, on the other, he is distancing himself in advance from their potential conclusions by adopting an ironic tone to describe their activity. Perhaps a similar kind of flirtation with Freudian ideas is also a feature of *Le Sang d'Atys*, extracts of which are, of course, incorporated in *Les Chemins de la mer*, sometimes in contexts that seem strongly to encourage a psychoanalytic interpretation.[69] Writing in 1934 about André Lafon's love of nature, Mauriac asks: 'ne pourrait-on se livrer ici à des variations freudiennes, chercher de quelles autres passions cette ferveur panthéiste tenait la place?' (*OC*, XI, 19). As ever, he elects not to go down this Freudian path. But I wonder whether his questions might not provide a hint that he was indeed consciously devising a 'Freudian' scenario in *Le Sang d'Atys*, especially as, immediately before the quotation given above, Mauriac compares Lafon with Maurice de Guérin, the poet with whom he consciously identified when writing *Le Sang d'Atys*.[70]

There is some doubt over precisely when Mauriac read Freud's work for the first time and over how carefully he read it.[71] However, whatever the precise year, it is certain that Mauriac was personally acquainted with Freud's ideas by the time he started working on *Le Sang d'Atys*. Unlike his contemporary Pierre-Jean Jouve (a fellow-Catholic), Mauriac's poetry is not overtly influenced by an interest in psychoanalysis.[72] But it seems possible to me that Mauriac may himself have been aware of (at least some of) the structures 'uncovered' by critics such as Quaghebeur. If this were so, it would mean re-evaluating the value of psychoanalysis as an interpretive tool in relation to his work. Not that such readings should be ruled illegitimate, simply that it would be desirable to reflect on the methodological

---

[69] See Paul Cooke, 'Le Poète et la poésie dans *Les Chemins de la mer*', *CM*, 11 (1997), 79–101 (pp. 88–89).

[70] '*Atys*, mon poème, est né moins peut-être du *Centaure* que de Maurice lui-même' (*OC*, VIII, iii); 'Maurice de Guérin, mon frère. *Le Sang d'Atys*: le poème qu'il aurait pu écrire. C'est à mes yeux sa secrète gloire' (*BN*, I, 85).

[71] See André Séailles, 'Mauriac et Freud devant l'inconscient et devant la foi', in *François Mauriac devant le problème du mal*, ed. by André Séailles (Klincksieck, 1994), pp. 19–35 (p. 20, p. 33).

[72] I am thinking particularly of Jouve's 1933 collection, *Sueur de sang*.

implications of the possibility that Mauriac may have chosen to incorporate certain 'Freudian triggers' *en connaissance de cause*.

There is one final aspect of the possible relationship between *Le Sang d'Atys* and psychoanalysis that is worth mentioning—one that takes us back to the significance of myth for Mauriac. It may be that Mauriac chose to incorporate such overt 'Freudian triggers' in this particular poem precisely because of its mythical background. It is undeniable that Freud's thought, and its influence on subsequent theorists such as Klein and Lacan, has had an immense impact on the modern world; its application to the human sciences and to literary studies proved particularly popular in the second half of the twentieth century. While some have tended to view psychoanalysis as a genuine science, others have adopted a more sceptical approach.[73] The extent to which Freud drew on mythical figures (such as Œdipus and Electra) in the formulation of his theories is an important aspect of this debate. It is not my purpose here to enter this debate (I would not, in any case, be competent to do so); rather, I simply draw attention to the fact that modern literary use of certain ancient myths cannot help but raise questions about the relationship between the text in question and Freudian thought. As Astier suggests, the only function (I would prefer to say: one of the main functions) of references to Œdipus in twentieth-century literature is to allude to psychoanalysis and the memory of Freud: 'Ainsi, peut-être, se crée peu à peu un mythe de la psychanalyse qu'il ne serait probablement pas impossible d'interpréter comme quelque mythe du mythe.'[74] I would suggest that *Le Sang d'Atys* could be read as a contribution to this mythologization of psychoanalysis.

Conclusion

As we follow Mauriac from *Les Mains jointes* to *Orages*, we see how the influence of figures such as Jammes, Sully-Prudhomme, Musset, and the converted Verlaine, gives way to that of Baudelaire. If Mauriac finds *Le Sang d'Atys* the least disappointing of all his texts, it is because he has tried to follow the same master: 'cherchant le secret

---

[73] See Malcolm Macmillan, *Freud Evaluated: The Completed Arc* (Cambridge: The MIT Press, 1997), pp. 591–627.

[74] Colette Astier, *Le Mythe d'Œdipe* (Colin 1974), p. 118.

d'un certain alliage, d'une matière dure [...] chercha[nt] à capter, cette
passion qui bouge encore, prise dans le filet serré de mots pour moi
irremplaçables' (*OA* 408). This quotation speaks of the density and
richness of poetic language; this is what Mauriac strives for in his later
poetry and it is a goal I believe he achieves. Perhaps even more than
Baudelaire, it is Racine and Valéry who serve as his principal sources
of inspiration in *Le Sang d'Atys*.[75] Cybèle's frustrated and partly in-
cestuous passion for Atys bears more than a passing resemblance to
Phèdre's passion for Hippolyte; and the alexandrines that Mauriac
uses to convey that passion certainly owe something to the style of
Racine.[76] Rather than seeking to imitate Valéry, Mauriac says that
reading *La Jeune Parque* and *Charmes* made him want to 'découvrir
les lois de [s]a propre rigueur', adding that it was this desire that gave
birth to *Orages* and *Le Sang d'Atys*: 'de toute mon œuvre, ce qui me
déçoit le moins'.[77] There are undeniable similarities between Mauriac's mythological poems and those of Valéry, but there are also
considerable differences, both in terms of poetic subtlety and because
of the ideological/ philosophical gulf separating the two authors.[78] The
clarity of Christianity's triumph at the end of *Le Sang d'Atys* is something Mauriac seemed to regret in later life. Interviewed on 5 January
1970, he confessed: '*Le Sang d'Atys* a quelque chose de surfait. J'ai
voulu faire un grand poème construit, comme on faisait alors. Je par-
tais d'une idée préconçue...'[79] Partisans of 'pure' poetry will almost
certainly criticize the cycle's strong narrative dimension and, especially, its overtly religious framework. But even readers who cannot
share Mauriac's religious convictions should be able to appreciate his

---

[75] 'En fait, la source première de mes poèmes est dans Racine. [...] La lecture de la
La Jeune Parque, [...], m'a confirmé dans ma religion racinienne' (*BN*, IV, 180).

[76] Guyonnet ('Mauriac et le mythe d'Atys', I, 422–61) establishes numerous parallels
between Mauriac's verse and that of his favourite poets from Racine to Valéry.

[77] François Mauriac, 'Supplément aux souvenirs', in *François Mauriac*, ed. by Jean
Touzot, pp. 121–41 (p. 126). Duhamel referred to Mauriac's 'maladie valérienne'—
quoted in *Correspondance François Mauriac–Georges Duhamel (1919–1966): le
croyant et l'humaniste inquiet*, ed. by J.-J. Hueber (Klincksieck, 1997), p. 208.

[78] Cf. Jacques Monférier, 'Mauriac et Valéry', *CFM*, 4 (1976), 112–20 (pp. 117–19).

[79] Quaghebeur, 'Une lecture du *Sang d'Atys*', p. 53. One is reminded of Valéry's
comments in 'Calepin d'un poète' (1928): 'Si tu veux faire des vers et que tu commences par des pensées, tu commences par la prose. / Dans la prose, on peut
dresser un plan et *le suivre!*' (*Œuvres*, I, 1449–50).

artistry. Durand may be guilty of hyperbole when he describes *Le Sang d'Atys* as 'un des sommets de la poésie française' (*OA* lxxvi), but the collection certainly merits a place among the foothills of Parnassus.

8. The End of the Affair: 'Ebauche d'Endymion'

Introduction
Although the archives of the Bibliothèque Doucet show that Mauriac occasionally turned to verse as a vehicle of expression after 'Endymion', this would be his last separately published poem.[1] I stress the word *separately*, because he did, in fact, publish one last piece of verse as the conclusion to an article that appeared in 1950.[2] Mauriac states that he came across this poem by chance 'en marge d'un cahier de brouillon' and suggests it was probably written at Malagar during the winter of 1942 or 1943. As it was only published as a kind of afterthought, I shall not be considering it here.

Precisely when he started work on 'Endymion' is not clear. The first reference in his correspondence comes in a letter to Georges Duhamel, dated 16 January 1941.[3] The poem originally appeared under the title 'Fragment d'Endymion' in the May–June 1942 issue of *Poésie 42*, edited by Pierre Seghers. As in *Le Sang d'Atys*, it is a story from Greek mythology that provides Mauriac with a framework for his poem. Mythological subjects proved popular with other French writers during the Occupation, but whereas authors such as Sartre (*Les Mouches*) and Anouilh (*Antigone*) used classical material to conceal a political message, Mauriac's choice of subject matter relates to more personal concerns. Perhaps his words in December 1939 about the imminent publication of *Le Sang d'Atys* could also be applied to the publication of 'Endymion' two-and-a-half years later:

> il fallait que cela sortît et précisément dans ce chaos où nous nous débattons. [...] Et puis tant de crevassses s'ouvrent de tous côtés, alors on jette ce qu'on cachait, le meilleur et le pire; il faut brûler ses vaisseaux, se 'sa-

---

[1] Massenet, *François Mauriac*, p. 325 reproduces the poem to be found at the end of 'Le Cahier rouge' (a diary covering the late 1940s). Four poems from *Orages* were republished in *Les Nouvelles littéraires* during 1948–49 in preparation for the collection's reissue in 1949, but I am discounting these as they are not new material.

[2] François Mauriac, 'Aspects de l'occultisme: témoignage de François Mauriac', *La Table ronde*, August–September 1950, 166–71 (pp. 170–71).

[3] *Correspondance François Mauriac–Georges Duhamel*, p. 125.

border' comme ces héroïques monstres allemands, ne rien réserver de soi
jusqu'au jour du jugement. (*NLV* 193)

I shall begin this final chapter on Mauriac's verse with a reading of
'Endymion' before going on to consider why he did not attempt to
extend his career as a poet.

A reading of 'Endymion'
The presence of the terms 'Ebauche' or 'Fragment' in the full title of
'Endymion' makes it clear that the poem is to be seen as a work in
progress. The line of dots both before and after the text in the *Œuvres
complètes* further underlines the poem's unfinished status.[4] The main
manuscript (MRC 50) gives no indication of the nature of the material
that Mauriac might have considered adding to the existing fragment. It
does, however, show how carefully he worked on the section he finally published. Mauriac was lavishing as much care on 'Endymion'
as he had on *Le Sang d'Atys*.[5] This may be an *ébauche*, but it is certainly not a *brouillon*.

According to the myth, Endymion was a handsome young shepherd (or king, in some versions) with whom Selene, the personification of the moon, fell passionately in love. Selene asked Zeus to grant
Endymion one wish: the youth chose eternal sleep so that he would
never grow old. The granting of this wish allowed Selene to visit her
lover regularly at night, conceiving no fewer than fifty daughters in
the process. It is easy to see how this myth would have attracted Mauriac. The story of a planetary goddess in love with a young man has an
obvious similarity with the story of Cybele and Attis. It is true that
Mauriac's Atys resists Cybèle (at least in *Le Sang d'Atys*), but the fact
that Endymion remains unconscious throughout his union with Selene
limits his degree of participation and responsibility in the relationship.
However, whereas Mauriac's association of the pine with the Cross
allowed him to rewrite the myth of Attis from a Christian perspective,
it is not obvious how he could have christianized the story of Endymion. In the poem's opening stanza, there are a few images that could
perhaps be viewed in a christic light. Séléné is said to prefer 'Ces

---

[4] References to the poem in this chapter will take the form of line numbers.

[5] As he writes to Jean Paulhan on 7 February 1941: 'je passe des journées de
désespoir sur un vers...' (*LV* 247).

corps désespérés qui n'ont pas de complices | Et que sur les prés noirs a cloués le sommeil' (ll. 9–10). One might relate the use of the verb *clouer* here to the Crucifixion and, indeed, relate the adjective *désespéré* to Christ's cry of desolation and his sense of isolation on the Cross.[6] A couple of lines later we read:

> Son corps offert au ciel comme aux flots d'une mer
> Est un pâle récif battu par cette eau sourde
> Et blanche que répand la vierge au flanc ouvert. (ll. 13–15)

The image of Endymion's 'crucified' body, offered to heaven, could be read in the light of certain theories of the Atonement.[7] Then, in the last two lines just quoted, the christic imagery is applied most clearly of all to Séléné: the 'water' that flows from the virgin's open side recalls the water that flowed from Christ's side when his virginal body was pierced by the soldier's lance.[8] However, in the absence of a plan indicating how this 'Ebauche d'Endymion' might have fitted into a larger whole, it is difficult to know how to interpret this christic imagery: is it a question of almost accidental verbal echoes, or was Mauriac attempting to weave a Christian dimension into his pagan material?

In 1943, Mauriac (under the pseudonym of Forez) contributed his *Cahier noir* to the clandestine Editions de Minuit. This short work assured his place among those courageous writers who contributed to the literary Resistance. Yet 'Endymion' is a long way from the politically committed resistance poetry of Aragon or Tardieu. As Touzot puts it, '"Fragment d'Endymion" marque une fidélité à la "poésie pure"…'[9] Elsewhere, Touzot shows how Mauriac uses proportionately fewer similes and more metaphors as one moves from the early verse to *Le Sang d'Atys*.[10] 'Endymion' reinforces this evolution: while

---

[6] Matthieu 27. 46.

[7] I am thinking particularly of those theories that view the Cross as a sacrifice made to the Father. For an overview, see Alister E. McGrath, *Christian Theology: An Introduction*, 2nd edn (Oxford: Blackwell, 1997), pp. 391–95.

[8] Jean 19. 34.

[9] *Mauriac sous l'Occupation*, ed. by Jean Touzot, 2nd edn (Bordeaux: Editions Confluences/ Centre François Mauriac de Malagar, 1995), p. 81.

[10] Touzot, 'Analogie et poème', p. 31, p. 42.

the poem contains only three similes (l. 13, l. 59, l. 79), there are about fifty instances of metaphorical language. The high incidence of adjectives occurring before nouns (twenty-three as opposed to forty-six placed after nouns) provides another indication of the overtly literary, or 'poetic', quality of the language.[11] The poem is located squarely within the French Classical tradition, being written in alexandrines that respect the *alternance des rimes* (though, as is standard in Mauriac's verse, there is no rigid rhyme scheme). We have seen how, in his early verse, Mauriac liked to toy with the conventions governing the caesura, using proclitics such as determiners and monosyllabic prepositions to provide the sixth syllable in dodecasyllabic lines. This practice is almost entirely absent from 'Endymion'.[12] Mauriac does not, however, carry his respect for the rules of Classical versification to extremes. There are, for example, a number of effective examples of *enjambement*, both between and within lines. A single example must suffice: 'Inerte, le fut-il jamais? Ce caillou pur | Et veiné: ce grand corps tout mouillé de rosée' (ll. 39–40). In the first line just quoted, the *rejet interne* emphasizes the adverb 'jamais', casting doubt on Endymion's innocence/ indifference. The *rejet externe* generates a similar emphasis on the words 'Et veiné': although visually Endymion may seem to be an impassive (and therefore 'pure') pebble, he is still a creature of flesh and blood (metonymically suggested by the term 'veiné'). Once again, therefore, any notion of total passivity on his part is called into question.

The poem is one hundred lines long and is divided into eight unequal stanzas of between nine and nineteen lines each. The overall structure is as follows:

> Stanza 1 (ll. 1–19): the narrator describes Séléné's dogs picking up Endymion's scent.
> Stanza 2 (ll. 20–28): Séléné addresses the sleeping Endymion.
> Stanza 3 (ll. 29–38): Séléné continues to address the sleeping Endymion.

---

[11] Cohen (*Structure du langage poétique*, p. 196) views adjectives that come before nouns as markers of poeticity.

[12] There are only two examples of the phenomenon, both of them relatively innocuous. In the line 'Inerte, le fut-il jamais? Ce caillou pur' (l. 39), 'il' occupies the sixth syllable, but the subject pronoun is strongly connected to its verb in the same hemistich via inversion. Three lines later, a *disyllabic* preposition occurs immediately before the caesura: 'Et sur l'herbe, parmi les figues écrasées' (l. 42).

Stanza 4 (ll. 39–52): the narrator, addressing Séléné directly, describes her desire to dehumanize Endymion.

Stanza 5 (ll. 53–66): the narrator describes how a goat obscures Endymion from Séléné.

Stanza 6 (ll. 67–76): the narrator describes Séléné's dogs picking up Endymion's scent again.

Stanza 7 (ll. 77–91): the moralizing narrator describes Séléné's descent to Endymion.

Stanza 8 (ll. 92–100): the moralizing narrator addresses Séléné directly.

We do not hear Endymion's voice at all, but Séléné's words account for roughly one fifth of the poem's length. Similarly, while we only ever see Endymion as immobile, Séléné seems to be constantly on the move.[13] It would be possible to attempt an allegorical reading of the poem in terms of the contemporary political situation—the silent, sleeping Endymion representing France's moral and political slumber; the predatory Séléné standing for the Occupier's rapaciousness—but such a reading would be difficult to sustain at the level of textual detail and there is no hint at all that Mauriac himself ever conceived of the poem along these lines.[14]

It seems far more likely that the poem should be read in terms of the recurrent theme of Mauriac's anxious fascination with sexuality. As in *Le Sang d'Atys*, the choice of a young man as the primary focus of desire is surely no coincidence.[15] In a review of *Le Sang d'Atys*, Robert Brasillach had written:

> Quel curieux poème! Ceux qui s'intéressent à son auteur feront bien de le scruter vers par vers, car je crois bien qu'il y a caché quelques secrets non encore révélés. Surtout, il s'y libère, il va au-delà de lui-même, il exprime peut-être ce qu'il ne s'avoue pas, il se déchaîne bien loin des entraves sociales et spirituelles. [...] Si je voulais plaisanter [...] je dirais que cet

---

[13] Séléné offers Endymion the opportunity to *fuire* and to *cheminer* (ll. 49–50), but he does not appear to respond. Also, when Séléné is no longer able to see Endymion, we read 'A-t-il fui?' (l. 63). The answer to the question is uncertain, but there is no description of any motion on Endymion's part.

[14] There is, however, the possibility that Mauriac's very real political concerns emerge unconsciously in this poem. Cf. Chantal Fouché's reading of *La Pharisienne* as a 'dénonciation véhémente et *inconsciente* de la montée du fascisme' in her article 'Une lecture politique', *CFM*, 13 (1986), 259–67 (p. 259; my italics).

[15] Cf. Croc, 'Lunettes freudiennes', p. 227: 'le poète, s'identifiant à la Lune, se complaisait dans la contemplation de l'éphèbe endormi, à une distance ... sidérale.'

> éminent académicien a attendu que le docteur Freud fût mort pour publier impunément son œuvre.[16]

Much the same might be said about 'Endymion'. The central image of Brasillach's review, that of secrecy and concealment (his title was 'Les Secrets de M. Mauriac'), is thematically significant in the poem. The verb *(se) cacher* occurs no fewer than four times (l. 1, l. 60, l. 89, l. 100). The first and last of these occurrences receive additional emphasis from their location in the poem's opening and closing lines. Earlier in the final stanza, we find the poem's only reference to the Christian God when the narrator refers to the 'noir azur où bat le cœur de Dieu' (l. 95). The Deity seems very distant, but still rather menacing. In order to touch Endymion 'd'un plus furtif rayon' (l. 98), Séléné therefore has to *hide* her face 'sous le masque changeant des rapides nuées' (l. 99). The rhetoric of concealment (sexual desire hiding from the Christian God) is particularly evident in this final stanza.

When Séléné first addresses the sleeping Endymion, she describes him in terms that recall Atys's metamorphosis into a pine:

> O grand arbre abattu, chargé de tes fruits lourds,
> Laisse-moi déceler sous ton écorce dure
> Les lieux tendres voués aux secrètes blessures [...]. (ll. 21–23)

In *Le Sang d'Atys*, the tree's verticality allowed Mauriac to introduce both a phallic emphasis and an aspiration towards the divine. Endymion's prone position means that both of these elements are toned down in the present poem. As far as phallic imagery is concerned, it is worth noting how Endymion's potentially phallic paraphernalia is explicitly discarded: 'Il a jeté sa peau de mouton et sa gourde, | Le bâton d'aulne frais encor poisseux et vert' (ll. 11–12). There is also the description of Endymion as Séléné's 'immobile enfant' (l. 62), followed by a reference to his 'face | Chérie où les péchés n'ont pas laissé de traces' (ll. 60–61). This infantilization further reduces Endymion's sexual status (as well as introducing the complicating factor of the mother–son relationship already found in *Le Sang d'Atys*).

In Mauriac's version of the myth, Séléné is certainly obsessed with Endymion's body, but their union is never depicted, nor is there

---

[16] Quoted by Risse, *Homoerotik*, p. 208.

any hint of the fifty daughters born as a result of their nocturnal en-
counters. Nevertheless, it seems as though Endymion's passivity
cloaks a powerful underlying desire. As the narrator says to Séléné as
she observes her lover: 'Tout te peint le sommeil d'une bête engourdie
| Ou d'un volcan qu'étreint sa lave refroidie...' (ll. 45–46). Here again
is the theme of concealment. Similarly, the goddess's description of
herself as 'très chaste' (l. 31) occurs in a stanza containing a number
of references to body parts and which therefore suggests a strongly
physical dimension to her desire. Indeed, despite the highly euphe-
mistic nature of Mauriac's descriptions,[17] this is a poem in which the
body features prominently, as can be seen from the list of body-related
lexical items in Table 16:

Table 16:

corps	9, 13, 40, 60, 91	sang	59, 92	gorge	41
front	18, 26, 44	boucles	43	hanche	31
genoux	36, 80, 91*	cheveux	18	joue	28
main	28, 29, 44	cuisse	31	poitrine	58
bras	27, 30	doigts	55	seins	16
face	60, 100	épaule	37	tête	43
jambes	16, 80	flanc	15	yeux	62

Notes

- Items have been arranged in terms of frequency and, when the number of occur-
  rences is the same, alphabetically.
- Figures refer to line numbers.
- The asterisk refers to an occurrence of the verb s'agenouiller.

Although there is a powerful physicality about the poem, it is important to note how Séléné's attempt to change Endymion differs from
Cybèle's metamorphosis of Atys. In the earlier poem, Cybèle may
dehumanize Atys by transforming him into a pine tree, but her act is
prompted by an altogether human desire for uninterrupted physical
union with her lover (hence the emphasis on the tree's phallic roots).
Séléné, on the other hand, seems to offer Endymion the opportunity to

---

[17] See for example lines 21–23 quoted above and compare the reference to 'l'éveil des
tendres violences' in line 33.

pass from the human realm into the divine—a transformation that would represent an altogether more spiritual form of union:

> Séléné jusqu'à lui jette une échelle d'or
> Pour qu'il fuie à jamais les terres habitées
> Et qu'il chemine seul sur les routes lactées,
> Détournant vers des dieux qu'il avait méconnus
> Un regard où l'humain ne se reflète plus. (ll. 48–52)

This part of the poem relates only indirectly to the original myth: Zeus may have granted Endymion immortality, but on condition that he remained eternally asleep.[18] Perhaps one could relate it to Mauriac's increasing interest in forms of possessive desire that transcend the purely sexual (this is an important theme in *La Pharisienne*, a novel whose composition may have overlapped with that of 'Endymion'). Unlike Atys, however, Endymion never appears to undergo the transformation that the goddess wishes to impose upon him. Just as he seems to be slipping away from the world of the living under Séléné's spell,[19] a male goat appears: 'Un bouc hésite, approche, et son ombre cornue | S'allonge, enténébrant cette poitrine nue' (ll. 57–58). As a result of its association with Pan, the goat has long been associated with male sexuality. If, earlier in the poem, phallic imagery seemed to have been set aside, the *enjambement* between the lines just quoted reintegrates a phallic dimension. It is as though the goat infuses Endymion with a basic animal energy, for the shepherd appears to have fled Séléné's potentially dehumanizing embrace. The stanza's final lines underline the sterility of the cosmic existence to which she had been calling Endymion:

> A-t-il fui? Séléné l'appelle en gémissant,
> Mais il n'est pas d'écho dans les muets espaces,
> Toute planète est sourde et les mondes sont morts
> Et le nom qu'elle crie expire sur leurs bords. (ll. 63–66)

In the poem's final three stanzas, the sensual nature of Séléné's desire returns to the fore. After the lifeless silence of the lines just

---

[18] *New Larousse Encyclopedia of Mythology*, trans. by Richard Aldington and Delano Ames, new edn (Hamlyn, 1968), p. 143.
[19] He is described as 'ce mort' (l. 53) and as a 'berger pétrifié' (l. 54).

quoted, noise and excitement are suddenly reinjected into the poem when a series of three /ʒ/ sounds (placed at the start of syllables 1, 7, and 12 for maximum emphasis) marks the reappearance of Séléné's dogs: '… Jusqu'au soir où les chiens jappèrent, fous de joie' (l. 67). However, as at the start of the poem (ll. 5–6), it is smell, rather than sound, that serves as the real stimulus:

> Plus riche que l'odeur de bouse et de marais,
> Séléné reconnut le parfum de sa proie,
> Cet encens cher aux dieux, qui monte des lieux bas. (ll. 69–71)[20]

It is at this point that the narrator reveals his own moral perspective for the first time: 'L'âme déjà liée aux délices du crime, | Elle avance un pied pur sur l'écume des cimes' (ll. 77–78). In these lines it is worth noting not only the deliberate echo of Pascal,[21] but also the way in which Mauriac makes effective use of sound to underscore the moralizing note: the repetition of the phonemes /l/, /m/, /d/, /e/, and /i/ in line 77 emphasizes the central concept conveyed by the term 'liée' (which itself figures immediately before the caesura);[22] the alliteration in line 78 should probably be read ironically, mocking the notion that Séléné can be described as pure. Indeed, her impurity is symbolized a little further on by the fact that she is exiled from her own light (ll. 85–86) and becomes as one with her hunting bitches before Endymion's body (ll. 87–88). In this context, the use of the verb 'descendre' in the final stanza could be seen as relating to a moral fall: 'Ce sang et cette boue interrompent ta course, | Tu ne peux pas descendre au-dessous de ce lieu' (ll. 92–93). The idea of a moral fall is certainly supported by the reference to Endymion's 'sang' and 'boue',[23] by the

---

[20] There is an affinity between Mauriac's portrait of Séléné (described as 'cette chasseresse' (l. 74)) and the traditional image of Artemis/ Diana as a hunter with a pack of dogs. H. J. Rose comments in *A Handbook of Greek Mythology, Including Its Extension to Rome* (Methuen, 1928) that Selene 'has again and again been identified with Artemis, with whom she has nothing in reality to do' (p. 34).

[21] The 'usage délicieux et criminel du monde' referred to in his *Prière pour demander à Dieu le bon usage des maladies* (1666)—see Pascal, *Œuvres complètes*, p. 606.

[22] Cf. lines 17–19 where the repetition of the phonemes—/ã/ (l. 17), /m/ (l. 18), and /i/, /m/, /e/, and /s/ (l. 19)—serves to underline the stillness produced by Séléné's spell.

[23] The negative moral connotations of 'boue' are even stronger than those of *chair*, the term one would normally expect to see coupled with 'sang'.

fact that the goddess's descent has reached its nadir, and by the fact that she is as far as she possibly can be both from the pagan divinities represented by the constellations (l. 94) and from the virtually invisible God of monotheism (l. 95). The description of her as 'trempée encor d'amour pris à sa source' (l. 96) perhaps suggests that Mauriac was thinking in terms of converting the goddess, since, from a Christian perspective, the source of love is the God who is love.[24] As was the case for the 'sinful woman' in Luke's gospel (traditionally identified with Mary Magdalene), Séléné's capacity for love might have provided the key to her 'salvation'.[25] However, in this unfinished poem, this possibility remains unexplored and the narrator concludes his text with a final value judgement, describing Séléné as 'malheureuse' (l. 100).

A farewell to verse

When Mauriac was asked in 1959 why he had stopped publishing poetry, he answered:

> Je n'ai pas continué *Endymion*... peut-être pour des raisons religieuses: c'était trop sensuel, trop charnel; ma poésie prenait sa source dans une partie si charnelle de mon être qu'il se peut—il se peut seulement—que le chrétien, en moi, ait arrêté cela... Mais je n'en suis pas sûr, après tout...[26]

The hesitant nature of this response suggests that it is far from constituting a satisfactory answer to the question. Mauriac had always seen the relationship between his art and his faith as a problematic one. As he commented some twenty years before writing 'Endymion': 'la sainteté, c'est presque toujours le silence. J'entrevois qu'André Lafon vivant n'aurait plus guère écrit que de fervents et brefs poèmes' (*OA* 61). There is therefore probably some truth in Mauriac's response to Mora. He was constantly aware of the potential moral influence of his writing, especially as certain Catholic journalists were quick to con-

---

[24] I Jean 4. 8.

[25] Jesus says of the woman: 'ses péchés, ses nombreux péchés, lui sont remis parce qu'elle a montré beaucoup d'amour' (Luc 7. 47). Claude Escallier brings out Mauriac's particular interest in the 'trois pécheresses' in the gospels—see her *Mauriac et l'Evangile* (Beauchesne, 1993), pp. 294–97.

[26] Edith Mora, 'François Mauriac pourquoi vous êtes-vous arraché à la poésie?', *Les Nouvelles littéraires*, 18 June 1959, p. 1, p. 7 (p. 7).

demn what they saw as his dangerous depiction of sexuality.[27] Yet it is difficult to see why 'Endymion' (which is less overtly sexual than *Le Sang d'Atys*) should have caused Mauriac particular concern in this respect.

Perhaps, though, it is not so much what the poem says as what it does *not* say that worried him. 'Endymion' may be less sexually suggestive than *Le Sang d'Atys*, but it also lacks the latter's overtly Christian dimension. Although, as I suggested in the previous section, there are a few places in the poem where Mauriac opens the door to a possible christianization of the myth, these references remain at the level of undeveloped hints. On 26 November 1941, Mauriac wrote to Jean Grenier: 'Je vous garde un *Atys*. Mais aujourd'hui, je suis honteux d'avoir cédé à cette frénésie païenne... Du moins le Christ n'est-il jamais absent même de mon paganisme' (*NLV* 213). Christ is, however, more or less entirely absent from 'Endymion'—the Christian God only appearing in the guise of the distant *deus absconditus* of line 95.

But there are other, perhaps more mundane reasons that may help explain Mauriac's decision to abandon poetry. Given his lack of recognition as a poet, he may simply have decided that the game was no longer worth the candle. There was something rather incongruous about one of the leading novelists of his generation, an Academician since 1933 who would receive no less an accolade than the Nobel Prize for Literature in 1952, continuing to publish poems that passed virtually unnoticed. From the mid-1930s onwards, Mauriac also devoted increasing amounts of time to political journalism, anchoring himself ever more firmly in what he calls 'l'histoire quotidienne et sanglante' (*OC*, XI, ii). Given the time and effort that went into producing *Le Sang d'Atys*, one wonders whether, even had he wished to do so, Mauriac would have found enough energy to write verse during the 50s and 60s when there were so many other pressing calls on his pen.

Mauriac's increasing involvement with political issues provides a final reason why he may have decided to abandon poetry. He had already started to reflect on the question of the writer's role in society

---

[27] See Jean Touzot, 'Quand Mauriac était scandaleux...', *Œuvres et critiques*, 2.1 (Spring 1977), 133–44.

in the early 1930s with *Le Mystère Frontenac*. In the novel's twenty-first chapter, Yves's hallucinatory vision of a métro station 'absorb[ant] et vomiss[ant] des fourmis à tête d'homme' (*ORTC*, II, 665) inspires thoughts of a future revolution when 'aucune fortune acquise ne permettra plus au moindre Frontenac de se mettre à part sous prétexte de réfléchir, de se désespérer, d'écrire son journal, de prier, de faire son salut'—or indeed, one might add, to write poetry—because 'les gens d'en bas auront triomphé de la personne humaine' (*ORTC*, II, 666). Mauriac was returning here to a contemporary debate with Gide over the merits of Communism. As Maucuer points out, Mauriac, like many other authors in the 30s, was wondering not just about the future of society, but also about the writer's role.[28] However, it has to be said that Mauriac's interest in this issue was still very limited at this stage: Yves's revolutionary thoughts come when he is on the verge of a nervous breakdown, having met with failure both in his personal relationships and in his vocation as a poet. Mauriac as omniscient narrator maintains an ironic distance from his semi-autobiographical hero.

By the late 1930s, however, Mauriac's authorial position seems to have shifted. In *Les Chemins de la mer*, Pierre Costadot expresses convictions that go far beyond Yves's sense of despair. Whereas Yves remains narcissistically obsessed with his own predicament, Pierre is genuinely sickened by the values of the world in general and, in particular, by the omnipresence of Mammon's influence. When financial considerations cause his brother Robert to break off his engagement to Rose Révolou, Pierre is faced with a choice between God and revolution (*ORTC*, III, 643). The manuscript adds a third option: that of pursuing a poetic vocation which 'l'isole[rait] du monde Costadot, l'en sépare[rait]' (*ORTC*, III, 1269). A little later in the novel, however, this third option is clearly discredited. Like Yves Frontenac (*ORTC*, II, 597), Pierre Costadot believes his 'seul devoir' consists in devotion to his art (*ORTC*, III, 678). At first, he tries to silence his conscience by suggesting that this poetic duty does not prevent him being on the side of the poor, but intellectual honesty causes him to reconsider: 'Pensée idiote: il n'existe pas de "côté des pauvres", mais deux méthodes pour exploiter les pauvres, à gauche et à droite' (*ORTC*, III, 678). Pierre's

---

[28] Maurice Maucuer, 'Yves Frontenac et les "fourmis à tête d'homme"', *CFM*, 7 (1980), 133–45 (pp. 141–42).

poetry does not allow him to hide from the world's evils: 'Le chemin que l'enfant-poète avait suivi, tout occupé de Cybèle et d'Atys, débouchait tout à coup sur la destinée de Landin, sur cette mer Morte' (*ORTC*, III, 690). While this image alludes primarily to Landin's homosexuality, it could also be seen, within the context of a political reading of the novel, as a transposition of the author's own situation: absorbed, at one level, in the writing of *Le Sang d'Atys*, but also increasingly aware that the road of European politics was about to reach a dead end. As he wrote to René Lalou in March 1938: 'C'est dur de vivre au temps des assassins triomphants... C'est étouffant...' (*NLV* 182). Pierre Costadot is unable to bear this feeling of suffocation: as soon as finishes his poem, he enlists in the *chasseurs d'Afrique* and dies during the First World War.

At the start of the nineteenth century—a period just as turbulent as the 1930s—the German poet Hölderlin asked: 'Wozu Dichter in dürftiger Zeit?'[29] Mauriac is asking a similar question in his 1939 novel, though without providing any significant answers. As Petit observes: '*Les Chemins de la mer*, c'est un peu le roman de la mauvaise conscience, celui des insolubles contradictions où se sent enfermé le poète d'*Atys et Cybèle*, bourgeois et "catholique de gauche"' (*ORTC*, III, 1200). Pierre Costadot's decision to leave France for Africa (and death) is obviously intended to recall Rimbaud's move to Abyssinia. The speed with which the narrator consigns his character to the grave may also, as Mauriac self-mockingly suggests, owe something to the narrative influence of the Comtesse de Ségur (*ORTC*, III, 925). But, more than anything else, Pierre's fate and the manner of its narration reveal Mauriac's inability, or unwillingness, to seek answers to the vast political and ethical questions raised by his novel.

It would not be until the Occupation that Mauriac would be in a position to provide an answer to Hölderlin's question. In the worsening international climate of the late 1930s, there was part of Mauriac that turned to art as a kind of refuge. Now, more than ever, he is convinced that 'la vocation de l'artiste tient dans une recherche désintéressée' (*OC*, XI, 226). And, in an article published just a month be-

---

[29] Friedrich Hölderlin, *Selected Verse*, ed. and trans. by Michael Hamburger (Harmondsworth: Penguin, 1961), p. 111; translated as: 'What is the use of poets at a time of dearth?'

fore the French defeat, he writes: 'avouons que nous sommes tentés, [...], nous poètes qui, à chaque instant, pouvons nous évader dans la création et dans le songe' (*OC*, XI, 306). In the early period of the Occupation, it seems as though Mauriac partly yielded to this temptation, writing both *La Pharisienne* and 'Endymion' and producing the first draft of *Le Sagouin* (*ORTC*, IV, 1210). However, it is noteworthy that after Mauriac's 'official' entry into the world of resistance writing when he contributed a text to the (unpublished) first issue of Jacques Decour's *Lettres françaises* in February 1942,[30] he does not turn again to creative writing until 1947 with his play *Passage du Malin* (his next novel, *Le Sagouin*, would not be published until 1951). The parallels between the dates are striking: as Mauriac completes his last poem, he begins his work as a resistance writer. As he writes in his most famous resistance text, *Le Cahier noir*:

> Le vieux Goethe, au seuil de son éternité, ne voulait plus donner un regard ni une pensée à la politique de ce monde, à ce qu'il appelait 'un brouillamini d'erreurs et de violences...' Ce brouillamini est notre affaire propre; il nous concerne et nous serons des lâches si nous cédons à cette autre facilité: celle du détachement. (*OC*, XI, 365–66)

Now, while the example of numerous other writers shows that there is by no means any necessary incompatibility between resistance and poetry (or creative writing generally), it seems clear that Mauriac, whether consciously or not, did see a distinction between the two in his own case. For Mauriac, poetry *was* a form of detachment from political realities, a retreat into a world of private desires played out in atemporal mythological frameworks. I showed in Chapter 5 how Mauriac's experiences during the First World War caused him to distance himself from the type of poetry produced in *Les Mains jointes* and *Un adolescent d'autrefois*. I would suggest that his experiences during the Second World War, leading to an impassioned and highly successful involvement in political journalism, proved a major contributory factor in his turning away from verse.

---

[30] Lacouture, *François Mauriac*, II, 147.

9. A Poetic Novelist

Introduction

The 'poetic' quality of Mauriac's prose has been affirmed by numerous critics over the years. Before the First World War, when Apollinaire visited Jacques Chardonne (who worked for the publishers Stock), he happened to pick up the manuscript of Mauriac's first novel, *L'Enfant chargé de chaînes* (1913). Chardonne apparently disliked the novel, but Apollinaire is said to have commented: 'C'est tout de même un poète' (*SR* 115). Reviewing *Le Nœud de vipères* (1932), Brasillach claimed that the novel's 'musique [...] correspond le plus exactement aux meilleurs vers de Baudelaire, même sonorité, mêmes évocations, même puissance charnelle et douloureuse'.[1] A decade and a half later, Palante compared Mauriac's novels to poems and described Mauriac the novelist as 'peut-être le dernier des poètes de la lignée symboliste'.[2] Cormeau provided many perceptive examples to demonstrate 'l'incantation poétique de la phrase' in Mauriac's prose.[3] And Raimond too saw Mauriac's novels as 'un peu des poèmes par leur structure, la priorité de l'évocation sur la dramatisation, une certaine vibration de la prose'.[4] The vast majority of critics would seem to agree with Delaunay's statement that: 'Le roman mauriacien est [...], avant tout, un roman poétique.'[5] Similar statements have also been made about Mauriac as an essayist, journalist, and dramatist.[6]

---

[1] Quoted by J. E. Flower, 'Mauriac et l'affaire Brasillach', *CM*, 9 (Autumn 1995), 59–73 (p. 61).

[2] Palante, *Mauriac*, p. 59.

[3] Nelly Cormeau, *L'Art de François Mauriac* (Grasset, 1951), p. 315.

[4] Raimond, *La Crise du roman*, p. 230.

[5] Gabriel Delaunay, 'Prix Nobel et "homme seul"', in *Mauriac* (Hachette, 1977), pp. 211–31 (p. 224).

[6] See, for example, Marie-Françoise Canérot, 'Les *Nouveaux Mémoires intérieurs*, poème de la vieillesse', *CFM*, 6 (1979), 113–22; Jean Touzot, 'Avant le *Bloc-notes*: la chronique, le billet, l'éditorial selon Mauriac', *CM*, 5 (Summer 1991), 49–69 (p. 56); and François Jacques, 'La Poésie dans le théâtre de Mauriac', in *Mauriac et le théâtre: actes du Colloque de la Sorbonne, 1991*, ed. by André Séailles (Klincksieck, 1993), pp. 262–70.

The question of precisely what constitutes the poetic dimension of Mauriac's novels is more difficult to answer. One possible line of enquiry might involve examining his presentation of characters who are themselves poets.[7] Such an approach is, inevitably, more thematic than linguistic or formal in orientation, but can still yield some useful insights. In this connection, it is interesting to note Todorov's analysis of Novalis's poetic novel *Heinrich von Ofterdingen* (1802). On the basis of quotations from Novalis's text, Todorov draws up a comparative table of the characteristic traits of heroes and poets.[8] He then goes on to suggest that it might be possible to use these features to help distinguish between the narrative novel and the poetic novel, and perhaps even to help identify 'le discours de la poésie, tel qu'il s'est pratiqué à l'époque romantique et depuis'. The problem, as he admits, is whether it is possible to pass from individuals (heroes and poets) to classes of texts.

A more obviously formal attempt at defining the poeticity of Mauriac's novels emerges from a focus on their structure. Petit's notes in the Pléiade edition of Mauriac's novels are often helpful in this respect. But the most focused piece of research is Canérot's analysis of the novelist's early works. Apart from the 'mince noyau dramatique' in Chapters 18–23 of *La Robe prétexte* (1914), she argues that this novel's structure is marked by discontinuity: 'Elle juxtapose "l'évocation" d'instants, de moments privilégiés, "remplis de la grâce d'un objet, d'un être ou d'un paysage", et fonde ainsi le roman en poésie.'[9] The term 'poésie' here denotes not any specific linguistic criteria, but an evocative form of writing in which temporal development is of minimal importance (the type of writing often associated with lyric poetry). Mauriac's chief inspiration in writing this sort of prose is Francis Jammes, who was not only a verse poet, but also one

---

[7] See, for example, Marie-Françoise Canérot, 'Le Thème de la vocation littéraire dans l'œuvre romanesque de François Mauriac', *CFM*, 5 (1978), 149–60 and Cooke, *Mauriac et le mythe du poète*.

[8] Todorov, *Les Genres du discours*, p. 106. The next quotation is from p. 107.

[9] Marie-Françoise Canérot, 'Les Premiers Romans de François Mauriac: des romans en quête de structure', *CFM*, 10 (1983), 80–89 (p. 82). Her quotations are from Raimond's *Crise du roman*.

of the masters of the turn-of-the-century *roman poétique*.[10] The other
major influence on Mauriac's early novels was Maurice Barrès whose
Culte du moi trilogy (1888–91) was viewed as a series of 'romans-
poèmes' by Paul Bourget.[11] Among Mauriac's early novels, it is in
L'Enfant chargé de chaînes that Barrès's legacy is most apparent:[12] in
the lack of dramatic conflict (a conventional novelistic marker); in the
general discussions of moral, political, and aesthetic questions; and in
the evocation of Jean-Paul's *états d'âme*.

    While this approach focusing on structure and general types of
narrative discourse reveals a number of parallels between Mauriac's
early novels and the *roman poétique* as practised by Barrès and
Jammes, it is perhaps less helpful as a means of establishing the poeticity of Mauriac's later novels. Hence the need for a stylistic approach to the question. The monographs by Bendz and Cormeau went
some way towards meeting this need. However, it was not until Touzot's work of the mid-1980s that the stylistic traits of Mauriac's fiction were analysed in real detail.[13] There have also been a handful of
articles on stylistic aspects of individual novels.[14] Although a full-
scale analysis of the 'poetic' qualities of Mauriac's prose (in various
genres) has yet to be undertaken, the aforementioned studies have all
contributed to a better understanding of the subject.

    There are two final approaches that could prove useful. The first
would involve an intertextual analysis of the way in which Mauriac
quotes from, or alludes to, the work of his favourite poets in his prose
texts. I intend to pursue this question elsewhere. The second (related)
approach would involve exploring the extent to which Mauriac's

---

[10] Mauriac would later refer to 'l'influence, pour ne pas dire l'imitation du Jammes de
Clara d'Ellébeuse' on *La Robe prétexte* (*ORTC*, I, 990).

[11] See Raimond, *La Crise du roman*, p. 202.

[12] As Lacouture points out (*François Mauriac*, I, 132), Mauriac's title provides an
'antithèse, complice peut-être, à *l'Homme libre* de Barrès'.

[13] See Jean Touzot, *François Mauriac, une configuration romanesque: profil rhétorique et stylistique* (Lettres Modernes, 1985) and *La Planète Mauriac: figure
d'analogie et roman* (Klincksieck, 1985).

[14] See, for example, Anne-Marie Naffakh, 'Roman et style poétique: les images dans
Le Désert de l'amour et *L'Agneau* de François Mauriac', *TCER*, 6 (December 1979),
37–49; Javier del Prado, 'Description de la nature et mise à l'écart du récit', *NCFM*, 8
(2000), 81–106; and Paule Lapeyre, '*Le Mal*: roman poétique de Mauriac?', *NCFM*,
10 (2002), 135–44.

prose texts make use of the themes and language to be found in his own verse. It is this second approach that will provide the main focus for my remarks in the remainder of this chapter. It is a type of intratextuality that has received very little attention so far in studies of Mauriac's *œuvre*. For example, although Petit's Pléiade edition of Mauriac's novels and plays provides numerous notes showing how phrases and images from one prose text recur in others, it is very rare for him to identify passages in the novels that draw on Mauriac's verse. It is worth noting that, although echoes of Mauriac's poems are more frequent in his novels than in other types of prose, traces of his verse can certainly be found in his non-fictional texts as well. The 1926 essay *Le Jeune Homme*, for example, contains a line from one of the poems in *Orages*: 'Qui souille le printemps? mais tout souille l'automne' (*ORTC*, II, 691; *Or* 434). There are also some intensely evocative passages in his autobiographical writings where we find elements that are used to great effect in his verse. In *Commencements d'une vie* (1932), for example, Mauriac's lyrical description of the pines, his identification with them, and the way in which he associates them with Christian suffering (*OA* 97–98) provide a number of strong parallels with *Le Sang d'Atys*. Owing to constraints of space, however, my remarks in this chapter will be limited to an analysis of Mauriac's novels, which I shall examine chronologically.

Early novels

We have already seen that Mauriac was very dismissive of his early verse. His evaluation of his early novels is equally severe, especially in terms of their weak characterization. But there is one aspect of these early works that escapes his mordant self-criticism—their poetic quality: 'Non que le meilleur de moi-même: le poète, ne s'y exprime déjà tout entier' (*ORTC*, I, 988).[15] But what precisely is the relationship between Mauriac's first two collections of verse and his first two novels?

The first point to consider concerns dates of composition (as opposed to publication). Mauriac places the dates '1909–1912' at the

---

[15] The quotation relates specifically to *L'Enfant chargé de chaînes*, *La Chair et le sang*, *Préséances*, and 'Le Visiteur nocturne'. But Mauriac says much the same about *La Robe prétexte* as well, associating his younger self as novelist with 'l'enfant de chœur' responsible for *Les Mains jointes* (*ORTC*, I, 990).

end of *L'Enfant chargé de chaînes* (*ORTC*, I, 79). As early as 1 November 1910, he wrote to tell Barrès that *Jean-Paul* (the novel's original title) was nearly finished, describing it as 'un petit livre commencé à vingt ans' (*NLV* 26)—a date which would put the novel's inception back to 1905–06. This was the period when Mauriac was involved with *Le Sillon*, an experience at the very heart of *L'Enfant chargé de chaînes*. The memory of his encounter with the movement's leader, Marc Sangnier, when the latter stayed at the Mauriacs' property in Langon, is transposed in the novel's ninth chapter. It is also worth noting that some parts of a letter written by Jean-Paul to Vincent (*ORTC*, I, 50) are taken almost verbatim from an entry in Mauriac's diary dated 25 December 1907.[16] So, although the bulk of the novel's text comes from a later date, there are a number of clear links with the period when Mauriac was working on *Les Mains jointes*.

The composition of *La Robe prétexte* is more difficult to trace, though the novel seems to have grown out of an initial short story ('Le Cousin de Paris') and its sequel ('Camille'), probably beginning to take definitive form during 1913. Since we cannot say for certain when Mauriac began work on 'Le Cousin de Paris', it is impossible to know whether there was any chronological overlap between the composition of the novel and that of the early verse. Mauriac certainly does not appear to have made as much direct use of earlier material as he did in his first novel, though his portrait of Camille derives, at least in part, from a 1906 diary entry about his cousin Louise.[17]

The broad plot lines of these early novels are certainly similar to those found in the early verse. Childhood memories dominate the first seven chapters of *La Robe prétexte* (cf. 'L'Enfance' section of *Les Mains jointes*),[18] while *L'Enfant chargé de chaînes* introduces us to a young man from the Landes who has just moved to Paris to study at the Sorbonne (cf. 'L'Etudiant' section of *Les Mains jointes*). Male friends such as Vincent Hiéron and José Ximénès play significant and supportive roles, whereas relationships with women (Marthe and Ca-

---

[16] See Mauriac, 'Ecrits de jeunesse', pp. 24–25.

[17] See Mauriac, 'Ecrits de jeunesse', p. 19 and Colin B. Thornton-Smith, 'Les Adolescentes d'autrefois dans *la Robe prétexte*', *CFM*, 11 (1984), 203–14 (pp. 208–10).

[18] Similarly, Jean-Paul's exclamation: 'O mon enfance, […], c'est vers vous toujours que je reviens' (*ORTC*, I, 13) clearly echoes the epigraph from Charles Demange at the start of the first section of *L'Adieu à l'adolescence* (367).

mille in particular, but also both Liettes) often prove more problematic (cf. 'L'Ami' section of *Les Mains jointes*). Both novels end with a return to the Landes, whether in mind or in body (cf. the final section of *Les Mains jointes*, 'Une retraite'),[19] though, in the case of *La Robe prétexte*, this return is followed by a final departure. I suggested in Chapter 2 that the plot lines of the early verse contribute to the delineation of Mauriac's *espace autobiographique*; the same is true of his early novels. Mauriac says of *L'Enfant chargé de chaînes*: 'j'y dessine d'un trait maladroit ma silhouette' and, of *La Robe prétexte*: 'là encore je me suis peint moi-même' (*ORTC*, I, 988, 989). Supporting evidence for these statements is readily available in Petit's notes for the Pléiade edition.

In addition to having a similar narrative shape, these early verse and prose texts also draw on similar lexical and semantic fields. Just as the term *âme* is omnipresent in the verse, so it is in the novels.[20] When Jean-Paul claims he was born with 'le goût de délicieusement s'intéresser aux âmes' and Jacques says he has 'le goût des âmes' (*ORTC*, I, 50, 133), they mirror the sentiments expressed in the poem 'Mon Dieu, plus que le charme...' (*AA* 389). Terms such as *médiocrité, tristesses, crépuscule, isolement, solitude, mélancolie, pleurer, peine* and their cognates occur repeatedly in *L'Enfant chargé de chaînes*,[21] just as we have seen they did in the verse.

Other similarities are more thematic in character. Neither Jean-Paul (*ORTC*, I, 6) nor the poet in 'Pourquoi faut-il...' (*AA* 387) receives any consolation from his travels. The reference to 'la divine amitié plus douce que l'amour' in the epigraph from Vallery-Radot and which finds expression throughout the third section of *L'Adieu à l'adolescence* (387) is echoed by Jacques's interest in the leading figures of Romantic Catholicism 'à qui l'amitié donnait de plus rares

---

[19] The term *retraite*, used in its religious sense, is actually found towards the end of both novels (*ORTC*, I, 68, 190).

[20] Touzot (*François Mauriac, une configuration romanesque*, p. 9) has counted seventy-five occurrences of the word *âme* in *L'Enfant chargé de chaînes* and describes it as 'le maître mot du livre' (p. 5).

[21] Here are just a few page references for each term from *ORTC*, I: *médiocrité* (4, 6, 15, 37, 38, 50); *tristesses* (6, 15, 24, 34, 37, 59); *crépuscule* (7, 33, 45, 48, 73, 77); *isolement* (7, 61); *solitude* (15, 41, 47, 55, 61, 68); *mélancolie* (4, 12); *pleurer* (16, 37, 42, 51); *peine* (23, 41, 47, 79).

joies que n'en donna l'amour au commun des hommes' (*ORTC*, I, 130). I have noted a degree of sexual ambivalence in the verse; in the novels we find certain gender confusions that perhaps point in a similar direction. Thus, one young woman tells Jean-Paul that he has the arms of a girl and another tells Jacques that some girls would envy him his white skin (*ORTC*, I, 43, 137). When Jean-Paul says: 'j'ai commencé à me délivrer de moi-même' (*ORTC*, I, 78), it is because of his new attachment to Marthe; in a similar way, the poet's childhood dies when he is in the arms of his beloved (*AA* 408). And Jacques's evocation of 'la volupté sacrée de la vie conjugale' (*ORTC*, I, 179) is mirrored throughout the final section of *L'Adieu à l'adolescence*. Finally, as if echoing the title of the 1911 collection, both novels end by evoking the possibility of bidding farewell to the past in terms that relate back to their respective titles (*ORTC*, I, 79, 191).

Then there are connections of a more stylistic nature. A similar periphrastic construction is used to describe Christ in both verse: 'le seul ami qui soit toujours fidèle' (*MJ* 340), and prose: 'le seul maître qui ne déçoive pas' (*ORTC*, I, 20). The narrator's address to Jean-Paul's childhood self in the second person singular (*ORTC*, I, 52) is reminiscent of the technique adopted in a poem such as 'Un jour clair et pesant…' (*AA* 385). Prayers making use of phrases such as *(O) mon Dieu/ Seigneur* are frequent in both *L'Enfant chargé de chaînes* and *L'Adieu à l'adolescence*.[22] Considerable attention is paid to olfactory impressions in all four texts.[23] And there are prose passages where the syllabic influence of verse is readily detectable. Here are a few examples of dodecasyllabic sentences from both novels:

1. Ah! je vois clairement ma médiocrité. (*ORTC*, I, 50)
2. Ah! dormir… dormir d'un sommeil indéfini… (*ORTC*, I, 60)
3. Il sentit sourdre à ses yeux la source des pleurs. (*ORTC*, I, 61)
4. Les ombrelles s'ouvraient comme de larges fleurs. (*ORTC*, I, 90)
5. Les arbres paraissaient engourdis de chaleur. (*ORTC*, I, 148)
6. Les feuilles des platanes étaient immobiles. (*ORTC*, I, 164)
7. Grand-mère, jalousement, détenait les clefs. (*ORTC*, I, 181)
8. Le salon sous ses housses paraissait en deuil. (*ORTC*, I, 182)

[22] See, for example, *ORTC*, I, 10, 23, 38, 58, 61, 62, 78 and *AA* 367, 368, 371, 372, etc.
[23] See, for example, *ORTC*, I, 48, 51, 59, 74, 121, 127, 141–42, 153, 189; *MJ* 325–31, 342, 362–63; *AA* 371, 382, 385–86, 388, 397, 399, 406–07.

The heroes of Mauriac's first two novels, Jean-Paul and Jacques, are themselves poets. Mauriac even presents them as the authors of some of his own verse: part of a stanza quoted by Jean-Paul is reproduced in 'L'Ami I' (*ORTC*, I, 34; *MJ* 339), while Jacques recites one of Mauriac's unpublished poems (*ORTC*, I, 148–49, 1052). Significantly, though, their poetry is seen as being of poor quality (*ORTC*, I, 4, 128). Is this just ironic self-deprecation on Mauriac's part, or is he already experiencing that dissatisfaction with his early verse that would become so apparent in later years? The presence of Mauriac's own verse in the early novels is by no means limited to the two instances just quoted, as can be seen from Tables 19 and 20 in the Appendix.

Constraints of space make it impossible to undertake a full analysis of these parallels here.[24] I shall limit myself instead to the general observation that Mauriac's first novel makes more extensive use of his verse than his second. Despite the fact that *L'Enfant chargé de chaînes* is less than three quarters the length of *La Robe prétexte*, it contains nearly twice as many lexical parallels with the verse and these parallels tend to be more extended than is the case in his second novel. This is probably due to the fact that the composition of *L'Enfant chargé de chaînes* coincided more closely with the early verse than was the case for *La Robe prétexte*.

The evidence presented in this section demonstrates that, whether viewed in terms of plot, theme, style, or lexis, there are numerous affinities between Mauriac's early verse and novels. The parallels are particularly strong between *L'Enfant chargé de chaînes* and *L'Adieu à l'adolescence*. There are, of course, many passages in the novels that are not directly related to the verse: the numerous dialogues between characters, for example, or those passages whose function is to advance the plot by narrating events. However, the remaining passages (particularly the descriptive ones), frequently display some kind of link with Mauriac's poems. The article referred to in note 24 will show that, while Mauriac is sometimes content merely to lift a pictur-

---

[24] For a detailed consideration of the parallels between Mauriac's first novel and his verse, see my forthcoming article (in *NCFM*), 'Echos des *Mains jointes* et de *L'Adieu à l'adolescence* dans *L'Enfant chargé de chaînes*'.

esque detail from his verse and incorporate it into his novel, there is generally some degree of overlap between the contexts surrounding the parallel quotations. These contexts relate to a limited number of well-defined areas: memories of childhood/ adolescence; religious experience; melancholia; the natural world (especially the landscape of the Landes); and the search for love. The language used in the poems tends to be slightly more condensed and occasionally more ornate (e.g., the use of inversion), but most of these differences are essentially due to the prosodic exigencies of versification. In other words, there is a high degree of stylistic similarity between these early prose and verse texts. Perhaps this is why, with hindsight, Mauriac was dissatisfied with his youthful efforts in both genres: the poetry is too much like versified prose and the novels rely too heavily on heroes who mirror the rather insipid lyric *je* of the verse.

Transitional novels

As the Great War progressed, Mauriac became increasingly dissatisfied with his pre-War output, confessing to his wife in July 1915: 'je frémis devant le néant de ce que j'ai fait jusqu'à cette heure' (*NLV* 59). This sense of inadequacy could only have been heightened when, towards the end of the War, Mauriac met for the first time Gide, Valéry, and Proust[25]—three writers whose work he already knew, but whose influence would soon begin to displace the likes of Barrès and Jammes.

Mauriac would have to wait until 1922 before enjoying real success and critical acclaim with the publication of *Le Baiser au lépreux*. But what about the transitional novels composed and/ or published between *La Robe prétexte* and *Le Baiser au lépreux*: how was Mauriac evolving as a novelist and how does this relate to his evolution as a poet over the same period? The works in question are *La Chair et le sang* (1920), *Préséances* (1921), and *Le Mal* (1924). Their publication dates are somewhat misleading, since *La Chair et le sang* was written during the period 1914–19, *Préséances* during 1918–20, and *Le Mal* during 1917–23 (*ORTC*, I, 1063, 1094, 1228). All three novels are

---

[25] Mauriac met Gide and Valéry at Mme Muhlfeld's *salon* in 1917 and Proust at Mme Alphonse Daudet's in February 1918.

quite different from Mauriac's pre-War work.[26] Canérot has shown a number of ways in which the style and structure of Mauriac's prose in the texts under consideration in this section move away from the model of the *roman-poème* towards a more conventional novelistic form.[27]

The element of self-absorption, so prevalent in Mauriac's pre-War work, is largely absent from these transitional novels. It is true that there is a significant autobiographical dimension to *Le Mal*, but even here there is less self-portraiture than in his first two novels. Mauriac is clearly attempting to broaden his vision as a novelist. But there are still a number of connections with the verse he wrote subsequent to *L'Adieu à l'adolescence*. In terms of the dramatic situations explored in these novels, the triangular relationships in both *Préséances* (Augustin–the narrator–Florence) and *La Chair et le sang* (Claude–Edward–May) partly reflect that of 'Le Disparu' (*le disparu–l'Ami–l'Amie*): in all three texts, a young man is the object of competition between a male and a female character. Indeed, in *Préséances*, Augustin is twice referred to as *ce/ le disparu* (*ORTC*, I, 385, 394) and, on the second occasion, this is in the explicit context of the Great War. A further thematic link with 'Le Disparu' concerns the portrayal of female desire: *l'Amie*'s sensuality is mirrored by the ostensibly 'pure' May: 'Aujourd'hui, voilà qu'elle se reconnaissait la sœur misérable, la sœur charnelle des filles d'Eve, esclave de la chair et du sang, sujette au même instinct, au même appétit que les bêtes: une femelle!' (*ORTC*, I, 255). The extraordinary virulence of this passage suggests something of a phobia on Mauriac's part. In a similar vein, just as *l'Ami* blames female love for killing off male childhood and exiling men from the 'candide Royaume' (Dis 417), so Fanny Barrett, contemplating the sleeping Fabien Dézaymeries, becomes aware of 'la chasteté de ce visage si mâle, cette noblesse des jeunes hommes

---

[26] Petit has shown that the original version of *Le Mal* is still 'très proche de *L'Enfant chargé de chaînes*, avec ses discussions religieuses et politiques' (*ORTC*, I, 1232), but these elements are absent from the definitive text.

[27] Canérot, 'Les Premiers Romans', pp. 84–86.

qu'une femme a mission de corrompre et qui survit à toutes les souillures, ce reste d'enfance sur sa face' (*ORTC*, I, 701).[28]

Generally, however, the relationship between the protagonists in *Le Mal* is closer to the situation portrayed in *Le Sang d'Atys*: Fanny's affair with Fabien (the son of her childhood friend) echoes Cybèle's passion for Atys. As the maternal earth goddess, Cybèle is metaphorically the mother of Atys; because of her friendship with Thérèse Dézaymeries, Fanny is metonymically the mother of Fabien. Colombe, presented as the antithesis of Fanny (*ORTC*, I, 711), could be viewed as fulfilling a similar role to that of Sangaris in the poem. When Fanny enters her dressing room and finds Fabien and Colombe burning with desire for each other, she attempts to commit suicide (*ORTC*, I, 718); her despair demonstrates the same depth of pain as Cybèle's fury when she discovers Atys and Sangaris making love (*SA* 455). There are other, more incidental, similarities between these transitional novels and *Le Sang d'Atys*. When Fabien goes riding in a vain attempt to forget Fanny, their is a physicality about the description (*ORTC*, I, 666) that reminds one of the sexual connotations of Atys's appearance on horseback (*SA* 450–51). In *Préséances*, God is presented as a hunter (*ORTC*, I, 372) just as He is in the poem (*SA* 444, 452). And, in the same novel, jellyfish ('méduses') are used both as an image associated with a negative view of ageing and as an objective correlative of the narrator's inner desolation (*ORTC*, I, 412, 427); similarly, they feature in one of the laments in which Cybèle compares herself unfavourably with Sangaris (*SA* 449).

However, the majority of links between these novels and Mauriac's verse relate to *Orages*—hardly surprising when one recalls the direct chronological overlap (the poems were composed during the years 1912–23). The term 'orage' is used as a metaphor for sexual passion in *Le Mal* (*ORTC*, I, 730), but the theme is foregrounded in all three novels.[29] The very title *La Chair et le sang* suggests a drama of

---

[28] Cf. a contemporary letter (November 1923) in which Mauriac, discussing Joseph Kessel's novel *L'Equipage*, refers to 'cette peinture exacte de l'amitié ou plutôt de la camaraderie héroïque que c'est la mission des femmes de détruire' (*NLV* 87).

[29] The social satire of *Préséances* means that the *libido sentiendi* is partially eclipsed by the *libido dominandi* as the narrator attempts to climb into the upper echelons of Bordeaux's 'aristocratie du bouchon' (*ORTC*, I, 1099). However, his sister Florence's sexual escapades help ensure that the theme of desire is never too far away.

bodily desire played out against a backdrop of religious concerns.[30] For the Apostle Paul, the phrase denotes humanity in its mortality and imperfection (its 'fallenness' in traditional Christian terms): 'Je l'affirme, frères: la chair et le sang ne peuvent hériter du Royaume de Dieu, ni la corruption hériter de l'incorruptibilité.'[31] This is exactly how the metonymy is used in the novel (*ORTC*, I, 197, 255, 280, 285, 310). The central conflicts of *Orages*—between flesh and spirit, sin and grace—are also at the heart of these novels. Fabien's oscillation between desire and renunciation (*ORTC*, I, 681) is precisely that of the poet in *Orages*. The association of desire and disgust, familiar from the verse (*Or* 430), recurs in the novels too (*ORTC*, I, 277, 302, 694). Specifically, in a manner reminiscent of the poem 'Assassin' (*Or* 431), Edward and Fabien long to be freed from their respective lovers once their sexual thirst has been slaked (*ORTC*, I, 259, 683).[32] The verb *rôder* is used to signal sexual curiosity just as it was in *Orages*.[33] The image of the 'marin' is used to evoke skill in negotiating the sea of love in both 'Sédentaire' (*Or* 427) and *Le Mal* (*ORTC*, I, 710). Fabien's 'yeux fuyants' (*ORTC*, I, 726) recall 'la fuite des regards' referred to in 'Tartufe' (*Or* 432); indeed, Fabien refers to himself as Tartufe (*ORTC*, I, 709), with Mauriac once again preferring Rimbaud's spelling to Molière's. Also, the figure of David occurs in these novels (*ORTC*, I, 227, 304, 409) as he does in *Orages* (445).

As with the early novels, there are moments when the syllabic sequences of French verse seem to haunt Mauriac's prose. Here are just a few examples:

1. Vainement leurs jeunesses s'attiraient / et l'une l'autre s'émouvaient, / il fallait qu'ils parlassent de cela: / à cet obscur drame charnel, / un autre s'ajoute qui le dépasse. (*ORTC*, I, 232; 10 + 8 + 10 + 8 + 10 syllables)
2. Une treille frissonne encore au vent marin. (*ORTC*, I, 429; 12 syllables)
3. L'Irlandaise riait, embrassait sa chérie. (*ORTC*, I, 652; 12 syllables)

---

[30] During its composition, Mauriac refers to *La Chair et le sang* as 'un roman assez terrible qui me lavera de tout soupçon de spiritualisme' (*LV* 71) and as a work 'qui tient les promesses du titre' (*NLV* 78).

[31] I Corinthiens 15. 50.

[32] Fanny tells one of her friends that she thinks of Fabien as her 'assassin' (*ORTC*, I, 729).

[33] See *Or* 432 and cf. *ORTC*, I, 225, 229, 250, 408, 411, 651, 669, 682, 732.

4. Les pins géants cernaient la maison de ténèbres. (*ORTC*, I, 654; 12 sylla-
    bles)
5. Seule éclatait sa bouche peinte et sans sourire. (*ORTC*, I, 660; 12 syllables)
6. Et le courant la confondit avec les mousses. (*ORTC*, I, 685; 12 syllables)
7. Aurait-il désiré qu'elle fût là ce soir? (*ORTC*, I, 709; 12 syllables)

Tables 21–23 in the Appendix show that are also numerous extended verbal parallels between the novels and the verse. While *Le
Mal* offers an 'average' number of parallels (seven), *Préséances* provides very few (only three). Given Augustin's status as a new Rimbaud and the fact that the anonymous narrator was himself something
of a poet as a schoolboy (*ORTC*, I, 420, 988, 335), this might seem
rather surprising. However, Mauriac's focus on social satire in this
novel perhaps made him feel that too overtly poetic a tone would be
inappropriate. In this first-person narrative, it may also be that Mauriac felt less inclined to use his 'own voice'. There is a certain self-
consciously literary character to the prose of *Préséances*. Partly this is
due to Mauriac's difficulty in producing convincing dialogue,[34] and
partly to his desire to use his narrator's prose as a means of contributing to the latter's characterization. If the narrator's text appears artifi-
cially literary at times,[35] it is no doubt because his style is intended to
reflect his superficial character.

The number of verse parallels for *La Chair et le sang*, on the
other hand, is very high (twenty-four). I would suggest that this is due
in large part to the use of Malagar as a setting. What had been merely
a 'décor' in *L'Enfant chargé de chaînes* becomes an integral part of
Mauriac's imaginative world in *La Chair et le sang* and also, to a
certain extent, in *Le Mal* (though not in *Préséances*). In Mauriac's
own mind, there is a clear connection between this discovery of *his*
atmosphere and the poetic quality of his writing; hence the telling

---

[34] For example, Florence says of her future husband: 'Tandis que je faisais la planche,
par de timides brasses il se rapprochait...' (*ORTC*, I, 347). The adjective placed before
the noun (there are a further thirteen examples in this chapter's three and a half pages)
and the placing of the adverbial phrase before the verb in the second clause (twelve
syllables in length) are hardly characteristic of standard speech. Cf. Blanche's perceptive comments on Mauriac's bookish dialogue (*François Mauriac–Jacques-Emile
Blanche*, p. 74).

[35] For a good example, see the first two paragraphs of Part I, Chapter 4 (*ORTC*, I,
346).

juxtaposition of sentences when he re-reads his early novels: 'Non que
le meilleur de moi-même: le poète, ne s'y exprime déjà tout entier.
L'atmosphère de Malagar baigne et pénètre *La Chair et le sang*'
(*ORTC*, I, 988).[36] Limitations of space prevent a full analysis of the
parallels between prose and verse in this novel, but such an analysis
(which I hope to publish elsewhere in due course) would reveal that
the parallels are rarely incidental: the contexts are mutually illumi-
nating, offering complementary perspectives on the common (and
often related) themes of sexual desire and the natural world. In the
absence of precisely dated manuscripts for all the texts concerned, it is
often impossible to say whether it was the verse that influenced the
prose or vice versa. And even if a full array of such manuscripts were
available, it still would not settle the issue definitively, since writers
may well carry certain images and formulae in their minds for a long
time before actually committing them to paper. What is clear is that
similar images and concerns characterize novels and verse alike; there
is an undoubted unity about Mauriac's varied literary production. As
Mauriac himself admitted, his world may well be somewhat limited in
scope (*OA* 90), but it is unmistakably *his* world and it is in *La Chair et
le sang* that it truly begins to take shape for the first time as the contours of the 'petite planète Mauriac' start to emerge (*ORTC*, I, 989).[37]
In *La Chair et le sang*, the landscape around Malagar provides Mauriac with the symbols and sense impressions he requires to create his
own imaginative universe. What one might call the mythic qualities of
this universe are beginning to help Mauriac's work transcend the
rather limited subjectivism of his early years.

Building a reputation
The previous two sections have shown a striking number of parallels
between Mauriac's verse and those novels whose composition either
preceded or overlapped the period of the Great War. In this section, I
shall examine the five texts that allowed Mauriac to claim a place
among the leading novelists of his generation: *Le Baiser au lépreux*
(1922), *Le Fleuve de feu* (1923), *Genitrix* (1923), *Le Désert de l'a-*

---

[36] On reading *La Chair et le sang*, Max Jacob wrote to Mauriac: 'Votre livre [...]
décèle un poète' (quoted by Lacouture, *François Mauriac*, I, 211).
[37] Which is why Lacouture's assessment of *La Chair et le sang* as 'son roman le plus
manqué' (*François Mauriac*, I, 123) strikes me as unnecessarily harsh.

mour (1925), and *Thérèse Desqueyroux* (1927). I have chosen *Thérèse Desqueyroux* as the cut-off point for this section primarily because its date of composition (begun in early 1926 and completed in October of the same year)[38] means that it is the last of Mauriac's novels to have been written prior to the 'official' start date for the composition of *Le Sang d'Atys* (1927). Much more has been written about these novels than about those considered in previous sections. However, the question of the relationship between these texts and Mauriac's poems has so far escaped critical attention.

The publication of *Le Baiser au lépreux* marked the moment when, as Mauriac puts it, 'en même temps que mon style, j'ai trouvé mes lecteurs' (*ORTC*, I, 990). Yet when he began work on the novel in January 1920 (*OA* 258), he was also working on such distinctly second-rate material as 'La Paroisse morte' (published in *La Revue des jeunes* in January 1921). It is obvious, therefore, that the success of *Le Baiser au lépreux* is not purely a matter of chronology. What are the qualities that made this short text qualitatively different from Mauriac's previous fiction? For Lacouture, it is because 'le *ton* y est, avec un personnage obsédant, une musique, et, d'un coup, cet alliage qui est le propre même du génie de Mauriac entre les battements du cœur humain et les frémissements de la forêt'.[39] For Canérot, on the other hand, it is less a question of style or atmosphere than of genuinely effective novelistic structures, that is, the fact that the novel 'se dépouille de tout développement extérieur au récit. [...] Le poète, l'homme de pensée et de foi cède le pas à l'inventeur de destins.'[40] The plot gains in importance; the hero is engaged in a series of events that shape his destiny; different characters act upon each other in significant ways; and the novelist utilizes a tight structure, almost as compressed and relentless as that of Classical tragedy,[41] to drive a dramatic situation towards its resolution. This rigorous structure leaves no room for the 'allure poétique' of the pre-War novels: 'Ce-

---

[38] Lacouture, *François Mauriac*, I, 293, 298.

[39] *Ibid.*, I, 218; his italics.

[40] Canérot, 'Les Premiers Romans', p. 86.

[41] Cf. Michel Dyé, 'Du roman-tragédie linéaire au théâtre: la ligne dramatique de l'écriture mauriacienne', in *François Mauriac et d'autres*, ed. by Bernard Swift, Rona Kanawati, and Angus Martin (Sydney: Macquarie University/ Société Internationale des Etudes Mauriaciennes, 2000), pp. 97–113 (pp. 100–01).

pendant Mauriac ne renonce pas à la poésie, sa vocation première. Il en fait une composante de son récit'.[42]

Canérot does not indicate how this 'poésie' manifests itself. Perhaps it has to do with the rhythm of Mauriac's prose. As with previous novels, it is not hard to find clauses or sentences whose rhythm is derived from that of the alexandrine. Here are a few examples taken from *Genitrix*:

1. Elle entendit grincer la porte du perron. (*ORTC*, I, 584)
2. la mort douce de ceux qui ne sont pas aimés. (*ORTC*, I, 598)
3. le murmure endormi d'un rêve végétal. (*ORTC*, I, 604)
4. Il était là, debout, dans le soleil atroce. (*ORTC*, I, 614)
5. [Ils avaient opposé à] l'inévitable mort la famille éternelle. (*ORTC*, I, 615)
6. Il n'est pas de martyre que dans le sublime. (*ORTC*, I, 624)

Then there are those passages where Mauriac remains attentive to the expressive possibilities afforded by phonemic clusters:

1. [Marie] inspecta le jardin vide, où la prairie chantait sous une palpitation de papillons. (*ORTC*, I, 532)
2. Tout était endormi, sauf ce froissement de feuilles… (*ORTC*, I, 808)
3. Penchée sur le jardin, Maria sentit sur ses lèvres cette saveur salée (*ORTC*, I, 814)
4. Maintenant c'est une main molle et mouillée (*ORTC*, I, 823)

Such features help create the poetic dimension of Mauriac's novelistic prose, since, as Jakobson suggests:

> Poeticity is present when the word is felt as a word and not a mere representation of the object being named or an outburst of emotion, when words and their composition, their meaning, their external and inner form, acquire a weight and value of their own instead of referring indifferently to reality.[43]

Given this definition of poeticity, one could also say that the various networks of imagery in these novels contribute to their poetic quality, since they help create a vertical axis of metaphorical significance that complements the horizontal axis of plot and character development. Each novel exploits particular semantic fields: in *Le*

---

[42] Canérot, 'Les Premiers Romans', p. 87.
[43] Jakobson, *Language in Literature*, p. 124.

Baiser au lépreux, there is considerable use of animal imagery; in *Le Fleuve de feu*, fire and water are to the fore, as well as hunting and fishing; in *Genitrix*, images related to warfare and worship are prominent; in *Le Désert de l'amour*, it is deserts and fire; and in *Thérèse Desqueyroux*, we find both fire and water imagery again, as well as networks revolving around imprisonment and pathways. I shall not explore any of these networks further, as they have nearly all been traced by other critics.

More relevant for present purposes are the direct verbal parallels between these five novels and Mauriac's verse collections (see Tables 24–28 in the Appendix). Although there is no obvious pattern here in terms of quantity, a pattern does emerge when we consider the distribution of the parallels. Eleven out of the thirteen parallels identified in the first two novels are with extracts from *Orages*, which is what one might have expected given that the composition of both novels was contemporaneous with that of *Orages*. By contrast, only half of the remaining parallels concern poems from *Orages*; there are now as many parallels with *Le Sang d'Atys*. Although Mauriac claims not to have started work on this cycle until 1927, he clearly incorporated certain images and expressions first used several years earlier. Whether this was a conscious process or not is impossible to say in the absence of appropriate manuscript evidence.

In addition to these overt verbal parallels (some of which are admittedly stronger than others), there are also a considerable number of similarities between novels and verse in terms of more general themes, imagery, and lexis. Consider, for example, a passage from *Le Baiser au lépreux* when Jean Péloueyre has gone into self-imposed exile in Paris:

> Il voyageait par la pensée sur ce corps que jamais il n'avait contemplé qu'endormi. Dans le sommeil, [...], le triste faune avait mieux appris à connaître ce corps que si, amant heureux, il l'eût possédé dans un mutuel délire. Il n'avait jamais tenu entre ses bras qu'un cadavre mais il l'avait réellement pénétré avec ses yeux. [...] La tête entre les mains, Jean Péloueyre s'excitait à la colère: il reviendrait au pays, s'imposerait à cette femme, jouirait d'elle, dût-elle en crever! Il en ferait un objet à son usage... (*ORTC*, I, 475)

There are a number of parallels here with the sentiments expressed by the lyric *je* of *Orages*. The opening image of mental voyaging recalls

the voyages of sexual desire evoked in 'Sédentaire' (*Or* 427). Jean
Péloueyre is described as a 'faune';[44] the same term provides the title
of a poem in *Orages* that focuses on the same kind of secretly desiring
male gaze displayed by Jean Péloueyre: 'Prométhée envieux du feu de
ton visage, | Je le vole à toute heure et rien ne me trahit' (430). The
same poem contains the line: 'Ton corps est violé dans mon cœur,
sans répit' (430); an even more shocking rape fantasy features in the
quotation from the novel given above.

The topos of sexual desire also underlies a number of similarities
between Mauriac's verse and *Le Fleuve de feu*. Like the poet of
Orages, Daniel Trasis is overwhelmed by the power of desire to the
extent that he too entertains a rape fantasy (*ORTC*, I, 515, 516). Suffering as a result of Gisèle de Plailly's apparent inaccessibility, Daniel
Trasis longs to sleep 'contre Cybèle accablée' (*ORTC*, I, 532) in a way
that recalls the Atys of *Orages* (427–28). For Lucile de Villeron, he is
'ce rôdeur' (*ORTC*, I, 543)—a term that recalls the poet's self-
description in the opening line of 'Tartufe': 'Je rôde, orage lourd,
autour de ta jeunesse' (*Or* 432). The emphasis that we find on the
human body in *Orages* is also to be found in the novel (*ORTC*, I, 547–
48). Describing Gisèle's body after she and Daniel have spent the
night together, the narrator comments: 'On l'eût dit tuée dans le sommeil' (*ORTC*, I, 548), a comment that reminds us of the frequent association of sex and death in *Orages*. Both Gisèle and Daniel experience
as lovers the dragging of time as each of them awaits some kind of
response from the other (*ORTC*, I, 563, 579)—a theme that is foregrounded in the poem 'Péché mortel' (*Or* 429). The title of this poem
is itself incorporated into the novel with the description of Gisèle's
daughter as 'son péché mortel mais à jamais vivant...' (*ORTC*, I, 566).
Gisèle's sense of disgust after losing her virginity—'Mais sa bouche,
à son insu, faisait la grimace du dégoût' (*ORTC*, I, 558)—recalls the
role played by 'le Dégoût' as God's accomplice in *Orages* (430). And
when we read of Daniel that: 'toujours il se sentait, l'acte étant ac-
compli, enclin au renoncement' (*ORTC*, I, 549), we can see a clear
parallel with the cycle of desire and renunciation that marks much of
Mauriac's poetry.

---

[44] Raymond Courrèges is also described as a 'faune' when he tries to make love to
Maria Cross (*ORTC*, I, 824).

The metaphor foregrounded in the title of *Orages* is found on a number of occasions in the novels, generally in relation to sexual desire. One thinks, for example, of the description of the new doctor in *Le Baiser au lépreux*: 'L'orage, c'était ce garçon pâle et furieux de désir et de qui les yeux paraissaient "chargés" comme le ciel' (*ORTC*, I, 494). *Le Désert de l'amour* provides numerous examples of these metaphorical or symbolic storms.[45] This novel also anticipates certain aspects of *Le Sang d'Atys*. The description of Maria Cross's forehead, 'ce front vaste et calme' (*ORTC*, I, 759), recalls the description of Cybèle: 'Reine à l'immense front' (*SA* 449). And the interest that Maria Cross as an older woman shows in the teenage Raymond Courrèges, an interest that has its maternal dimension as she seeks to compensate for the loss of her son François (*ORTC*, I, 815), partly reflects the relationship between Cybèle and Atys.[46] *Le Désert de l'amour* also emphasizes the association between men and trees that would later prove so important in *Le Sang d'Atys*. In addition to the reference to 'la jeune forêt humaine' given in Table 27 in the Appendix (an image used to describe the seventeen-year-old Raymond Courrèges and his school friends), we read: 'L'accablement des arbres était humain: on eût dit qu'ils connaissaient la torpeur, la stupeur, le sommeil' (*ORTC*, I, 819). In Mauriac's world, human beings are tree-like and trees are like human beings. The association between the two is even more prominent in *Thérèse Desqueyroux*: here, pines have a heart; they suffer from rickets; they seem to make signs to the heroine; they form a 'foule' just as men do; and the noise that the wind makes in their upper branches is human.[47] Mauriac's imagination is clearly close to starting work on *Le Sang d'Atys*.

When Amrouche pointed out the fourth parallel between *Le Désert de l'amour* and *Orages* given in Table 27, Mauriac answered: 'Oui, justement, parce que c'est contemporain; j'ai vraiment conçu des romans comme *Thérèse*, comme *Le Désert de l'amour*, je les ai vraiment conçus comme des poèmes' (*SR* 200). It is difficult to know exactly what Mauriac meant by this, since the five novels reviewed in

---

[45] See *ORTC*, I, 784, 787, 805, 811, 812, 814, 824.
[46] This theme first emerges in Daniel Trasis's fear of 'la poursuite d'une femme acharnée et vieille' (*ORTC*, I, 504).
[47] See *ORTC*, II, 52, 104, 99, 100, 86, 106.

this section are those in which he achieved a mastery of the novel form precisely because he moved away from the type of *roman-poème* practised, in different ways, by Barrès and Jammes. Hence Rivière's enthusiasm for *Le Désert de l'amour* (awarded the Grand Prix du roman de l'Académie Française in 1925): 'Cette fois, vous y êtes tout à fait. [...] C'est un roman, un vrai.'[48] This judgment is particularly interesting given Rivière's comments in his influential article, 'Le Roman d'aventure' (1913). In this, Rivière stated that: 'L'époque symboliste a été le règne de la poésie: il semble bien que nous entrions aujourd'hui dans l'âge du drame et du roman.'[49] From Rivière's perspective, Mauriac's early works (whether in verse or prose) would be classified as belonging to the Symbolist era. When Rivière wrote: 'Dans l'œuvre qu'enfin vous me présenterez, je veux ne plus trouver trace des plaintes de votre cœur, de vos mélancolies, ni de vos élans et n'avoir affaire qu'à des événements', he could almost have been addressing himself directly to his fellow-Bordelais.

In his novels of the 1920s, Mauriac rises to the challenge laid down by Rivière. But while this fiction is certainly more conventionally novelistic than his earlier work, we have also seen that it retains a significant 'poetic' dimension. I have shown that this is partly due to various types of parallels with his verse. But it is also due to the fact that, compared to previous novels, a greater economy of means results in more intense texts whose powerful sensuality and concentrated metaphorical networks can justifiably be described as poetic.

Mature novels
This section will focus on Mauriac's novels published between 1928 and 1939: *Destins* (1928), *Ce qui était perdu* (1931), *Le Nœud de vipères* (1932), *Le Mystère Frontenac* (1933), *La Fin de la nuit* (1935), *Les Anges noirs* (1936), and *Les Chemins de la mer* (1939). In one way, it is perhaps rather odd to include *Destins* in this group, as this is a novel written at the height of Mauriac's religious 'crisis',

---

[48] *François Mauriac et Jacques Rivière*, p. 46. Similarly, Griffiths sees *Le Désert de l'amour* as representing Mauriac's real break with the traditional Catholic novel—see Richard Griffiths, '1920–1925: du "roman catholique" traditionnel au roman mauriacien', *CFM*, 11 (1984), 23–39 (p. 32).
[49] Jacques Rivière, *Nouvelles Etudes* (Gallimard, 1947), p. 250. The next quotation is from pp. 264–65.

whereas the others all post-date his 'conversion' of November 1928. The significance of this religious experience is such that it is commonplace for critics to distinguish between a pre- and post-1930 Mauriac. However, I prefer to group *Destins* with the novels of the 1930s for two reasons: firstly, the sequence of novels from *Destins* to *Les Chemins de la mer* coincides with the official composition dates of *Le Sang d'Atys* (1927–38); and, secondly, this sequence of novels also shows Mauriac's efforts at broadening his scope as a novelist.[50] *Destins* may be a weak title, but it underlines Mauriac's interest in studying the interactions of a group of characters, rather than pursuing the somewhat narrower focus of his earlier novels. It may well be true that this broader approach can be related to his conversion,[51] but it is a process that begins in what is perhaps his least Christian novel. The attempt to paint on a larger fictional canvass could also be seen in terms of an effort to produce more traditionally 'novelistic' texts, more in line with the broad social sweep of classic nineteenth-century fiction. If this is so, does it mean that these novels are less 'poetic' than their predecessors?

In one sense, the answer to this question would have to be in the affirmative. If the novelist writes longer texts with more space devoted to developing the relationships between characters and inventing more involved plots, the text's lyrical dimension, even if it remains present, will seem less prominent. This hypothesis is supported by the statistics given by Touzot for the average number of images per page for all Mauriac's novels up to and including *La Pharisienne* (listed below in order of publication):[52]

Table 17:

L'Enfant chargé de chaînes	1.09	*Thérèse Desqueyroux*	2.87
La Robe prétexte	2.06	*Destins*	2.17
La Chair et le sang	2.55	*Ce qui était perdu*	1.96
Préséances	2.73	*Le Nœud de vipères*	2.38
Le Baiser au lépreux	3.50	*Le Mystère Frontenac*	1.89

[50] See Petit's notes (*ORTC*, II, 995, 1060; III, 1035, 1194–95).
[51] As implied by Marie-Françoise Canérot, *Mauriac après 1930: le roman dénoué* (SEDES, 1986), p. 61.
[52] Touzot, *François Mauriac, une configuration romanesque*, pp. 146–47.

Le Fleuve de feu	4.26	*La Fin de la nuit*	1.38
Genitrix	3.72	*Les Anges noirs*	1.90
Le Mal	3.69	*Les Chemins de la mer*	2.07
Le Désert de l'amour	3.19	*La Pharisienne*	1.09

Images are often seen as being related to a text's poeticity.[53] If this is so, then the statistics in Table 17 provide an empirical guide to one level of poeticity within Mauriac's novels. The number of images rises as one moves through the first six novels and then declines through the next six. There is no such neat pattern for the final six novels, though one notes that the intensity of images is, in all cases, relatively low. The difference between the figures for *Thérèse Desqueyroux* and *Destins* supports the decision to include the latter novel in the present section. With the exception of *La Fin de la nuit*, the figures for the novels under consideration in this section all fall within a relatively narrow band from 1.89 to 2.38.

There is also the issue of narrative point of view. Although manuscript evidence reveals that Mauriac was frequently tempted by the first-person narrative, the vast majority of his novels are, in fact, written from the perspective of an omniscient third-person narrator. In the novels to be considered in this section, however, there are two significant exceptions to this rule: Louis's letter-cum-diary that makes up the bulk of *Le Nœud de vipères* and Gradère's lengthy prologue to *Les Anges noirs*. These narrative voices are subtly different from Mauriac's usual authorial voice and this may effect the degree of lyricism in the respective texts.[54] For example, it is noticeable that shortly after Louis becomes more human,[55] there is an increase in the degree of personification in his text (especially in Chapter 18). The amount of dialogue used is another important factor. In both *Ce qui était perdu* and *Les Anges noirs*, dialogue accounts for a considerable proportion of the text. While it is true that the dialogue in Mauriac's early novels

---

[53] See, for example, Cohen, *Structure du langage poétique*, p. 48.

[54] This is not to suggest that the texts are devoid of 'poetic' passages. With his customary flair, Jean Touzot discusses the poeticity of *Le Nœud de vipères* and *La Pharisienne* (another first-person narrative) in 'Histoire et partition poétique', *CFM*, 14 (1987), 237–49. He does not, however, note any connections between these novels and Mauriac's verse.

[55] 'Cette tête de Méduse [...] se métamorphosait, devenait simplement humaine' (*ORTC*, II, 499).

is often rather bookish, the dialogue in these later novels approximates more closely to natural speech. Inevitably, the scope for lyricism as traditionally conceived is therefore much reduced. Location is also a factor: *Ce qui était perdu* and *La Fin de la nuit* are both set predominantly in Paris (as are important sections of *Le Nœud de vipères*, *Le Mystère Frontenac*, and *Les Chemins de la mer*) and it is clear that Mauriac finds the capital a less 'poetically charged' setting than the countryside around Bordeaux. Finally, there are elements within particular texts that tend to militate against a lyrical style: the planning and execution of a murder in *Les Anges noirs*, for example, or the comic notes injected into *Les Chemins de la mer* in the chapters given over to the monologues of Landin's sister.

Yet, despite the fact that these novels seem less closely related to Mauriac's verse than was the case for his earlier fiction, one can still identify a number of close textual parallels between the two corpora, as can be seen from Tables 29–35 in the Appendix. Although there is no great variation in the number of parallels found, it is perhaps significant that the lowest number of parallels are to be found in novels that are, in some way, atypical for Mauriac: *Ce qui était perdu* because it is set in Paris and consists largely of dialogue; *Le Nœud de vipères* because it is a first-person narrative; and *Les Anges noirs* because of the centrality of Aline's murder. Two of the highest number of parallels, on the other hand, coincide with the beginning and end of the period when Mauriac was working on *Le Sang d'Atys*. Perhaps the influence of his verse weighed more heavily on his mind when he was beginning and completing this poem. The close lexical similarities between *Destins* and *Le Sang d'Atys* in Parallels 5 and 8 of Table 29 certainly suggest that the borrowing is entirely conscious on these occasions.[56] The two parallels between *Destins* and *Les Mains jointes* are more unexpected until one remembers that Mauriac's first collection of verse had been republished in 1927. Mauriac had contributed a new preface to this edition and had clearly re-read his early verse by way of preparation.

Le Mystère Frontenac is another novel for which six parallels have been identified (Table 32). But, if one compares these with the five identified for *La Fin de la nuit* (Table 33), the average length of

---

[56] Cf. Paul Croc, *'Destins' de François Mauriac* (Hachette, 1972), pp. 18–20.

the parallels differs considerably between the two texts. Whereas it is a question of relatively brief notations in *La Fin de la nuit*, often related to human physical appearance, the parallels are generally longer, less verbally precise, and more focused on the natural world in *Le Mystère Frontenac*. This latter novel is generally regarded as one of Mauriac's most 'poetic' novels[57]—indeed, Mauriac himself describes it as 'un poème' (*LV* 210). There are two main reasons for this: firstly, Mauriac draws extensively on vivid childhood memories of holidays spent among the pines of the Landes; and, secondly, the novel foregrounds Yves Frontenac's own development as a poet. The net result is the creation of a lyrical tone that is particularly intense in Chapter 4 (which narrates Yves's birth as a poet), Chapter 9 (when the miracle of childhood is recreated through Blanche's absence and Oncle Xavier's prolonged visit), and the last section of Chapter 22 (when Yves imagines the family's ultimate reunion above the pines of Bourideys).[58]

As with Mauriac's earlier novels, there are also a number of parallels between prose and verse that are not based on direct lexical similarities. These range from small details such as the description of Tota Revaux's arm as 'un reptile hésitant dont la main eût été la tête' (*ORTC*, III, 285), an image that is echoed in the description of Atys's limbs as 'doux serpents' (*SA* 449), to a much more diffuse feature such as the 'atmosphère panique' that Mauriac discerns in *Destins* (*ORTC*, I, 991) and that is very much the climate of *Le Sang d'Atys*. The characters of this poem are clearly present in the novelist's mind even if he does not refer to them directly very often. The triangle formed by Elisabeth Gornac, Bob Lagave, and Paule de La Sesque in *Destins* recalls the relationship between Cybèle, Atys, and Sangaris. Elisabeth's quasi-maternal bond with Bob (*ORTC*, II, 114) recalls not only the Cybèle–Atys relationship, but also that between Phèdre and Hippolyte. This Phèdre–Cybèle theme recurs in Thérèse Desqueyroux's relationship with Georges Filhot and in Mathilde Desbats's passion for Andrès Gradère (*ORTC*, III, 1020, 1032–33). Atys's meta-

---

[57] It is the only novel in this section for which Petit identifies a poetic dimension (*ORTC*, II, 1238, 1241).

[58] For detailed discussions of these scenes, see my *Mauriac et le mythe du poète*.

morphosis is echoed in the frequent associations made between humans and trees, especially pine trees.[59]

The linking of sexuality and death that was so prominent in *Orages* emerges even more clearly in these novels. Thérèse's heart condition means that her feelings prompted by Georges Filhot's desire threaten, quite literally, to kill her (*ORTC*, III, 136, 143). The description of Gradère's murder of Aline has unmistakably sexual overtones, especially in the original manuscript (*ORTC*, III, 1029). The association between sex and death is particularly prominent in *Les Chemins de la mer*, culminating in the 'côtés scabreux' of Landin's murder (*ORTC*, III, 689).[60] The shock of his father's suicide causes the sixteen-year-old Denis Révolou to view love-making as 'le geste qui ensemence de futurs cadavres' (*ORTC*, III, 571), a particularly pessimistic image even in Mauriac's world. The similarity between this image and the final line of the poem that narrates Atys's self-emasculation— 'Le sang trouble d'Atys ensemençait le monde' (*SA* 461)—suggests that, for Mauriac, it is only through the sublimation of sexuality that death can be overcome.

It is clear, then, that the novels of Mauriac's maturity continue to bear the influence of his verse in a variety of ways. However, I have not yet mentioned the most important of the associations between prose and poetry to be found in the texts produced during this period. I am referring to Mauriac's decision to incorporate significant sections of *Le Sang d'Atys* in *Les Chemins de la mer*. While, as we have seen, Mauriac includes brief quotations from his own verse in his earliest novels, the degree of self-quotation in *Les Chemins de la mer* is of an altogether different order.

While the finished text of *Les Chemins de la mer* is deeply indebted to *Le Sang d'Atys*, it is clear from the first version of the text, composed in August 1937, that Mauriac did not initially intend including extracts from the poem in his novel (*ORTC*, III, 1203–24). There are two obvious explanations for Mauriac's change of mind. The first is that he may have wished to gauge the critical response to his poem before deciding whether to publish it in its entirety (one

---

[59] See *ORTC*, II, 588, 667, 670, 673; III, 251, 347, 565, 570, 571, 610, 611, 626, 631, 672, 696.

[60] For additional connections between sex and death, see *ORTC*, III, 569, 570, 663, 669, 688.

remembers how much time and effort he had devoted to this poem).[61] But why choose to publish extracts in a novel rather than in a specialist journal? Perhaps (and this is the second reason) because Mauriac, hugely successful as a novelist, but still virtually unrecognized as a poet, hoped to generate more potential readers for *Le Sang d'Atys* by obliging them to read extracts in his new novel.

As I have examined the relationship between verse and prose in *Les Chemins de la mer* in some detail elsewhere,[62] it would be superfluous to repeat that analysis here. However, it might be useful to list precisely which parts of the poem are present in the novel:

Table 18:

	Extract	*CM*	*SA*
1	Whole of 'Sommeil d'Atys'	555	449
2	Repetition of last 4 lines of 'Sommeil d'Atys'	562	449
3	Stanza 1 of 'Plaintes de Cybèle'	582	447
4	Stanza 2 of 'Plaintes de Cybèle'	583	447
5	Whole of 'Trahison d'Atys'	602	455
6	Repetition of line 12 of 'Trahison d'Atys'	604	455
7	Stanzas 1 and 2 of 'Atys à Cybèle'	612	448
8	Stanza 3 of 'Plaintes de Cybèle'	639	448
9	Stanzas 8 and 9 of 'Cantique de Cybèle'	641–42	452
10	Stanza 5 and lines 1–2 of stanza 6 of 'Cantique de Cybèle'	642	451–52
11	Lines 6–29 of stanza 1 of 'Atys en état de grâce'	686–87	461–62
12	Stanza 13 of 'Cantique de Cybèle'	701	453
13	Line 1 of stanza 11 of 'Cantique de Cybèle'	701	452
14	Lines 1–3 of stanza 12 of 'Cantique de Cybèle'	701	452

Notes
- The figures under *CM* (*Les Chemins de la mer*) are page references to *ORTC*, III.
- The figures under *SA* (*Le Sang d'Atys*) are page references to *OC*, VI.

[61] It was Gide who encouraged publication after he heard Mauriac read the poem at Malagar during the summer of 1939 (Lacouture, *François Mauriac*, II, 103). A few weeks later, Mauriac wrote to Paulhan, offering him the poem for the *NRF*, but only if publication of the entire cycle could be guaranteed (*LV* 236).
[62] Cooke, 'Le Poète et la poésie dans *Les Chemins de la mer*'.

In other words, the novel reproduces about 30% of the poem (118 lines out of 390). The manuscript reveals that the percentage would have been higher had Mauriac not made certain cuts.[63] Although the order of the extracts quoted does not follow that of the verse cycle, most of the poem's main themes are present, with the exception of the war of the Atys and the ultimate reconciliation with the Lamb.

Although the majority of the novels considered in this section are less obviously connected to Mauriac's verse than is the case for the novels of the 1910s and 1920s, we have seen that the links are never entirely absent. Moreover, in the last of his novels of the 1930s, the association between prose and verse is more strongly foregrounded than ever before. Although Mauriac was certainly not the first writer to incorporate lengthy sections of verse within a prose narrative (one thinks, for example, of Novalis's *Heinrich von Ofterdingen*), it was certainly not a common practice. Balzac, who himself combined the two genres in *La Muse du département* (1843), felt the need to defend his decision in the following terms: 'Quoique l'alliance des vers et de la prose soit vraiment monstrueuse dans la littérature française, il est néanmoins des exceptions à cette règle.'[64] Is Mauriac's juxtaposition of these codes in *Les Chemins de la mer* 'monstrous', or does his novel prove one of the 'rare exceptions'?

The decision to include extracts from *Le Sang d'Atys* in *Les Chemins de la mer* certainly creates some problems. One of these concerns the question of credibility. The notion that an inexperienced adolescent aged between sixteen and eighteen should be responsible for the poem with which Mauriac had struggled throughout his maturity is a little hard to believe, especially as Pierre tells Denis that the subjects of his poetry 'ne [les] concernent pas', since they have not yet started loving 'pour de vrai' (*ORTC*, III, 602). Like Augustin (*Préséances*) and Yves Frontenac before him, Pierre is, of course, modelled on the precocious poetic genius of Rimbaud. Mauriac therefore allows Pierre to ask himself in *style indirect libre* whether he might not be a genius, adding: 'Il n'est nullement grotesque de se le dire à soi-même' (*ORTC*, III, 678). But, of course, since Mauriac is himself the author of

[63] See *ORTC*, III, 1244, 1268, 1272, 1273, 1298.
[64] Honoré de Balzac, *La Comédie humaine*, ed. by Pierre-Georges Castex and others, 12 vols (Gallimard, 1976–81), IV: *Études de moeurs: Scènes de la vie de province* (1976), p. 657.

Pierre's poem, it would indeed be at least immodest (if not grotesque) for him to pursue this idea too far.

Perhaps a more fundamental problem concerns the respective aesthetic qualities of the prose and verse. Although Mauriac regarded the story of Rose's broken engagement as one of the high points of his art (*ORTC*, III, 925) and, near the end of his life, cited *Les Chemins de la mer* as one of the novels of which he remained proud (*BN*, V, 14), he was not always so favourably disposed towards it. On 28 December 1937, for example, he wrote to his daughter, Claire: 'J'écris un roman assommant. On voit bien que c'est pour le percepteur' (*LV* 422). Certainly critics have never considered this novel as one of Mauriac's finest. Petit observes that the natural world is less present in *Les Chemins de la mer* than in most of Mauriac's other novels, partly as a result of the location (Léognan being based on the family property of Château-Lange, rather than on Malagar or Saint-Symphorien) and partly because it is the poem which assures the presence of nature within the novel (*ORTC*, III, 1420). There seems to be an implicit critique here that the novel's prose is rather flat in comparison with its verse. More trenchantly, Lacouture sees *Les Chemins de la mer* as a 'roman avorté' that is only really redeemed by the verse extracts it contains.[65] And, for Touzot, the novel demonstrates that 'la citation et la paraphrase des poètes trahissent toujours un affaiblissement de la veine romanesque'.[66]

Nevertheless, despite these shortcomings, the novel does illustrate in exemplary fashion the close relationship that exists between Mauriac's verse and his fictional prose. The juxtaposition of the two texts may not always be very flattering for the prose, but it is important to note how each text demands to be read in the light of the other.[67] Although not a testamentary text in the manner of *Le Mystère Frontenac* or *Un adolescent d'autrefois*, *Les Chemins de la mer* does appear to have been produced at a significant juncture in Mauriac's development as a writer. When, in November 1937, his first play, *Asmodée*, was performed to great acclaim at the Comédie-Française,

---

[65] Lacouture, *François Mauriac*, II, 97.

[66] Jean Touzot, 'Les Voies de la poésie dans le roman', *La Licorne*, 11 (1986), 9–16 (p. 11).

[67] This is clearly demonstrated in my article 'Le Poète et la poésie'.

he immediately penned an article entitled 'Le Romancier peut se re-
nouveler par le théâtre et le cinéma' (*ORTC*, III, 962–63). This title is
an implicit admission of a sense of novelistic exhaustion, something
that also emerges clearly from his 1939 essay, *Les Maisons fugitives*
(*ORTC*, III, 908). And, as shown in Chapter 8, he was also becoming
increasingly engaged in political journalism. Perhaps, then, *Les Chemins de la mer* should be seen as the text in which Mauriac begins his
protracted farewell to both verse and the novel. If the text does indeed
have this quasi-testamentary function, then perhaps the explicit manner in which it brings together verse and prose should be read as an
encouragement to view all of Mauriac's previous novels in terms of
the interaction of these two codes.

Last novels
In this final section, I shall consider the five novels Mauriac wrote
after the publication of *Le Sang d'Atys*, that is: *La Pharisienne* (1941),
Le Sagouin (1951), *Galigaï* (1952), *L'Agneau* (1954), and *Un adolescent d'autrefois* (1969). Due to its unfinished state, I shall not be
considering *Maltaverne*, published posthumously in 1972. The only
one of the five novels to have been composed while Mauriac was still
writing poetry destined for publication was *La Pharisienne*. One
might therefore expect this group of novels to display fewer parallels
with Mauriac's verse than those examined earlier in this chapter.

Tables 36–39 in the Appendix partly support this hypothesis. *La
Pharisienne* offers a few close verbal parallels with Mauriac's verse
(Table 36), especially with *Le Sang d'Atys*. This is not surprising
given that the poem was initially published in the *NRF* in January
1940 and that Mauriac was working on the novel only six months
later.[68] But the parallels are certainly not numerous. If reasons were to
be sought for the relative scarcity of parallels in what, for Mauriac, is
a long novel, one could point to the fact that he opted for a first-person
narrator (hence a slightly different style) and that one of his major
concerns was to counter Sartre's claim that he was not a genuine nov-

---

[68] According to Lacouture (*François Mauriac*, II, 125), the novel was written from
July to November 1940.

elist—hence an uncharacteristically close attention to questions of narrative technique.[69]

Le Sagouin is the only one of Mauriac's novels for which I have been unable to find a single extended verbal parallel with his verse. One reason for this may be that the novel is rather different from the rest of Mauriac's fiction due to its proximity to a *conte* (*ORTC*, IV, 1212–13).[70] But, even here, we find the personification of trees that is so familiar from his verse (*ORTC*, IV, 325, 371). This association between men and trees is also found in *L'Agneau* (*ORTC*, IV, 507). As shown in Table 38, this novel only offers two, very brief, verbal parallels with Mauriac's verse. It is interesting, therefore, to note Durand's observation that *L'Agneau* offers a spare, concentrated narrative in which Mauriac 'refuse les digressions, le relâchement, le lyrisme'.[71] One final parallel with the verse that should be noted comes from Jean de Mirbel's reference to Ganymède (*ORTC*, IV, 508). Like the subject of Mauriac's poem, Xavier de Dartigelongue could be described as a 'Ganymède chrétien' (*Or* 444). The allusion to this mythological character relates to the theme suggested by the novel's original title, *La Griffe de Dieu* (*ORTC*, IV, 1337).

Galigaï, on the other hand, presents a rather different picture. No doubt this is partly due to the fact that one of the main characters, Nicolas Plassac, is a poet based fairly transparently on Mauriac's friend, André Lafon (*ORTC*, IV, 1256). This also helps explain why a number of the parallels relate to Mauriac's early verse (Lafon, it will be remembered, died during the First World War). As in Mauriac's verse, we find sexual desire in the novel associated variously with hunger, powerful smells, hunting, and death (*ORTC*, IV, 389, 399, 417, 426). And, in addition to the seven clear parallels listed in Table 37, there are also passages that offer broader links with Mauriac's verse. Here, for example, is the description of Gilles and Nicolas as they are watched by Mme Agathe on a summer evening:

---

[69] See Caroline Casseville, 'Présence et absence de Sartre à travers *La Pharisienne*', *NCFM*, 8 (2000), 189–98.

[70] One critical study of the novel devotes a chapter to its 'poésie', though the term is used rather loosely, and never in connection with Mauriac's verse—see Luisa Borella, '*Le Sagouin*' *de François Mauriac* (Firenze: La Nuova Italia Editrice, 1980), pp. 67–74.

[71] Mauriac, *L'Agneau*, ed. by François Durand, p. 13.

Ils étaient penchés sur le jardin. Ils devaient dire: 'Ça sent bon la terre mouillée...' car quelques larges gouttes s'étaient déjà écrasées sur les feuilles flétries du tilleul. [...] Les deux garçons étendirent leurs mains pour recevoir la pluie qui maintenant tombait avec violence. Agathe se leva, revêtit son imperméable. Le chêne l'abritait. Un brusque éclair l'aveugla; un écroulement dans les nuées livides fut recouvert par l'immense plainte chuchotée de la pluie. La fenêtre fut refermée. La glace luisait toujours qu'interceptait parfois l'ombre d'un des garçons. (*ORTC*, IV, 392–93)

Elements of this description can already be found in the second part of 'A la mémoire de R. L.':

> Le jardin rafraîchi s'ouvrait à la nuit claire,
> Et sur les prés brûlés dans la torpeur du jour
> L'orage était passé comme un immense amour.
> Une odeur de mouillé venait des terres molles,
> Et ton bras doucement pesait sur mon épaule. (*MJ* 362–63)

As in the prose passage, a garden is refreshed by nocturnal rain after a hot summer day; the earth gives off a distinctive smell; and there is physical contact between two young men. The very muted homoeroticism of the poem becomes more explicit in the novel where there is an unmistakably homosexual undertone to the friendship between Gilles Salone and Nicolas Plassac. Further frustrated desire emanates from Mme Agathe whose passion for Nicolas is unreciprocated. The triangular relationship presented in the prose passage quoted above, in which a jealous older woman spies on the closeness of a younger couple, recalls the passage from *Le Sang d'Atys* in which Cybèle secretly observes Atys and Sangaris making love:

> L'orage qui rôdait à travers les ramures
> Éclaira d'un feu bref deux mondes confondus,
> Deux pâles univers l'un dans l'autre perdus:
> Atys et Sangaris, dont la blancheur humaine,
> L'espace d'un éclair, déconcerta ma haine.
> Je tordis sur leurs corps mille bras furieux,
> Mais l'âpre paradis où ces corps m'avaient fuie,
> Le Plaisir, les rendait indifférents aux dieux
> Et la foudre inutile embrasait de ses feux
> Leurs jeunes flancs luisants de sueur et de pluie.
> Alors je fis silence autour de ce bonheur.
> Mes branches s'égouttaient sur la double torpeur,
> Sur le double sommeil de cette chair souillée

D'où montait le parfum de la terre mouillée. (*SA* 455)

The rain, the lightning, the smell of the damp earth, and the silence of the concealed observer who hates her rival—these elements are common to the verse and the prose passage and suggest that the latter derived (perhaps unconsciously) from the former.

The influence of *Le Sang d'Atys* is also evident in Mauriac's last completed novel, *Un adolescent d'autrefois*. When Marie tells Alain Gajac that he is 'composé d'un alliage où ce qui vient du Christ se confond avec ce qui vient de Cybèle...' (*ORTC*, IV, 775), she is presenting him as a kind of living embodiment of Mauriac's poem. The terminology used by Alain when he says he deceived his mother during his affair with Marie—'je la trompais' (*ORTC*, IV, 750)—suggests a quasi-sexual infidelity. The relationship between Mme Gajac, Alain, and Marie therefore mirrors that between Cybèle, Atys, and Sangaris. When Alain and Marie make love at Maltaverne, the wonderful night they spend together turns out to be unrepeatable and, on subsequent occasions, this unique experience gives way to 'le dégoût' (*ORTC*, IV, 775).[72] There is a lexical similarity here with the concluding stanza of 'Autre péché' (*Or* 430), but there is also a parallel with the way in which 'le bonheur' that initially characterized the love-making of Atys and Sangaris soon dissolves into the language of moral unease: 'Atys sort confondu de sa propre déroute' (*SA* 455, 456).

Unlike the semi-autobiographical protagonists of Mauriac's first two novels, Alain Gajac does not appear to write poems himself. When M. le Doyen calls him 'un poète', he means simply that the young man has a fertile imagination (*ORTC*, IV, 672). However, there are certainly ways in which Alain's text could be regarded as poetic. When he writes: 'Quelle étrange alchimie au-dedans de moi transfigurait toutes ces choses de néant' (*ORTC*, IV, 760), one is reminded of Mauriac's comment about 'les poètes de sept ans' who 'détiennent un pouvoir de transfiguration qui fait bon marché des apparences' (*OA* 373). Although this highly self-conscious narrator is aware of the facility of certain poetic clichés (*ORTC*, IV, 675), his style is strongly lyrical on occasions, especially when describing the landscape around Maltaverne (clearly modelled on Malagar). Pines are frequently per-

---

[72] Alain inherits this 'dégoût' from his mother (*ORTC*, IV, 723).

sonified and even divinized (*ORTC*, IV, 673). Elsewhere the pines
bleed, bless, watch, and wave (*ORTC*, IV, 786, 787, 810, 811). Here is
a more extended example of the narrator's lyricism, focusing on a
stream rather than trees:

> Je me retrouvai dans cette ténèbre lactée d'un soir de lune, [...], attentif au
> ruissellement de la Hure, à cette calme nuit murmurante, à cette même
> clarté qui baignera la pierre sous laquelle le corps que je fus finira de pour-
> rir. Ce temps qui coule comme la Hure et la Hure est là toujours et sera là
> encore et continuera de couler... Et c'est à hurler d'horreur. (*ORTC*, IV,
> 704)

The mingling of darkness and milky moonlight, the bubbling brook,
and the personification of a murmuring night create a distinctly lyrical
atmosphere in the first sentence, an atmosphere that is punctured by
the closing image of a rotting corpse (a distant echo of Baudelaire's
poem 'La Charogne', perhaps). This reminder of human transience in
the first sentence contrasts with the endlessness of natural cycles
evoked in the second sentence where the play of (semi-)vowel sounds
(/u/, /y/, and /ɥ/ in particular) and the alliteration in /k/ add to the sense
of infinite repetition. Then, in the third sentence, Alain's sense of
injustice at the contrast between his ephemeral existence and the eternity of the natural world is captured in a verb ('hurler') that provides a
phonemic amalgamation of 'Hure' and 'couler', the two most significant words in the preceding sentence: the magical Hure has become a
source of 'horreur' (again, one notes a phonemic similarity in the
terms).

Alain, then, is not only 'attentif au ruissellement de la Hure', he
is also attentive to the poetic function of his own text. When he writes:
'Il pleut *s*ur les *ch*ênes de la *Ch*icane. Ce *ch*uch*o*tement indéfini a*j*oute
encore à l'i*s*olement de *c*ette lande perdue' (*ORTC*, IV, 783), the nine
italicized sibilants reveal again his interest in the phonemic expres-
siveness of language. Elsewhere, repetition of a particular phoneme
reveals something more akin to a psychological obsession. Thus,
Alain's recollection of his dead father concludes: 'En face d'elle le
fauteuil du pauvre papa était vide. Père, il ne restait de toi accrochée
au-dessus du lit de maman que ta photographie agrandie par Nadar...'
(*ORTC*, IV, 726). There are no fewer than twelve /a/ sounds in these
two sentences—and /a/ is, of course, the only vowel sound in the word

'papa'. The father's chair may be vacant, but his memory continues to haunt the son's imagination in ways that recall Mauriac's earliest (unpublished) verse.[73]

Table 39 shows how clearly Alain's text recalls the verse that Mauriac actually published. But there are further similarities in addition to these extended verbal parallels. When Alain writes: 'Ma douleur jouissait d'elle-même' (*ORTC*, IV, 722), one cannot help thinking of the self-indulgent melancholy of Mauriac's early verse. Similarly, the ease with which Alain cries recalls the lachrymose tendencies of the poet in *Les Mains jointes*. And Alain's comment on his tearfulness—'Toute ma religion ne tenait qu'à ce geste d'enfant malheureux qui pour tant d'autres serait à la fois une absurdité et une lâcheté' (*ORTC*, IV, 730–31)—is reminiscent of the terminology used by Mauriac in the 1927 preface to his first collection of verse (*MJ* 323–24). Alain's sexual ambivalence—'A vingt et un ans, je pouvais être la proie du premier venu, de la première venue' (*ORTC*, IV, 741)—recalls aspects of Mauriac's early verse. The same is true of Alain's description of Marie at Maltaverne: 'Dans sa robe claire d'été, sous son chapeau de paille, elle était une autre Marie que celle de chez Bard, la jeune fille que je n'avais pas connue' (*ORTC*, IV, 755). This idealized 'jeune fille' is very similar to the vision of the beloved in 'Laissez l'ombre envahir...', with her 'simple chapeau de paille' and her 'robe [...] claire' (*AA* 405). Keller, one of Alain's student acquaintances, had described *Le Sillon* to him as an 'amitié'. Alain comments: 'On s'aime, c'est de l'amour, et il n'y a pas la chiennerie' (*ORTC*, IV, 788)—words which recall the *amitié/ amour* contrast found in some of Mauriac's early poems. Finally, the circularity of Mauriac's early verse, where the poet ends up returning more or less to where he began, is reflected in the passage from Flaubert's *Education sentimentale* used by Alain to sum up his own life: 'Il ne revint pas, parce qu'il n'était pas parti...' (*ORTC*, IV, 768).[74]

---

[73] The absent father is the subject of some of the poems dating from 1901–03 in MRC 2 and MRC 3 held at the Doucet. For a fuller discussion of the absent father in Mauriac's novels, see my article 'The Paternal Reverie in Mauriac's "Mémoires imaginaires"', *French Studies*, 50 (1996), 299–310.

[74] The end of *Un adolescent d'autrefois* is, in fact, more open than this quotation suggests. However, the unfinished *Maltaverne* reveals the essentially static nature of Alain's subsequent career: he is 'l'homme d'un seul livre' (*ORTC*, IV, 825).

In this section, I have been considering novels whose publication was increasingly far removed from the period when Mauriac published his verse. It is hardly surprising, then, that these novels published during the last thirty years of his career should offer fewer direct similarities with his verse than those published before the Second World War. Far more surprising is the fact that such similarities exist at all—but they do, especially in *Galigaï* and *Un adolescent d'autrefois*. We have seen that the parallels are particularly numerous in the latter. It is surely no coincidence that Mauriac should choose a title for his last completed novel that recalled that of his second collection of verse. Indeed, one could say that *Un adolescent d'autrefois* essentially reproduces the broad plot lines of *Les Mains jointes* and *L'Adieu à l'adolescence*. The themes of the *domaine/ parc* (Maltaverne), the privileged male friend (Donzac), the mother (Mme Gajac), the beloved (Marie), religious scruples, the departure to Paris, student life, and the fleeting attraction of social commitment (*Le Sillon*) are all present in Mauriac's novel as they were in his early poetry.

Significantly, however, Mauriac's final completed novel also contains one very important new element: the rape and murder of Jeannette Séris (nicknamed 'le Pou'). It is the sound of Alain's foot snapping a piece of wood that makes Jeannette run off to her death (*ORTC*, IV, 792). She runs because she is frightened of Alain, knowing how much he hates her. The irony is that 'le Pou' is not (as Alain believes) a scheming pawn in Mme Gajac's machinations, but a twelve-year-old girl who genuinely loves him and who is in turn genuinely loved by Alain's mother (*ORTC*, IV, 796–801). Alain's self-absorption tragically blinds him to all of this. But, as he comes to realize the truth, the crime leads to an obsession on his part with 'le mystère du mal' (*ORTC*, IV, 820)—a subject which impressed itself increasingly on Mauriac in his post-1930 work. It is not the kind of subject he found easy to tackle in verse. Although *Un adolescent d'autrefois* provides many fine examples of Mauriac's lyrical prose and shows how that prose continues to draw on the themes and lexis of his verse, it also provides an implicit critique of the self-indulgent values that underpin this lyricism. If Alain Gajac had been less a prisoner of his past and less obsessed with his own anxieties, Jeannette Séris might never have died.

Conclusion

Although there have been a few very general surveys of Mauriac's poetry and some more in-depth discussions of individual collections, the present study is the first to have examined the whole of his verse corpus in detail.[1] Mauriac's verse has always been the poor relation of his prose. Yet it was as a poet that he began his literary career in 1909 and, as late as January 1968, we find him defiantly claiming the title of *poet*: 'je sais bien, quoi qu'on en puisse penser aujourd'hui, que Barrès ne s'était pas trompé et que je suis poète' (*BN*, V, 16). Indeed, at one point he even describes the poems of his maturity as the *only* part of his *œuvre* that was truly special to him (*OA* 463). There is, therefore, no doubt that he was profoundly disappointed by the reading public's neglect of his verse.[2] When he refers to 'cette indifférence, cet oubli qui assassine les poètes' (*OC*, XI, 176), one senses that he is speaking from the heart.

My principal aim in this study has been to go some way towards remedying this neglect. There are three reasons why I felt this project was worth undertaking. Firstly, as a Mauriac scholar, I was aware there was an important gap in the secondary literature that needed filling. Major writers need to be viewed from a variety of angles so that stereotyped or incomplete appreciations of their work can be avoided. I would not claim that Mauriac's verse is the most important part of his *œuvre*, but it certainly deserves more attention than it has generally received from *mauriaciens*, especially given the emphasis that Mauriac himself always placed on his status as a poet. As Kushner points out, 'les recueils de poèmes incarnent à leurs dates respectives le drame essentiel du poète.'[3] It is certainly true that the major stages in Mauriac's development as a writer (with the exception

---

[1] With the exception, as noted in the Introduction, of the juvenilia.

[2] Mauriac confessed in 1968: 'On n'a jamais voulu considérer en moi le poète. [...] J'ai souffert de ce refus.' See François Chapon, 'Le Fonds François Mauriac', in *Mauriac et les grands esprits de son temps*, ed. by Noël Herpe and others (Bibliothèque Historique de la Ville de Paris, 1990), pp. xi–xvi (p. xiv).

[3] Eva Kushner, *Mauriac* (Desclée de Brouwer, 1972), p. 60.

of his final period as 'le premier journaliste de France'[4]) can be identified with particular clarity as one moves through his verse. In the first
two collections, we see a young writer trying to find his own voice,
but still strongly indebted to precursors such as Musset, Verlaine,
Sully-Prudhomme, and Jammes. In the poems dating from the First
World War, especially 'Le Disparu', Mauriac begins to move away
from the sentimental religiosity of his early verse as he enters a significant transitional phase. With the poems of *Orages*, we are caught
up in the fierce struggle between faith and desire that would later cul-
minate in Mauriac's famous 'crise' of the mid-to-late 1920s. Finally,
in *Le Sang d'Atys* and 'Endymion', the engagement with mythological
material gives a deeper, more general resonance to Mauriac's concerns as a writer. Séailles is surely right, then, when he asserts that the
importance of Mauriac's poems 'ne saurait être sous-estimée dans
l'ensemble de sa création'.[5] As shown in Chapter 9, the influence of
Mauriac's verse is readily detectable in nearly all of his novels; indeed, the echoes of the verse in his prose provide one of the main
reasons (though by no means the only one) why it is appropriate to
consider him a poetic novelist.

The second reason why a study of Mauriac's verse is important
relates to the wider literary scene. It is, perhaps, inevitable that literary
history should focus on innovative currents, especially in our post-
Romantic age when innovation and individuality are so highly prized.
But, if one of the aims of literary history is to provide as full an account as possible of the various trends in literary production, then it
cannot afford to focus solely on writers whose work broke new
ground or on overtly avant-garde movements. Mauriac certainly has a
distinctive voice as a poet, but his use of traditional verse forms makes
him appear rather conventional. We have seen that he was no slave to
the rules of Classical versification, but he never strayed beyond the
limited degree of flexibility that had been current since the second half
of the nineteenth century. Guyonnet gets the balance right when she
observes that 'la versification de Mauriac est "sage", ce qui ne signifie
pas pour autant médiocre', adding: 'Nourrie de lectures classiques,

---

[4] Pierre de Boisdeffre, *Une histoire vivante de la littérature d'aujourd'hui (1939–
1964)*, 5th edn (Librairie Académique Perrin, 1964), p. 304.
[5] Séailles, *François Mauriac*, p. 143.

elle peut paraître réactionnaire en plein vingtième siècle.'[6] Somewhat perversely perhaps, the older Mauriac tended to glory in this aesthetic conservatism. Discussing modern art in 1962, he defined himself as being 'seul, dans le wagon de queue, dans un compartiment déserté où je me rencogne, à l'arrière-garde de l'arrière-garde', and five years later he admits to 'une certaine forfanterie [...] d'appartenir à l'arrière-garde!' (BN, III, 218; IV, 527). Such comments probably did little to commend Mauriac to a whole generation of critics, but, now that the polemical dust has settled, perhaps it is time to examine his production more objectively. In particular, there is a need to view Mauriac's poetry in the context of the general relationship between religion and literature in the first half of the twentieth century.[7] Virtually no work has been done on the so-called 'spiritualist' group which brought together Mauriac, André Lafon, Robert Vallery-Radot, and Eusèbe de Brémond d'Ars. There is still no history (literary or sociological) of Les Cahiers de l'Amitié de France. Nor has there been a definitive survey of the range of 'Catholic' poetry produced in twentieth-century France,[8] a survey that would certainly need to include a chapter on Mauriac. One could also envisage an interesting study on the different uses to which classical mythology has been put in modern French poetry. In other words, my study of Mauriac's verse could feed into a number of broader projects and, if this study encourages further analysis from other scholars, it will have served a useful purpose.

The third and final reason for studying Mauriac's verse is that, particularly in his later work, he is a much better poet than is generally imagined. The early verse is by no means devoid of value for Mauriac scholars, or for those with a more general interest in early-twentieth-

---

[6] Guyonnet, 'Mauriac et le mythe d'Atys', I, 451.

[7] Pace Cornell who seems dubious that 'discuss[ing] Mauriac in relation to Catholic verse' will yield any significant results. See Kenneth Cornell, The Post-Symbolist Period: French Poetic Currents, 1900–1920 (New Haven: Yale University Press; Paris: Presses Universitaires de France, 1958), p. 151.

[8] There has, however, been some useful recent work on the relationship between poetry and aspects of the sacred in modern French poetry from Baudelaire to Bonnefoy. See, for example, Jean-Pierre Jossua, Pour une histoire religieuse de l'expérience littéraire, 4 vols (Beauchesne, 1985–98) and Jérôme Thélot, La Poésie précaire (Presses Universitaires de France, 1997).

246 MAURIAC: THE POETRY OF A NOVELIST

century poetry, but its 'period charm' is unlikely to detain the reader for long on purely aesthetic grounds. His last two collections success-fully combine moral anxieties, intellectual tensions, powerful imagery, subtle sound-patterning, and prosodic adroitness in such a way as to offer the reader a varied and rewarding experience.

Does Mauriac the novelist conceal a great poet, as Alyn sug-gests?[9] Is he, alongside Claudel, 'sans doute le plus grand poète en notre temps de la Révélation, de la Faute et du Rachat'?[10] The an-swers to such questions are so dependent on personal preferences that they are perhaps hardly worth asking. Mauriac himself saw little point in producing league tables for poets (*OC*, XI, 159–60). 'Ce qui nous importe,' he wrote in 1936, 'c'est bien moins de classer un auteur, de lui donner un numéro d'ordre, que de se rendre compte de son exis-tence en tant que "monde"—s'il est une planète (fût-elle minuscule), s'il a son atmosphère propre, sa flore et sa faune' (*NLV* 172). Judged in these terms, it would have to be said that Mauriac *is* a successful author. There is indeed 'une petite planète Mauriac' (*ORTC*, I, 989) and, I would argue, its contours are more clearly discernible in his poems than in his novels. The distillation demanded by verse means that it is in this medium that 'les termes de [s]on vocabulaire per-sonnel' (that is, the central concepts that underpin all his writing)—'bien, mal, conscience, vie intérieure, responsabilité, foi, espérance, im-pureté, pardon' (*BN*, V, 59)—find their purest expression.

Mauriac once remarked that *Orages* and *Le Sang d'Atys* formed the glacier from which all his novels had flowed (*BN*, IV, 180). The statement would have been more accurate had he also mentioned the verse published prior to *Orages* which, as I have shown, had a signifi-cant influence on his pre-1920 fiction. But this caveat in no way de-tracts from his main point: namely, that an appreciation of Mauriac the poet is crucial for any evaluation of Mauriac the novelist.

---

[9] Alyn, 'Avant tout, un poète', p. 11.
[10] Séailles, 'Défense et illustration d'un poète', p. 301.

Appendix

Although not necessarily exhaustive, these tables offer a reasonably complete picture of the interpenetration of verse and prose texts in Mauriac's *œuvre*:

Table 19:

	L'Enfant chargé de chaînes (*ORTC*, 1)	Verse
1	la photographie de sa mère, ce sourire triste, flottant sur des traits adorés (8)	Leur sourire flottant sur des traits adorés, | Dans l'album où sont les vieilles photographies? (*AA* 367)
2	l'obscure maison de campagne, [...] sa bonne odeur de placard et de coing (13)	La maison de campagne obscure sent | Les coings (*MJ* 331)
3	l'album à photographies, où des messieurs et des dames souriaient qu'on ne connaissait plus (13)	l'album où des photographies [...] | Encore des inconnus avec des inconnues | —Sourires effacés qui ne disent plus rien... (*AA* 404)
4	le vent faisait un bruit monotone et doux dans les pins ondulants... (13)	Le vent [...] a des voix assoupies | Dans les grands pins blessés, aux cimes ondulantes. (*MJ* 332)
5	un ciel pâle et comme lavé—un ciel strié par les vols des martinets. Une odeur de campagne flotte sur la ville (32)	Le ciel pâle et taché d'ardoise semble attendre | Les vols des martinets qui n'y sont pas encor. | La rue a une odeur d'été, [...] (*AA* 388)
6	Une sirène pleurait à travers les brumes du port. (41)	En écoutant pleurer, dans les brumes du port, | Les appels prolongés et tristes des sirènes (*AA* 372)
7	des soirs pesants et lents à mourir, où l'on pleure sans cause, où le cœur s'éveille (42)	Où, dans les soirs lents à mourir, le cœur s'éveille (*AA* 405)
8	le samedi soir, [...] dans la cour solitaire. Des moineaux piaillaient autour des miettes du goûter. (42)	Ce soir, [...] | Comme ils doivent piailler les moineaux, dans la cour | Où toujours il restait du pain après quatre heures! (*AA* 371)
9	Et Jean-Paul se rappelle cette même route à cette même heure, quand, petit garçon aux yeux pleins de sommeil, il rêvassait dans la victoria... Comme ce soir la lune le poursuivait d'arbre en arbre (48)	Mon enfance [...] | Avec quelle douceur ce soir t'a rappelée! | [...] On s'endormait dans la victoria. [...] | Et que nous étions, d'arbre en arbre, poursuivis | Par la lune... (*AA* 369)
10	Les grands vents d'équinoxe se	Les grands vents d'équinoxe ont

11	lamentaient à travers les pins (51) ces vieux cantiques des veilles de 15 Août, [...] *Dieu de paix et d'amour, lumière de lumière.* (52)	pleuré dans les bois (*AA* 381) le vieux refrain des veilles de quinze août: | *'Dieu de Paix et d'amour, Lumière de Lumière...'* (*AA* 368)
12	La vitre ruisselait comme un visage plein de larmes (58)	La vitre ruisselant comme un visage en pleurs (*AA* 393)
13	l'accablement des siestes. (59)	le doux accablement des siestes. (*AA* 407)
14	le large apaisement de *la Sonate au clair de lune...* (59)	L'apaisement de *la Sonate au clair de lune...* (*AA* 403)
15	le collège clair et la chapelle odorante. Un jeune homme balance l'encensoir (68–69)	comme au clair collège de naguère, | Ils balancent, fronts hauts, le lys et l'encensoir. (Dis 421–22)
16	la prière du soir [...] ces formules qui viennent du lointain de son enfance: *Dans l'incertitude où je suis si la mort ne me surprendra pas cette nuit, je vous recommande mon âme, ô mon Dieu...* Comme son cœur d'enfant se serrait jadis devant le mystère de la mort, ainsi évoquée! (69)	Et l'oraison du soir montait de nos jeunesses. | O formules! *'Dans l'incertitude où je suis, | Si la mort ne me surprendra pas cette nuit...'* Comme je me souviens de ce soudain silence, | Après les mots: *examinons notre conscience...* (*AA* 368)
17	Il erre dans les allées symétriques. [...] Un peu de lune pâle est dans l'azur. (72)	Un peu de lune pâle est dans l'azur. [...] | C'est donc l'âme, ô mon Dieu, des heures en allées (*AA* 379)
18	les tocsins haletants qui se répandaient de village en village. Ils aimaient l'âcre odeur de résine brûlée (73)	Quand le tocsin sonnait, de village en village | [...] l'odeur des pins brûlés... | [...] après le tocsin haletant... (*AA* 406–07)
19	soirs complices (78)	Soir complice (*AA* 376)
20	Vous entendiez dans le grand silence des landes, les cahots d'une charette, [...] la salle à billard où restaient accrochés les chapeaux de soleil des grandes vacances. (78)	Nous n'entendrons, dans le grand silence des landes, | Que les lointains cahots d'une charrette lente... | [...] Dans la salle à billard, les chapeaux de soleil | Evoqueront pour nous les vacances passées. (*AA* 407–08)

Table 20:

	La Robe prétexte (ORTC, 1)	Verse
1	La veille, nous avions, [...], orné des reposoirs. (91)	La veille, on s'effarait autour du reposoir. (*MJ* 326)
2	les siestes accablées (139)	le doux accablement des siestes (*AA* 407)
3	une obscure tendresse (140)	une tendresse obscure (*MJ* 347)
4	l'odeur de la terre mouillée (149)	Une odeur de mouillé venait des terres molles (*MJ* 363)

5	Jamais l'ombre d'une chapelle n'avait été aussi douce à ma tristesse. (154)	O toi qui n'aimes plus que l'ombre des chapelles (*MJ* 340)
6	une rade pleine de départs pour les îles… (161)	Un départ éternel endeuillait cette rade (*AA* 373)
7	le vieux domaine (182)	le vieux domaine (*MJ* 329)
8	nous ne récitions plus en commun la prière du soir (184)	Réciter en commun la prière du soir. (*AA* 383)
9	Les mêmes tournantes allées (184)	ses tournantes allées (*AA* 373)
10	l'enfant que je fus (187)	l'enfant que je fus (*MJ* 325)
11	le domaine abandonné (191)	Ce parc abandonné (*MJ* 363)

Table 21:

	La Chair et le sang (*ORTC*, I)	Verse
1	Un souffle chaud qui ferait croire à l'orage (201)	comme un souffle chaud d'orage (Dis 416)
2	un verger offre au soleil les fruits qui, par instants, tombent et s'écrasent sur le sol durci. (204)	et le verger dont le sol est si dur | Qu'en leur chute il meurtrit les prunes reine-claude? (*MJ* 330)
3	la terre chaude et douce et complice de la chair des hommes et de qui l'odeur, aux soirs orageux, est celle même du désir… (208)	La terre fendue et chaude | Est complice de ton sang. | […] Ce soir, l'odeur de la terre | Est celle de ton désir. (*Or* 429)
4	les aveugles et sourdes constellations, avec leurs noms de mauvais dieux! (208)	J'invoque une étoile sourde | Au doux nom de mauvais dieu. (*Or* 430)
5	le grand silence de la campagne où Pan sommeille. (211)	Ce silence de la campagne où Pan sommeille. (*Or* 441)
6	un obscur élan de joie végétale (215)	cet élan de végétale joie (*Or* 441)
7	la volupté des labours exténués (215)	les labours exténués (*Or* 442)
8	Sieste: Claude regarde les hommes, comme une armée anéantie, joncher la prairie. Autour des meules, ils étendent leurs bras crucifiés. (224)	A l'heure où des faucheurs l'armée anéantie | Ecrasait l'herbe sous des corps crucifiés (*Or* 442)
9	Il rêve que ses pieds s'enracinent, que ses mains étendues se tordent et que sous la poussée de la sève, sa tête, dans les nuées, agite une chevelure de feuillages sombres. (224–25)	Rêve que désormais immobile, sans âge, | Les pieds enracinés et les mains étendues, | Tu laisses s'agiter aux orageuses nues | Une chevelure odorante de feuillage. (*Or* 441)
10	les cimes immobiles, qui font silence sur le sommeil des jeunes maîtres. (225)	Leurs jeunes flancs […] | Alors je fis silence autour de ce bonheur. | […] le double sommeil de cette chair souillée (*SA* 455)
11	Une cigale éclate, grince longuement, puis trouve son rythme et bat comme	Une seule cigale éclate, grince et bat | Comme le cœur souffrant de Cybèle

	le cœur souffrant de Cybèle engourdie. (225)	engourdie. (Or 428)
12	à la vie du fleuve, à cette circulation de la terre vivante. (226)	Et ton sang éternel sera, comme les fleuves, | La circulation de la terre vivante. (Or 441)
13	Ce même soir, qui était la veille du 15 Août, Claude dès qu'il eût diné, vint à la terrasse. De brèves fusées mouraient sur les domaines lointains où des familles fêtaient une Marie. (247)	Ce soir, leurs cloches vont sonner pour le quinze août, | Et je verrai la lueur brève des fusées | Au dessus de lointains et vieux domaines, où | L'on fête, avec des cris joyeux, une Marie... (AA 386)
14	ce ciel nocturne d'août traversé de bolides perdus. (248)	l'août [...] | Tend ses ciels traversés de bolides perdus. (VAL 469)
15	Un monde inconnu de sentiments, de délicatesses (248)	un monde inconnu de délices (AA 377)
16	elle aussi, jeune plante, en face de ce bel arbre embrasé (266)	ce qui te consume, ô jeune plante humaine (Or 443)
17	la proie inerte de son désir. (276)	cette inerte proie. (EE 465)
18	au soleil de mars [...] la tache jaune et mouillée d'une fleur. [...] la sève qui tremblait, se gonflait au bout des branches noires, dilatait les poisseux et gluants bourgeons. (277)	Mars gonflait les durs bourgeons gluants. | Le jaune des crocus tachait les prés acides. (SA 450)
19	Un peu de lune pâle se fondait dans un azur vierge (281)	Un peu de lune pâle est dans l'azur. (AA 379)
20	A cette heure de défaite, il appelait l'assouvissement si proche de la mort (282)	Vous m'avez consolée en ces nuits de défaite, | Morne assouvissement, parfait comme la mort... (Dis 419)
21	les lilas déjà mourants (283)	les mourants lilas (Dis 421)
22	repaître ses yeux du spectacle d'un jeune corps violé (284)	Ton corps est violé dans mon cœur (Or 430)
23	la pluie lui arracha son parfum le plus secret. (287)	l'odeur que m'arrache l'averse (SA 449)
24	la chaîne de deux bras (288)	l'anneau de deux bras (SA 449)

Table 22:

	Préséances (ORTC, 1)	Verse
1	aux branches du passé touffu (356)	à travers | Les branches du passé touffu (VAL 468)
2	j'avais peur de Dieu (370)	Un Dieu couvert de sang dont Cybèle avait peur. (SA 460)
3	qui souille le printemps? (375)	Qui souille le printemps? (Or 433)

Table 23:

	Le Mal (*ORTC*, I)	Verse
1	ces invisibles eaux où s'agitent les chevelures des longues mousses— [...] nymphes enlisées (654)	Les gaves dont les eaux par les cailloux brisées | Agitent les cheveux des nymphes enlisées (*SA* 448)
2	La lande n'était qu'un infini cri de cigales. (655)	La lande [...] | Crie indéfiniment de toutes ses cigales (*Or* 443)
3	le tocsin haletant de l'incendie. (655)	le tocsin haletant... (*Or* 407)
4	des lacs d'un azur sombre (667)	Des lacs de sombre azur (*AA* 368)
5	Debout au centre de la fournaise (678)	Seul debout, en ces jours de feu et de poussière (*Or* 442)
6	ce corps éclairé du dedans (695)	Ton corps laiteux et roux, éclairé du dedans (*Or* 439)
7	le Dieu jaloux (727)	un Dieu jaloux (*Or* 443)

Table 24:

	Le Baiser au lépreux (*ORTC*, I)	Verse
1	il a retenu la receveuse des postes à l'extrême bord de l'adultère. (460)	Jusqu'à l'extrême bord nous fûmes | De la volupté défendue (*Or* 431)
2	Une après-midi à l'époque des premières chaleurs [...] cette odeur de pain de seigle qui était l'haleine de la métairie (497–98)	Telle est l'après-midi que les hommes ont peur | Et dorment, dans l'odeur de pain des métairies. (*Or* 428)
3	Comme la campagne se délivre de l'hiver, cette femme se délivrait de lui (473)	jardin nu, mais délivré de son hiver, | Délivré comme moi, (*Or* 432)
4	la volupté du lit désert. (475)	O nuit de mes deux mains contre le lit désert! (*Or* 435)

Table 25:

	Le Fleuve de feu (*ORTC*, I)	Verse
1	cette ruse du regard, toujours ailleurs qu'au seul visage qui l'attire. (513)	La ruse de mes yeux d'être toujours ailleurs | Ne leur dérobe pas la face qui les blesse. (*Or* 432)
2	Il [...] se brûlait au feu de ce corps étendu. (521)	me brûlant au feu de ton corps endormi (*Or* 436)
3	les genoux blessés contre les carreaux... (527)	à genoux aux carreaux de la chambre, | Vous saignez sous le joug (*Or* 444)
4	La verdure avait souillé de sève sa robe de piqué (528)	L'herbe où tu dors te souille de sa sève. (*SA* 461)
5	l'indéfinie vibration des prairies	la prairie entière vibre et crie (*Or*

6	(545) les jambes pures de Gisèle l'éclairant mieux que la lampe posée sur le tapis.	428) Cette lampe que tu posas sur le tapis | L'éclaire moins que tes jambes pures.
7	(548) Gisèle de Plailly, qui, […], l'été presque nue sous sa robe de toile, s'étendait sur la pierre de la terrasse pour en éprouver la chaleur (552)	(*Or* 439) la terrasse | Est brûlante où j'aimais à quinze ans de m'étendre | Pour braver le soleil comme la mort en face. (*Or* 443)
8	Le fleuve de feu est au-dedans de nous. (554)	Le pays de la soif est au dedans de nous. (*Or* 440)
9	les tocsins haletants (575)	le tocsin haletant (*AA* 407)

Table 26:

	Genitrix (*ORTC*, 1)	Verse
1	Des orages rodèrent (622)	L'orage qui rôdait (*SA* 455)

Table 27:

	Le Désert de l'amour (*ORTC*, 1)	Verse
1	la jeune forêt humaine (753)	l'humaine forêt (*SA* 459)
2	il ne discernait pas les lignes pures de sa face (754)	un monde meurtri. | […] J'en suis les pures lignes. (*SA* 452)
3	je supprime le monde autour de cette sombre figure angélique. (767)	J'anéantis le monde autour d'Atys qui dort. (*SA* 449)
4	ses paupières sont les bords ravagés d'une mer (767)	Des yeux avaient les bords ravagés d'une mer. (*Or* 427)
5	deux lacs confus sont assoupis aux lisières des cils. (767)	J'ai vu des lacs dormir aux lisières des cils (*Or* 427)
6	le printemps est souvent la saison de la boue […] cet adolescent pouvait n'être que souillure (796)	Qui souille le printemps? (*Or* 434)
7	une écume amère (814)	l'amère écume (*Or* 431)
8	ce flot trouble en elle, de ce remous obscur? (818)	flot trouble et de boue épaissi. (*Or* 436) Cette eau vaseuse et ces remous (*Or* 432)
9	cette brève étreinte que la honte dénoue… (828)	Trop longtemps j'ai souffert de dénouer l'étreinte (*SA* 457)

Table 28:

	Thérèse Desqueyroux (ORTC, II)	Verse
1	Nous nous arrêtons au bord, à l'extrême bord de la dernière caresse (45)	Jusqu'à l'extrême bord nous fûmes | De la volupté défendue (*Or* 431)
2	c'est lui qui me résiste, et moi qui souhaiterais d'atteindre ces extré-mités inconnues dont il me répète que la seule approche dépasse toutes les joies (45)	De toute sa douceur, il dit: non! et résiste | Au chaud baiser du soir sur son âme inquiète, | A l'amour, dont la seule approche le rend triste (*AA* 376)
3	pins sans nombre. (46)	Atys sans nombre (*SA* 458)
4	les coqs semblaient déchirer le brouillard (84)	Mes branches déchiraient lentement le brouillard (*SA* 447)

Table 29:

	Destins (ORTC, II)	Verse
1	Dix heures: sur la vigne, la brume tremblait. (136)	la brume tremblante annonce | L'accablement d'une après-midi torride (*MJ* 329)
2	et parfois, un oiseau n'achevait pas sa roulade, comme en rêve. (142)	Un oiseau s'interrompt de chanter comme en rêve. (*SA* 461)
3	ce couple muet qui suspendait le temps (145)	ses prunelles | Qui suspendaient le Temps (*Dis* 419)
4	des dos roux de bœufs émergeaient des vignes (146)	Les dos sombres des bœufs vont émerger des vignes (*Or* 443)
5	elle n'avait jamais vu, sous des pau-pières, dormir cette eau trouble,—ce secret d'ardeur, de fatigue, de ruse. (146)	Mais sous les cils toujours sommeille une eau confuse, | Dort un secret d'ardeur, de fatigue et de ruse. (*SA* 456)
6	jusqu'à ce que les collines ne fussent plus que des vagues d'ombre. (150)	Les coteaux sont des vagues d'ombre immobiles (*MJ* 330)
7	leurs deux corps complices, indif-férents à ce ciel, à ces astres témoins d'une gloire et d'une puissance infinies. (154)	Mais l'âpre paradis où ces corps m'avaient fuie, | Le Plaisir, les ren-dait indifférents aux dieux (*SA* 455)
8	Peut-être Elisabeth désirait-elle obscurément suivre sur ce corps une piste, et, comme un voyageur retrouve la cendre d'un camp aban-donné, s'arrêter longuement à une meurtrissure. (203)	Mais sur ce corps plus roux qu'un désert, et plus nu, | Les pistes que je suis ont d'étranges méandres. | La trace y brûle encore d'un chasseur inconnu. | D'un camp abandonné je reconnais les cendres. (*SA* 452)

Table 30:

	Ce qui était perdu (*ORTC*, II)	Verse
1	Désir tapi au plus secret de son être (279)	L'odeur te fait mourir de mon désir tapi. (*Or* 430)
2	un bel œil sombre et trouble (368)	Ton œil, trouble océan (*SA* 452)

Table 31:

	Le Nœud de vipères (*ORTC*, II)	Verse
1	les soirs d'été, j'écoutais leurs voix pures, cet air de Lulli: *Ah! que ces bois, ces rochers, ces fontaines …* (430)	cet air de Lulli qui m'obsède, | Dont nos voix emplissaient le parc et la nuit tiède: | … '*Ah! que ces bois, ces rochers, ces fontaines…*' (*AA* 368)
2	un azur trouble (508)	Cet azur trouble (*SA* 456)

Table 32:

	Le Mystère Frontenac (*ORTC*, II)	Verse
1	les écorces des pins luisaient comme des écailles, leurs blessures gluantes captaient le soleil déclinant. (566)	En vain ce corps si doux se recouvre d'écailles | Et saigne, jeune pin, par de longues entailles (*SA* 458)
2	les longues chevelures vivantes des mousses. (566)	les cheveux des nymphes enlisées, | Longues mousses (*SA* 448)
3	Le jet sans défaut des pins rapprochait les étoiles: elles se posaient, elles nageaient dans ces flaques de ciel que délimitaient les cimes noirs. (570)	Nos regards s'élevaient vers les chantantes cimes | Des pins—qui découpaient d'immobiles abîmes, | Des lacs de sombre azur où tremblaient des planètes… (*AA* 368)
4	les prairies seules vibraient follement. (596)	la prairie entière vibre et crie (*Or* 428)
5	les pins continueraient d'aspirer au ciel, de s'étirer, de se tendre. (673)	Un jeune pin tendu vers l'essence divine | Fait des signes au ciel avec ses longues mains. (*SA* 457)
6	la forêt humaine (673)	l'humaine forêt (*SA* 459)

Table 33:

	La Fin de la nuit (*ORTC*, III)	Verse
1	son front trop vaste (148, 156)	Reine à l'immense front (*SA* 449)
2	l'ombre des feuilles tigrait la chair	ce torse tigré par l'ombre des

	(130)	fougères (*SA* 449)
3	un secret d'ardeur, de science et de ruse (145)	un secret d'ardeur, de fatigue et de ruse (*SA* 449)
4	autour de ces yeux qui l'avaient tant fait rêver, un monde meurtri (157)	Ton œil, trouble océan, ronge un monde meurtri. (*SA* 452)
5	les bords brûlés d'une mer morte (157)	cette cendre au bord des mers Mortes (*Or* 445)

Table 34:

	Les Anges noirs (*ORTC*, III)	Verse
1	la terre mouillée nous enveloppait de son odeur (235)	le parfum de la terre mouillée (*SA* 455)
2	inerte comme ce caillou (249)	Inerte, le fut-il jamais? Ce caillou pur (EE 465)
3	cet océan dont la marée de toutes parts nous ronge (350)	océan qui me ronge. (*SA* 447)

Table 35:

	Les Chemins de la mer (*ORTC*, III)	Verse
1	ces cheveux indistincts comme une forêt confuse. (569)	Et l'obscure forêt au bord du front désert (*SA* 447)
2	il respira dans son cœur l'odeur de la terre mouillée, des branches lourdes de pluie. Il crut recevoir, comme les recevraient Rose et Robert, des gouttes tièdes sur son front. (611–12)	Mes branches s'égouttaient sur la double torpeur, | Sur le double sommeil de cette chair souillée | D'où montait le parfum de la terre mouillée. (*SA* 455)
3	cette vibration des prairies (618)	la prairie entière vibre (*Or* 428)
4	malgré toutes les ronces et tous les ajoncs qui me font saigner, je suis une route tracée… (666)	Les ronces de mon cœur griffaient leurs jambes nues | Et mes branchages fous faisaient saigner leurs mains. (*SA* 451)
5	Le chemin que l'enfant-poète avait suivi, […], débouchait tout à coup sur la destinée de Landin, sur cette mer Morte. (690)	Les routes où tes pieds ont saigné, tous les bouges | Et cette cendre au bord des mers Mortes ou Rouges (*Or* 445)
6	Les grands cils avaient été ravagés (695)	Des yeux avaient les bords ravagés d'une mer. (*Or* 427)

Table 36:

	La Pharisienne (*ORTC*, III)	Verse
1	Et le silence régna: des cigales, un chant de coq, un bourdonnement de mouches. (734)	Bourdonnement des mouches […]. | Chant d'un coq […]. | Silence lourd étreignant la maison… (*MJ* 331) J'entoure ton sommeil d'un bourdonnement sourd | De mouches que le cri perdu d'un coq traverse. (*SA* 449)
2	ma chair encore endormie. (754)	La chair encore endormie (*SA* 448)
3	l'orage qui ne rôdait plus derrière les pins, grondait au fond de plus d'un cœur. (759)	Mais l'orage enchaîné des musiques futures, | En nos cœurs séparés et déjà confondus, | Grondait… (Dis 418) L'orage qui rôdait à travers les ramures (*SA* 455)
4	les paupières sont les bords ravagés de la même eau verte aux reflets de varech et d'algue. (780)	Des yeux avaient les bords ravagés d'une mer. (*SA* 427)

Table 37:

	Galigaï (*ORTC*, IV)	Verse
1	les coteaux dorment dans un flamboiement immobile. (382)	Des vagues de coteaux dorment dans la lumière (*MJ* 330)
2	Des gouttes d'eau brillaient sur son pelage doré. (382)	Sur ton épaule brille une goutte de pluie, (*SA* 458) ce léger pelage | Dont la flamme montant du ventre jusqu'au cœur (*SA* 451)
3	les feuilles flétries du tilleul (393)	les tilleuls flétris (*SA* 461)
4	La terre était dure et, tout près de son oreille, le pré aride vibrait. (393)	la Terre où je me couche. | […] Sous un corps, la prairie entière vibre et crie (*Or* 428)
5	ce sombre ciel embrasé et palpitant au-dessus d'une terre délivrée des hommes et où régnaient les arbres. (402)	Un ciel prodigieux palpitait sur nos têtes. | Nos regards s'élevaient vers les chantantes cimes | Des pins (*AA* 368)
6	un lac de néant où une large étoile tremblait. (407)	Des lacs de sombre azur où tremblaient des planètes… (*AA* 368)
7	Mais dans l'encadrement de la fenêtre, se dressait cette créature éphémère qui lui cachait Dieu. (417)	Cybèle à qui le ciel est caché par ton corps! (*SA* 452)

Table 38:

	L'Agneau (***ORTC***, IV)	Verse
1	il demeurait pareil à un jeune pin dans la nuit. (525)	Marsyas, […] ǀ Je te confonds avec ce jeune pin (*Or* 443)
2	Il tendait les mains en écran et ses gros souliers fumaient. (550)	Tes lourds souliers au feu fument d'un long chemin (VAL 468)

Table 39:

	Un adolescent d'autrefois (***ORTC***, IV)	Verse
1	la brume annonciatrice d'un jour torride (755)	la brume tremblante annonce ǀ L'accablement d'une après-midi torride (*MJ* 329)
2	ses boucles blondes au vent de la course paraissaient vivantes: oui, des serpents vivants (677)	Les dociles serpents de tes boucles mêlées ǀ Obéissent aux vents (*SA* 453)
3	cette terre […] qui, elle, nous possédera. (745)	Du temps que j'étais fou, j'ai possédé la terre. (*Or* 427)
4	Son enfer était au-dedans de lui. (748)	Le pays de la soif est au dedans de nous. (*Or* 440)
5	le brouillard que les branches des pins semblaient arracher d'eux. (758)	Mes branches déchiraient lentement le brouillard (*SA* 447)
6	Ah! me coucher sur la terre nue (801)	la Terre où je me couche. (*Or* 428)
7	Elle regardait l'eau dormante de l'écluse que ne ridait aucun souffle. (809)	Ton reflet s'endormait dans mes sources cachées ǀ Dont un souffle ridait l'eau froide (*SA* 447)
8	cette eau endormie (809)	une eau endormie. (*Or* 434)

Bibliography

This bibliography contains all items referred to directly in the study and a number of additional entries relating to the general subject of Mauriac and poetry. Unless otherwise stated, books in French are published in Paris and books in English are published in London.

Abbreviations

CFM	*Cahiers François Mauriac*
CM	*Cahiers de Malagar*
NCFM	*Nouveaux Cahiers François Mauriac*
TCER	*Travaux du Centre d'études et de recherches sur François Mauriac*

Bibliographies

Goesch, Keith, *François Mauriac: essai de bibliographie chronologique, 1908–1960* (Nizet, 1965)

Granger, Laurence, 'Supplément bibliographique', *NCFM*, 4 (1996), 297–310

Books by Mauriac (by date of publication)

De quelques cœurs inquiets: petits essais de psychologie religieuse (Société Littéraire de France, 1919)

Petits Essais de psychologie religieuse, 2nd edn (L'Artisan du Livre, 1933)

Orages (Grasset, 1949)

Œuvres complètes, 12 vols (Fayard, 1950–56)

Journal V (Flammarion, 1953)

D'autres et moi, ed. by Keith Goesch (Grasset, 1966)

François Mauriac–Jacques-Emile Blanche: correspondance (1916–1942), ed. by Georges-Paul Collet (Grasset, 1976)

Lacordaire, ed. by Keith Goesch (Beauchesne, 1976)

Mauriac avant Mauriac, ed. by Jean Touzot (Flammarion, 1977)

Œuvres romanesques et théâtrales complètes, ed. by Jacques Petit, Bibliothèque de la Pléiade, 4 vols (Gallimard, 1978–85)

Lettres d'une vie (1904–1969), ed. by Caroline Mauriac (Grasset, 1981)

Souvenirs retrouvés: entretiens avec Jean Amrouche, ed. by Béatrice Avakian (Fayard/ Institut National de l'Audiovisuel, 1981)

L'Agneau, ed. by François Durand, GF, 431 (Flammarion, 1985)

Les Paroles restent, ed. by Keith Goesch (Grasset, 1985)

Paroles perdues et retrouvées, ed. by Keith Goesch (Grasset, 1986)
François Mauriac et Jacques Rivière: correspondance 1911–1925, ed. by John E. Flower, Textes Littéraires, 68 (Exeter: University of Exeter, 1988)
Nouvelles Lettres d'une vie (1906–1970), ed. by Caroline Mauriac (Grasset, 1989)
Œuvres autobiographiques, ed. by François Durand, Bibliothèque de la Pléiade (Gallimard, 1990)
Bloc-notes, ed. by Jean Touzot, Points Essais, 269–73, 5 vols (Grasset, 1993)
Le Feu secret, ed. by Jean-Louis Curtis (Orphée/ La Différence, 1993)
Mozart et autres écrits sur la musique, ed. by François Solesme (La Versanne: Encre Marine, 1996)
Correspondance François Mauriac–Georges Duhamel (1919–1966): le croyant et l'humaniste inquiet, ed. by J.-J. Hueber (Klincksieck, 1997)
La Paix des cimes: chroniques 1948–1955, ed. by Jean Touzot (Bartillat, 1999)
François Mauriac et Jean Paulhan: Correspondance, 1925–1967, ed. by John E. Flower (Editions Claire Paulhan, 2001)

Articles and shorter works by Mauriac (by date of publication of edition used)
'Poèmes', *Mercure de France*, 85 (May–June 1910), 420–24
'Nocturne', *Les Cahiers de l'Amitié de France*, 2.4 (March 1913), 78–80
'Elégie', *Les Cahiers de l'Amitié de France*, 3.4 (April 1914), 201–05
'L'Acte de foi', *Le Divan*, no. 79 (May 1922), 276–78
'Poèmes', *Intentions*, 1.6 (June 1922), 1–2
'Aspects de l'occultisme: témoignage de François Mauriac', *La Table ronde*, August–September 1950, 166–71
'Le Bloc-notes', *L'Express*, 12 January 1961, p. 40
'Ecrits de jeunesse', ed. by Jean Touzot, *CFM*, 10 (1983), 7–55
'Un poète de dix ans', in *François Mauriac*, ed. by Jean Touzot, Les Cahiers de l'Herne, 48 (Editions de l'Herne, 1985), pp. 59–60
'Supplément aux souvenirs', in *François Mauriac*, ed. by Jean Touzot, Les Cahiers de l'Herne, 48 (Editions de l'Herne, 1985), pp. 121–41
'Lettres à sa mère (1907–juin 1911)', in *François Mauriac*, ed. by Jean Touzot, Les Cahiers de l'Herne, 48 (Editions de l'Herne, 1985), pp. 61–77
'Lettres de François Mauriac à Robert Vallery-Radot', ed. by Yves Leroux, *CFM*, 12 (1985), 29–81
'La Correspondance entre François Mauriac et Claire Mauriac, sa mère [Extraits, 1907–1914]', ed. by John Flower, *NCFM*, 5 (1997), 25–48
'Lettre à Henri Guillemin [extrait]', in Maison Charavay, *Bulletin d'autographes à prix marqués*, no. 828 (2000), p. 41

Books and theses on Mauriac

Alyn, Marc, *François Mauriac*, Poètes d'aujourd'hui, 77 (Seghers, 1960)

Bendz, Ernst, *François Mauriac: ébauche d'une figure* (Gothenburg: Elanders Boktryckeri Aktiebolag, 1945)

Borella, Luisa, *'Le Sagouin' de François Mauriac* (Firenze: La Nuova Italia Editrice, 1980)

Canérot, Marie-Françoise, *Mauriac après 1930: le roman dénoué* (SEDES, 1986)

Chapon, François, ed., *François Mauriac: Manuscrits – Inédits – Editions originales – Iconographie* (Bibliothèque Littéraire Jacques Doucet, 1968)

—— *Catalogue de fonds spéciaux de la Bibliothèque littéraire Jacques Doucet, Paris: Fonds Jouhandeau et Fonds Mauriac* (Boston, MA: Hall, 1972)

Cooke, Paul, *Mauriac et le mythe du poète: une lecture du 'Mystère Frontenac'*, Archives des Lettres Modernes, 274 (Lettres Modernes/ Minard, 1999)

Cormeau, Nelly, *L'Art de François Mauriac* (Grasset, 1951)

Croc, Paul, *'Destins' de François Mauriac* (Hachette, 1972)

Escallier, Claude, *Mauriac et l'Evangile* (Beauchesne, 1993)

Fabrègues, Jean de, *Mauriac* (Plon, 1971)

Guyonnet, Anne-Marie, 'Mauriac et le mythe d'Atys', 2 vols (unpublished doctoral thesis, University of Paris IV, 1978)

Jarrett-Kerr, Martin, *François Mauriac* (Cambridge: Bowes & Bowes, 1954)

Kushner, Eva, *Mauriac*, Les Ecrivains devant Dieu, 30 (Desclée de Brouwer, 1972)

Lacouture, Jean, *François Mauriac*, 2 vols, Points Littérature, 206–07 (Editions du Seuil, 1990)

Massenet, Violaine, *François Mauriac* (Flammarion, 2000)

Mauriac, Jean, *Malagar: entretien avec Eric des Garets* (Pin Balma: Sables, 1998)

Mauriac, Pierre, *François Mauriac: mon frère*, ed. by Jacques Monférier (Bordeaux: L'Esprit du Temps, 1997)

Monférier, Jacques, *François Mauriac du 'Nœud de vipères' à 'La Pharisienne'*, Unichamp, 10 (Geneva: Editions Slatkine, 1985)

O'Connell, David, *François Mauriac Revisited* (New York: Twayne, 1995)

Palante, Alain, *Mauriac: le roman et la vie* (Editions Le Portulan, 1946)

Risse, Dorothee, *Homoerotik bei François Mauriac: zur literarischen Gestaltung eines Tabus*, Studia Romanica, 105 (Heidelberg: Universitätsverlag C. Winter, 2000)

Séailles, André, *François Mauriac* (Bordas, 1972)

Simon, Pierre-Henri, *Mauriac par lui-même* (Editions du Seuil, 1953)

Speaight, Robert, *François Mauriac: A Study of the Writer and the Man* (Chatto and Windus, 1976)

Swift, Bernard C., *Mauriac et le Symbolisme* (Bordeaux: L'Esprit du Temps, 2000)

Touzot, Jean, *François Mauriac, une configuration romanesque: profil rhétorique et stylistique*, Archives des Lettres Modernes, 218 (Lettres Modernes, 1985)

——, *La Planète Mauriac: figure d'analogie et roman* (Klincksieck, 1985)

——, ed., *Mauriac sous l'Occupation*, 2nd edn (Bordeaux: Editions Confluences/ Centre François Mauriac de Malagar, 1995)

Articles and chapters on Mauriac

Alyn, Marc, 'Avant tout, un poète', *Le Figaro littéraire*, 7–13 September 1970, pp. 11–12

——, '"Si je suis né poète"', in *Mauriac*, Collection Génies et Réalités (Hachette, 1977), pp. 115–39

——, 'Le Désir, messager de l'irrationnel dans les poèmes d'*Orages*', *CFM*, 15 (1988), 77–87

——, 'Stèle pour un poète méconnu', in *Mauriac et les grands esprits de son temps*, ed. by Noël Herpe and others (Bibliothèque Historique de la Ville de Paris, 1990), pp. l–liii

Bataille, J.-M., 'La Chambre de la mère', in *Présence de François Mauriac: actes du Colloque organisé à Bordeaux pour le Centenaire de Mauriac (10–12 octobre 1985)* (Bordeaux: Presses Universitaires de Bordeaux, 1986), pp. 131–40

Baudorre, Philippe, 'François Mauriac, lecteur de Rimbaud', *NCFM*, 8 (2000), 221–31

Bercot, Martine, 'Le Mythe d'Attis dans *Genitrix*', *CFM*, 13 (1986), 239–47

Bikoi, Félix Nicodème, 'Mauriac et Mallarmé', *NCFM*, 5 (1997), 279–88

Bourcheix, André, 'François Mauriac et André Lafon', *CFM*, 4 (1976), 27–41

Canérot, Marie-Françoise, 'Le Thème de la vocation littéraire dans l'œuvre romanesque de François Mauriac', *CFM*, 5 (1978), 149–60

——, 'Les *Nouveaux Mémoires intérieurs*, poème de la vieillesse', *CFM*, 6 (1979), 113–22

——, 'Les Premiers Romans de François Mauriac: des romans en quête de structure', *CFM*, 10 (1983), 80–89

——, 'Nocturne mauriacien', in *Présence de François Mauriac: actes du Colloque organisé à Bordeaux pour le Centenaire de Mauriac (10–12 octobre 1985)* (Bordeaux: Presses Universitaires de Bordeaux, 1986), pp. 149–59

Casseville, Caroline, 'La Symbolique du destin à travers le mythe d'Atys', *NCFM*, 6 (1998), 241–49

——, 'Présence et absence de Sartre à travers *La Pharisienne*', *NCFM*, 8 (2000), 189–98

Chabaneix, Philippe, 'François Mauriac poète', *Bulletin de la Librairie Ancienne et Moderne*, no. 140 (December 1971), 254–55

Chapon, François, 'Le Fonds François Mauriac', in *Mauriac et les grands esprits de son temps*, ed. by Noël Herpe and others (Bibliothèque Historique de la Ville de Paris, 1990), pp. xi–xvi

Chevallier, Simone, 'Quelqu'un marchait à nos côtés', *La Voix des poètes*, no. 40 (Winter 1970), 28–30

Cooke, Paul, 'Problems of Establishing an Autobiographical Identity: The Case of François Mauriac', in *Locating Identity: Essays on Nation, Community and the Self*, ed. by Paul Cooke, David Sadler, and Nicholas Zurbrugg (Leicester: De Montfort University, 1996), pp. 17–30

——, 'The Paternal Reverie in Mauriac's "Mémoires imaginaires"', *French Studies*, 50 (1996), 299–310

——, 'Le Poète et la poésie dans *Les Chemins de la mer*', *CM*, 11 (1997), 79–101

——, 'Les Obstacles au bonheur dans la poésie de François Mauriac', in *Le Bonheur dans la littérature européenne contemporaine*, ed. by Michel Reffet (Sarrebourg: Association Européenne François Mauriac, 1998), pp. 36–45

——, 'Les "Sources" de François Mauriac', *Rencontres avec Jean Sullivan*, 11 (1999), 84–95, 168–70

——, 'Présence des mythes dans la poésie de François Mauriac', *NCFM*, 9 (2001), 67–87

——, 'Echos des *Mains jointes* et de *L'Adieu à l'adolescence* dans *L'Enfant chargé de chaînes*', *NCFM* (forthcoming)

Croc, Paul, 'Lunettes freudiennes', in *François Mauriac: Psycholectures/ Psychoreadings*, ed. by J. E. Flower (Exeter: University of Exeter Press, 1995), pp. 218–31

Daniel, Jean, 'François Mauriac et le journalisme', in *Mauriac*, Génies et Réalités (Hachette, 1977), pp. 141–59

Décaudin, Michel, 'Les Premiers Poèmes de Mauriac', in *François Mauriac 1: la poésie de François Mauriac*, ed. by Jacques Monférier, La Revue des Lettres Modernes, 432–38 (Lettres Modernes/ Minard, 1975), pp. 9–23

——, 'Mauriac et ses poètes', in *François Mauriac*, ed. by Jean Touzot, Les Cahiers de l'Herne, 48 (Editions de l'Herne, 1985), pp. 295–98

Dédéyan, Christian, 'Notes pour une poétique de François Mauriac', *La Voix des poètes*, no. 40 (Winter 1970), 43–45

Delaunay, Gabriel, 'Mauriac et la terre d'Aquitaine', *La Voix des poètes*, no. 40 (Winter 1970), 16–20
——, 'Prix Nobel et "homme seul"', in *Mauriac, Génies et Réalités* (Hachette, 1977), pp. 211–31
Durand, François, 'Les Jeunes Héros de Mauriac devant l'amitié', *CFM*, 11 (1984), 147–56
——, 'Mauriac devant la grande guerre', in *Présence de François Mauriac: actes du Colloque organisé à Bordeaux pour le Centenaire de Mauriac (10–12 octobre 1985)* (Bordeaux: Presses Universitaires de Bordeaux, 1986), pp. 81–87
——, 'Richesse et ambiguïté mythiques du *Sang d'Atys*', *NCFM*, 9 (2001), 89–99
Dyé, Michel, 'Du roman-tragédie linéaire au théâtre: la ligne dramatique de l'écriture mauriacienne', in *François Mauriac et d'autres*, ed. by Bernard Swift, Rona Kanawati, and Angus Martin (Sydney: Macquarie University/ Société Internationale des Etudes Mauriaciennes, 2000), pp. 97–113
Escallier, Claude, 'Poésie et credo mauriacien', *NCFM*, 5 (1997), 75–87
Faguet, Emile, 'Les Poésies de M. François Mauriac', *Revue des Deux Mondes*, 1 November 1912, 196–204
Favre, Yves-Alain, '*Le Sang d'Atys*: poétique et poésie', in *Présence de François Mauriac: actes du colloque organisé à Bordeaux pour le centenaire de Mauriac (10–12 octobre 1985)* (Bordeaux: Presses Universitaires de Bordeaux, 1986), pp. 243–54
——, 'Sensations, passions et signes dans *Le Sang d'Atys*', *CFM*, 15 (1988), 88–93
Flower, J. E., 'Mauriac et l'affaire Brasillach', *CM*, 9 (Autumn 1995), 59–73
Fouché, Chantal, 'Une lecture politique', *CFM*, 13 (1986), 259–67
Frontenac, Yves, '*Orages* ou la dualité du miroir', *Australian Journal of French Studies*, 22 (1985), 138–41
Griffiths, Richard, '1920–1925: du "roman catholique" traditionnel au roman mauriacien', *CFM*, 11 (1984), 23–39
Guibert, Armand, 'Un Mauriac moins connu ou la poésie d'un prosateur', *La Voix des poètes*, no. 40 (Winter 1970), 10–14
Guyon, Bernard, 'Mauriac–Péguy', *CFM*, 4 (1976), 175–86
Huet-Brichard, Marie-Catherine, 'Mauriac–Guérin: le dialogue ininterrompu', *TCER*, 32 (December 1992), 11–25
Jacques, François, 'La Poésie dans le théâtre de Mauriac', in *Mauriac et le théâtre: actes du Colloque de la Sorbonne, 1991*, ed. by André Séailles (Klincksieck, 1993), pp. 262–70
Kanters, Robert, 'François Mauriac et la grâce poétique', *CFM*, 6 (1979), 102–12
Lafargue, Marc, 'La Poésie', *Les Marges*, no. 25 (January 1911), 15–28

Landry, Jean-Pierre, 'Mauriac, lecteur de Pascal', *CFM*, 14 (1987), 111–31

Lapeyre, Paule, '*La* [sic] *Sang d'Atys*, poème de François Mauriac: mythe fondateur d'une vie, d'une œuvre et d'une pensée', in *Hommage à Claude Faisant (1932–1988)*, Publication de la Faculté des Lettres et Sciences Humaines de Nice, 3 (Les Belles Lettres, 1991), pp. 267–78

——, 'Antée/ Atys: vie, mort et survie tellurique dans la destinée et l'œuvre de François Mauriac', *NCFM*, 9 (2001), 57–66

——, '*Le Mal*: roman poétique de Mauriac?', *NCFM*, 10 (2002), 135–44

Legrand, Yolande, '"Les grands pays muets…": de Vigny à Mauriac', *TCER*, 18 (December 1985), 23–58

Le Hir, Yves, 'La Versification de François Mauriac', in *Le Vers français au 20ᵉ siècle: colloque organisé par le Centre de Philologie et de Littérature Romanes de l'Université de Strasbourg du 3 mai au 6 mai 1966* (Klincksieck, 1967), pp. 65–84

Leroux, Yves, 'De la poésie de Maurice de Guérin à la poésie de François Mauriac', in *François Mauriac 1: la poésie de François Mauriac*, ed. by Jacques Monférier, La Revue des Lettres Modernes, 432–38 (Lettres Modernes/ Minard, 1975), pp. 111–31

——, 'L'Enfance et la solitude dans la poésie de Marie Noël et de François Mauriac', *CFM*, 5 (1978), 36–50

——, 'Mauriac poète dans les *Mémoires intérieurs* et les *Nouveaux Mémoires intérieurs*', *CFM*, 6 (1979), 123–36

Le Touzé, Philippe, 'Les Trois Nocturnes', in *Pascal–Mauriac: l'œuvre en dialogue. actes du Colloque du Sénat, 4–6 Octobre 1999*, ed. by Jean-François Durand (L'Harmattan, 2000), pp. 195–210

Madaule, Jacques, 'François Mauriac et Paul Claudel', *CFM*, 4 (1976), 197–212

——, 'La Poésie de l'enfance dans l'œuvre de François Mauriac', *CFM*, 11 (1984), 77–89

Massabki, Dom Charles, 'François Mauriac et l'abbaye Sainte-Marie', in *François Mauriac*, ed. by Jean Touzot, Les Cahiers de l'Herne, 48 (Editions de l'Herne, 1985), pp. 425–27

Maucuer, Maurice, 'Yves Frontenac et les "fourmis à tête d'homme"', *CFM*, 7 (1980), 133–45

Monférier, Jacques, 'Avant-propos', in *François Mauriac 1: la poésie de François Mauriac*, ed. by Jacques Monférier, La Revue des Lettres Modernes, 432–38 (Lettres Modernes/ Minard, 1975), pp. 4–6

——, 'Mauriac et Valéry', *CFM*, 4 (1976), 112–20

Mora, Edith, 'François Mauriac pourquoi vous êtes-vous arraché à la poésie?', *Les Nouvelles littéraires*, 18 June 1959, p. 1, p. 7

Naffakh, Anne-Marie, 'Roman et style poétique: les images dans *Le Désert de l'amour* et *L'Agneau* de François Mauriac', *TCER*, 6 (December 1979), 37–49

Nemo, Maxime, 'Poète et romancier', *La Voix des poètes*, no. 40 (Winter 1970), 47–50

Parry, Margaret, 'Mauriac and D. H. Lawrence', in *François Mauriac: Visions and Reappraisals*, ed. by John E. Flower and Bernard C. Swift (Oxford: Berg, 1989), pp. 181–200

Pény, Jean-Marie, 'Plaidoyer pour des vers mal aimés', *CFM*, 10 (1983), 174–89

Petit, Jacques, 'Mauriac et le surréalisme', *CFM*, 7 (1980), 41–52

Pradelle, François, 'Les Feuillets gallicans du *Cerf-Volant*', *Le Cerf-Volant*, no. 72 (1970), 38–45

Prado, Javier del, 'Description de la nature et mise à l'écart du récit', *NCFM*, 8 (2000), 81–106

Prévost, Jean, 'De Mauriac à son œuvre', *La Nouvelle Revue française*, 34 (January–June 1930), 349–67

Quaghebeur, Marc, 'Mauriac ou la poésie', *Revue générale*, 10 (1970), 13–22

——, 'Mauriac poète', *La Quinzaine littéraire*, 1–15 October 1970, pp. 14–15

——, 'Mauriac poète: interstices', *Les Lettres romanes*, 25.2 (1971), 178–99

——, 'Méandres créateurs de Mauriac poète', *La Revue nouvelle*, 55 (1972), 354–64

——, 'Yves Frontenac désert', *Cahiers Internationaux de Symbolisme*, 21 (1972), 39–50

——, 'Une lecture du *Sang d'Atys*', in *François Mauriac 1: la poésie de François Mauriac*, ed. by Jacques Monférier, La Revue des Lettres Modernes, 432–38 (Lettres Modernes/ Minard, 1975), pp. 51–68

Quillard, Pierre, 'Les Poèmes', *Mercure de France*, no. 304 (February 1910), 685–90

Sartre, Jean Paul [sic], 'M. François Mauriac et la liberté', *La Nouvelle Revue française*, 52 (January–June 1939), 212–32

Séailles, André, 'Mauriac et Baudelaire', in *François Mauriac 1: la poésie de François Mauriac*, ed. by Jacques Monférier, La Revue des Lettres Modernes, 432–38 (Lettres Modernes/ Minard, 1975), pp. 95–110

——, 'François Mauriac lecteur de Rimbaud: affinités et contrastes', *CFM*, 5 (1978), 95–112

——, 'François Mauriac et Jean Racine, ou l'enfer des mal-aimés', in *François Mauriac*, ed. by Jean Touzot, Les Cahiers de l'Herne, 48 (Editions de l'Herne, 1985), pp. 299–306

——, 'Défense et illustration d'un poète', *Revue des deux mondes*, February 1986, 280–303

——, 'Mauriac et Freud devant l'inconscient et devant la foi', in *François Mauriac devant le problème du mal: actes du Colloque du Collège de France, 28 septembre–1ᵉʳ octobre 1992*, ed. by André Séailles (Klincksieck, 1994), pp. 19–35

Simon, Pierre-Henri, 'François Mauriac poète', *La Voix des poètes*, no. 40 (Winter 1970), 24–26

Suffran, Michel, 'François Mauriac poète du réel et de la grâce', *La Voix des poètes*, no. 40 (Winter 1970), 32–40

——, 'François Mauriac et la "poésie de roman"', in *François Mauriac 1: la poésie de François Mauriac*, ed. by Jacques Monférier, La Revue des Lettres Modernes, 432–38 (Lettres Modernes/ Minard, 1975), pp. 69–93

——, 'François Mauriac et Francis Jammes, ou le dialogue avec soi-même', *CFM*, 4 (1976), 72–97

Swift, Bernard C., 'François Mauriac et le don d'atmosphère: la poésie de la nature et de l'innocence', *CFM*, 13 (1986), 357–63

——, 'François Mauriac and French Literary Symbolism', in *François Mauriac: Visions and Reappraisals*, ed. by John E. Flower and Bernard C. Swift (Oxford: Berg, 1989), pp. 97–115

——, 'Mauriac entre l'aventure et une rigueur valéryenne', *NCFM*, 5 (1997), 53–64

——, 'Mauriac et Proust: la poésie de l'endroit', *NCFM*, 7 (1999), 89–100

Thornton Smith, Colin B., 'Les Adolescentes d'autrefois dans *la Robe prétexte*', *CFM*, 11 (1984), 203–14

Touzot, Jean, 'Analogie et poème, ou les deux saisons de l'imagerie mauriacienne', in *François Mauriac 1: la poésie de François Mauriac*, ed. by Jacques Monférier, La Revue des Lettres Modernes, 432–38 (Lettres Modernes/ Minard, 1975), pp. 25–49

——, 'Quand Mauriac était scandaleux…', *Œuvres et critiques*, 2.1 (Spring 1977), 133–44

——, 'L'Eau et le rêve chrétien: réflexions sur l'imagerie des *Nouveaux Mémoires intérieurs*', *CFM*, 6 (1979), 77–88

——, 'Les Voies de la poésie dans le roman', *La Licorne*, 11 (1986), 9–16

——, 'Histoire et partition poétique', *CFM*, 14 (1987), 237–49

——, 'Avant le *Bloc-notes*: la chronique, le billet, l'éditorial selon Mauriac', *CM*, 5 (Summer 1991), 49–69

——, 'Les Trois Avatars de la revue rivale', *NCFM*, 8 (2000), 199–210

Trigeaud, Françoise, 'Province intérieure et roman poétique chez François Mauriac', *CFM*, 2 (1975), 53–64

Welch, Edward, 'Le Carnaval perverti de François Mauriac', in *Masque et carnaval dans la littérature européenne: actes du Colloque de Ljubljana,*

Université de Ljubljana, 9–11 juillet 2000, ed. by Edward Welch (L'Harmattan, 2002), pp. 39–53

Works of literary criticism and theory

Artaud, Antonin, *Le Théâtre et son double*, Folio Essais, 14 (Gallimard, 1985)

Astier, Colette, *Le Mythe d'Œdipe* (Colin 1974)

Attridge, Derek, 'Closing Statement: Linguistics and Poetics in Retrospect', in *The Stylistics Reader: From Roman Jakobson to the Present*, ed. by Jean Jacques Weber (Arnold, 1996), pp. 36–53

Banville, Théodore de, *Petit Traité de poésie française* (Charpentier, 1891)

Bénichou, Paul, *Le Sacre de l'écrivain, 1750–1830: essai sur l'avènement d'un pouvoir spirituel laïque dans la France moderne* (Corti, 1973)

Bethlenfalvay, Marina, *Les Visages de l'enfant dans la littérature française du XIXᵉ siècle: esquisse d'une typologie*, Histoire des Idées et Critique Littéraire, 176 (Geneva: Droz, 1979)

Blanchot, Maurice, *L'Espace littéraire*, Folio Essais, 89 (Gallimard, 1989)

Boisdeffre, Pierre de, *Une histoire vivante de la littérature d'aujourd'hui (1939–1964)*, 5th edn (Librairie Académique Perrin, 1964)

——, *Les Poètes français d'aujourd'hui (1940–1986)*, Que sais-je?, 1543, 3rd edn (Presses Universitaires de France, 1987)

Bonnet, Henri, *Roman et Poésie: essai sur l'esthétique des genres. La littérature d'avant-garde et Marcel Proust*, 2nd edn (Nizet, 1980)

Bremond, Henri, *Racine et Valéry: notes sur l'initiation poétique* (Grasset, 1930)

Briolet, Daniel, *Le Langage poétique: de la linguistique à la logique du poème* (Nathan, 1984)

Burke, Seán, *The Death and Return of the Author: Criticism and Subjectivity in Barthes, Foucault and Derrida* (Edinburgh: Edinburgh University Press, 1992)

Clancier, Georges-Emmanuel, *La Poésie et ses environs* (Gallimard, 1973)

Cohen, Jean, *Structure du langage poétique* (Flammarion, 1966)

Combe, Daniel, *Poésie et récit: une rhétorique des genres* (Corti, 1989)

Cornell, Kenneth, *The Post-Symbolist Period: French Poetic Currents, 1900–1920* (New Haven: Yale University Press; Paris: Presses Universitaires de France, 1958)

Davies, Margaret, *'Une Saison en enfer' d'Arthur Rimbaud: analyse du texte*, Archives des Lettres Modernes, 155 (Minard, 1975)

Dérieux, Henry, *La Poésie française contemporaine: 1885–1935* (Mercure de France, 1935)

Dunstan Martin, Graham, 'High Formal Poetry', in *Poetry in France: Metamorphoses of a Muse*, ed. by Keith Aspley and Peter France (Edinburgh: Edinburgh University Press, 1992), pp. 204–18

Eigeldinger, Marc, 'Formule spirituelle de la poésie de Pierre Jean Jouve', in Jean Starobinski, Paul Alexandre, and Marc Eigeldinger, *Pierre Jean Jouve: poète et romancier* (Neuchâtel: La Baconnière, 1946), pp. 81–153

Etiemble, *Le Mythe de Rimbaud*, 5 vols (Gallimard, 1952–67)

France, Peter, *Racine's Rhetoric* (Oxford: Clarendon Press, 1965)

Gibson, Robert, *Modern French Poets on Poetry* (Cambridge: Cambridge University Press, 1961)

Griffiths, Richard, *The Reactionary Revolution: The Catholic Revival in French Literature 1870–1914* (Constable, 1966)

Jakobson, Roman, *Questions de poétique* (Editions du Seuil, 1973)

——, *Language in Literature*, ed. by Krystyna Pomorska and Stephen Rudy (Cambridge, MA: Harvard University Press, 1987)

——, 'Closing Statement: Linguistic and Poetics', in *The Stylistics Reader: From Roman Jakobson to the Present*, ed. by Jean Jacques Weber (Arnold, 1996), pp. 10–35

Jossua, Jean-Pierre, *Pour une histoire religieuse de l'expérience littéraire*, 4 vols (Beauchesne, 1985–98)

Kibédi Varga, Aron, *Les Constantes du poème: analyse du langage poétique*, 2nd edn (Picard, 1977)

Lalou, René, *Histoire de la poésie française*, 8th edn (Presses Universitaires de France, 1967)

Le Guern, Michel, *L'Image dans l'œuvre de Pascal* (Colin, 1969)

Lejeune, Philippe, *Le Pacte autobiographique* (Editions du Seuil, 1976)

Lemaitre, Henri, *La Poésie depuis Baudelaire* (Colin, 1965)

Leuwers, Daniel, *Introduction à la poésie moderne et contemporaine* (Bordas, 1990)

Lewis, Roy, *On Reading French Verse: A Study of Poetic Form* (Oxford: Clarendon Press, 1982)

Lindley, David, *Lyric* The Critical Idiom, 44 (Methuen, 1985)

Mossop, D. J., *Pure Poetry: Studies in French Poetic Theory and Practice, 1746 to 1945* (Oxford: Clarendon Press, 1971)

Raimond, Michel, *La Crise du roman: des lendemains du Naturalisme aux années vingt*, 3rd edn (Corti, 1968)

Raymond, Marcel, *De Baudelaire au surréalisme*, rev. edn (Corti, 1952)

Richard, Jean-Pierre, *Poésie et profondeur*, Points Littérature, 71 (Editions du Seuil, 1976)

Rivière, Jacques, *Nouvelles Etudes* (Gallimard, 1947)

Rousselot, Jean, *Histoire de la poésie française, des origines à 1940* (Presses Universitaires de France, 1976)

Sabatier, Robert, *La Poésie du XXe siècle*, 3 vols (Albin Michel, 1982–88)

Sartre, Jean-Paul, *Qu'est-ce que la littérature?*, Folio Essais, 19 (Gallimard, 1986)

Scott, Clive, *French Verse-Art: A Study* (Cambridge: Cambridge University Press, 1980)

Sellier, Philippe, 'Qu'est-ce qu'un mythe littéraire?', *Littérature*, 55 (1984), 112–26

Steiner, George, *Real Presences: Is There Anything 'in' What We Say?* (Faber, 1989)

Suhamy, Henri, *La Poétique*, Que sais-je?, 2311 (Presses Universitaires de France, 1986)

Thélot, Jérôme, *La Poésie précaire* (Presses Universitaires de France, 1997)

Todorov, Tzvetan, *Les Genres du discours* (Seuil, 1978)

Vadé, Yves, 'L'Emergence du sujet lyrique à l'époque romantique', in *Figures du sujet lyrique*, ed. by Dominique Rabaté (Presses Universitaires de France, 1996), pp. 11–37

Vaillant, Alain, *La Poésie: initiation aux méthodes d'analyse des textes poétiques* (Nathan, 1992)

Works of literature

Apollinaire, Guillaume, *Œuvres complètes*, ed. by Michel Décaudin, 8 vols (Balland et Lecat, 1966)

Aury, Dominique, ed., *Anthologie de la poésie religieuse française*, Poésie, 309 (Gallimard, 1997)

——, and Jean Paulhan, eds, *Poètes d'aujourd'hui* (Editions de Clairefontaine, 1947)

Balzac, Honoré de, *La Comédie humaine*, ed. by Pierre-Georges Castex and others, Bibliothèque de la Pléiade, 12 vols (Gallimard, 1976–81)

Baudelaire, Charles, *Œuvres complètes*, ed. by Claude Pichois, Bibliothèque de la Pléiade, 2 vols (Gallimard, 1975–76)

Bercot, Martine, Michel Collot, and Catriona Seth, eds, *Anthologie de la poésie française: XVIIIe siècle, XIXe siècle, XXe siècle* (Gallimard, 2000)

Catullus, *The Poems of Catullus*, trans. by Peter Whigham (Harmondsworth: Penguin, 1966)

Char, René, 'Les Dentelles de Montmirail', *La Nouvelle Revue Française*, no. 97 (1 January 1961), 1–6

——, *Œuvres complètes*, ed. by Lucie Jamme and others, Bibliothèque de la Pléiade (Gallimard, 1983)

Claudel, Paul, *Œuvres en prose*, ed. by Jacques Petit and Charles Galpérine, Bibliothèque de la Pléiade (Gallimard, 1965)

Décaudin, Michel, ed., *Anthologie de la poésie française du XXe siècle: de Paul Claudel à René Char*, Poésie, 168 (Gallimard, 1983)

Delvaille, Bernard, ed., *Mille et cent ans de poésie française: de la 'Séquence de Sainte Eulalie' à Jean Genet* (Laffont, 1991)

Fouchet, Max-Pol, ed., *Anthologie thématique de la poésie française*, 12th edn (Seghers, 1958)

Gide, André, ed., *Anthologie de la poésie française*, Bibliothèque de la Pléiade (Gallimard, 1949)

Guerard, Mme M. J. Adolphe, ed., *La Corbeille de l'enfance: choix gradué de cent jolis morceaux de poésies* (Avize: [n. pub.], 1853)

Hölderlin, Friedrich, *Selected Verse*, ed. and trans. by Michael Hamburger (Harmondsworth: Penguin, 1961)

La Rochefoucauld, *Maximes*, ed. by Jacques Truchet (Garnier Frères, 1967)

La Ville de Mirmont, Jean de, *Œuvres complètes*, ed. by Michel Suffran (Seyssel: Champ Vallon, 1992)

Mallarmé, Stéphane, *Œuvres complètes*, ed. by Carl Paul Barbier and Charles Gordon (Flammarion, 1983)

Maxence, Jean-Louis, ed., *Anthologie de la poésie mystique contemporaine* (Presses de la Renaissance, 1999)

Musset, Alfred de, *Poésies complètes*, ed. by Maurice Allem, Bibliothèque de la Pléiade (Gallimard, 1957)

Ovid, *Fasti*, trans. and ed. by A. J. Boyle and R. D. Woodward (Penguin, 2000)

Pompidou, Georges, ed., *Anthologie de la poésie française* (Hachette, 1961)

Proust, Marcel, *A la recherche du temps perdu*, ed. by Jean-Yves Tadié and others, Bibliothèque de la Pléiade, 4 vols (Gallimard, 1987–89)

Racine, Jean, *Œuvres complètes*, ed. by Georges Forestier, Bibliothèque de la Pléiade, new edn (Gallimard, 1999–)

Ragon, E., ed., *Morceaux choisis de prosateurs et de poètes français des XVIIe, XVIIIe et XIXe siècles: cours élémentaire* ([n. pub.], 1886)

Rimbaud, Arthur, *Œuvres*, ed. by Suzanne Bernard and André Guyaux (Garnier Frères, 1981)

——, *'A Season in Hell' and 'Illuminations'*, trans. by Mark Treharne (Dent, 1998)

Valéry, Paul, *Œuvres*, ed. by Jean Hytier, Bibliothèque de la Pléiade, 2 vols (Gallimard, 1957)

Vallery-Radot, Robert, *Les Grains du myrrhe: 'Les Chants de Chryseis', 'Les Dents du Sylvain', 'Au seuil de la Demeure' (1904–1906)* (Bibliothèque Internationale d'Edition/ Sansot, 1907)

——, ed., *Anthologie de la poésie catholique (des origines à 1932)* (Les Œuvres Représentatives, 1933)

Van Bever, Ad., and Paul Léautaud, eds, *Poètes d'aujourd'hui: morceaux choisis* (Mercure de France, 1900)

Verlaine, Paul, *Œuvres poétiques*, ed. by Jacques Robichez (Garnier Frères, 1969)

Anthologie de la nouvelle poésie française, new edn (Kra, 1928)

Works of religion, thought, history, and reference

Augustine, Saint, *Expositions on the Book of Psalms*, ed. by C. Marriott, E. B. Pusey, and H. Walford, 6 vols (Oxford: Parker, 1847–57)

Chevalier, Jean, and Alain Gheerbrant, *Dictionnaire des symboles*, 2nd edn (Robert Laffont/ Jupiter, 1982)

Claudel, Paul, and André Gide, *Correspondance: 1899–1926*, ed. by Robert Mallet (Gallimard, 1949)

Eliade, Mircea, ed., *The Encyclopedia of Religion*, 16 vols (New York: Macmillan, 1987)

Frazer, James George, *Adonis, Attis, Osiris: Studies in the History of Oriental Religion*, 3rd edn (Macmillan, 1907)

Freud, Sigmund, *The Pelican Freud Library*, trans. and ed. by James Strachey and others, 15 vols (Harmondsworth: Penguin, 1973–86)

Genouvrier, Emile, Claude Désirat, and Tristan Hordé, *Nouveau Dictionnaire des synonymes* (Larousse, 1977)

Gibson, John C. L., *Genesis*, 2 vols (Edinburgh: The Saint Andrew Press, 1981)

Grimal, Pierre, *The Penguin Dictionary of Classical Mythology*, ed. by Stephen Kershaw, trans. by A. R. Maxwell-Hyslop (Penguin, 1991)

Ignatius of Loyola, Saint, *The Text of the Spiritual Exercises of Saint Ignatius*, 4th edn (Burns and Oates, 1913)

Loisy, Alfred, *Les Mystères païens et le mystère chrétien* (Nourry, 1914)

McGrath, Alister E., *Christian Theology: An Introduction*, 2nd edn (Oxford: Blackwell, 1997)

Macmillan, Malcolm, *Freud Evaluated: The Completed Arc* (Cambridge: The MIT Press, 1997)

Marshall, I. H., and others, eds, *New Bible Dictionary*, 3rd edn (Leicester: Inter-Varsity Press, 1996)

Pascal, Blaise, *Œuvres complètes*, ed. by Jacques Chevalier, Bibliothèque de la Pléiade (Gallimard, 1954)

Pépin, Jean, *Mythe et allégorie: les origines grecques et les contestations judéo-chrétiennes*, rev. edn (Etudes Augustiniennes, 1976)

Robertson, John M., *Pagan Christs: Studies in Comparative Hierology*, 2nd edn (Watts, 1911)

Rose, H. J., *A Handbook of Greek Mythology, Including Its Extension to Rome* (Methuen, 1928)

Schmidt, Joël, *Dictionnaire de la mythologie grecque et romaine* (Larousse, 1965)

Vermaseren, Maarten J., *Cybele and Attis: The Myth and the Cult*, trans. by A. M. H. Lemmers (Thames and Hudson, 1977)

Wenham, Gordon J., *Genesis 1–15*, Word Biblical Commentary, 1 (Waco: Word Books, 1987)

La Bible de Jérusalem, new edn (Desclée de Brouwer, 1975)

New Larousse Encyclopedia of Mythology, trans. by Richard Aldington and Delano Ames, new edn (Hamlyn, 1968)

Traduction œcuménique de la Bible, new edn (Alliance Biblique Universelle/ Le Cerf, 1991)

Index

This index lists all personal names given in the main body of the text, with the exception of the names of characters in novels. The names of historical, biblical, and mythological characters are given in their English version only. The index also covers the names of authors (but not editors or translators) referred to in the footnotes.